John Wrathall Bull

Early experiences of life in South Australia and an extended colonial history

John Wrathall Bull

Early experiences of life in South Australia and an extended colonial history

ISBN/EAN: 9783337153885

Printed in Europe, USA, Canada, Australia, Japan

Cover: Foto ©ninafisch / pixelio.de

More available books at **www.hansebooks.com**

EARLY EXPERIENCES OF LIFE

IN

SOUTH AUSTRALIA,

AND

AN EXTENDED COLONIAL HISTORY.

BY

JOHN WRATHALL BULL,

SON OF THE LATE REV. JOHN BULL, M.A., INCUMBENT OF ST. JOHN'S, WALTHAMSTOW.

"Let the great world spin for ever down the ringing groove of change."

WITH ILLUSTRATIONS.

E. S. WIGG & SON,
Publishers,
ADELAIDE, SOUTH AUSTRALIA.

AND

SAMPSON LOW, MARSTON, SEARLE, & RIVINGTON,
"CROWN BUILDINGS," 188, FLEET STREET, LONDON.

1884.

HIS EXCELLENCY

SIR W. F. C. ROBINSON, K.C.M.G.,

GOVERNOR-GENERAL AND COMMANDER-IN-CHIEF OF THE COMBINED

COLONY OF SOUTH AUSTRALIA, THE NORTHERN

TERRITORY, AND DEPENDENCIES,

This History

IS RESPECTFULLY DEDICATED

BY

THE AUTHOR.

PUBLISHERS' NOTE.

The *first* edition of this work was privately printed by the author for circulation in South Australia only. This new and enlarged second edition may therefore be regarded virtually as a new work.

LONDON, *October* 8, 1883.

PREFACE

TO THE SECOND EDITION.

IN complying with the demand for a second edition, the Author feels it necessary to commence the early history of the colony of South Australia by recording the steps which were taken to obtain from the Imperial Government the Act of Parliament by which the colony was founded: as well as further to extend the work from where the first edition ended—namely, from the departure of Captain Grey to the end of the administration of Sir Wm. F. D. Jervois, K.C.M.G., C.B., R.E.—during which period the colony has made rapid strides politically and materially.

The history opens as follows. So early as the year 1831, a numerous body of influential gentlemen were associated together in England for the purpose of establishing a colony in the southern part of New Holland, on Wakefield's new principle of colonisation —*i.e.*, to open and establish new colonies, by devoting the funds from sales of land to the cost of deporting a working population. Under the auspices of that association a considerable number of persons, some with small capitals, was collected together, who desired to go out as settlers to the proposed new colony, which was to be established in a slice of country, from the southern and western parts of the large province of New South

Wales, its western boundary to be the colony of Swan River. After a long and unsuccessful negociation with His Majesty's (William IV.) Government to obtain the desired Charter, these proposing emigrants were disbanded. A large amount of time, trouble, and money was thus thrown away in a grand endeavour to relieve the mother country of redundant labour, by converting a needy home population into prosperous colonists, and to occupy, convert, and fructify a portion of the waste and desert parts of a colossal empire.

No further steps were taken until the beginning of the year 1834, when a fresh society was formed with the same objects, under the name of the South Australian Association, and it was determined that the proposed colony should be founded, not as previously intended by Royal Charter, but by an Act of the Imperial Parliament. To carry into effect the original project in this amended form, an extended committee was elected, embracing the greater portion of the previous body, and with other influential names added. This committee was composed of the following gentlemen, viz. :—W. Woolryche Whitmore, Esq., M.P., *Chairman*; A. Beauclerk, Esq., M.P.; Abraham Borradaile, Esq.; Charles Buller, Esq., M.P.; H. L. Bulwer, Esq., M.P.; J. W. Childers, Esq., M.P.; William Clay, Esq., M.P.; Raikes Currie, Esq.; William Gowan, Esq.; Samuel Mills, Esq.; Sir William Molesworth, Bart., M.P.; Jacob Montefiore, Esq.; George Ward Norman, Esq.; G. Poulett Scrope, Esq.; Dr. Southwood Smith; Edward Strutt, Esq., M.P.; George Grote, Esq., M.P.; Benjamin Hawes, Esq., M.P.; J. H. Hawkins, Esq., M.P.; Rowland Hill, Esq.; M. D. Hill, Esq., M.P.; W. Hutt, Esq., M.P.; John Melville, Esq.; Colonel Torrens, M.P.;

Preface. vii

Daniel Wakefield, Jun., Esq.; H. Warburton, Esq.; H. G. Ward, Esq., M.P.; John Wilks, Esq., M.P.; Joseph Wilson, Esq., M.P.; John Ashton Yates, Esq.; George Grote, Esq., M.P., *Treasurer;* Robert Gouger, Esq., *Hon. Sec.*

After great exertions by the association in the same year (1834), the incorporating Bill was passed through the Imperial Parliament, having been greatly advanced by the support and influence of the Duke of Wellington (4 & 5 Wm. IV. cap. 95). Under this Act a commission was appointed to manage the proposed work of colonisation, and to settle the principles upon which it was to be carried out; Wakefield's scheme being adopted. The Act provided that no convicts should ever be sent to South Australia, and that a Constitution should be granted as soon as its population reached 50,000 souls.

The commissioners first appointed were:—Colonel Torrens, F.R.S.; George Fife Angas, Esq.; William Hutt, Esq.; John George Shaw Le Fevre, Esq.; Alex. McKinnon, Esq., M.P.; Samuel Mills, Esq.; Jacob Montefiore, Esq.; George Palmer, Jun., Esq.; John Wright, Esq.; George Barnes, Esq., *Treasurer;* Rowland Hill, Esq., *Secretary.*

It has been considered an act of justice to publish the names of the far-seeing patriots who, against great opposition, were the agents in founding this most prosperous colony, now one of the *largest* customers of British manufactures, affording happy homes for a most loyal section of the great British Empire, and still crying out for immigrants with capital, as well as hands to work.

The name of the colony, which has often led to absurd mistakes being made by residents in the mother country and elsewhere, was adopted by the committee of the association in 1834. As the colony of Victoria was not separated from the province of New South Wales until after the proclamation of South Australia, the latter was at that time the most southern settlement in Australia, the site of Melbourne being occupied by a solitary sheep-farmer. A reference to a map of Australia will show, however, that from the eastern boundary of the colony the coast trends considerably to the south.

CONTENTS.

	PAGES
PREFACE .	v to viii

BOOK I.

CHAPTER I.

Visits of explorers to Kangaroo Island during the years 1802 and 1819 . . . . 1 to 4

CHAPTER II.

First "squatters" on Kangaroo Island—Arrival of ships with settlers, emigrants, and staff of the South Australian Company—First trade with Sydney . . . . 4 to 12

CHAPTER III.

Arrival of Colonel Light, Surveyor-General—Extracts from letters of Vice-Admiral Pullen—Postscript—Mr. Henry Mildred . 12 to 25

CHAPTER IV.

Arrival of Captain Hindmarsh, R.N., first Governor of South Australia—Tales "for the marines"—Resignation of Colonel Light—Recall of Captain Hindmarsh—G. M. Stephen, Esq., appointed Acting-Governor—A questionable transaction . . . 25 to 32

Contents.

CHAPTER V.

PAGES

First trip in the "bush" by a private party—A "Corroboree"—Attempt to reach Encounter Bay overland . . . . 32 to 38

CHAPTER VI.

"Church and State"—First Colonial chaplain—Rev. T. Q. Stow and other missionaries . . . . 38 to 50

CHAPTER VII.

Arrival of the Author and his family—Pick-a-back—"Suspended" Birthday ball at Government House—Novel carriages—Conjugal love—Postscript—Sad end of Samuel Stephens, Esq., Manager of South Australian Company . . . . . . 50 to 56

CHAPTER VIII.

Attempt to murder Sheriff Smart—The Riot Act read—Clever capture of Morgan. . . . . 56 to 63

CHAPTER IX.

Murders of settlers by the natives—A neat weapon—Infanticide—Murder of Captain Barker, before the settlement of the colony . . . . 63 to 75

CHAPTER X.

Arrival of first herd of cattle from New South Wales, conducted by Charles Bonney, Esq. . . . . 76 to 80

CHAPTER XI.

Arrival of Governor Gawler—"Berry good cockatoo gubbernor"—Our first volunteer force—Captain Frome—Bamboozling the Governor—A palatial residence—Judge Cooper . . . 80 to 87

CHAPTER XII.

Arrival of Pastor Kavel with German emigrants, assisted by G. F. Angas, Esq.—Founding of German townships . . . 87 to 93

CHAPTER XIII.

Erroneous opinions entertained of the general character of the country north of and around Adelaide by Captain Sturt and Mr. Eyre—Extracts from diary of first exploration of the latter—First runs in the "Far North" . . . . . . 93 to 99

CHAPTER XIV.

Captain Sturt's exploration of the interior by order of the Imperial Government—Death of Surveyor Poole, second in command—Fails to reach centre of continent . . . . . 99 to 104

CHAPTER XV.

First Wesleyan ministers—An interposition of Providence—Wreck of the brig "Fanny"—The Rev. Mr. Draper . . . 104 to 116

CHAPTER XVI.

Massacre of captain, passengers, and crew of the brigantine "Maria" on the coast of Encounter Bay by Milmenura tribe of natives 116 to 129

BOOK II.

CHAPTER I.

Early fires in the city—Bush fires—Great fall in prices of live stock—A practical joke—A very *moist* banquet . . . . 130 to 137

CHAPTER II.

Mineral discoveries—Glen Osmond silver lead mine—Kapunda and Burra Burra Copper Mines—"Nobs and snobs" . . 137 to 144

CHAPTER III.

Journey across the mount Lofty Range—"Reckless driving"—An "overlander"—Murder of an old native—"King John," a native help . . . . 144 to 155

CHAPTER IV.

Progress of agriculture—Invention of the reaping machine . 155 to 163

CHAPTER V.

Career and capture of bushrangers—Attempts to escape from gaol—Execution of Curran and Hughes—Capture of Green, Wilson, and Morgan . . . . 163 to 177

CHAPTER VI.

Final careers of Foley and Stone, escaped convicts—Encounter with Stone in the ranges . . . . 177 to 185

CHAPTER VII.

Occurrences on battle run pointed out by Stone—Stockkeeper Hart's crimes and escape—Suicide of Moorhead . . . 186 to 192

CHAPTER VIII.

Providential escape of Captain Sturt from natives on the Murray—Troubles with the Rufus tribe of natives—Capture by them of overland travelling flocks of sheep—Major O'Halloran sent against the natives—Recalled by Governor Gawler—Private party under Lieutenant Field defeated by the natives—Governor Gawler recalled . . . . 192 to 206

CHAPTER IX.

Progress of the colony during Colonel Gawler's administration—Vice-regal visit to the Murray—Mr. Jas. Hurtle Fisher, first Resident Commissioner—Final career of Colonel Gawler . . 206 to 219

CHAPTER X.

Continuation of history of contest with the Rufus natives—Defeat of the natives by Major O'Halloran—Salvation of an overland cattle party . . . . 219 to 243

CHAPTER XI.

Governor Grey—Ruin of pioneers by the policy he was instructed to pursue . . . . 243 to 253

CHAPTER XII.

Governor Grey's bills on the Home Government also repudiated—The Governor ordered to New Zealand on account of the Maori war . . . . 253 to 261

CHAPTER XIII.

Arrival of Lieut.-Col. Robe—Grant in aid to religious bodies—Royalty on minerals—Dr. Short, first Anglican bishop—St. Peter's Collegiate School—St. Peter's Cathedral . . . 261 to 264

BOOK III.

CHAPTER I.

Cattle-stealers in the Black Forest—Murder of Gofton—Trial, conviction, and execution of Joseph Stagg—Strange self-accusation of Trooper Lomas . . . . 265 to 275

CHAPTER II.

PAGES

Career of Storey—First actions in 1838—Subsequent appearance in 1841 as Chief of the "Black-faced Robbers" . . . 275 to 282

CHAPTER III.

Loss of the ship *Lady Dennison*, with convicts, *en route* to Tasmania—Voyage of the brig *Punch* with convicts—Failure of attempt of convicts to seize the ship. . . . . . . 282 to 289

CHAPTER IV.

Settlement of Port Lincoln—Visit of Lady Franklin—Murders of settlers by natives on out-stations in Port Lincoln District—Party of soldiers dispatched against the natives—The "campaign" a failure . . . . 289 to 303

CHAPTER V.

Relief party in search of Mr. Dutton—List of natives executed for murders committed in the Lake and Port Lincoln districts 303 to 310

CHAPTER VI.

Arrival of Governor Young—Royalty on Minerals Act repealed—"Black Thursday"—Port Adelaide Railway Act passed—Discovery of Gold in New South Wales and Victoria—Exodus of males from South Australia—Escort established and gold tokens issued—The Author's experiences as a digger—Navigation of the River Murray—Constitution Bill referred back to the colony. Postscript—River Murray navigation in 1883 . . . . . 311 to 321

CHAPTER VII.

Governor Sir R. G. MacDonnell—Constitution Act—First Parliament opened—Railway extension—The Real Property Act—No Man's Land annexed—Arrival of Governor Daly—Northern Territory annexed—Arrival of H.R.H. the Duke of Edinburgh—Death of Sir Dominic Daly—Prince Alfred College. Postscript—Camels in South Australia . . . . 321 to 331

Contents.

CHAPTER VIII.

	PAGES
Stuart's explorations .	332 to 344

CHAPTER IX.

Stuart's final and successful expedition .	345 to 360

CHAPTER X.

The Northern Territory—First attempt to form settlement at Escape Cliffs—McKinlay's exploring trip—Removal of settlement to Port Darwin—Wreck of S.S. *Gothenberg* and loss of Judge Wearing, his *suite*, and other passengers . . . . 360 to 376

CHAPTER XI.

Arrival at Palmerston of Parliamentary Party	376 to 383

CHAPTER XII.

Reports of the Minister of Education and other visitors to the Northern Territory . . . . 384 to 394

CHAPTER XIII.

Arrival of Sir James Fergusson—The overland telegraph line . 394 to 399

CHAPTER XIV.

Sir Anthony Musgrave—Bishop Bugnion—Sir W. W. Cairns—Sir W. F. D. Jervois—Sir William's farewell speech—Concluding remarks . . . . 399 to 406

APPENDIX.

	PAGES
Australian statistics	. 407
Notes on the Queensland Sugar Plantations by the Hon. J. L. Parsons, Minister of Education	. 407 to 413
First steamer from London to Adelaide, South Australia	. 414
Rum Jungle Creek Nurseries, Northern Territory (near Southport)	. 414
Useful information for parties who intend to visit or to invest funds in South Australia	. 415
Corporation of the City of Adelaide	. 415
Bank of South Australia	. 416
Elder, Smith, & Co.	416
Orient line of steamers	. 416

LIST OF ILLUSTRATIONS.

FRAMEWORK OF PUNT IN WHICH MCKINLAY AND PARTY RETURNED FROM THEIR EXPLORING TRIP.

ARRIVAL OF MCKINLAY AND PARTY AT ESCAPE CLIFF, NORTHERN TERRITORY.

VIEW OF ADELAIDE IN 1836, SHOWING THE VICE-REGAL RESIDENCE.

CHAMBERS' PILLAR, NEAR THE CENTRE OF THE CONTINENT.

EARLY EXPERIENCES OF LIFE

IN

SOUTH AUSTRALIA

BOOK I.

CHAPTER I.

BEFORE the relation of the early occurrences in forming a new Colony, it will be profitable to go back a few years and quote from the published voyages of the following maritime explorers, viz., Captain Flinders and the French navigators Baudin and Freycinet, as well as the accounts given by Captain Sutherland at a later period.

In the year 1802, Captain Flinders, in his Majesty's ship *Investigator*, after he had explored the coast to the west of Encounter Bay, there fell in with the French expedition under Captains Baudin and Freycinet; and to commemorate such a friendly encounter, named that portion of the coast Encounter Bay; at this time the two countries were engaged in a deadly war. By a few days only Captain Flinders was the original discoverer of the Gulfs of St. Vincent and Spencer, which he also named.

On the morning after casting anchor in Nepean Bay, Captain Flinders writes :—" On going towards the shore a number of dark brown kangaroos were seen feeding upon a grass plat by the side of the wood, and our landing gave them no disturbance. I had with me a double-barrelled gun, fitted with a bayonet, and the gentlemen (my companions) had muskets. It would be difficult to guess how many kangaroos were seen, but I killed ten, and the rest of my party made up the number to thirty-one taken on board in the course of the day. The least of them weighed sixty-nine, and the largest one hundred and twenty-five pounds. These kangaroos had much resemblance to the large species found in the forest lands of New South Wales, except that their colour is darker, and they were not wholly destitute of fat. The whole ship's company were engaged in the afternoon in skinning and cleaning the kangaroos, and a delightful regale they afforded after four months' privation from almost any fresh provisions. In gratitude for so seasonable a supply I named this southern land 'Kangaroo Island.'

"These poor animals suffered themselves to be shot in the eyes with small shot, and in some cases to be knocked on the head with sticks. I scrambled through the brushwood and over fallen trees to reach the higher land with the surveying instruments, but the thickness and height of the wood prevented anything else being distinguished. There was little doubt, however, that this extensive piece of land was separated from the main land, and accounted for the extraordinary tameness of the kangaroos and the presence of seals upon the shore, thus also proving the absence of human inhabitants, of whom no traces were found.

"On a day following, the scientific gentlemen landed, and in the evening eleven more kangaroos were brought on board, but most of these were smaller, and seemed to be of a different species (qy. wallaby?). Some of the party saw large running birds, supposed according to description to be the emu or cassowary.

"A thick wood covered almost all that part of the island visible from the ship, but the trees in a vegetating state were not equal in size to the generality of those lying on the ground, nor to the dead trees which were still standing. Those on the ground were so abundant that in ascending the higher land a considerable part of the walk was made on these fallen trunks. They lay in all directions, and were nearly of the same size and in the same progress of decay; whence it would seem that they had not fallen from age, nor yet been thrown down in a gale of wind, but had succumbed before a general conflagration.

"The soil of that part of Kangaroo Island examined by us was judged to be much superior to any before seen either upon the south coast or upon the islands."

The above quotation is confirmed by the reports of the French navigators and Captain Sutherland, as they all agree in the descriptions they give, which represent such an extraordinarily different condition of the island, both as to the size of timber and the animals they found on their visits, from what was found when the first ships arrived in Nepean Bay, to form the first settlement there, under the direction of the Board of Commissioners in London. Remarkable changes like these can only be accounted for by such an overwhelming conflagration as in the opinion of Captain Flinders must have happened before his visit.

The French navigators also give an account of the vast number and large size of the kangaroos which they found on the island. They took full advantage of the opportunity to secure a number, and "took on board twenty-seven alive, besides numerous carcases." They found no traces of man.

Captain Sutherland, who was employed by some merchants of Sydney to obtain a cargo of salt and seal-skins from the island, writes:—"On the 8th January, 1819, we arrived at Kangaroo Island from Sydney after a pleasant voyage of 14 days, and anchored in Lagoon Bay (part of Nepean Bay) in about four fathoms of water close in shore. Two boats were dispatched with five men in each to discover the salt lagoon, and to ascertain on what part of the bays seals most resorted. Another boat with three men also started to seek from whence a supply of water could be obtained. During our ramble from this boat a shallow well with a small supply of fresh water was found, with a flat stone near it with writing cut upon it, giving the names of the captains of the French expedition, and the date of their visit. Not far from this spot, and close to Point Marsden, Nepean Bay, we dug a well, behind the sand bank, about four feet deep, which immediately filled with fresh water. The period during which I stayed on and near the island was from the 8th of January to the 12th of August in the before mentioned year. The soil was thickly covered with timber and brushwood. Some of my men landed at several different places on the main. I never saw or heard of any native dogs on Kangaroo Island, and from the very great number of kangaroos I do not believe there are any. Some of the kangaroos I killed weighed one hundred and twenty pounds. I have known our men to have taken as many as fifteen in one morning. We never made use of any part of them but the hind quarters."

He also says he travelled across the island in company with two sealers who had been living on the island some years, but he does not give their names.

The concurrent testimony in the reports which have been quoted should remove all doubts which may have been entertained as to the number of kangaroos said to have been originally found there, and also as to their tameness. The excessive timidity of these marsupials in all other parts of Australia is universally known; in those localities, however, they had been joint occupiers with native aboriginal hunters.

As to the timber which the discoverers report to have found covering the country differing so greatly from the saplings found by our first arrivals, it may be remarked that an explanation will occur to those colonists who have had experience in heavily timbered or close scrubby districts. To such persons it is well known that when a strong bush fire occurs, and is extinguished by rain before it has quite consumed the trees or scrub, the vitality of which it has destroyed, after a sufficient time has elapsed to allow fresh saplings or strong scrub to make considerable growth, a succeeding fire, aided by the dry material left, will make a clean sweep of the country, and the subsequent state of the locality will be either open ground or a close eucalyptus scrub. A few scattered ancient trees, which were perhaps always detached, may possibly survive, and this is considered to be a reasonable explanation of the state of the island as to timber when our colonists arrived, and that the kangaroos had also been nearly exterminated by the overwhelming fires.

As to the future fruitfulness of the island, it is a reasonable expectation that as clearing progresses it will become a prosperous agricultural district, but probably at a great cost to the farmer. A few small farmers are at the present time taking up and clearing portions of the island, the soil of which is found to produce good crops of excellent malting barley, but is not so well suited for the growth of wheat. The climate is both pleasant and healthy.

CHAPTER II.

FOR the following account of Kangaroo Island and its first occupants, the author is partly indebted to information obtained from two of the original islanders many years after he himself became a settler on the mainland, in addition to information he had previously gained. He is thus enabled to correct one erroneous impression early extant, that they were principally runaway convicts, the fact being that the majority of the early inhabitants were men who had left whaling and sealing vessels or surveying ships at various times before the founding of the Colony. One of them, George Bates, arrived on the island in the year 1824, and was engaged in sealing and hunting, and occasionally in making visits to search the beach of Encounter Bay for the bones of stranded whales. On one occasion, shortly after the whaling stations were formed at the Nob and what is now called Victor Harbour, he and some mates had collected whalebone on the beach near the mouth of the River Murray, which they estimated to be worth over £200. This was taken from them by the recently-arrived authorities, and sent by Captain Hart to be sold in Sydney, and yet no salvage was given to them, which they deemed a great hardship. When George Bates forwarded the above information, he stated his age to be seventy-eight years.

In the year 1835 William Thompson, a seaman, landed on Kangaroo Island from the cutter *William*, Captain Wright, after he had fulfilled his engagement in a sealing voyage. He then joined William Walker, who had been some time on the island. At the time Thompson landed there were about seven male white settlers, engaged in sealing and catching wallaby, and in preparing the skins for export. The first settler was Waller, who was said to have been on the island fourteen or fifteen years before Thompson became a resident, say 1819. He had assumed the title of Governor of the island, and to his rule the others yielded such obedience as was necessary in so primitive a state of society. Several of the men had coloured women living with them, some obtained from Tasmania and the others from the tribes occupying the Cape Jervis and Encounter Bay districts. One of these women, not satisfied with her promotion from the position of slave to one of her own race to that of help to a white man, took to the water and swam across the straits, nine miles wide at the narrowest part. Despite the dangers of the powerful currents, and the multitudes of sharks, for which this passage (now called Backstairs Passage) is notorious, she landed safely in her own country. Some four or five years after this extraordinary swim was accomplished, this woman was pointed out to the writer, and she was then a fine specimen of her race.

These primitive inhabitants of the little settlement had cleared small patches of land from the scrub, which they cultivated or worked with strong hoes, thus producing vegetables and wheat, which latter was ground between two flat stones, and from the meal produced they made their unleavened bread or dampers, which were baked in wood ashes.

The late Captain Hart, when in the employment of Mr. Griffiths, of Launceston, was in the habit of visiting the island to trade with the islanders for their seal and wallaby skins and salt, gathered from various lagoons in that part of the island, and to furnish them with goods in exchange. The settlers had pigs and fowls, and varied their diet with the flesh of wallabies, wild-fowl, and fish.

One of the earliest islanders was a young man of the name of G. Meredith, whose father was an inhabitant of Tasmania, in a large way of business. He had been dispatched by his father in a small vessel amongst the islands to catch seals, and had the misfortune to wreck his vessel on Howe's Island, and escaped in a boat with a Dutchman, who was known afterwards as Jacob Seaman. They had with them, on landing on the island, a Tasmanian black woman, called Sal, who had lost half of one of her feet when young, by sleeping with them too near the fire. She was owned by Meredith. He took up his residence at Western River, on the coast of the island opposite the Althorpes. He had also with him two native boys whom he had procured from the mainland, and whom he was training to be of great use to him in his sealing trips. In one of his boat voyages with the black woman and the two boys, he landed on the part of the coast now known as Yankalila, and whilst there encamped Meredith was killed by his black boys, of which sad occurrence the black woman afterwards gave the following account to the islanders:—" Whilst their unsuspecting master was sitting near the camp-fire partaking of porridge, the boys stole behind him." It was supposed that they had been instigated to commit this act of treachery by some black fellows, who afterwards took possession of the black woman, the boat, and all its contents, with which they made their way to Encounter Bay. In the then unsettled state of the country no steps were taken in the matter, as this occurred before the first colonists from England arrived. The boat, it was reported by the islanders, was for some time used by the Encounter Bay natives in sealing and fishing, and was ultimately lost by getting adrift from their careless fastenings. Sal eventually managed to escape to the island, and joined a settler (an American black), named George Brown. He had been engaged as headsman in one of the whaling companies. After the colonists arrived George Brown left the island, and was engaged at the first occupation of Holdfast Bay. He had become acquainted with an emigrant girl who was in the service of Captain Lupson, our first harbour master, who was, I may mention, officially and privately held in universal esteem and respect. Brown was legally married to this young woman, and they left a family, who are now in respectable positions. Sal, after parting from Brown, joined William Cooper, one of the sealers, who acted as interpreter to Colonel Light in his intercourse with the aboriginals on the mainland.

It was more than twelve months after William Thompson became a resident on the island that the first South Australian ships arrived from London. The *Duke of York*, a barque which had left Torbay on the 17th or 18th of April, 1836, arrived on July 29th, with passengers and emigrants, and dropped anchor in Nepean Bay at noon. This was the first vessel which arrived with colonists. Passengers—Mr. Samuel Stephens, first manager of the South Australian Company in the colony; Mr. Thomas Hudson Beare, second in command under the Company ; Mrs. Beare and four children, with Miss C. H. Beare (afterwards Mrs. Samuel Stephens); Mr. D. H. Schryvogle, clerk; Hy. Mitchell, butcher; C. Powell, gardener; Neale, carpenter; Wm. West, labourer,—the last four being emigrants.

The Board of Commissioners in London granted to the management of the South Australian Company a most extraordinary, not to say questionable favour, in accepting and passing the entire crew of the *Duke of York*, as well as those of the *John Pirie, Lady Mary Pelham, Sarah and Elizabeth*, and the *South Australian*, as emigrants, so that the lists which were published (and have lately been republished) as to the numbers of emigrants arriving by those ships were really incorrect. The party from whom this information comes was a passenger in the *Duke of York*, and adds:—"Hardly one of these men remained here. A few of them returned years afterwards, and settled in the colony." Information was not further given whether those who returned succeeded in getting passed as emigrants a second time, but that they were paid for as emigrants the first time by the commissioners was positively stated.

All on board the *Duke of York* were ready to go ashore as soon as the vessel was made snug, and a landing was effected in a little bay, at the spot where the Rapid Bay and Cape Borda submarine cable has been since brought ashore. The time the passengers set their feet on the land was 2 P.M. The first duty then performed was the reading of the Church of England service, in which all joined. Captain Morgan concluded the service by an extemporary prayer or thanksgiving for the prosperous voyage which had been granted to them. Just before the party left the *Duke of York*, a magnificent rainbow appeared in the heavens, and the captain remarked it was a good omen. The rambling and weary party returned late on board; still sleep was not obtained, owing to the excitement of their new position. Between 12 and 1 o'clock the vessel heeled over, and the commotion was general. All were rushing to the boats; but the captain allayed the universal alarm by explaining that he had anchored in too shallow water, and the ship had swung round and grounded on a muddy bottom in an ebbing tide, of the rise and fall of which he had been ignorant.

The following day tents were pitched; and that night the passengers remained on land, and felt the chill of a very severe frost. On the morrow guns and ammunition were the order of the day. The new arrivals early in the morning had been greatly astonished by the clamour of a number of laughing jackasses, as those birds (a variety of the kingfisher) are called. At first some of the people believed the blacks were laughing at them, and had arrived to make an attack. A few days after they landed, some of the sealers living on the island paid them a visit, and brought a splendid supply of vegetables, including a quantity of very fine water melons. Though not quite ripe, these were quickly disposed of. It was not long before patches of land were cleared of the tall scrub, which abounded on all sides. The seeds of vegetables were sown, and soon green food was indulged in.

On the 4th of August two large boats with twenty men started on a trip across Backstairs passage, and a landing was made at Rapid Bay—afterwards so named by Colonel Light. On the way back they fell in with the *John Pirie*, Captain Martin, who was on the look-out for a whaling station. It is here proper to mention the fact that Mr. Menge, who had been engaged and sent out by the South Australian Company to examine the country for minerals, was one of the boat party, and pronounced the ranges to be highly metalliferous.

At a meeting of the few scattered inhabitants, Mr. S. Stephens called on the self-elected primitive Governor Waller to abdicate, which he did magnanimously. The manager purchased all his stock and crops on his small squatting farm, situated about ten miles from Nepean Bay, and since known as "The Farm." I may here mention that Mr. Stephens married a lady passenger on the voyage out, and she was subsequently long known and respected as his widow. I shall later in this history relate the fatal accident by which Mr. Stephens lost his life.

The first selections of land were made at Kingscote, and unfortunately so, for the Company and some private individuals, who at once commenced to work and build houses, &c., which were shortly abandoned after the arrival of the Surveyor-General, Colonel Light, in the brig *Rapid*, on the 20th August, 1836. Colonel Light brought with him, as his staff, Lieutenant Field, R. N., Mr. J. S. Pullen (now Vice-Admiral), Messrs. W. Hill, Wm. Jacob, and G. Claughton, surveyors; Dr. Woodford, Mr. Alfred Barker, mate, and other survey hands.

Of the above are surviving at the time of publishing this work, Messrs. Wm. Jacob, Hiram Mildred, William Hodges, and John Thorne. There is also now residing in England Vice-Admiral Pullen, who has risen by his extraordinary merits, and by his services on one of the expeditions to the North Pole in search of Sir John Franklin's remains, also in Besika Bay and other parts of the world.

Colonel Light, after sufficient examination of the island, as a first place of settlement, pronounced it to be unsuitable, although it possessed in Nepean Bay a grand harbour scarcely surpassed in any known country. In a short time most of the officers, servants, goods, and plant were removed to Port Adelaide or Holdfast Bay. The buildings, gardens, &c., were left to be generally occupied by the original islanders. Colonel Light promised them that they should not be disturbed in their original squatting holdings; but this promise he was not able to fulfil. When the colonists arrived no kangaroos were to be seen on the island; the first sealers, however, reported that when they became residents a few remained, but were soon killed off. At this time, however, the appellation of Kangaroo Island is a misnomer. But Thompson says that he saw bones of kangaroos at Hog Bay and several other places. Hog Bay was reported to be so called from pigs found there by sealers, supposed to have been left by the French navigators, as at that place there was writing in French, cut in a rock near a spot where they obtained fresh water. Mr. C. W. Stuart has kindly furnished me from his notes with the account of his landing at the island, which is interesting as mentioning the arrival of a cargo of goods which had been shipped to find a market in Swan River Settlement, but which were purchased by Mr. S. Stephens, and formed the first opening of trade between the infant colony of South Australia and the much older colony of New South Wales. Mr. Stuart says:—" In September, 1833, I left London in the barque *Atwick*, 500 tons, Captain Hugh McKay, bound for Hobart Town and Sydney. The latter place we reached after a fortnight's detention at Hobart Town, in a little less than five months from Gravesend. I left the ship in Sydney with little less grief than I had felt at leaving home. After recruiting for a few weeks at a friend's house in Sydney, to whom I had letters, I took a passage in the *Lambton* cutter to Port Stephens, about 180 miles to the north of Port Jackson. Here I remained about two years, my attention chiefly directed to cattle, the country near the coast being well adapted for cattle and horses. While still living at Port Stephens, early in 1836 I received from London a land order for a preliminary section of land and a town acre, in a new colony to be called South Australia. My determination was soon made to start to Sydney and to find my way to Nepean Bay, Kangaroo Island, as directed, where they were first to rendezvous. My friends did all they could to persuade me to remain in New South Wales, hinting that the new colony must be a failure—land at one pound an acre and free labour against land at five shillings an acre, as it was in Sydney; and convict labour available. On arriving in Sydney, I found that South Australia was scarcely known there; and as to communication with Kangaroo Island there was none. The late Emanuel Solomon had at that time a place of business in George Street, on which was posted a notice that the schooner *Truelove* was to sail for Swan River on a day mentioned, and would take passengers from Sydney to that place. I went into the office and asked Mr. Solomon if the *Truelove* would put into Nepean Bay, Kangaroo Island. He was astonished at my question and said he did not know, and asked my object in inquiring. On my telling him I wanted a passage there, and information about the

new colony, he seemed to think that I had been duped,
and advised me not on any account to go to Kangaroo Island
till I knew positively that some vessels had arrived there from
England. He told me to see the captain of the *Truelove*, who
would give me more information on the subject than he could.
I saw the captain of the *Truelove*, Colton. His advice to me
was much the same as Mr. Solomon's, but at the same time, for
a certain sum, he would take me to Nepean Bay, and, wind and
weather permitting, he would remain there twenty-four hours,
and if no ships from London had arrived, and I did not like
to remain, he would take me on to Swan River and back
to Sydney for the same money. It was a liberal offer, and I
accepted it. A few days after I went on board the *Truelove*,
with about one ton of stores and two kangaroo dogs. After a
pleasant run of fourteen days we were caught in a heavy S.W.
gale, and being near the island, the vessel was hove to for the
night. Next morning at daylight a brig was descried seven
miles ahead, evidently steering for Nepean Bay. We followed
her, and a few hours later let go our anchor near to her in
Nepean Bay, and she proved to be the *John Pirie*, belonging to
the South Australian Company, and had just returned from
Hobart Town. There were then lying in Nepean Bay the
ships *Cygnet* and *Africaine*, and the brig *Rapid*. I went on
shore immediately in the ship's boat, and on landing was
surprised to see the (to me) strange appearance of the people
just come from England, many of them clad in smock frocks,
with gaiters, &c. On asking where the Governor was to be
seen, I learnt that he had not yet arrived, but I was introduced
to the Manager of the South Australian Company, Mr. Samuel
Stephens. Mr. Stephens was very courteous; and on my
telling him my name, and informing him that I had land orders,
he warmly welcomed me, asked me to his tent to lunch, and
introduced me to Mrs. Stephens. The *Truelove* was the first
vessel that had arrived in Nepean Bay from Sydney, and being
laden with stores and provisions on a trading venture for Swan
River, Mr. Stephens asked me to take him on board and introduce him to the captain. The consequence of this introduction was that Mr. Stephens bought the cargo of the *Truelove*,
and sent her back to Sydney for more necessaries. The day
after I landed I was introduced by Mr. Stephens to the following colonists: Mr. J. Hallett, Captain Duff, Messrs. C. S. Hare,
T. H. Beare and M. Smith, Esq., solicitor, and to the sons of

the last two gentlemen, W. L. Beare, Esq., Justice of the Peace, of Clare, and H. J. Smith, Esq., S. M. Narracooste, the only survivors at this time.

CHAPTER III.

COLONEL LIGHT arrived in the brig *Rapid* and landed on Kangaroo Island on the 20th August, 1836. Extracts from his published journal, at the present time out of print, are now given.

"Having sailed from Nepean Bay, after deciding that the island was a locality not suitable on which to fix the capital, I put into Rapid Bay, from thence sailed up the Gulf, and came to anchor in $\frac{1}{4}$ less 5 fathoms on September 24th, 1836. Opposite to the brig appears a very extensive flat, to the northward and east of which mangroves were to be seen lining the shore.

"*September 25th.*—Left the ship to examine what appeared to be an inlet, and on passing up the same at about half a mile the boat grounded; on getting off I returned on board. On the report of Mr. Hill, second mate, that he had seen from the mast-head a considerable river, I again left the ship in the hatch boat to explore, and after walking along the beach without success, returned to the brig. At 4 P.M. an opening was plainly seen from the brig. I had gone along the shore southward. Mr. Field during my absence had gone in the jolly-boat and had entered and sounded the mouth of a considerable river, which I determined to explore next day.

"*September 26th.*—At 9 A.M. entered the river; the first reach runs about two miles. After passing the channel we came into a good wide river; on going some distance and finding it did not accord with Captain Jones' description of the harbour he discovered, I determined to run higher up the Gulf, and to examine this place at a future period, and returned to the brig.

"*September 27th.*—After running up the Gulf, at 3 P.M. anchored in three fathoms. From this position could see the head of the Gulf as laid down by Flinders. Dispatched Mr. Field in the jolly-boat; on his return he reported no harbour could exist there; returned to the last anchorage. I now despaired of ever finding the beautiful harbour described by Jones.

"*September* 28*th*.—At half-past 6 sent Mr. Pullen and Claughton in the hatch-boat. They having shaped their course along shore, we got under way to run with easy sail as nearly abreast the boat as we could. We had after a little time the satisfaction of seeing them enter an inlet, and soon after disappear. I was now full of hope that Jones' harbour was at last found, and at 1 P.M. came to an anchor in our former berth to await the return of the hatch-boat. At half-past 2 Mr. Field went in the jolly-boat to look at the same river I had been in on the 26th.

"Mr. Field met Mr. Pullen in the gig, who had left the hatch-boat at anchor at the northern entrance; each party, after communicating, separated, Mr. Field returning to the brig, Mr. Pullen to the hatch-boat. I now remained in great anxiety between hope and fear. A report brought back by Mr. Field that Mr. Pullen had seen no *fresh water* damped me much, and I could only remain till his return before determining what course to pursue.

"*September* 29*th*.—Mr. Pullen returned and reported his entrance by the northern channel, and no fresh water met with. He further stated that there were two separate channels. This was so different to the account given by Jones that I felt a great disappointment.

"*September* 30*th*.—Left the ship in the surveying boat, and got into the harbour by a small channel about a mile to the northward of the southern entrance, and with a fine breeze from the north-west passed up a reach fully three miles in extent to the southward, carrying three or four fathoms all the way. We went on the island (Torrens) and found *no fresh water*. At the end of this reach a large inlet appeared still keeping a southwardly direction; but I was anxious to examine the creek to the eastward in a line with Mount Lofty. Into this I bent my course with the strong hope of finding it prove the mouth of some fresh-water stream from the mountains. On the rise of the tide I returned to the hatch-boat, which being now afloat, we got under way, and having now fully persuaded myself that no part of this harbour could be that described by Captain Jones, I resolved on returning to the brig to run again down the coast (south) and see if by any chance we could have missed so desirable a shelter."

I here bring forward Captain Jones' account as given subsequently in Colonel Light's diary, on which he so unfortunately depended, and in doing so endured great trouble and loss of time.

Captain Jones' report:—"The inlet (miscalled Sixteen-mile Creek) is a stream of fresh water, at about fifteen or twenty miles north of this river. I (Captain Jones) discovered a fine harbour, sheltered by an island, which is about three miles in circumference, with abundance of fresh water upon it, as well as some streams running into the harbour from the main land."

Continuation of the diary:—" *October 1st.*—At 6 A.M. made sail for the brig, at half-past 8 got on board and got under way once more in search of Jones' harbour."

So much for the misfortune of having relied on an exaggerated description of what Captain Jones saw. Thus Colonel Light again turned his back on what he ultimately adopted as Port Adelaide, making light of the work accomplished by Mr. Pullen, in the first passage up the Sixteen-mile Creek, in his truthful but less florid report, furnished to his superior officer on September 29th.

On the subject of the ultimate adoption of Port Adelaide, it is only necessary to continue to give extracts from Colonel Light's diary, to be followed by information gained from Admiral Pullen's letters, recently received.

"*October 1st.*—Running down the coast south, was enchanted with the extent of the plain to the north (qy., west?) of Mount Lofty. All the glasses of the ship were in requisition. At length, seeing something like the mouth of a small river (Glenelg Creek), and a country with trees so dispersed as to allow the sight of most luxuriant green underneath, stood in, and anchored in three and a half fathoms, in mud and seaweeds, about one and a half miles from the mouth of the river (Pattawalonga).

"*October 3rd.*—At 9 A.M. went on shore to examine plains. A gardener (with a spade), named Laws, was landed. The gig's crew were desired to pull along shore and stop at the mouth of the river. Messrs. Claughton and Woodford accompanied Laws, keeping some way inland to examine the soil, while Pullen and myself kept along the beach. We proceeded about two miles, but found nothing but a wide indenture of the coast. We walked five miles further, and then returned to the place where we landed. At 4 P.M. all returned on board. I was much gratified at the report Laws gave me of the soil, he being a good judge.

"*October* 4*th*.—Went on shore at 9 A.M. to examine the plain. I cannot express my delight at seeing no bounds to a flat of fine rich-looking country, with abundance of fresh-water lagoons. The little river, too, was deep. After walking some distance through long grass returned to the beach at 2 P.M., and getting into the gig pulled on board.

"*October* 5*th*.—Sent Messrs. Claughton and Jacob to trace the river up. At 1 P.M. these gentlemen returned, and said the river at four miles up was fresh. It was then a very narrow stream bending to the N.E., and appeared to have its source in the plains.

"The brig proceeded down the coast. At 1.30 P.M. hove-to on the 10th abreast a river—(qy., Onkaparinga?). A native woman on board had mentioned this, and I sent Mr. Pullen in the gig to examine the entrance. At 2.10 he returned, and reported his seeing a large river for some distance, but, the sand bar having much surf over it, he was nearly upset. Again disappointed in my hopes of finding Jones' harbour, I now felt fully convinced that no such thing could exist on this coast, at least as described by him.

"*October* 11*th*.—At 5.45 got under way. At noon we observed a boat coming towards us. At 2 P.M. hove-to; the boat brought Mr. John Morphett and Mr. Samuel Stephens. They reported the arrival of the *Cygnet* at Nepean Bay, and the landing of stores, and that the people were hutting themselves. I now resolved on going into Rapid Bay, and after landing some stores there, to send the brig to Kangaroo Island to fetch over the assistant surveyors, that they might be employed in the survey on this side the gulf during my examination of Port Lincoln, &c.

"*November* 2*nd*.—Divided the surveying party into two, Mr. Kingston having the largest party, and Mr. Gilbert with the greater part of the stores, to embark on board the *Rapid* for Holdfast Bay. Mr. Finniss, with his party, including Mr. Jacob, Mr. Hiram Mildred, and others to remain at Rapid Bay, each party to make as many observations as possible during my absence at Port Lincoln or elsewhere.

"*November* 6*th*.—At 4 P.M. the *Africaine*, Captain Duff, arrived at Rapid Bay with Mr. Gouger, Colonial Secretary, Mr. Brown, Emigration Agent, and other passengers. Mr. Gouger questioned me as to where we should settle. I could only recommend his proceeding to Holdfast Bay for the present, but stating that I could not guarantee permanent settlement there With Captain Duff I embarked at 10 A.M. on the 7th.

"*November 8th.*—Landed at Holdfast Bay, was met by Mr. Field and Mr. Morphett, who had been out exploring. The accounts given by these gentlemen, though not unfavourable, did not cheer the spirits of the new comers. Messrs. Field, Kingston, and Morphett had made a few miles inland, and had found a fresh-water river (the Torrens) much larger than any yet seen. Looking generally at this place I am quite confident it will be one of the largest settlements, if not the capital, of the new colony; the creek will be its harbour.

"*November 20th.*—Sailed for the creek (*i.e.*, Sixteen-mile Creek, Port Adelaide), taking Mr. Kingston with me. At 6 P.M. we came to anchor in the first reach, all hands overjoyed at the little brig's berth in so snug a spot.

"*November 21st.*—Left the brig by the hatch-boat with Messrs. Kingston, Morphett, and Pullen, to examine the southern reach which I had before left unnoticed."

Extract from letter to the Commissioners :—"*November 22nd* (dated). The Harbour. I could not leave this coast without looking once more at this harbour. We steered at once for this beautiful anchorage, and ran the brig in, where we now lie at single anchor although it is now blowing a gale of wind from the south-west with thick rainy weather. We were more than delighted to find the creek running into the plain so far. I am now more than ever persuaded that it is connected with the fresh-water lagoons. It is one of the finest little harbours I ever saw. We had three fathoms water and very often four fathoms at dead low water in sailing up. I have sent Mr. Kingston to trace the connection between the head of the salt-water creek and the fresh-water, and to make his way back to the Glenelg camp by land."

"*November 25th.*—Got under way and out of the harbour with a light breeze. At 1 P.M. anchored in Holdfast Bay."

Extract from Mr. Kingston's letter :—" I kept along the banks of the river (creek) about two miles, when I think it had its source in the marshes (lagoons) in which I found the river (before alluded to) losing itself. The following day I crossed the river (Torrens) running down from (direction of) Mount Lofty. I again traced the plain, being able to view the course of the river by the reeds, until I found it again running through a regular bed."

Colonel Light, after giving instructions to Mr. Kingston to follow up his discovery of the running river Torrens, left for Port Lincoln. What he found there is described in another chapter. On his return to St. Vincent's Gulf on December 17th, "at daylight, Mount Lofty and the range of hills were seen. At 10 A.M. came to anchor, and went ashore to see our party. The time now lost in much extra labour, and the arrival of many people from England made me anxious to find some place to locate the land purchasers and others, and from every answer from the sealers and from the view I have had of the western coast (of the Gulf) I felt convinced I should never find anything more eligible than the neighbourhood of Holdfast Bay. As for Encounter Bay, I resolved on leaving that to a future period, for the following reason:—I never could fancy for one moment that any navigable entrance from the sea into the lake could possibly exist. On looking at Flinders' chart, and considering the exposed situation of that coast, moreover the very circumstance of so large a lake being there, was a convincing proof to me that the Murray could not have a passage sufficiently deep or wide to discharge its waters into the sea. Deep and fine harbours with good entrances are only found where the shore is high, hard, or rocky; sand alone can never preserve a clear channel against the scud of the sea such as must inevitably be thrown on the coast about Encounter Bay.

"On my arrival at Nepean Bay reports of the sealers I obtained, confirmed the opinion I held that there was no such thing as a harbour along the coast, I therefore thought I should be throwing away valuable time in examining there.

"*December* 18*th*.—At half-past nine got under way with the *Tam o' Shanter* for the harbour. At six entered the first reach and came to anchor; about 11 A.M. the *Tam o' Shanter* struck on the edge of the western sandspit, having three fathoms of water within half her own length; she remained here until the 22nd; about 4 P.M. she was hove off, both crews assisting, and both ships made sail for the higher part of the harbour. I preceded both ships in my hatch-boat.

"It was really beautiful to look back and see two British ships for the first time sailing up between mangroves in fine smooth water, in a creek that had never before borne the construction of the marine architect, and which at some future period might be the channel of import and export of a great commercial capital. Having got both ships up the harbour, I shall leave my narrative of the marine part of the expedition and proceed to my work on shore.

"*December* 24*th*.—Walked over the plain to that part of the river where Mr. Kingston had pitched his tent (the site of the future capital). My first opinions with regard to this place became still more confirmed by this trip. Having traversed over nearly six miles of a beautiful flat, I arrived at the river, and saw from this a continuation of the same plain for at least six miles more to the foot of the hills under Mount Lofty, affording an immense plain of level and advantageous ground for occupation. Having settled future work with Mr. Kingston, I returned to make arrangements for finally leaving the ship.

"*December* 28*th*.—Pitched my tent near Mr. Kingston's at the side of the river. I heard of the Governor's arrival at Holdfast Bay, but having much to do had not time to go down to meet him.

"*December* 30*th*.—His Excellency the Governor arrived at our camp, and we walked together that he might see the spot I had selected. His Excellency expressed his sense of the beauty of the place, but said it was 'too far from the harbour.' But, nevertheless, the site was adopted, on which is now built the most beautiful city in the Southern Hemisphere. Colonel Light, in deference to the Governor, entertained the idea of placing the city on the banks of the Torrens about one and a half miles lower down, but finding both above and below his first choice marks of the river overflowing its banks, he fortunately returned to it."

As bearing on the question of selecting Port Adelaide as the principal port of the province, the following extracts from Vice-Admiral Pullen's letters to the late A. Barker, Esq., who was also an officer on board the brig *Rapid*, are given :—

" I see in portions of Colonel Light's journals which have appeared in the papers that not one mention of my name is made in them in connection with the discovery of Port Adelaide. I believe I was the first in it (*i.e.*, the southern reach of the present harbour). You cannot forget the brig dropping me with the hatch-boat on September 28, 1836, when I got into an opening above the present entrance and finally anchored in the North Arm, thence proceeding southerly in the gig I passed up the long southern reach. On my return I met Mr. Field in the jolly-boat. On the next day I sailed out in the hatch-boat by Light's Passage, and on arriving on board the *Rapid* reported what I had discovered in my trip up the long southern reach, on receiving which the Surveyor-General decided to return with me the next day, on which occasion he confined himself to an examination of an eastern branch of the creek, and a patient search for fresh water.

"I have to complain of much the same treatment as to the Murray Mouth, as I was the first to enter that river from the sea. I feel great interest in that champion stream, and in the colony generally, in the establishment of which we had something to do, and which seems to be flourishing wonderfully. I am now giving all the help I can to an engineer to go in for the docks in the port just above the North Arm. A few days ago I was called on by a gentleman to tell me that such a thing was likely to be undertaken, whom I informed that it was possible I might be able to give him some important information. The spot chosen is near where I got turned out in the water on the capsizing of the hatch-boat, by the force of a heavy squall, in beating up for the head of the creek (Old Port). I do not remember the names of my men, but it was a narrow escape, especially for poor Nation, who was with us. I heard of his sad death with great regret."

Note.—As to the circumstances which confused Colonel Light in the essential difference between the state of the water he found in the Sixteen-mile Creek, and the somewhat exaggerated account of it given by Captain Jones, such a discrepancy may be explained from the different season of the year when the creek was seen by them. It is natural to suppose, although the date of Jones' visit is not given, that he arrived and found the fresh state of the heads of the various branches of the main creek after a heavy and continued rain-fall, when the freshets were still running, and that fresh water had displaced the salt at and below their unapproachable heads, as we know is the case more or less periodically at the present time. Jones may also have landed on Torrens Island when he found lodges of rain water on it. I may mention that when ships were lying at or a little below the Old Port (Misery) I heard reports of buckets being let down from ships' sides and fresh water obtained.

In further explanation it is observed that the time when Colonel Light made his inspection of the island, and of the easterly branch creek which points towards Mount Lofty, was late in the month of November, probably after a dry season. Moreover, his idea was a natural one, that a main stream might be found joining the eastern head of the creek, and thus he was led to neglect the southern reach on which Mr. Pullen had reported, the course of which runs parallel to the coast, and separated from it only by a narrow sandy strip of land. It is seen by these now published facts brought side by side that to Admiral Pullen and Sir G. S. Kingston belong the credit of proving that the sixteen-mile salt water creek and the constantly running water of the River Torrens have a connection, although after dry months the surface junction disappears.

I continue to extract from the Admiral's letters to show his work when a master's mate at the Murray Mouth, and his taking a boat in and reaching what was called Port Pullen, now the Goolwa. The Admiral says :—

"Port Pullen, I suppose, will follow (in the loss of his name), for the sketch I have lately seen of the entrance to the Murray is nothing like what I furnished after I had succeeded in passing through the mouth. There too I nearly lost my life, for on going in in a boat expressly built for the river work I was thrown out into the surf. If I had lost my presence of mind and let go the steer oar, which the man pulling the after oar called on me to do, I should never have been writing this. I do not know how many times I passed down the south-east branch, now the Coorong, but the last time was when I went to hunt the murderers of the poor shipwrecked passengers and crew of the unfortunate *Maria*. When I first found the mangled bodies of men, women, and children, all in a nude state, I am certain that if there had been any natives present I could not have answered for the consequences, my men being in so exasperated and excited a state. Duncan was one of my men. He deserved a better berth than he has ever held since I have known him. He came home with me in the Lord Glenelg. The last time I saw him was in Valparaiso, in 1849; he was boatman's mate in the *Nereus*, a Government store-ship, and I was lieutenant in H.M. ship *Asia*."

"Whilst engaged at the Murray Mouth the Governor, and Surveyor Nixon, were with me on Barker's Knowle when I was first sounding in and out. I have seen several plans and sketches of the Channel, but only one of them agrees with the course it had when I sailed in in the cutter *Waterwitch*, and the river only found that course a few days before I ordered the cutter to Encounter Bay, for the purpose of sailing her in. Indeed, the course direct out had changed so suddenly that I had no time to sound the new one, which winded so much that I felt very anxious about it, but I could not give up, so risked it and happily succeeded.

"I can give you but little account of the events of the first days of the colony, except from recollection, for when I started on the survey of Lake Alexandrina, while fitting out at Encounter Bay, I was burned out, and what notes I had, with everything else I possessed, were destroyed except a pair of trousers I seized hold of, when I tumbled out of my cot to escape the burning element, then all over the roof, leaving me no time to get my watch from under the pillow. That fire commenced in another part of the building, in which I had placed my instruments, &c., as more secure, but they all went, and I was helpless, and had to walk the whole way to Adelaide to replenish everything (over eighty miles).

"After some little time I returned and pitched my first camp, and surveyed what is now called Port Elliot, a mere notch in the coast, with an island or islet called by the then Governor Pullen's Isle, since known, I believe, as Lipson's, so blotting out all reminiscences of one of the earliest pioneers in the work.

"My next adventure happened at one of the survey camps (Hill's), where a vicious beast of a Timor pony I had in use threw me, and I was four days insensible, away from my own camp, and no doctor nearer than Adelaide, which accident happened in this way. I had gone to Encounter Bay from my camp in the morning for some purpose in connection with my work, when on my return I called at Hill's camp, and found Mr. Nichols, the coroner, there. He had lost his horse, and I was asked if I found it on my way, would I return with it. I discovered the horse with the survey horses, and brought them all in, and whilst sitting carelessly with a slack rein on my beast whilst the men secured the horses, I was thrown. I do not know whether I fell with my head against a tree, or if the pony kicked me on the head. This was on Wednesday afternoon, and not until the Sunday following did I recover my recollection, when I woke up in a tent in Hill's camp, with old Dr. Wright and one of my men bending over me. The doctor had arrived that morning, and on seeing the state I was in, almost black in the face, thought it was all over with me. Now, from that day to this I never knew how it occurred. I found all my hair off when I recovered my senses, and my left arm much sprained, which I had to wear in a sling for some time.

"Shortly after returning to my camp I received a letter from the Surveyor-General, saying, that Governor Gawler, with a party, wished to embark in my boats and go up the Murray, and if I had not sufficiently recovered, one of the surveyors was to take my boats (Mr. Calder, I think), but this I could not allow, and by the time proposed I was ready, and directly the party reached my camp, a start was made. Two ladies went with us—Mrs. Sturt and the Governor's eldest daughter. We stopped at the North-West Bend, and there a camp was formed. A small party started off to explore, and the result of that ride was a sad one, when poor Bryant was lost. The Governor was nearly gone also. In fact all the party came into the camp in a most exhausted state, also Sturt and Inman, who had separated from the Governor. One horse had been killed to save human life.

"When at Valparaiso I was superintending the loading a small brig chartered by the Commander-in-Chief of the Station to take stores and provisions to the Sandwich Isles for the Arctic ship in Behring's Straits.

"I went in the brig to join that ship, having been sent from England to join her at Panama, which port she did not visit, and I lost my passage, and it was not until June, 1849, I got on board of her, and ten days afterwards left in her boats to search the Northern Arctic coast of America in quest of Franklin; that ship I have never seen from that day to this. I wintered two years and a half with the fur traders of the Hudson Bay Company, entering the Rivers Mackenzy, and passing right through Northern America to York Factory, bottom of Hudson's Bay, and got home with my men in one of their ships in October, 1851.

"The next year I went out again to Davis Straits, Lancaster Sound, and Beachy Isle, and was shut up in the ice two years. The ship I commanded was the only one of that expedition that returned to England of the squadron of five which left home in 1852; the crews returning with me and two ships which had brought us supplies, which ships heaved in sight the day I got my ship clear of the ice with all four crews on board.

"I was glad to see these two ships, so we hauled into

the edge of the floe again, and they took a share of the men I had on board, and we reached England again in time to take part in the Russian War, where, at the bombardment of Jeddah, I had no less than eleven of the murderers of our consuls executed by decapitation. I got more than two salutes of thirteen guns each from two of our men-of-war, who arrived after I had finished the bombardment. I also received a letter from the Secretary for Foreign Affairs in acknowledgment of that affair.

"When in the Red Sea, sounding for the first cable for the purpose of connecting India with the western world, I had an audience with the Pasha of Egypt. This was in 1861, after my return from the Arctic regions, on which occasion he remarked to me, 'Why, your Government first freeze you and then send you here to be thawed.' After that service was completed I was in hopes I should have had something of the same sort of work to do in connection with South Australia; but no, the Lords of the Admiralty did not seem to enter into the spirit of enterprise sufficiently to spare one of Her Majesty's ships for the purpose. I would gladly have ventured in the undertaking, rotten as my old ship was, even to the necessity of taking out of her two of her heavy guns. In fact an engineer of the name of Gibson had commenced a correspondence with me on the subject. Nothing would have given me more pleasure than in taking my old H.M. ship *Cyclops* into Port Adelaide. Hard as my life has been in all my services, I have, by God's blessing, good health, and have much indeed to be thankful for, still I cannot help grumbling at having at this time nothing to do, which is about the hardest work I ever had.

"I still feel great interest in the Murray Mouth, and, indeed, in all else in the colony. I should like to hear of that river being brought into closer connection with Adelaide and the port by rail. The sea mouth must be such a heavy undertaking, and no means of estimating the end of the cost, so that it had better be dropped for the time. I am afraid though that amongst you there are so many conflicting interests that you don't pull together. It seems to me that every one is for himself, and no one for the good of all, and no downright public feeling and thought for the benefit of the country.

"I am very glad to hear that your new Governor takes such an interest in the colony, and that he advocates a railway to Port Darwin. I saw in one of the papers (the *Ad-*

vertiser) the speech of Sir William Jervois at the Mayor's dinner. I consider it a very good one, and to the point, and that he confirms my views also as to the sea mouth and Port Victor. Such opinions have been published in my letters some time ago.

"I met Sir William Jervois in Bermuda when I was there on marine surveying purposes. He was there to consider the best means of fortifying the islands, and I was called on to advise as to the best style of marine monsters (ironclads) to act in conjunction with the land forts.

"I believe that Adelaide (S. A.) will eventually be the chief settlement in Australia. The telegraph line across to Port Darwin has given a great impetus to the colony."

It has given the author great pleasure in being able to publish the foregoing *résumés* of Admiral Pullen's public services, both in the Imperial and Colonial services.

Postscript.—Mention may with propriety here be made of the late Mr. Henry Mildred, who was one of the few who joined in the work of founding the colony.

Mr. Henry Mildred was born at Portsea, England, in March, 1795. For some years before South Australia was spoken of as a colony, Mr. Mildred had determined to emigrate. The new colony of South Australia presented such attractions that he dispatched his son, Hiram Mildred, in the brig *Rapid*, under Colonel Light, to South Australia, intending to follow himself with the remainder of his family. At this time the South Australian Company retained his services to proceed to the North of England to purchase the appliances required for a ship building yard, a patent slip, and steam saw and corn mills. On his return he proceeded to the colony with the manager, Mr. David McLaren, in the barque *South Australian*, which arrived at Kangaroo Island on the 22nd April, 1837. After some delay, part of the plant was removed to the mainland and the engine and mills were erected near Adelaide, being known as the Company's Mill. The other parts of the plan were abandoned by the company. An offer was then made to Mr. Mildred to continue in the service of the Company, which he declined.

He accepted a seat in the Municipal Council in 1841, and took an active part in all public questions of the day. He was a most determined opponent of the project to introduce the Parkhurst boys, and greatly assisted in causing the scheme to be abandoned. In 1850 he was appointed a justice of the peace, and in 1858 a special magistrate. In 1857 he was elected a member in the House of Assembly for the district of Noarlunga. In April, 1860, Mr. Mildred was returned for East Torrens, and sat a second time for the same district. In 1866 three vacancies occurred in the Legislative Council, and of ten candidates Mr. Mildred was returned second on the list. The honourable gentleman retained his seat till 1871, when it became vacant by effluxion of time and he then retired from public life. He died in the year 1877, aged 82 years. In his public life he was consistent and active, in private life exemplary, and it may be said he left no enemies.

Mr. Henry Mildred left two sons and one daughter, who are still living. Mr. Hiram Mildred, the eldest, is a member of the Council of the City of Adelaide; his second son, Henry, who some time ago sat in Parliament for East Torrens, is a solicitor; the daughter is the wife of Mr. J. Varley, special magistrate, of Kapunda.

CHAPTER IV.

CAPTAIN HINDMARSH arrived in the ship *Buffalo*, 28th December, 1836, to take up his office as first Governor of South Australia. With him came the Rev. C. B. Howard, first Colonial chaplain, Osmond Gilles, Esqre., treasurer, with a few other officers and some emigrants. On landing, the governor proclaimed the colony in the presence of government officers and settlers on the spot, under a bent gum tree at Glenelg, near the mouth of the Pattawalonga Creek.

My intention is to avoid a relation of the little political squabbles which disturbed the harmony of the first few months of the colony, but it is necessary to record something of the causes which produced the disagreements. Captain Hindmarsh was strongly impressed with the importance of the grand waterway of the Murray and its tributaries, and pressed his views perhaps too warmly on the Commissioner of Crown Lands and the Surveyor-General. He also objected to the site chosen for the city, and desired to have it placed adjacent to the port; but Colonel Light, after careful examination of the country nearer the landing place, adhered to his first choice. Thus arose two parties in the colony and much excitement was caused. The governor had no official voice in the matter, but nevertheless it must be admitted that he put a correct value on the importance of utilising the grand stream which, coming from the heart of Australia, finds its mouth at Encounter Bay. In this matter, however, Captain Hindmarsh was in advance of the times, for as far as this colony is concerned, the Murray flows mostly through poor country, and in 1838 we knew little or nothing of the value of the pasture lands about the upper Murray and its tributaries, and the Riverina trade was then a thing of the future. Yet the value of the River Murray as a navigable watercourse, with its far-stretching feeders, having been proved by Captain Sturt, in his successful boat trip down the Murray and back, all that was required in the first place was to remove snags in its channel and provide harbour accommodation through or near its embouchure. Lieut. Pullen, R. N., was early after his arrival with the Surveyor-General, detached by him to explore and survey the mouth of the Murray with a small boat's crew and a whale boat under his command. I was, as far as I know, the only individual who rode down to meet Mr. Pullen after he entered the river mouth in an open boat, and I spent a night with him where he was engaged in surveying the channel past Goolwa, as it was subsequently named. He had expressed his confidence that he would be able to succeed in entering the mouth with a sailing craft, and this feat he subsequently accomplished in the cutter *Waterwitch*, which afterwards foundered off Moorundie, where she was anchored. It will hardly be believed by strangers that after doing this he was coldly received in Adelaide, and left us in disgust. I must mention that before he left the colony he accompanied Captain Hart in assisting to bring overland a herd of cattle from Portland Bay which had been purchased by the brothers Hack from Dr. Imby, of Twofold Bay, employment very different from the high and honourable professional services he has subsequently rendered to the nation.

A small number of marines were left as a sort of body guard to the Governor. I may here give some accounts of them under the influences of drink even when on duty.

Of these men one had been told off to act as guard over the Treasury. I furnish this instance as related to me by the Treasurer himself. He had spent the evening with a few convivial friends (a not unusual occurrence in those early days), and on leaving the company for his own dwelling (a small wooden cottage), he had to pass near the *tent* then used as the Treasury, and in which was a large safe, his own private property, lent to the Government. As the moon was shining brightly, he could see the tent but not the sentinel. Feeling that something was out of place, he approached the tent, and found the guard lying down, with his musket beside him ; so, although he was not on his legs, he could not be said to have deserted his post. The marine was addressed thus, in a loud voice, " Brown, what the d—— are you doing?" and received a sharp kick in addition ; but this only producing a grunt, some further and more violent kicks were applied. On this the sleeper was aroused so far as to sit up and rub his eyes. He was then asked what he was about—did he know where he was? "Yes, sir ; yes, sir." "Well, then, where are you?" To this he blurted out, "Aboard the *Buffalo*, sure, sir ; but who are you, sir, kicking me? Oh, Lord, what shall I do—it's the Treasurer himself ! Oh, sir, do not report me ; good sir, I shall be ruined !" "Well, then, get up and attend to your duty, you drunken rascal ; in the morning I will let you know what I shall do." The Treasurer added, after relating the above, with sundry strong words which I have omitted, " The truth is, as there was only one shilling and sixpence in the safe, a guard might have been spared." The Government were aground at this time as to cash, but immediately afterwards a supply was obtained through the Treasurer's private means.

I will add one more example of the way in which these marine guards sometimes performed their duties during the short time they were so employed, which came under my own observation. I was returning home late one day after sunset, having taken a long ride to the north of the city, and desired to make the north-east corner of South Adelaide as laid out. The night was dark, and on crossing the Torrens near where the Company's Bridge now stands, I was attracted by a log fire, and also could see a tent. As I got near I became aware I had arrived at the encampment where a few prisoners, chained by the legs to a trunk of a tree, were kept under charge of marines. This was about the centre of the ground now occupied by our charming Botanic Gardens. When I got sufficiently near I found no one about, but on closer inspection discovered guards as well as prisoners all in a sound sleep ;

the sentinel, who ought to have been patrolling around the spot, was lying on his back cuddling his brown bess, and with an empty black bottle beside him. I conjectured that he had not taken his final and finishing drop until he had seen his comrades and prisoners safe in a helpless state of drunkenness. I did not consider it politic or necessary under the circumstances to disturb the slumbers of the guard, and I suppose that on the change of guards in the morning all matters were found to be in due form, as no prisoners escaped. The services of the marines were not retained after the retirement of Captain Hindmarsh. From one of the original Government officers I had the following information :—The Governor, wishing to review and inspect his guards, ordered the corporal to bring them up for that purpose. After due notice and some trouble their non-commissioned officer could only muster in a presentable state about half the squad for the Vice-Admiral's inspection. On this disgraceful display, as a matter of course, His Excellency's remarks were more warm than complimentary, but I do not think his reproof of the absent delinquents had more effect on those present than the remarks from the pulpit so often heard by the regular attendants at church have upon the stray sheep that are missed from the ecclesiastical fold.

I believe that nearly the whole of the marines, after spending a jolly time in the colony, were taken away by Captain Hindmarsh when he left Adelaide for Sydney in the month of July, 1838, in the *Alligator*, gun brig. I think the corporal or sergeant was the only one left; he was a respectable man, and resided at Glenelg until his death. As to his rowdy men, they were soon put under discipline calculated to produce reformation after having been placed in a false position on shore under insufficient restraint.

I must not omit to do justice to Colonel Light, who early retired from his duties. As Colonel Light vacated his office before my arrival, I have little to say as to the causes of this step, further, than that the Commissioners in London desired to introduce some radical changes in the principle of surveying the lands, and were much dissatisfied on account of the delays, which appeared to them uncalled for, although they were in a great measure occasioned by their own injudicious arrangements. It is but justice to add, that Colonel Light, at the time of his arrival, was suffering from serious indisposition. Of Colonel Light's zeal and efficiency in the service there can be but one opinion, and his bearing was always that of a most efficient officer and a gentleman. The manner in which he performed his first and critical duties in selecting the site of the city and temporary old port cannot be too highly spoken of, especially as, although he had some good and well-qualified officers under him, they were all new to the work of laying out and surveying a new country, and amongst them were a large proportion of men of little or no experience as surveyors. Then he was hurried and pestered by the arrival of immigrants and settlers before he had time even to examine the country as he must have desired to do. If all these circumstances are properly weighed, how much must he have suffered in mind when he had to surrender the work, on which his heart was so deeply set, before his choice of sites were fully proved to be the best possible to have been made, even had the circumstances been more favourable as to the time and means he had at his command. It is also a matter to be regretted that his name is not associated with more pleasing localities than Light Square and the " Dirty Light " (a watercourse so called), with the exception of Light's Passage. After his lamented death, which occurred in 1839, about one year after his resignation, when the proposal to raise funds to erect the monument to his memory was broached, to be placed in its present position, there were several objections urged, and a suggestion was made to substitute some useful work, such as a bridge or jetty, especially as up to that time no such works had been erected in the colony. I had not the pleasure of being intimately known to him, and yet as an old colonist I desire that our obligations to him should be acknowledged by some more worthy memorial than has yet been raised in his honour.

The misunderstandings and bickerings which had been stirred up between the Governor, Captain Hindmarsh, and some of the officials over whom he had no control, soon led the Home Government to recall him. He had experienced a most harassing time, and on being recalled by Lord Glenelg had the consolation of being informed by him " that it was without censure, and to avoid the removal of responsibility from the South Australian Commissioners in London as to the peaceable government of South Australia, and that his confidence in Captain Hindmarsh was such as to lead the Home Government to give him without delay another appointment," which he soon got with honours added.

The Governor was regretted by a large portion of the colonists; he was a warm-hearted, bluff sailor, whom to know was to esteem and to respect. Captain Hindmarsh had served under Nelson, of glorious renown, from whose hands he had the honour to receive a presentation sword, accompanied with high compliments on his gallant conduct and the uniform discharge of his professional duties. Captain Hindmarsh obtained his various steps of promotion by merit.

He finished his career in the public service, after receiving knighthood from her Majesty, as Governor of Heligoland, one of England's important stations in time of war.

Captain Hindmarsh, on vacating his Government (1838), appointed G. M. Stephen, Esq., the Attorney-General, as Acting-Governor. Mr. Stephen, during his short reign, conducted the Government in a very efficient style, but as to private matters he did not escape censure. He embarked in a private land transaction, which brought him into great trouble. Out of this land speculation two criminal charges were brought against him, from which, however, he got clear. Respecting this matter, he brought a libel action against the late Mr. George Stevenson, who had been Private Secretary to Captain Hindmarsh, but the jury found a verdict for the defendant.

It is not necessary to go into particulars, excepting so far as to relate circumstances to his credit in this transaction, in a matter on which I can speak, as having been involved with him, but without any pecuniary advantage. On his taking up the Port Gawler Special Survey he applied to me for pecuniary assistance, stating that he was short of £500 of the necessary amount of the purchase-money. He told me the locality in which he had made his selection. As I had seen the country a few days before, I was quite satisfied he had secured a good thing for himself, and that there would be small risk, if any, in assisting him. It was not convenient for me to lend him the amount. On my telling him this, he proposed that I should draw upon him for the sum he required. To this I consented, and afterwards procured the discount of the acceptance for him. After he had obtained the land he negotiated the sale of it with two wealthy gentlemen, recent arrivals from India. On these parties becoming dissatisfied with their bargain (I had reason at the time to think through bad advice)—they were persuaded they had paid too dear for their whistle—and finding they could under the land regulations obtain for themselves direct from the Government land at £1 per acre, desired to back out of the arrangement; but on finding they could not do this, they instituted criminal proceedings against the seller, charging him with giving a false description of the land, and of altering a figure in one of the documents. He was brought up to the Supreme Court, and charged with fraud and forgery. The bill for £500 on which I was liable was current at the time of these trials. The general opinion was that Mr. Stephen would be cast, and I felt sure of losing the amount in which I had become liable. However, to the defendant's credit, on the morning of the second trial (*i.e.*, on the charge of forgery) I met him entering the Court, and, although I endeavoured to avoid him, he came towards me, and produced his acceptance cancelled, saying, " I have taken up your draft, and here it is." I further mention that at the time Mr. Stephen presented me with the cancelled draft, Mr. George Stevenson saw the action, and immediately afterwards told me I should be required as a witness for the prosecution; but I was not called on, as I answered I knew nothing personally of the transactions except what would redound to the defendant's credit. Now, it was almost universally expected that on this charge he would have been found guilty. Although by the verdicts of the juries he got clear of the charges brought against him, he was generally blamed for having gone into land speculations; and at any rate was chargeable with conduct unbecoming the high position he held. It must be admitted that his action in releasing me from liability, whilst his own position appeared so doubtful, was honourable in the extreme. It is but justice to him to add that the land, which he had so soon resold for a good profit, is now I may say worth ten times the amount he realised for it. For myself, I may say that I made no charge for the accommodation, nor did I ever receive anything, directly or indirectly, as a return for it. I was satisfied with my escape at the time, and think it only justice to one who held the position of Acting-Governor to mention circumstances to his credit.

I should mention that Colonel Gawler had arrived and displaced Mr. Stephen before the trials took place. At that time the following highly complimentary remarks appeared in the *Register* of February 21st, 1839:—" We do not think it possible for the most inveterate opponent of the system of government adopted in South Australia to deny to Mr. G. M. Stephen the praise of having borne his honours meekly, &c. Our own favourable opinion of his acts have been too distinctly expressed to need repetition, &c., &c."

CHAPTER V.

IN the early part of 1837 the establishments of the Government and of the South Australian Company were removed from Kangaroo Island to temporary encampments at Holdfast Bay and Port Adelaide. There were at this time only two horses in the colony—one belonging to the Company and one to Mr. John Morphett (now Sir John). No stable had yet been built nor any fences put up, and the horses were kept on tether-ropes to feed on the luxuriant kangaroo grass growing about the lagoons at the termination of the River Sturt.

One morning these valuable animals were discovered to have got away from their tether-ropes. An immediate search was made around the neighbourhood by several men, some going south and towards the hills, and others northerly to the Reed-beds and near the spot whereon the City of Adelaide now stands. Success not having attended the search, Mr. C. W. Stuart (who held the position of overseer of stock) determined to start the next day to seek traces of the lost horses. He was accompanied by Mr. Allen, who desired to have such an opportunity to botanise; H. Alford, an employé of the Company; and Nat, a sealer from the island. (Mr. Allen was afterwards the manager of the first Botanical Gardens, which were commenced on ground between the present slaughter-house and Thebarton Bridge.) An early start was made on foot by the horse hunters, each carrying three days' rations and two bottles of water. Mr. Stuart's fine kangaroo dog Hector also accompanied them. They travelled south, in sight of the Gulf. The weather was hot, and their water was expended before the day was far spent, and the bottles were cast away—the first tokens of civilization left in that part of the country.

About 4 o'clock Nat said to Mr. Stuart—"When we get to the top of that rise we shall see the outlet of a river; the water is salt, but there are native wells under the sandhills." (He had landed there when sealing.) On arriving at the summit of the gentle mound, and whilst enjoying the charming prospect of the river meandering in a serpentine course through natural meadows, smoke was seen to arise from a clump of honeysuckle trees, or *Banksias*, and a native camp was soon perceived, with the smoke of fires rising upwards towards the deep blue sky.

All doubts were soon dissipated and fears aroused by the sudden appearance of a considerable number of natives of all ages and sexes. Their first impulse was to retire, but the natives had early seen them, and in a short time men, women, and children rushed towards them to indulge their curiosity with the sight of white men. The native men set up a great shout, and, coming to the front, brandished their spears, and appeared to invite or dare the whites to approach and engage them.

Mr. Allen and Alford were in great alarm on this their first sight of natives; and they exhibiting threatening actions, Nat also seemed disconcerted, and muttered, "Full moon, come down to fish and hold a corroboree; they must be Onkaparinga and Encounter Bay blacks." Mr. Stuart had been much among aboriginals in New South Wales, and was well acquainted with their habits; he was therefore calm and collected. Nat now explained to him that the black woman whom he had on the island belonged to one of these tribes, and he was aware that they were not pleased at her absence. He understood a few of their words, but thought it better for him to keep as much out of sight as possible. Mr. Stuart kept in front with his fowling-piece in hand. On one side of him Alford was placed, Mr. Allen behind, and Nat on the other side, as much out of sight as possible. Mr. Allen was in a most excited state, and kept saying that they must be prepared to die like men. At length eight warriors came forward with spears in their hands. Hector was parading to and fro, growling most angrily, with his tail and bristles erect. Fearing he might precipitate a collision, he was chained to a small tree. The blacks came on in single file, but in such an open manner that it was felt that they were not bent on mischief. A tall fellow was ahead of the others, who was afterwards known as Tam o' Shanter. On their approaching within six paces of the leader of the English force (Mr. Stuart), he commenced an address in his unknown tongue, the others viewing the whites with intense astonishment. Tam, as he spoke, pointed to the sea. In answer to him, signs were made that the party required water to drink; and the word "cowie,

cowie" was repeated. For some time Mr. Allen addressed the
black leader, repeating that they had landed to introduce Mr.
Wakefield's principles of colonization, and that they begged to
apologise for the intrusion on their country, &c., &c. Tam
o' Shanter, not understanding Mr. Allen's polite speech, got
impatient and stepped up to Mr. Stuart, and first took from
his head his cabbage-tree hat and touched up his hair, and then
opened his waistcoat and shirt-front to examine his skin; then
lifted up one of his feet, and, like a vet., examined his boot.
The others also had to submit to a similar examination—at
which Mr. Allen expressed great anger, saying he had never
been treated in such a manner before. They did not attempt
to take anything until they discovered the sugar and salt pork;
of the first they partook, also of the fat of the pork, which they
devoured greedily. They were much frightened of Hector.
They next examined the guns, and when satisfied handed them
back to the owners of them. Mr. Stuart, wishing to show them
the use of guns, placed his to his shoulder and fired high in the
air. Tam then seized it, and placed it to his own shoulder in
the same manner, and there held it, seemingly expecting it to
go off as it had done before, and after a short time cast it down
in disgust. Having now satisfied their curiosity, one of them
said, "Cowie," and led the party to one of their native wells,
and then left them. As the place was well adapted for a camp
it was adopted, and by the time the sun was getting low a bush
tent was made—a shelter being necessary as the party had no
blankets. Pots of tea having been made, as they were discussing their diminished provisions, two old women appeared,
bearing on small sheets of bark a supply of fried fish, which was
a most acceptable addition to their fare. Although all the rest
of the travellers were satisfied of the friendly dispositions of the
blacks, Mr. Allen continued to express his fear that none of
the party would be allowed to depart, or ever reach the camp
at Holdfast Bay, as he believed they were in the midst of can-
nibals. All being tired an early coil was adopted, but before
sleep closed their eyes musical sticks were beaten in time, and
a blaze of fire shot up in the natives' camp, and a grand corroboree was commenced. Mr. Allen and Alford, never having
heard such a performance, were somewhat alarmed, but Mr.
Stuart and Nat by their laughter reassured them. There was a
large concourse of performers. The men, as usual on such
festivities, were adorned with white stripes on their faces and

breasts, and down the arm and leg bones. Hector was chained at his owner's feet and kept quiet, and sleep soon closed all eyes. In the morning Mr. S. rose early, and looking on the serpentine channel of the river, at a short distance from the camp, to his surprise saw a numerous concourse of wild fowl on the bosom of the quiet water. Hector was unchained and accompanied his master, armed with his fowling-piece. A swan was soon shot, which Hector brought to land, and this was hung on a tree out of reach of the blackfellows' dogs. Other swans were followed by the sportsman. At this time by growls Hector gave notice that some one was approaching, and two young black men joined company, intimating they had heard the gun and wished to join in the sport. They had throwing-sticks with them. In a short time two more swans were approached, and, on rising, a shot was fired, and one dropped into the water with its wing broken. One of the black youths jumped into the river at the same time Hector did, and gave chase, but the dog reached the wounded bird first. The black endeavoured to intercept him, and a contest took place; but the boy had to dive to escape Hector's fangs, who landed with his prize in triumph. This little display of strife did not break up the friendly relations of those engaged in the sport, but after this occurrence the blacks did not interfere with Hector's department, but were satisfied to carry the game. The water birds were so abundant, and had not before been scared by gunners, so that six ducks were soon bagged, with which a return was made to the camp. There was a duck for each of the party and to spare. Tam o' Shanter was presented with one of the swans, and the old women who had so kindly improved their previous supper had the other bestowed upon them. Mr. Stuart was soundly rated by Mr. Allen for running such a risk in going out alone without rousing any of his companions, who had been exceedingly anxious about him when they awoke and found him absent.

After breakfast the men, two at a time, indulged in a swim in the river, and then followed up the same to seek a place where the horses, if they had travelled south, might have crossed. A large number of the blacks accompanied them. In the afternoon Mr. Stuart shot a fine wild turkey, which was retained for their own use for that day and until they reached home. On their arriving near the part of the river now called the Horseshoe they first saw the footprints of the horses, and on pointing such out to a young blackfellow he went down all-fours and endeavoured to imitate the galloping of a horse, and then pointed over the range, intimating by signs that the horses were feeding there. On the ground being further examined it was perceived that horses had been feeding in that bend of the river for a day or two, and, if they had not been disturbed, might have been easily shut in by bushes and caught; but as they had got out of such a favourable place, and were now out in the clear, it was considered to be useless for men on foot to pursue them further, and as more horses were expected by the next ship from Launceston it was decided to return, as traces to be followed had been met with. After passing a miserable night, with occasional showers of rain, without shelter or blankets, an early start was made in the morning for Holdfast Bay, distant about twenty-one miles. Many of the natives kept with them. On reaching the high land near what is now known as O'Halloran Hill, the *Buffalo* and other ships lying at anchor in Holdfast Bay were visible. The blacks who were in company expressed their astonishment by yells and dancing. After half-an-hour's rest Tam o' Shanter and five or six of the men of the tribe kept up with the returning party, the remainder keeping in the rear as if they were in doubt as to the treament their men would meet with. On the double party reaching the tents they were met by Governor Hindmarsh. There had been some anxiety about their fate. His Excellency expressed himself shocked that Mr. Stuart should have brought the naked black men amongst the tents of the numerous immigrants, and immediately called on Mr. Gilbert, the Government storekeeper, to supply the men with clothing, which being brought forth, some of the sailors, who were ashore from the *Buffalo*, took the natives in hand to dress and pet, pressing on them pipes and grog, which at the time the blacks declined, preferring sugar and fat pork; but alas! how soon they acquired a taste for the indulgences offered! The dressed-up black men displayed anything but comfort or content in their unaccustomed array, which on becoming apparent, the Governor, on advice, was considerate enough to order blankets to be exchanged for the unpopular garments, and the men soon retired greatly pleased with the blankets enveloping them, and rejoined their anxious and doubting families. Before they left, although they were fashionable enough not to express surprise at any of the unaccustomed sights which met their eyes, yet at the appearance of a wax doll with moving eyes they could not contain their admiration. The doll was in the hands of a little girl just landed.

The first expedition into the bush attempted or entered upon by officials was in the same year (1837), when the Commissioner of Crown Lands (Mr. J. H. Fisher) and the Surveyor-General (Colonel Light) started to reach Encounter Bay overland. Mr. Stephen Hack was with them to render his assistance as an incipient bushman; a corporal's guard of marines was obtained from the *Buffalo* to act against any hostile natives whom they might encounter. Tents and swag were conveyed in a Government bullock-dray. There was a horse-dray and saddle horses for the officials, who had also the attendance of their own servants and some other men. The first day they made the Messrs. Hack's sheep station, near the coast, and distant in a direct course from Glenelg about twelve miles. The ground was found to be soft from recent rains. It was now discovered that the outfit of the party was too ponderous for the cattle, and on the following morning Mr. Hack was sent back to secure the services of Mr. John Chambers to bring out drays and some additional requirements, and to convey the marines with their outfit back to their ship.

On the following day Mr. Chambers arrived with his drays at the encampment. He did not set out on the starting tracks of the Government drays, but hit them on the top of what is now known as Tapley's Hill. He also found the ground heavy enough to try his cattle. At sundown the bullocks, which had been put on good feed, were placed under the charge of a night watchman (one of the drivers) fully armed, who was to be relieved in the usual manner. All other hands having turned in, in their first sleep the watchman rushed in, giving the alarm that a number of natives were coming down the hill, uttering their war cries. All hands quickly turned out, and the sounds which had alarmed the watchman were soon heard approaching nearer and nearer. The marines under the corporal had soon their muskets loaded, and were drawn up ready to receive the advancing foe. Colonel Light charged the men to be steady and not to fire at random, but only at the word of command, and to take good aim. The yells were continuously kept up; none of the party had previously heard such piercing cries; but as the numerous throats from which they proceeded approached nearer, doubts from some of the most courageous of the party began to be entertained as to the kind of animals keeping up such an unusual concert, it also being known that the largest carnivorous brutes found in Australia were dingoes.* It was soon decided that a false alarm had been given, and a general return was made to the blankets; but the guard declined to return to his duty unless he had the protection of an armed marine with him. The drays and cattle belonging to Mr. Chambers remained at the camp one day to recruit for the return journey of twelve miles. During the night a sheep which had been obtained from Mr. Hack's flock was dressed, and placed for safety in Colonel Light's own tent, provided for the advancing exploring party.

On the following morning the carcase was missing, supposed to have been used up by the marines, to whom a taste of fresh meat was at that time a rarity; the officials were therefore well pleased when their guards started on their return march, with their tents, &c., in Mr. Chambers' drays. The exploring party continued to push southwards, and after passing the spot where Aldinga is now, made the foot of the ranges, where the town of Willunga has been since erected. Here they decided to return to the settlement, feeling it imprudent in their weakened state to encounter the perils of the untracked and difficult country before them, and the wild blacks of the coast districts. Mr. Chambers had returned the marines to their ship, at anchor in Holdfast Bay, and thus ended the first Government exploring trip.

CHAPTER VI.

IN the charter which was obtained by an Act of the Imperial Parliament, it was provided that a colonial chaplain should be appointed, and an income of £300 a year be set apart out of the colonial funds for his support. This was the only special privilege given to the branch of the Episcopal Church of England in the new colony; and, so far as it went, was an approach

* The wild dogs (dingoes) at an early period were in the habit of serenading the first settlers in the manner above described, forming packs of considerable numbers, so that a kind of concert was kept up, and sleep was impossible.

to a connection of religion with the State; but some time afterwards, against the wish of a majority of the colonists, grants in aid of public worship and sites for churches and glebes, were given by the colonial government to such of the various bodies, in proportion to the numbers belonging to each, as would accept them. This grant-in-aid was, after a few years, withdrawn by a vote of the legislative council. Churchmen are now, at any rate, content with the condition of equality in which their Church has been placed with other Christian communions.

Our first colonial chaplain, the Rev. C. B. Howard, was specially adapted for the important post he had to fill as a missionary priest. No sooner was the site of the city fixed by the Surveyor-General, and the small population somewhat concentrated, than Mr. Howard desired to commence his ministerial duties. To carry this out conveniently, in the absence of any building in which services could be held, he borrowed a large sail from a ship captain in port, to be used until a temporary room could be provided. Having progressed so far, the next difficulty to be overcome was how to get the sail conveyed to the infant city. All other means failing, he applied to his friend and fellow-passenger, Mr. Osmond Gilles, the colonial treasurer, who had a truck at the Old Port, for the use of it. This was at once granted; but then came the obstacle of a want of hands to drag the load seven miles along the dusty track, in blazing hot weather. This difficulty seemed to be insurmountable, as all hands were fully occupied in landing baggage and cargo, and in various other occupations. Saturday had arrived, and so there was no other alternative for the two enthusiasts, who had already and alone commenced the arrangements, but to put themselves in harness to drag the load. Let those who knew the *stout* treasurer imagine him in the pole and the rev. chaplain in the lead, with a rope over his shoulder, and then fancy them, having toiled so far, about five miles, crossing the gullies as they were then at Hindmarsh, before that township was laid out, and they will be able to realise the figure they cut at the bottom of the first gully, with the treasurer sprawling on the ground, overpowered in his fruitless endeavours to hold back and steady the pace. As neither poler nor leader was hurt, they sat down and had a hearty laugh while the fallen one dusted himself. How they managed to cross the Torrens I do not know. I have no doubt they had assistance there from a few people who were busily engaged in erecting tents and huts on the encampment between North Terrace and the river. The sail having been rigged to the best of their ability, the services of the church were held beneath it the next day, and regularly until a temporary wooden building was ready.

The Church of England next had the use of a room situated in the Arcade in Currie Street, which was used on week days as a court house. This was so small that many of the congregation had to remain outside, and here I and my family had the privilege of attending the ministrations of the colonial chaplain until the present Trinity Church was completed. The broad and truly catholic principles exhibited by our dearly-beloved clergyman cannot be too highly spoken of. His zeal and that of the treasurer in their desire to erect a substantial church, in place of the flimsy wooden-framed one sent out from England, led them to become responsible in the sum of £1,000 to the contractor for the stone structure now in use. As the last ministerial duty the Rev. Mr. Howard performed was over the remains of one of my family, I may be permitted to give an account of it as a doubly bitter experience. Some months after I with my family had settled in the bush, *i.e.*, nearly three years after landing, we were called upon to suffer the loss of a dear child under two years of age. No place of worship had at that time been erected out of the city, nor had any other than the West-terrace cemetery been set apart by the Government. The Rev. Mr. Howard, although at the time in a weak state of health, came to us in our distress to perform the funeral service over the remains of our boy. The treasurer had sections in my neighbourhood, on one of which he had promised to give several acres as a graveyard, but it had not been conveyed or consecrated. One adult had already been buried there in the open and wild bush. After the service had been impressively delivered, and we were returning from the grave, reflecting on the unprotected place in which I was leaving the earthly remains of my child, I became almost overwhelmed, and paused in the bed of the creek we were crossing, and there I received from my dear pastor a long, kind, consolatory address. Sad to say, they were the last words I was to be favoured with from his lips.

On mounting his horse, he departed from this wild spot, and I saw him no more. On reaching his parsonage, weary and faint, he retired to his bed. Soon after, as I was informed, a person who said he required to see him on pressing business, was allowed an interview, and prostrate as he was, there and then served him with a writ for the amount in which he had become responsible jointly with the treasurer, on account of the contract with the builder of the church. Melancholy to relate, his death followed within a few days, hastened, it was feared, by the shock he received from the service of the writ (1843). The lamentation and grief at his loss was universal, and he was followed to the grave by the inhabitants *en masse*. I should here explain that the claim for the debt on the church was principally met afterwards by the treasurer, who surrendered one of his best sections, and so our modest first church was cleared from liability; but our pastor's life had passed away before he was permitted to see the work completed on which he had exercised such untiring exertions, and he had sunk under the weight of them. Of the Rev. C. B. Howard I can only repeat what has been so often said of him, that he abounded in Christian charity, and consequently was beloved and respected even by those of the colonists outside our communion. He was an Evangelical broad churchman in the highest sense, and rejoiced, as all true churchmen do, in the comprehensiveness of our Church and history. Such a clergyman, occupying the post he filled, by his example did very much to produce the harmony which prevailed in the colony in his day, and since, as to religious matters, especially exhibited in the pleasing actions of Christians of all denominations contributing to the building funds for the erection of places of worship under whatever name they might be called. I would say, as to non-essential differences, let them continue to prevail, if Christians of all denominations join in loyal and united support of good government, and work together in harmony for real liberty without licence. When we old colonists of the small number surviving, after many hard struggles in our own private affairs, now turn our eyes from Trinity Church, across the river and park lands, and see on the opposite rise the beautiful and imposing cathedral which the venerable and respected Bishop Short was able to complete so far, and know also that he had been aided in funds by the liberality of members of other religious bodies, we cannot but rejoice thereat, and feel that the good examples set in the early days of the colony have been followed. It is also a source of gratification to see the many beautiful and characteristic sacred buildings which have been erected at so large a cost, and with so much taste, by other communions. On the lamented death of the first colonial chaplain, the Very Rev. Dean Farrell was appointed to succeed him. At the death of Dean Farrell the office of colonial chaplain was abolished.

Having devoted so much space to our first colonial chaplain, I now desire to do justice to another eminent fellow-worker with him in pastoral duties, who, although not of the same communion, was in a high degree successful in gathering a flock under the banner of the same Spiritual Master—I mean the Rev. T. Q. Stow. I was a witness to the praiseworthy manner in which he devoted himself to the task he had undertaken. I then, as I have often since, wondered how a minister of his high talents and popularity could have been induced to leave England, where he must have commanded a first-class position in the Congregational Church, to undergo the toils and privations of pastoral life in a new and wild country. Though he had the support of the Colonial Missionary Society to depend upon, in addition to the free-will offerings of his flock in South Australia, he drew upon the funds of the Society as little as possible, and for this reason for some years educated a few private pupils, and afterwards engaged in farming until the times of struggling and depression in the colony had passed away, and the pioneer Independent Church and congregation became self-supporting. It will be seen from this that the privations Mr. Stow endured were voluntary, and were borne in the true missionary spirit. It is also to be recorded that he assisted with his own hands in building the first Congregational church, which was constructed of pines and reeds, and was situated on North Terrace, a little to the west of Morphett Street. A pleasing contrast to this is exhibited in the present large and influential body of Independents. The esteem in which the father of the Congregational Church in South Australia was held is marked by the beautiful Stow Memorial Church, which loving members of his communion and the public have erected to his memory, and by the monument over his grave in West Terrace cemetery. He was spared to his people until the colony greatly increased in population and prosperity.

To the late Rev. Mr. Stow may also be justly applied the remarks I extract from the *South Australian Magazine* of January, 1842, which are there applied to the Rev. C. B. Howard, the first colonial chaplain—"To him is doubtless to be attributed much of that cordiality and good feeling which has existed among all denominations of Christians from the establishment of the province up to this hour." This may be again repeated at the end of 47 years.

The author has great pleasure in giving the history, from small beginnings, to the successful and extensive operations of the Roman Catholic Church in this province, which rapidly advanced after the arrival of the Right Rev. Bishop Murphy. He is indebted to the Right Rev. Bishop Reynolds, the present liberal and truly Christian head of that Church, for copious extracts from their records, as follows :—

"Among the very first settlers in South Australia the number of the Catholics was proportionally great. The spiritual wants of those about Adelaide, Brighton, and Morphett Vale were attended to by Mr. Phillips, whose house served as an oratory, where as many as wished assembled each Sunday for prayer reading and for catechcism.

"Early in 1839 the Catholic inhabitants deputed Messrs. Phillips, Johnson, and Counsell to make known the great need of a priest in their midst, and through them a petition was sent to Sydney, to Archbishop Polding, who sent his vicar-general, the Very Rev. W. B. Ullathorne, D.D., to visit the little flock in South Australia. He arrived in June, 1840. On his arrival the Catholics mustered in goodly numbers. The house in which they had previously met was too small in which to open service. Dr. Ullathorne applied to Mr. D. McLaren, then manager of the South Australian Company, to allow him the temporary use of a school-room, which was used at times as a chapel, but was then vacant. The respectful application was refused with rudeness; the words used, taken from Dr. Ullathorne's report, were, ' he would not aid me in my Popish practices.' Many of the non-catholics expressed their indignation at such narrow-minded bigotry."

Mr. Neal, who had at that time a large store in Waymouth Street, placed it at the disposal of the Catholics, as Dr. Ullathorne says in his report :—" A very large room was given us by a liberal *Protestant gentleman*, where I erected a temporary altar, where, surrounded by crockery, hardware and miscellaneous articles, I preached my first public sermon in the capital of South Australia. I had previously met a few of my people in a cottage on East Terrace, where also I offered the sacrifice of the mass for the first time.

"After organising the Catholics to collect the means to erect a place of worship, and to pay the passage of a priest, whom he promised to procure for South Australia, Dr. Ullathorne returned to Sydney. The Rev. Mr. Benson was duly appointed by the Vicar Apostolic, and left Sydney by the brig Dorset, February 14, 1841, for his mission in South Australia. He was a quiet, delicate gentleman and scarcely ever left the city. He hired a wooden building which stood near the corner of Topham and Waymouth streets, and lived in a small slab hut in rear of his temporary chapel. The building will be remembered by old colonists as having previously served for a time as a police court. Father Benson's health completely gave way during the heat of January, 1843. He returned to Sydney in the following April, and afterwards left for England, and died at Wolverhampton, in 1868, at the ripe age of 73.

"In 1842 Pope Gregory XVI. raised Sydney to an Archiepiscopal See, and gave to the first archbishop, the late Venerable John Bede Polding, O.S.B., Hobart Town, Perth, and Adelaide, as suffragan sees. The choice of the Pontiff compelled Dr. Murphy, Vicar-General of the Archbishop, to become first Bishop of Adelaide. The Rev. Edmund O'Mahony was sent *pro tem.* to Adelaide by the Metropolitan, to prepare for the coming of the bishop. He visited every district where he heard of any of his flock residing. He had for some time to work alone, as Father Benson had left *via* Sydney for New Zealand, and was single-handed until November 9, 1844, when the Right Rev. Francis Murphy, D.D., arrived per ship *Mary White*, accompanied by Father Michael Ryan, whom the bishop subsequently appointed as his vicar-general. The good bishop and his two priests found that the 'harvest was indeed great, and the labourers very few,' yet he was not discouraged, but set about the work at once, although he accepted the highly onerous office with great reluctance, knowing the uphill work he would have to encounter. He hired a building in Pirie-street, and this served as his pro-cathedral until the opening of St. Patrick's Schoolhouse at West Terrace. The episcopal residence—or, as they were accustomed to call it, the Brick Cottage (the palace)—was in Wakefield Street, and became in after-years the Dublin Arms. Incongruous changes! Bishop Murphy took on himself the sole charge of the city, and dispatched Fathers O'Mahony and Ryan to distant districts. They visited Catholic families about the Gilbert, the Dirty Light, Armagh village, or, as it was then called the Hutt River Special Survey

"The spreading gum trees on the Gilbert, and the late Patrick Butler's barn, served those good missionaries as churches. Distant shepherds' huts were also visited, and the consolations of their religion brought to many bush homes. On one of their return trips to Adelaide they were 'bushed,' having lost their way somewhere about the head of the Wakefield. The night turned out wet and cold. Father Ryan, who had a robust constitution, did not suffer from any ill effects of that miserable night, but poor Father O'Mahony's weaker constitution was not able to sustain the strain put upon it, and here he caught a severe cold which brought on a rapid consumption. He left Adelaide for his deanery at East Maitland towards the year 1845. Before he left he made a census of the Catholics of South Australia, who then numbered only 1,273, the entire population being at that time 19,317.

"The first church erected in South Australia by the Catholics was St. Mary's, Morphett Vale, on a site given by the late Mr. A. Anderson. This was solemnly dedicated by Bishop Murphy on the 8th of December, 1844. St. Patrick's, West Terrace, was originally intended as a school, and first served the double purpose of school and pro-cathedral. The first stone of the building was laid on the 12th December, the same year."

In November, 1845, Father Jas. Watkins, on his passage to Adelaide, was wrecked on the beach to the east of the mouth of the River Murray, in the brig *Mariner*. The passengers and crew reached the sand dunes without loss of life, and were soon visited by a large number of natives, whose anxiety to exercise their wrecking propensities led them to display such manners as to excite in the unfortunate shipwrecked people great dread and fear for their personal safety. The brig was carried high and dry, and divested of masts, so that much of the passengers' luggage and cargo was soon scattered along the sandhills. Communication was forwarded to Adelaide of the wreck and the doubtful position of the people. The following particulars I obtained from Messrs. Tolmer and Alford :—

Sergeant-Major Alford, with Sergeant Lamb and Private McLean, left the barrack-yard to go to the rescue of the shipwrecked people about midnight. When the party reached the wreck, no people, blacks or whites, were in sight. The beach and sandhills were strewed with cargo. Numerous footprints of natives were seen and followed over the sandhills, until they arrived at an encampment on the bank of the Coorong formed of spread sails, around which a great number of natives were seen, who on perceiving the quick approach of the three horsemen, and recognising them as police, immediately scattered, some of them dropping plunder from the wreck. On their disappearance the wrecked people showed themselves. The first person who spoke to the arriving party was Father Watkins, who in his joy at their opportune visit dropped on his knees and said, "Thank God, we are saved." Then the captain presented himself to the police, saying, "You have found me hard at work making a punt to get the passengers across the Coorong, as we were frightened the blacks meant mischief. I have only one gun with a broken lock, and they have used threatening signs and language to induce us to abandon cargo, &c., to their undisturbed plunder."

The sergeant-major informed them that he had been dispatched by the Government to render every assistance, and, to carry that out, he would in the morning take one man with him, leaving the other trooper as their guard, and make his way to Encounter Bay, and dispatch boats to remove them and their luggage down the Coorong, from whence they would be conveyed to Adelaide. The blacks did not, after this, show themselves in any number. They had not forgotten the punishment which had been inflicted on them by Major O'Halloran for the murders which had been committed a few years before.

About the same time that Father Watkins was cast on our shores by the wreck of the *Mariner*, Father Ryan left the central station in Adelaide on a visit to the scattered flock of Roman Catholics in the Qatiara district, and had a very dangerous encounter with the natives in the Maria Creek country, but was not injured.

The Rev. Ralph Drummond, the first minister of the United Presbyterian Church, arrived in this colony in June, 1839, in the ship *Sir Charles Forbes*, and commenced the services of his church in a small chapel in Angas Street, still standing. In the performance of his first duties to the scattered members of his Church here he had to take many long and toilsome journeys on foot about the Finniss, Strathalbyn, and Mount Barker districts, in order to visit wide-apart members of his flock, and scattered settlers of other communions whom he desired to benefit spiritually. He continued to officiate as pastor of the church he had opened in this colony till the year 1856, when he had toiled here seventeen years. In the year 1871 he completed the fiftieth year of his ministry. On the expiration of this term of his fixed official duties, an address was presented to him by the Revs. J. Lyall and J. Davidson, on behalf of the Presbytery, expressing most cordial congratulations on his having attained his jubilee as a minister of the Gospel, and regret that his then state of health would not admit of a public celebration on such an interesting occasion. Mr. Drummond expired at Mitcham on the 26th April, 1872, at the age of eighty years.

The first minister of the Established Presbyterian Church of Scotland who came to the colony to gather together a flock of members of his Church, was the Rev. Robt. Haining, who landed at Port Adelaide at the end of 1841, from the ship *Orissa*, of London. It is gratifying, as showing true Christian union, to be able to state that the opening services he held, on the first Sunday after his arrival, were in Trinity Church, North-terrace. The Rev. C. B. Howard, the incumbent, gave the use of his church on that occasion, himself giving aid in leading the psalmody. Then for two Sundays Mr. Haining preached in the Congregational church in Freeman Street, Mr. Stow taking advantage of this opportunity to pay missionary visits to several districts a day's ride or more from Adelaide. Arrangements were at the same time being made by the Presbyterians of the old Kirk for hiring a small place of worship which had been erected by the Wesleyan Methodists, and was afterwards sold to the Baptist body and used by them. It stood in Hindley Street, immediately west of the site of the present theatre. Here Mr. Haining gathered his first congregation around him, and here he continued to officiate until a larger edifice was erected in Grenfell Street in 1844, which in its turn was abandoned to secular purposes on the erection of the present church in Wakefield Street, known as St. Andrew's Church, of which he continued minister until the infirmities of advanced years compelled him to retire from ministerial work. Besides regular morning and evening services in the city, Mr. Haining for some time took part in maintaining a Sunday afternoon service at Port Adelaide in the original wooden church, on the site where now stands St. Paul's Anglican church, which was erected with the understanding that it should be available for divine service alike for the Anglican and Presbyterian forms of worship, an arrangement which was carried out in a most brotherly spirit by the Rev. (afterwards Dean) Farrell, and the Rev. Mr. Haining officiating alternately, each according to the form of his own Church, the congregations embracing with few exceptions the same individuals at either service. A pleasing instance this of Christian union.

An amusing anecdote is told of one of Mr. Haining's visits to the Port Adelaide Church, and is worthy of Dean Ramsay's collection. Mr. Haining was glad to get some friend to accompany him on these visits, and on one occasion, having with him in the old hired gig Mr. Wotherspoon, W.S., then resident in Adelaide, the following incident occurred:—Mr. Haining was driving, and when he came to the crossing of the Torrens at Thebarton, where there was then no bridge, and the banks of the river were steep and worn into deep holes, he let one of the wheels jerk violently into a hole, and was pitched out. The accident was supposed to have occurred in consequence of Mr. Haining slackening the reins while he took a pinch of snuff—he was an inveterate snuffer. He rolled down the dusty bank, and was nearly going into the shallow stream when his friend jumped out and stopped him. After brushing the dust from his clothes as well as they could the journey was resumed. Presently Mr. Wotherspoon said in a solemn manner, " Mr. Haining, I'm sorry to see you've disobeyed one o' the injunctions o' Scripture the day." " Indeed," replied Mr. Haining, " and what is it?" " Why d'ye no mind what Joseph said to his brethren—' See that ye fall not out by the way'?"

I have given an account of the first Independent minister who arrived amongst the very earliest colonists (the Rev. T. Q. Stow). I may now mention two others who came to the colony somewhat later. The Rev. Ridgway William Newland arrived about the year 1839, and soon after settled at Encounter Bay, where for many years, as he himself said, "he preached righteousness and wrought agriculture." He was a man of remarkable vigour, both of body and mind, just the right stamp for a pioneer colonist. He has walked the entire distance from Encounter Bay to Adelaide in a single day, fifty-six miles, swimming two rivers on the journey. He was a good preacher, and one who was not afraid to "call a spade a spade." He was very outspoken and unsophisticated, as an illustration of which I may mention that on one occasion having come to Adelaide on business, and been unexpectedly detained over Sunday, he was solicited to preach for the Rev. T. Q. Stow, who had been taken suddenly ill. Mr. Newland, having expected to return home by the Saturday night, had not brought his Sunday suit with him, and it being summer-time had only light clothes and a holland coat, and that not fresh from the laundress. He replied to the messenger, "O, yes, I'll come and preach if the people of Freeman Street will not object to hear me in this coat." The people of Freeman Street were as sensible in this respect as Mr. Newland, and heard him with pleasure, while he preached with more comfort probably than if he had had a black coat on, the day being hot. Mr. Newland did a great deal of good in the neighbourhood where he lived, and brought up a large family. He died at a good old age, some years ago, from the effects of an accident.

The next Congregational minister who came to this colony was the late Rev. J. B. Austin, who arrived at the close of the year 1843 with a family of eight children. He, like Mr. Newland, had not come with the intention of taking up the ministry as a profession; but finding that the spiritual wants of the place were not adequately provided for, he felt it to be his duty to exercise the gifts he possessed, and he soon commenced Sunday services at Macclesfield, where he resided. There being at the time no place of worship, nor even a room large enough to accommodate the small congregation of about five-and-twenty persons, Mr. Austin, with the help of his son, used to pitch a tent on the flat early every Sunday morning. It was unsafe to pitch it over night, as the cattle came and chewed the ropes. Divine service was for many months held in the tent as reverently, and perhaps as profitably, as in the more pretentious and substantial ecclesiastical edifices of the present more civilised times. Mr. Austin also established preaching stations at Echunga, Mount Barker, and Strathalbyn, where he continued to hold services in rotation, sometimes at three different places in the same day, and riding from sixteen to twenty-four miles. He died on the 31st January, 1882, aged 82, greatly regretted.

The Rev. Thomas Playford, who arrived in the colony in the year 1844, belonged to the "Christian Society" founded in London by the Rev. Robert Atken, who had seceded from the Church of England. Mr. Playford was born in Yorkshire in 1795; and was in the regiment of Life Guards at the Battle of

Waterloo. Soon after his arrival in the colony he commenced preaching in the little chapel in Hindley Street before mentioned, near where the Theatre Royal now stands, and from his earnest and impressive manner, as well as from the fact of his preaching on the near approach of Christ's second coming and personal reign upon earth, he drew many to hear him. In the year 1848 a new chapel was built for him in Bentham Street, and there he continued to exercise the pastorate for twenty years without remuneration. He was greatly respected, and led a useful and blameless life until the year 1873, when he died in the month of September, soon after entering his 79th year. Mr. Playford left a large family, all grown up, the eldest of whom, the Hon. Thomas Playford, M.P., has for some years ably represented the district of East Torrens in the House of Assembly, and has held the position of Commissioner of Crown Lands in two or three ministries. It may not be out of place here to notice the high positions attained in the colony by other sons of the earliest ministers of the Gospel in South Australia. The eldest son of the late Rev. T. Q. Stow was one of our most talented judges, the second is Editor of the *Advertiser* newspaper, and the third Senior Judge's Associate. The eldest son of the Rev. James Way, a Bible Christian minister, is Chief Justice of the Colony, and has been four times Acting-Governor of the Province. Mr. Way's second son is one of our leading medical men.

CHAPTER VII.

ON the 30th April, 1838, the second year after the proclamation of the colony, from the good ship *Canton* I landed with my family in the colony. The ship was at first anchored off the present site of the Semaphore Jetty, at an easy distance; on board were a large number of cuddy passengers as well as intermediates, about 300 emigrants, besides horned stock, sheepdogs, and swine, and a large cargo.

At the time Captain Hindmarsh held the rather ambiguous position of Governor. In addition to my wife and two children and a brother and sister, I had three young men under my charge, and one maid-servant. The captain, with consideration for passengers who had a large party on board, invited me and three male passengers to accompany him in the first and only boat going to land that day. Although the tide was high, our boat grounded half a mile from the beach. The captain then ordered out of the boat five of the sailors, on one of whom we had each to mount pick-a-back. The captain, being heavy, selected the stoutest Jack tar. I had a very lively young fellow under me, who made good headway. I looked back when we had made about half-way, and perceived that the captain's carrier was allowing him to sink nearer and nearer the water, and that he would soon be dropped (as I was afterwards told, intentionally). With my usual impetuosity, I ordered my bearer to drop me with my feet downwards, and return to the skipper's assistance, forgetting I had on a tight pair of Wellington boots. I nevertheless felt pretty comfortable whilst wading the remainder of the distance to the shore. Then came the climb over the sand hummocks, then the drag of three-quarters of a mile through sandy scrub and flaggy plants, and occasionally bog.

At length we made the side of the creek, and discovered on the opposite bank a bush shanty and a few wurlies, these erections constituting the old port. On crossing to what was then, with some propriety, called Port Misery, to our great joy we found we could get good beer at the moderate price of two-and-sixpence per bottle, of which we partook freely. A gig then, I think, the only one in the colony, was waiting for the captain, but we, to our grief, had to tramp the seven miles, and now something like the skinning of my feet commenced. The country appeared most charming, as we walked over a plain which had been swept clean by a bush fire a few weeks before we landed. The fire had been followed by copious rains, and the surface over which we travelled had the appearance of carrying a fine, early wheat crop, presenting a prospect so cheering, that my discomforts were nearly lost sight of.

On approaching the North Adelaide hill, my attention was drawn to a crowd of, say 200, people surrounding a large gum tree. I could not at first observe what had attracted them, until a sudden stampede took place, many rushing away in all directions with yells and cries, and then I saw an unfortunate man suspended by the neck from an outstretching limb of the tree. By one of the stampeders I was coolly told that it was a *regular and legal affair*, that the hangman had only bungled his business and bolted, followed by the execrations of the spectators, and that the sheriff, in mercy, was finishing the poor wretch. This was the explanation given me at the time, but on further inquiry I was informed that the constables quickly caught the escaping hangman, who was brought back to complete his revolting task, and that so far as Sheriff Smart was concerned, he was horror-struck and completely unnerved. With this explanation I was satisfied I had adopted a country where *civilisation* was known and *practised*.

I crossed the River Torrens, at that time a tiny stream, neither so wide nor deep as now, and the bed generally green with grass and reeds, under which surface I believe the main part of the stream was then percolating out of sight through gravel. In London I had seen a plan with a fine sheet of water, with vessels at anchor, under Government House. I was limping sorely, and soon got my boots off by unseaming one side of each, in one of the primitive refreshment booths in a small canvas town, on the ground now occupied by the present railway station.

We heard before we left the old port that the ship was ordered to return and anchor in Holdfast Bay, and then knew that we had no chance of getting on board that night. The accommodation and comforts I was able to procure on this my first night in the colony were not cheering or pleasant. My bed was formed of a couple of bags stretched across two side poles, lodged on four corner forks fixed in the ground, without blankets or pillows, in an outer canvas shed. I sought out and found an old friend who had landed some eight months earlier, and he kindly chartered for me a bullock dray to take me the next day to the beach at Holdfast Bay, to bring up my living charge and baggage.

By noon next day I found all safely landed at the mouth of the bay creek, on the corner sand hill near a native well of fresh water, from which we took copious draughts, and were thankful. A few reed huts had been erected, but the township was not laid out. The authorities had decided to reserve at this landing place a section to be at a future time formed into a township. Before this was done a land order was tendered at the land office, and a claim put in for the section; after some hesitation on the part of the Commissioner of Crown Lands and the Surveyor-General the grant was made. The following are the names of the fortunate speculators :—Messrs. O. Gilles, Mat Smith, W. R. Wigley, and W. Finke.

I was told that my wife, sister, and children, had been carried as I had been, from the boats to shore by the sailors. The fact was we were a very jolly party, and the roughness of things we took to be amusing. A pleasant ride across the plains, in defiance of many heavy jolts over wombat holes and logs, and we at length reached what is known as South Terrace, and found our friends' encampment near the spot where now stands St. John's Church. Our tents pitched, we were invited to a sumptuous repast consisting of kangaroo stew and parrot pie, relieved with ship pork and biscuits and colonial damper; of course no vegetables were procurable. The freshness of the atmosphere, the brilliancy of the sky, and the extreme verdure of the plains and hills satisfied us, and with grateful hearts we passed our first night in our adopted country under canvas.

In the early days of the colony grumblers were ashamed to open their mouths. On rambling about one curious feature for a new country was discovered around the tents and shanties, and in spots a few miles away in the bush, viz., congregations of empty bottles here and there, and plentiful too in their emptiness. Perhaps these might be fairly taken to account for the general joviality of the people; nevertheless, I am persuaded that much of the life and animation so universally exhibited, by the ladies as well as the stouter sex, was genuine, for we all felt we had come to a fine country as pioneers to found a new kingdom, but then, like the young donkey frisking about, all our trials had yet to come. I should mention that on one of the first acres which was taken possession of and occupied, two brick pillars, imposing by their ugliness, had been erected to form a gateway, through which to approach a wooden shanty of two or three rooms, and on one of the pillars was a board giving notice that "any person found trespassing on these grounds (*i.e.*, a bare acre) will be prosecuted with the utmost rigour of the law." This, also, was comforting, as a forward step in civilisation.

Shortly after our arrival our gracious Queen's birthday was commemorated by a ball at Government House, to which we had the honour to be invited. We were still under canvas; the ladies were in distress; trunks had to be unpacked, &c., &c.; and, worse than all, no conveyances for hire had yet been introduced, and the line we had to travel to Government House was diagonally across the then forest city, with no clearings or even direct tracks. The pressing difficulty was overcome by a kind neighbour offering us a ride in a waggon drawn by three horses in chain-harness, and driven by a real waggoner, with his long whalebone whip, all just imported from Tasmania. Well, the ladies soon got over the difficulties of such a conveyance, that is to say, such as the want of seats, steps to get in and out with, and such usual carriage belongings as were absolutely indispensable, by suggesting that the side rails should be clothed with railway rugs strapped on, a carpet on the bottom, and a high chair for steps. The ladies being young, lively, and energetic, the ascent was accomplished with our assistance, and without accident or ruffle. Our pace was necessarily slow, as our driver walked by the side of his team, driving with a "gee-up," and stopping with a loud "whoa" at the government porch. We arrived late, and unfortunately had left the chair behind, while the seats at Government House were fully occupied. Servants were not numerous, and those who were about were otherwise engaged, and the ladies had to alight by springing into the arms of the gentlemen from the back of an unusually high waggon. In the party were three officials high in the service. Two of the company had been in the home yeomanry cavalry—one as a commissioned and one as a non-commissioned officer. These appearing in uniform added to the imposing appearance of our party, which consisted of six ladies and six gentlemen. On entering the ballroom our eyes were dazzled by the brilliancy of the scene, to which we formed a striking addition, thanks to our military friends. Such a display of elegantly-dressed ladies could hardly have been expected to emerge from such confined and temporary dwellings as those in existence at that time. Dancing was kept up without flagging, as although the guests were chiefly married people, they were endowed with the spirit and energy necessary for early colonists. The entertainment was in all respects a success, and kind and hospitable Governor Hindmarsh and his charming family everything that could be desired. The pleasure experienced by the guests was equal to any they had ever met with under any other and more advanced state of society.

We departed early, and did not see any other vehicle, although there must have been some half-dozen or so coming and going at other times during the evening. We were afterwards kept in countenance by hearing that one lady, a special beauty and highly connected, had been conveyed from her home to the vicinity of the vice-regal residence in a bullock dray. The inconveniences and trifling deprivations now experienced, and of which we hear such grave complaints, rather amuse the old settlers, and remind them of such scenes as the above. Before chimneys were built, and cooking was performed out of doors, it was not an unusual thing to see in showery or even in sunny weather a lady watching the kettle, camp-oven, &c., under an umbrella at a log fire.

On one of my early rides, in company with my wife, south of the city, when all the country was open, and the hand of man had not defaced the natural park-like landscape, as we were crossing the Brownhill Creek, in an open glade, we started a pair of emus. We immediately gave chase. We had no dogs with us, but after a short gallop we overtook the female, which appeared to be in some way disabled. The male had at first dashed off at a great pace, but on looking back and seeing the danger which threatened his mate, he returned and darted between our horses and the hen, and so cut us off from our intended prey; and this he continued to do, striking at the horses' heads, and causing them to swerve as often as we approached his distressed partner. He completely foiled us, and as we felt his devoted attachment and noble courage deserved consideration at our hands, we desisted from further chase. I was greatly surprised at his bold attacks. His own life was greatly endangered, as by degrees our horses seemed to become interested parties in the sport, and did not exhibit so much fear as on his earlier assaults, nor care for his noisy defiant clucks, deeply sounded in his chest. His departure was most pleasing to witness, in the affectionate joy he exhibited. I never saw anything so courageous in any subsequent encounter I had with emus, although I have had more than one upstanding fight with old men kangaroos.

Postscript.—The author will, in this place, relate the fatal accident which so early closed the career of Mr. Samuel Stephens, the active and energetic first manager of the South Australian Company.

The writer and his wife on the day of the accident were returning from the cattle station on Bull's Creek, after a long ride through the Mount Barker district, and called at Hahndorf, at the coffee shop kept by old ex-sergeant Lubasch, for rest and lunch. Whilst the frugal meal was preparing they took a turn in the recently formed garden, and as they were returning to the cottage four men on horseback alighted at the cottage and rushed into the room where the ordered lunch was spread, which three of them, without ceremony, appropriated, in spite of the landlord's remonstrances. The fourth gentleman (Mr. Stephens) left his companions, and mounting his horse, galloped off towards Adelaide. The writer and his wife, also displeased at the action of the intruders, followed his example at a smart pace, but not sufficient to overtake him, although occasionally hearing the hoofs of the horse ahead of them.

Having to call at a cottage on the Glen Osmond section, they passed down that spur and so lost the sound of the horse's feet, Mr. Stephens having taken the more direct and easy Beaumont Spur, the one most in use, on which half-way down he was soon after found lying insensible; his horse had fallen, and as the unfortunate gentleman had fallen on his head he did not recover consciousness or survive many hours. The whole of the few inhabitants of the colony felt the deepest regret for such a sad termination of the useful career of one so universally esteemed.

CHAPTER VIII.

The relation of circumstances which occurred before I landed will generally be given in the words of witnesses. The first account thus given is from an individual, Henry Alford, who was actively engaged for the Government, originally as a special constable, and afterwards in a much higher post. He arrived as an articled servant, to the South Australian Company, and landed in August, 1836.

The free settlers, as well as Government officials, were obliged to employ banished men (not asking if they were expirees or runaways), who had been well trained to work as convicts, and were skilful splitters, sawyers, pincers, and builders of huts. High wages were paid to them. The port being free at first, drinkables abundant, and licences granted indiscriminately, even to bush huts, the usual consequences of this state of things followed amongst such a class of men as ex-convicts, free from restraint, with plenty of money at their command, who had only to take an occasional rest to spend their earnings in debauchery, and then resume work for a fresh supply. Captain Hindmarsh had a small party of marines left with him from Her Majesty's Ship *Buffalo*, some twelve or more in number, with a corporal; but up to this time no police force had been organised. A serious riot having occurred, got up by the drunken old lags, the Governor ordered out the marines, with loaded muskets; the Riot Act was read by the Attorney-General, but this producing no effect, the marines were ordered to load and fire with ball cartridges. Some of the rioters were wounded, and a few taken into custody, and sentenced to short terms of imprisonment. Shortly after this the Government Store was broken into, and fire arms and ammunition, besides other goods, were stolen. The Governor had appointed S. Smart, Esq., a legal gentleman from Tasmania, as sheriff. This gentleman entered on his duties with commendable zeal, and as he knew most of the Vandemonians, as they were called, was also well known by them, and marked for death. His hut was attacked after dark by three men. It was not difficult to make an entry into tents or even the temporary huts then in use without giving previous alarm, and as such dwellings were very small, a pistol presented from the door would be but a yard or two from the person aimed at. One of the ruffians instantly fired, the ball missing Mr. Smart's head, but the powder singeing his ear. As he did not fall, the intruders immediately bolted, as he had fire arms at hand, which, however, they did not give him time to use. The alarm was given, but the men escaped; and it may well be supposed what fear was experienced by the few surrounding inhabitants that night. The next day no time was lost. The Governor called for volunteers to come forward to be sworn in as special constables. A few loyally responded to the call, and very shortly two of the men who had made the attack on the sheriff were taken and committed, the one who fired the ball (viz., Magee) was afterwards found guilty and sentenced to death, and was hung; the third man, Morgan, escaped, and was afterwards reported to be lurking in the neighbourhood of the recently formed whaling stations at Encounter Bay. The Governor, on receiving this information, requested three of the special constables to go and execute a warrant, and bring in Morgan, dead or alive, and they undertook the task. Their names were Henry Alford (afterwards Inspector of Police, and one of the smartest and pluckiest men that ever joined the force), Anderson, and Hately. A description of their journey in pursuit of Morgan will be given in Mr. Alford's own words. It will be as well to explain that about this time three suspicious strangers suddenly arrived in the canvas town, no one knowing from whence they came, or by what means they had made the settlement. A few days after their arrival, a report was brought in that a strange horse was lying dead in the forest to the south of the settlement. A great cry was raised, on which the strangers vanished. They were afterwards ascertained to be escaped lifers from Sydney, named Foley, Stone, and Stanley. Before giving the account of the journey of the special constables in pursuit of Morgan an account of his origin and family should be given. He was reported to be one of seven children, whose father and mother had been transported to Tasmania for crimes committed at home. He was a remarkably fine young man, under age at the time he was sought for, of a pleasing countenance, fine figure, and over six feet high, and it was said that his brothers and sisters were equal in stature and in good looks. It has been stated to me that two of Morgan's sisters were married to highly respectable landowners in Tasmania, and were remarkable for their beauty, as well as for their becoming demeanour in the station of life to which they had attained. The following is Mr. Alford's account:—

"Our party of three specials was speedily formed, with the addition of one native blackfellow as our guide. Our outfit was a blanket each, with biscuits, tea, and sugar, and a little bacon, for eight or ten days, and one glass bottle each in which to carry our water. The arms supplied were one old musket, one horse pistol, and a pair of pocket barkers. We received minute instructions as to our course, &c., and started on, to us, an unknown country, with none but native tracks, and as such useless for us to follow. Our instructions were to make the whaling stations at Encounter Bay and to keep the gulf in sight, and we had a warrant to bring in Morgan, alive or dead. The direct distance as now travelled by a good road is 65 miles. The course we were ordered to take, with the numerous bends we had to make to head creeks and deep gorges, would not be less than 95 miles, perhaps more. Our first day's journey we finished at a deep creek, where we fortunately found good water.

"Our bottles had been exhausted some miles back. The next morning, after an early breakfast, our black guide exhibited great uneasiness, and objected to the course we proposed to take, and kept pointing more inland, giving us to understand by signs we should not find water in the direction we wished to go. We persisted in our course, and the native soon took an opportunity to abandon us to our fate. We were told before we started that on rounding Cape Jervis we should see the Pages, three small islands a few miles off the south coast, and nearly opposite the western horn of Encounter Bay. After we sighted them from a high and precipitous shore, we had to fight our way through many miles of dense scrub; but, fortunately, we had to cross plenty of good water. In eight days from starting we made Hack's Whaling Station, our food exhausted and our strength gone, as may be readily understood by those who know the country over which we made our weary way.

"Before I proceed further I must hark back and say a little more about our difficulties on our outward tramp. The horrors of our return journey being now so deeply impressed on my memory that more trifling matters are easily forgotten. I came into the whaling station barefoot, having long before worn the soles off my boots on the rocky country over which we had passed; my feet were blistered and bleeding. Our provisions had been scanty enough, and not of such a nutritious character as to keep up strength and stamina. Having reported ourselves to Captain Hart, in command of the station (who had not long before been wrecked on the same coast, but many miles to the east, on Moonlight Point), we were supplied with all we required, and enjoyed a few days' rest. On making inquiries, we found that our man was in the neighbourhood, planted and well armed, and further, that the whalers were in sympathy with him, so that we were advised to adopt stratagem, and that our lives would be in danger if the object of our visit was known or suspected. We therefore agreed upon the story, that we had come down to be ready to receive cattle which were expected to be landed at the Bay. After a few days of rest, spent in making cautious inquiries, we heard that Morgan was hiding at a spot about midway between the two whaling stations, so as to obtain his supplies of provisions from his friends in the two parties.

"Many escaped prisoners were working as whalers. After

we had received the above information as to Morgan's position, we proceeded to the next station, viz., Wright's, and here our mate H—— discovered a runaway lifer from Van Diemen's Land, in which island he (H——) had resided. We decided to use this man as a decoy duck. After threatening him with arrest, although we had no warrant for such a threat and no power or authority from the Government of Tasmania for such action, our decoy duck consented to our terms. We had determined to grab our man, and were not particular as to the means we employed. We promised the lifer we would let him go free if he honestly assisted us in securing Morgan. This he agreed to do.

"He commenced by advising us to return to Hack's station, and he would accompany us, and would point out the hut which Morgan would visit for his supplies that night. This course was pursued, and we were planted by him in a position commanding the hut. He then left us, telling us to give the man Morgan time to become settled before we stirred. Our confederate proved true to us by refraining from giving counter information, which might have cost us our lives. Having waited a sufficient time, and with darkness shrouding us, we crawled quietly to the hut, and rushing in found Morgan reclining in a bunk. We were able to seize him before he could rise and reach his gun, which was beside him loaded, and his capture was made and handcuffs on him in almost no time. As he was only a youth, though over six feet high, and I was the youngest of the party, the post of being handcuffed to him was assigned to me, the votes being two to one against me. We now made an immediate start back to Wright's station, from which establishment we had to get our supplies for the return march. The office (*i.e.*, alarm) had soon been given to his friends (as the fraternity say), our real characters were quickly circulated, and we were saluted in anything but polite language. As we hastened away a gun was fired to call for aid from Granite Island, from whence some men pushed off in a boat with the intention to intercept us. As we succeeded in heading them, language not to be repeated was roared after us. 'Oh, you —— ——; that is your —— game of landing cattle,' &c., &c., to which we replied we were well armed and would sell our lives dearly. Having arrived safely at Wright's, I was relieved, and Morgan was braceletted and otherwise secured. Here we remained the following day.

" We had been sworn in as special constables, and were yet only amateur policemen, but we were elated and eager for work in our new profession, so made inquiries as to prior entanglements of other individuals, and heard of two young men as being in that quarter who were wanted in Adelaide, and who had committed a trifling robbery. Thinking we were doing our duty we arrested them also, although we had no warrant, but as they were green and young beginners in the course of crime they quietly submitted. We had now each a prisoner to guard, and with whom to make our way back to the settlement. These young men, however, gave us no trouble, and on the way their conduct was good. The following day we started, taking provisions only sufficient to last us five or six days, hoping to reach our destination in that time by adopting a direct course, as preferable to our coasting track. Morgan, putting on an appearance of good and quiet behaviour, offered to pilot us by a short and easy cut. The provisions and swag were equally divided between the two fresh prisoners and the guards, Morgan being free of any load. To him I was again coupled with the steel cuffs. Unfortunately for all parties, we followed the guidance of Morgan, who kept as much easting as possible. We soon lost sight of the sea. We travelled for two days, having departed from the sea on our left, and after tramping many miles, on ascending high land we discovered the lakes at the mouth of the River Murray to our right. We now perceived our error in trusting to Morgan, who was leading us into a trap, as it was afterwards supposed that Stanley and Stone were harbouring in that direction. We called a halt and encamped for the night. Up to this time I had been coupled with Morgan. I was considerably below him in stature and strength, and thus it may be imagined what punishment I endured in working through scrub and over rough ground. Having secured our chief prisoner for the night, we lay on the range till morning, when we decided to tack back to obtain a sight of the sea. This course we continued on all that day, but no sea was discovered. At night we camped at a tea-tree swamp, near the range now called Mount Magnificent. At this time we had remaining food sufficient for two days only for the whole party. The usual securing of Morgan being made, we remained for rest. Early next morning Morgan refused to budge a step, and we had to remain that day, as he said he was ill, though he was brisk and lively enough as long as he thought he was leading us into a trap. We discovered he had been saving some of his biscuits in his pockets, of which we deprived him. That night we camped on the same ground.

"The following morning, after an early breakfast, we called on Morgan to get up and walk. This he declined to do in the most foul language, calling on us to shoot him, as he might as well be shot as be taken in to be hung. Our reply was, we had a warrant to take him in dead or alive, and that we should so act. After waiting patiently, time enough for him to relent, and finding him still obdurate, we decided to make him fast to a young gum-tree by passing his arms around it, and then locking his wrists with the handcuffs. This was the only course open to us, unless we set him free, or complied with his demand to put a ball through him, to either of which alternatives we decidedly objected. With some struggling we so fastened him that he had only just room to move round the tree, a position it shocked us to leave him in. We informed him he could not be released under four days at least, and must be that time without food and water, and so left him. In two hours we felt we could not leave a fellow-creature to such a cruel fate, and so returned and begged him to consent to travel. His answer, as before, was that of a desperate and determined man—he would not move. In such a dreadful predicament we finally left him; but our own position was critical enough, with short allowance for one day, and an unknown distance to encounter, which in our state might take three days to cover. We had no known place before us to reach nearer than Adelaide, and felt we might sink by the way. As to Morgan, we found he was not to be daunted. His intention was after we left him to break the handcuffs, but they proved too strong for him. We pushed on as rapidly as possible, and, fortunately, took and kept a correct course, and, though late, the same day made Onkaparinga River at the Horseshoe, and here to our great joy we found the camp of a land selector, who was there for the night on his way south. From him we obtained refreshment and food, and here we remained. We were too much exhausted to make a very early start next day, but, weary and foot-sore, at night reported ourselves at Government House, to Governor Hindmarsh. His horror and excitement at our sad tale was great.

"He immediately called a Council, when it was decided to establish a regular police force and to appoint a superintendent.

A horse was purchased at an enormous cost of £110, a superintendent was appointed, Mr. Inman, and all arrangements made to dispatch him and the officials back to the prisoner, with necessary supplies. A No. 1 (*i.e.*, myself) and Hateley appeared, but A No. 2 could not attend muster, and so we departed and made the Horseshoe, where we encamped for the night. Here I remained, the superintendent and Hateley making an early start to reach the prisoner, expecting to find him either dead or gone."

At the end of the fourth day of Morgan's self-imposed awful confinement he was found by them alive. Having released him and refreshed him with weak spirit and water and food, the party encamped there for the night. Morgan confessed in pitiful terms his regret at his obstinate conduct, and described his sufferings as something fearful, what with the wild dogs at night, which he had to keep off by kicking and tramping round the tree, and the flies and mosquitoes on his face and raw wrists; such miseries may be imagined but not described. He had frantically struggled to snap his shackles, but they were too strong and only cut deeper and deeper into his flesh. Well, marvellous to relate, this man of iron, after one night's rest and a moderate supply of food, walked the whole distance into town, over twenty miles, the course being rough and hilly with no track. He was tried for his life on a capital charge, was found guilty, and sentenced to transportation for life. His future career will be subsequently given.

CHAPTER IX.

IN the early days of the colony a most impolitic order was issued by the Government to the settlers as to the treatment of the natives, viz., that they were not to employ them in work, in order to avoid any approach towards slavery. I do not know if this emanated from the home authorities, but I suspect it did. At all events such bastard sentimentality was not generally responded to or obeyed. On the one hand were the settlers requiring a number of little jobs to be done, and on the other the natives in want of food and the requirements of civilisation as to clothing, which they were immediately called on to respect; their skin which nature had afforded them, with on stated occasions a few stripes of white or red paint, and sometimes a small girdle round the loins, being all they had previously found necessary, except when in cold weather they chose to wear wallaby or opossum rugs on their shoulders. Nevertheless, if the Government had from the first treated them as the natural owners of the land and lords of the soil, to whom an ample provision had to be set apart to enable them to lead an idle and independent life, there would have been some justice if not sense in such a proposition. But as in the progress of settlement of their country by our intrusion their game must be either destroyed or driven back, they would have been without means of subsistence in the absence of an appropriate equivalent. The question is, has justice been done them? I say it has not, and I think the contrary will not be asserted.

As to the order not to employ them, I for one, when applied to by them for food or clothing, made it a rule to give them a job more or less slight, and paid them accordingly, thinking if their necessities drove them to beg, degrading habits would be set up, and that it was our duty to induce them to adopt habits of thrift and industry. It is proper to relate that after the arrival of Colonel Gawler right steps, as far as they went, were adopted. Mr. Cronk retired as interpreter on the appointment of Captain Bromley. Dr. Wyatt, who had been appointed as Protector of Aborigines by Captain Hindmarsh, was succeeded by Dr. Moorhouse, who had his appointment from home, and who, with the scanty means supplied to him, did all in his power to ameliorate the condition of the natives and raise them in the scale of humanity, following up the attempts Dr. Wyatt had made. But such a desirable object has scarcely ever been attended with success to any such extent as philanthropists desire, proving that low and depraved feeding and habits acquired during ages reduce even man to a state of physical degradation from which an improvement is next to an impossibility, at any rate with adults. One of the first steps adopted in this colony for their benefit was the establishment of a school for the young, and as some of the scholars in subsequent years became my servants I shall with pleasure show that some moral good arose from that establishment, and that good impressions were not lost in all instances by such scholars after many years of wandering and mixing chiefly with untaught members of their own or other tribes. The policy of placing the school in the city, nevertheless, was accompanied with great evils and drawback, as it of necessity led to the adults sitting down there also, and thus the worst vices of the town were only too readily acquired and adopted by them. If the Government, instead of a few detached sections which have been from the first set apart as aboriginal reserves, had appropriated or devoted blocks of sufficient extent near fishing and hunting grounds, and there formed native stations, such as that afterwards founded at Poonindie by Archdeacon (now Bishop) Hale, and at Point McLeay under the Aborigines' Association—and had continued to carry out a system of reserves of land, with grants of money, all over the colony, in anticipation of settlement, a righteous justification would have been gained for our occupation of their land without conquest or purchase, and in compensation for the destruction of their game, and natural habits and laws. We had been received as friends, and now where are the original lords of the soil, and in what state are the few who remain in any of our settled districts?

Before any measures had been adopted for their improvement it is recorded that one white man was killed near the river below the town. This was previous to my arrival. The name of the man was Pegler. It was ascertained from some of the Adelaide tribe that he was killed by two natives named William and George, brothers. Their native names I have not learned. He was pierced through the heart by a sharpened kangaroo bone, passed in a slanting direction down from the neck, whilst under the influence of drink. This man, it was said, had insulted the natives by intruding on them at a corroboree, and had placed himself between two black women belonging to the men who killed him, and was ordered off. On his retiring he was followed and found asleep by the two brothers, one of whom killed him. The blacks gave as a further reason that some of their dogs had been killed by a white man. On the information reaching the Governor, the Protector, Dr. Wyatt, and another officer (Inspector Inman) were sent down to inquire into the sad affair.

The information Dr. Wyatt obtained was a confirmation of what had gained currency; the names William and George had been given them by the whites, their native names lost. In addition to particulars received from Dr. Wyatt will be added an account from Mr. George James of what he did in assisting to arrest these two natives.

Dr. Wyatt early devoted much time and attention to gain a knowledge of the language of the natives, and succeeded in obtaining about 1,000 native words in common use. In this research he discovered that they had found the necessity for creating fresh words to represent objects new to them, one for instance for trousers, quite a new article to them and requiring a name; their new word expressed leg-covering, a compound word, evincing much ingenuity. Dr. Wyatt, in company with Mr. Charles Mann (then Advocate-General) was subsequently directed by the Governor to visit Encounter Bay to inquire into the murder of a sailor of the name of Driscol, belonging to the ship *South Australia*. The native who killed Driscol was found by them on board the ship in irons, and evidently under very harsh treatment. It appeared on inquiry that a fight had taken place between Driscol and the black man about one of his lubras; that the sailor had been guilty of very bad conduct, and had criminally assaulted one of the women; a desperate fight occurred resulting in the death of the white man; and that the charge could only be laid for manslaughter. The difference between this death and that of the man Pegler was that the one was in a stand-up fight, and the other by the passing the sharpened bone into the vitals when the man was in an insensible state.

From Mr. G. James I have received the following account of his spirited assistance in capturing the two brothers as follows :—

" As I was crossing the river at the ford I heard shouts from a number of people, who were chasing a black man; they shouted out, 'Stop him! Stop him! He murdered Pegler.' As he flew past me he threw a waddy at me, by which I was partially stunned, as it struck me on the forehead. Although he had thus a good start, I speedily followed him, but before I could overhaul him he gained a gum tree and quickly climbed up by the cut steps in the thick bark. I followed him by the same means. On his gaining a limb high up he commenced to break off pieces of dead branches, which he continued to throw at me and a man who followed me up, named Robert, who pressed me to allow him to pass. Immediately he did so he was struck on the head with a piece of wood which wounded him and produced much blood, which fell on me. By this time a number of people had arrived, one with a gun with which the black was threatened, but still he refused to come down or cease throwing, when a shot was fired, but he still declined to surrender himself. At the request of Mr. Inspector Inman I climbed higher although he still continued to throw at me. At this time Mr. Giles Abbott, who had an axe, pretended to be cutting the tree down, and at this move he came down and surrendered himself, was handcuffed and taken to the marines' tents, amidst the lamentations of some of the blacks."

Mr. James goes on to relate that during the evening of the same day he was sent for by the Governor, who asked him to accompany a file of marines to search the wurlies of the blacks, as information had been brought to him that the other black implicated in the murder of Pegler was there. He goes on to say, "I accompanied the file of marines; on arriving at the black camp I saw four lubras standing before the opening of a wurlie. On looking round I observed a small black boy of the Adelaide tribe (Cowandilla, which means water) pointing at the wurlie behind the black women. I at once saw we had a friend and pushing between the women I pulled away a few green boughs, and there lay the fellow we wanted, nude and well greased, but the marines surrounded us, each with his old brown bess in his hand, and so he gave himself up to be handcuffed, and was coupled to his brother. These two, George and William, were placed in one of the tents, under the guard of one of the marines. During the night they both escaped with their irons on, which irons, in the morning, were found by a bullock driver, looking for his bullocks, in the bed of the Torrens above Adelaide." About six months after one of them, George, was caught, tried, and hung for the murder of a shepherd on Mr. Jas. Hallet's station.

A subsequent case of deliberate murder was performed on the same principle as the first on Pegler, only the stabber was passed upwards into the vitals. I will endeavour to describe the instrument which had such deadly effect with so little to be seen on the surface of the skin of the murdered men. It was made in one case out of the shank-bone of a kangaroo; in the other of the shank-bone of an emu, say twelve or fifteen inches in length, shaved down by pieces of quartz or glass, as it were, split in half, and one end worked to an extremely fine point, which the close texture and the strength of the bones allowed, in the form of a scoop, the sides also carrying fine sharp edges. I was told soon after I arrived that the old men or doctors of the tribes had devised this mode of taking the lives of the white men, so as on the withdrawal of the instrument, and pressing down the small half-circular flap, little blood could escape, and the spirit would not pass out, as they believed, to trouble them. In relating circumstances exhibiting their original and native habits, I can mention one described to me by Dr. Wyatt of a very touching character.

It has been always asserted that one of the shocking customs of the natives of this continent was infanticide. I give the facts related to me by the doctor, which prove that the destruction of recently-born female children was a tribal policy and custom, and a sad crime against nature and motherly feelings.

Amongst the early settlers were many who had the kindest feelings towards a race of human beings just one step removed above the beasts that perish. One lady (Mrs. Finlayson) especially interested in their behalf, having heard that a lubra had been confined of a female child, and that the tribe were about to kill it, sent to Dr. Wyatt, urging him to visit the blacks' encampment without delay, with which request the Protector immediately complied. Arrived at the wurlies on the north side of the river, the woman was pointed out to him. He found her sitting up, with the recently-born female child lying on the bare ground by her side, nothing having been done to the poor uncovered infant. Close at hand stood a vile-looking black fellow, just on the point of killing the child. A stop being put on proceedings, the mother was remonstrated with, to which she replied that the act decided on by the tribe had her consent, as one of their customs.

Dr. Wyatt observed a stout boy, about four years of age, standing and taking nourishment from the mother's breast, who was conveniently sitting on the ground. He had been advised by the kind and motherly woman who had sent him down to endeavour to get the mother to put the infant to her breast. After some persuasion she did this, and then motherly affections were excited, as the lady had predicted, and the life of the child was saved. It is well here to mention that I have on several occasions seen a boy of three or four years of age standing up and taking his nourishment from the mother in a similar manner, and on my inquiring where the recent infant was, I have been told that it was dead, and I admit that at the time I did not suspect that the child had been killed. From Dr. Wyatt I have been informed that the reasons given to him for such a barbarous custom were that the tribes being generally at war, they stole females from one another, and so each tribe wished to have as few young girls to tempt their enemies as possible. Such barbarous customs are almost too revolting to be related, but true history demands it. As the tribes on the settled part of the country became partially civilised, I believe such a cruel custom was seldom, if ever, resorted to, but a kind of barter took the place of it, of which I became cognisant. A young man having a sister could exchange her for a girl of another tribe, with the father, the brother, or cousin of the girl he desired to acquire, giving his own relative in exchange. Such cases I became aware of in my intercourse with the natives as an employer of them.

I have now to relate the sad murder of a quiet and confiding shepherd by three blacks, in order to obtain a sheep. With a friend, Mr. Osmond Gilles, I had formed a joint sheep station about four miles to the north of Adelaide, each having a separate flock and shepherd, we dividing the expense of the hut. My friend's shepherd's name was Duffield; my flock, under the charge of a man named Miles, ran west; Duffield's flock ran east. This was at the time the farthest out station. Miles had followed me from England, and stipulated that I should furnish him with a gun and a brace of small pocket-pistols, with suitable ammunition. He held the blacks in such dread that he would not allow them to come near him. He never went out without his gun in his hand and pistols in his pocket, and when he chanced to meet any of the blacks, he would wave them off to keep at a distance, and would produce from his pocket one of his pistols, and say, "Picaninny gun, plenty more." I give these particulars to account for the cautious and planned proceedings the murderers adopted to kill his comrade, Duffield, who, unfortunately for himself, acted on all occasions in a confiding manner with the natives, and gave every encouragement to them, allowing them to walk about with him, saying, when his mate remonstrated with him, "Poor creatures, we are taking their country from them!" but he put his trust in them once too often. He never carried arms. On their attack on him they acted as if they thought he might have "picaninny guns" in his pocket, the same as his mate. On the alarming news being brought to me that Duffield was lying on the plain dying or dead, I lost no time in going out with a conveyance, and finding the poor fellow prostrate, and suffering the greatest agony, I brought him into town that he might have all the attention his case required. With much difficulty he told me that three black men were walking with him quietly, one on each side of him and one behind, conversing in friendly terms. One of them asked him suddenly for a sheep. On his saying "No," he received a severe blow from the one behind him with a heavy waddy, and fell down insensible, but shortly became conscious, and felt he had been pierced upwards, from just below his ribs. He said he saw one of them withdraw the instrument he used. He spoke with such difficulty that I thought his vitals had been pierced; yet on examining him at the spot he pointed out, I could perceive very small marks of blood, and the wound was closed, and was to all appearance such as would be seen after a heavy pressure of a man's thumb nail; the small flap must have been pressed down, as I have stated in Dr. Wyatt's account of the death-wound inflicted on Pegler; but in this case a most treacherous and cruel action was committed without provocation. Duffield was without loss of time placed under medical treatment. On examination it was found that the fine and sharp instrument used had been passed a short distance under the skin and then pressed downwards, and had passed through the lungs. I must explain that Duffield, as he informed me, was on his back—that is, on his head and shoulders; that a black named Rodney was placed between his legs, which were held up by a black behind Rodney's back, and so the sharp bone was conveniently used. The instrument used was a finely-sharpened and thin leg-bone of an emu.

Every attention was exercised to relieve the sufferer, but nothing could save him. He lingered about forty-eight hours. Singular to relate, the shepherd's faithful dog, unaided, gathered the scattered sheep, took them home, crossed the river with them, and placed them in the fold, less only three stolen or lost. Duffield gave the name of the principal murderer as Rodney, a villainous fellow, who had not long before this killed his lubra; Cronk, the interpreter, found her body and buried it. Whilst I was attending on the poor sufferer Duffield, unknown to me a meeting of the inhabitants took place, as great excitement was caused, and some intemperate men proposed that a party should go out armed, and take summary vengeance on the blacks. Unfortunately, at this time, the Governor, Colonel Gawler, was away from the seat of government on an exploring expedition. Dr. Wyatt, the Protector, was also absent at Encounter Bay, with Mr. Mann, the Advocate-General, on official business, inquiring into the death of Driscol at that southern station. In this unfortunate complication of difficulties, moderate measures were happily adopted at the meeting, as by a resolution passed, in the absence of the proper authorities, four gentlemen were requested to investigate the matter, viz., Messrs. D. McLaren, J. B. Hack, and one whose name I forget, with Mr. John Brown, Immigration Agent. Mr. Brown for some time declined, not wishing to interfere out of his department, but eventually was persuaded to act, desirous to prevent any retaliatory action. On the return of Governor Gawler, he sent to Mr. Brown a written censure on his conduct, and calling for an apology or his resignation. Mr. Brown's explanation not being satisfactory, he was summarily dismissed. I am not able to say if misunderstandings antecedent assisted to cause the Governor to take this severe step, but I have reason to think such was the case.

Although Rodney was such a barbarous aboriginal, he was allowed to escape after being captured, and as far as I remember did not turn up again. He might have been killed by his own tribe, as was customary among them, to get rid of a troublesome member. I am sorry to say that the above sad murders, harrowing as they were, were exceeded far in atrocity by others committed on the natives, and bring to remembrance one instance of a brutal murder of an old black man by an overland white man, on whom retribution soon fell. There were also instances of more serious collisions between the two races. On the whole, however, I can say that this colony stands alone in the infrequency of such sad occurrences as compared with other communities in this part of the world, which had gone forth to carry out the divine command "to increase and multiply, and replenish the earth and subdue it."

Captain Bromley had been appointed interpreter and protector of the natives in place of Cronk. The new protector might be said to have lived with the blacks as he had a small cottage at their location on the north side of the river, and opposite to where the gaol has since been built. Here the Government had erected for the accommodation of the natives, huts or kennels, open towards the rising sun, and which with much trouble some of the blacks were induced to use for a time. But this was too great a departure from their previous habits, as such permanent sleeping places would require to be kept clean, and then as their bits of fires, according to their custom, were placed in front of the open part, when an east wind was blowing the dwellings were uninhabitable, and they could not effect a change of front, as they do with their customary wurlies formed of leafy boughs, which they cleansed when they moved to a fresh sleeping-place by putting a fire-stick in them. Here Captain Bromley lived, until he was found dead in a water-hole in the river; and here the blacks congregated when they were not away on hunting and fishing excursions. The interpreter's duties were to serve out flour, sugar, tea and blankets at certain times, and report to the Government anything serious which might happen. For some little time before the interpreter's death, great dissatisfaction had been created amongst the natives on account of an inferiority in the quality of the rations with which he had to supply them. At this time flour had become very scarce and dear, and in place of that, oatmeal somewhat damaged, had been substituted. This they threw about in disgust, and with much grumbling and great complaints to Captain Bromley. The sugar was also said to be inferior. It was Captain Bromley's habit to fetch his own water from the river. On the morning of his death he had as usual gone down with his can, and was afterwards found dead in the water-hole. Suspicions were excited against the blacks; he was found with his hands clenched, but with no marks of violence on his person, and there was no evidence to show that, as some people said, he had been pushed in, and held down under water by the natives, who were certainly at that time in a most angry mood about the altered rations.

The question of the displacement of an aboriginal race has always been attended with great difficulties, but is one of those necessary processes in the course of Providence to bring about the improvement of the human race and the promised latter days. From my own experience with our natives, low as they have sunk, I am convinced that with ample means granted, and time, much good may be worked on them; but at the same time the introduction of civilised habits seems to be fatal to their continued existence, independently of the vices and diseases we have brought among them, to our disgrace, which have hastened their destruction.

Before I took up my residence beyond the ranges I became acquainted with a Captain Beevor, who had a small sheep station towards the river Murray. On one occasion he complained to me of the blacks being very troublesome to him, and that he and his men had to be constantly on the look-out to keep them away from his sheep. Shortly after this we heard that one of his men had accidentally shot a black. Whether the occurrence reached the ears of the authorities or not I do not know; at all events no steps, as far as I was aware of, were taken to inquire into the matter, nor did I ever speak to him on the subject. Shortly after this occurrence he called on me in passing my place, and told me he had given up his station, and was leaving for a distant part of the colony, namely, to form a station at Port Lincoln, and was about to remove his sheep overland. The next account I heard of him was that he had gone on an exploring expedition on the Port Lincoln side of the province. Then in a few years the news came that when encamped on the margin of an extensive patch of scrub, at some distance from Port Lincoln, early in the morning, he had walked a short distance from his tent, and had sat down, when without any warning he was killed by a large spear, thrown by an unseen hand. No natives were known to be in the neighbourhood, nor did any after this murder show themselves. It was not long afterwards that his friend Mr. Dark, a surveyor, was also killed by the natives.

The only explanation I ever heard of the way in which the native was killed by Captain Beevor's shepherd was that on his rising one morning early, on looking out he perceived a native approaching the sheepyard, and that he motioned him to go away; as the warning was not complied with he fired, not aiming at the man, but the ball striking a stone ricochetted, and in rising struck the approaching native, who sprang into the air and fell dead on his face. From my own knowledge of Captain Beevor, I accepted this explanation as true, as did his other neighbours, knowing that he would not have allowed or sanctioned an act of wanton cruelty to a native. It is a sad reflection that the white man, in seeking to occupy the countries the aboriginal races have previously wandered over, should have been under the necessity of taking their lives; but I do without hesitation assert that in South Australia the instances of wilful and unjustifiable destruction of them have been few in comparison to the cases of necessity. For myself, I am thankful indeed that although I was much out in the bush, and exposed to danger from the blacks, I was never brought into collision with them. I certainly kept on good terms with them, but I do not assume that my escape was in consequence of my treatment of those who were acquainted with me, but that I kept a sharp look-out when likely to meet with strange or wild blacks, as we called them, and never allowed such to come within range of their spears.

A very few instances of unprovoked murder of whites by the natives have come within my own knowledge. The killing of Captain Barker on the eastern side of the mouth of the Murray occurred some years before the foundation of our colony, and I believe the tribe by which he was killed were afterwards guilty of other murders in our time, as such took place in the same district. Captain Barker, a brother officer of Captain Sturt, both of the 39th regiment of the line, then quartered in Sydney, was ordered by Sir Ralph Darling, Governor of New South Wales, on his way from Western Australia, " to visit and inspect the Gulf of St. Vincent and Encounter Bay, to explore and examine the country, to ascertain if the favourable report of it furnished by Captain Sturt on his return from his boat trip down the Murray River, to near its embouchure, founded only on the distant views which he was able to obtain of the country in passing up and down the river, was borne out by an actual inspection of it." I gather the following facts from the report of Mr. King, who accompanied Captain Barker. It appears that he, with a party, left their ship (we may presume at Holdfast Bay), and travelled on foot to the top of Mount Lofty, from whence, it may well be said, he had on all sides of him a most extensive and splendid prospect. From this elevation he made his way, principally through a dense forest, till he came to the exceedingly rich flats near Mount Barker (named after him), and continued on from thence to Lake Alexandrina and the Lower Murray or the Goolwa. Wishing to get a good view of the outlet to the sea, he left his party and swam across one of the channels, with his compass fastened on his head. He was seen after leaving the water to ascend a high sand hummock, and then disappeared from their sight never to be seen again alive or dead by his people. As he did not return he was subsequently sought for by them, accompanied by a white sealer and a native woman from Kangaroo Island, and they ascertained he had been killed, and that his body was thrown into the stream and was carried out to sea. Here was a noble man cut down in the performance of the arduous duties he had almost completed. Of him, his comrade and friend, Captain Sturt, wrote :—" He was in disposition, as he was in the close of his life, in many respects similar to Captain Cook. Mild, affable, and attentive, he had the esteem and regard of every companion, and the respect of every one under him. Zealous in the discharge of his public duties, honourable and just in private life, a lover and follower of science, indefatigable and dauntless in his pursuits, a steady friend, an entertaining companion. In him the King lost one of his most valuable officers, and his regiment one of its most efficient members." I conjecture he was cast into the rapid swirl with his compass untouched, as they evidently got rid of his remains and all he had about him effectually, as nothing has since been discovered of anything he had with him. I think they dreaded to touch the compass, as they would think it to be some mysterious part of his person, as some of them thought the first man on horseback formed, with the horse, one animal, and, as was related to me by a river black who first saw Captain Sturt in his boat, and the one following him, he believed them to be two animals with "plenty heads and long arms." When it is considered that the whites, who have taken possession of so much of this fifth quarter of the world, as it has been called, have spread themselves out so widely, we may well wonder that so few lives have been lost, especially as some of us know how careless the majority of the people have been, and in how many instances, as reported in other colonies, our countrymen, to their disgrace, have treated the aboriginals with insult and injustice. Having met some further particulars on my first visit to Mount Barker about seven years after Captain Barker fell, I felt much on the painful subject. I came upon a camp of blacks at or near the spot where he left his party, and amongst them was a woman who could speak a few words of English. She had been recently stolen from the Adelaide tribe, and had been told by the black who had caught her, by what I could make out, as follows : That the tribe would not have killed him (Captain Barker), only he ran away and would not stop when they gave him friendly signs, and so a spear was thrown at him, which made him tumble down. She could not tell me of anything taken from him. I could gather that he was cut off by some who were secreted in ambush, and whom he had passed, so that he could not return towards his party.

CHAPTER X.

THIS chapter contains an interesting narrative of the first overland expedition with cattle from Sydney to South Australia. That expedition was one of the early and essential instruments in the successful conversion of a vast wilderness into a fruitful garden, and in assisting in the establishment of a colony now one of the brightest jewels in the British Crown.

I am entirely indebted to Mr. Charles Bonney for the account which follows, and feel especially obliged to him, knowing how fully his time is occupied by his important official duties:—

"The first overland expedition was fitted out by Joseph Hawden, Esq. The cattle, about 300 head, were mustered on the River Goulburn, just below the point where the Sydney Road then crossed it. A start was made on the 26th January, 1838. I had joined the party a day or two previously, and had undertaken the duty of leading the drays and choosing the line of route, the cattle being generally some little distance in the rear. The course we had intended to take was to follow the Goulburn to the point where Mitchell supposed he had left it when he turned to the southward after exploring the River Darling, and then to take his track to the southward, to follow the course of some of the rivers which he had crossed, and which he described as flowing to the westward, hoping that we might thereby avoid what was anticipated to be a difficult country to get through with cattle, in the neighbourhood of the Murray Cliffs, described by Captain Sturt.

"We found as we followed the course of the Goulburn, instead of its running in the direction of Mitchell's supposed point of departure from its banks, a littte north of west, it tended more and more to the north, and sometimes east of north, until we suddenly came upon the junction of a large river coming from the eastward. Knowing that we were somewhere about 100 miles to the eastward of what Mitchell had described as the junction of the Goulburn with the Murray, and yet feeling certain that the river before us could be none other than the Murray, we were very much puzzled at first to reconcile Mitchell's account with what we saw. However, at last we hit upon the solution of the difficulty, which afterwards we proved to be correct, that he had mistaken a channel of the

Murray, for the junction of another river, and thus we pursued our course along the left bank of the Murray until we came to Mitchell's track. We then followed the course he took to the southward, passing the hill he named Mount Hope, because from its summit he saw a line of trees which seemed to mark the course of a large river flowing to the westward. We also had a view from the summit of Mount Hope, but it was Mount Disappointment to us. The line of trees described by Mitchell evidently marked the direction of a watercourse flowing to the northward to join the Murray. However, we followed Mitchell's track till we came to a log bridge, which he had thrown over the river, seen from Mount Hope, which he named the Yarrayne. His grand river had dwindled down to a dry creek, with only a little water left in some of the holes at distant intervals. The question then was what course should we follow? Go on to some of the other rivers which Mitchell had described, or return to the River Murray, which we had left, and trust no more to Mitchell's accounts? My advice to go back to the Murray was followed. To do this we continued on the course of the Yarrayne to its junction with the Murray, and continued to follow down on the left bank of that river until we thought we were below the junction of the Darling, when we crossed to the other or north side, but soon found we had crossed a little too early, the junction of the Darling being still below us. However, as we were travelling in a very dry season, and the rivers were all very low, the crossing of the Darling gave no trouble. After this we kept the right bank of the River Murray until we had passed the North-west Bend, and made three days' journey on its southerly course. We then left the river, and after a very hard day's work got through the scrub, and camped at the foot of the range. Following the course of the range to the southward until we found an opening, we passed immediately to the north of Mount Barker, where we saw the first signs of civilization in the shape of horse-tracks. From the summit of the mount we had a view of Lake Alexandrina, and being misled by Sturt's map, in which the junction of the river and the lake was shown as being in the same latitude as Adelaide, we kept a south-west direction in travelling through the ranges, and after coming upon the Onkaparinga followed its course until we came out at the Horseshoe. Here we found a party of kangaroo hunters (Sladden and others), and learned from them the direction and distance of the settlement, as Adelaide was then called, which we reached on the 4th of April, 1838, having performed the journey in ten weeks. Thus ended the first overland journey from New South Wales to South Australia after Captain Sturt's boat expedition—a journey accomplished without any disaster or difficulty worth mentioning, and almost without the loss of a single head of cattle.

"After we left Mitchell's Yarrayne everything went smoothly; we had no trouble whatever with the natives. At Swan Hill we established friendly relations with them, and from that point until we left the river they always sent forward messengers to the next tribe, to give notice of our approach, and we used to find the tribe drawn up to meet us, on which occasions they gave vent to their astonishment, in an audible manner, at the sight of what was to them such a strange race. On one occasion only were we in danger of coming into collision with them. I had left the drays and proceeded in advance to look out for a road, and the party had come up with a tribe of blacks, drawn up, as usual, at the edge of a lagoon, which the drays had to go round; and the blacks wishing to have another look at the strange white creatures, took a short cut across the lagoon to meet them, when our men became frightened, and took it into their heads that the blacks were going to attack them, and halted the drays and got out their firearms. The blacks, seeing what was going on, handled their spears in self-defence. Fortunately at this moment I returned, just as the fight was about to commence. Having been a great deal among the blacks, and being well acquainted with their habits, I at once saw the mistake the men had made, and ordered them to put down their guns. I then rode up to the natives, and by signs induced them to lower their spears, and so peace was restored. The natives on many occasions proved very useful to us, and the paths which they had made in travelling up and down the river afforded an unfailing guide as to the direction we ought to take in order to cross the great bends it frequently makes. On one occasion we came to a point on its course where the river swept away to the south as far as the eye could reach, without any appearance of a return to its general western course. A well-beaten native track led off north of west, and it became a weighty question whether we should trust to the usual guidance of a native path or keep to the river. It was evident that if the path led to the river it would not reach it for many miles, and I was inclined to adopt the safer course of keeping to the river; but Hawden thought we might venture to follow the path, and we did so. We travelled on till late in the afternoon, and still there was no appearance of the river gums in the western horizon. Hawden, who had ridden on ahead, anxious to look out for the river, came hurriedly back, and wanted me to turn to the southward and strike in for the river; but I showed him that it was too late then to alter our course, and that we should probably find the river further away to the south than in the direction we were going. We accordingly pursued our course along the native track, and just before dark we were fortunate enough to come upon a fine sheet of water, which Hawden named Lake Bonney. One of the overland parties who came down after us determined to stick to the river, and it took them nearly a week to get round the bend. When we arrived at that part of the river where the cliffs commence, my great difficulty was to know when to keep to the river flats and when to take to the high land. On the flats it was much better travelling than on the sandy plains on the top of the cliffs, but the river would sometimes take a sudden sweep round to the cliffs and compel us to climb to the high land, when we might have to go back two or three miles before we could find a place up which the drays could be taken. At last we fell in with three natives, who gave us to understand by signs that they belonged to a tribe lower down the river, and that they would accompany us. One of them I adopted as a guide, and made him understand what I wanted, and such was his intelligent and quick apprehension that, though he had never seen a white man before, he seemed to know almost by instinct where a dray could pass and where it could not. He acted as my guide for three or four days, and during the whole of that time he never once led us wrong. Old colonists will remember my friend in old 'Tinberry,' whose portrait figures in Eyre's Australia.

"At the time we commenced our overland journey the second expedition was being fitted out under the leadership of Mr. E. J. Eyre. Both my party and his had, without concert, fixed on the same line of route—that was, to follow the course of the rivers which Major Mitchell said he had discovered south of the Murray, and which it was supposed would join and form what Captain Sturt thought to be a river running into the Murray above the Great Bend, but which was subsequently discovered to be merely an anabranch of the river. Eyre, however, struck across from Mount Macedon, and cut Mitchell's track a little south of the Yarrayne Bridge, where he arrived about a fortnight after we had been there. He saw our tracks going back towards the Murray, and not having had so much experience of Mitchell's inaccuracies as we had found, he placed accordingly more reliance on his description of the rivers he had met with further south, and in consequence he continued on Mitchell's track, and tried to get to the westward by following the courses of several rivers one after the other, but they all ran out in the scrub until he came upon the Wimmera, which he found to end in a lake, to which he gave the name of Lake Hindmarsh, after the then Governor of South Australia. He next tried to push through the scrub to reach the River Murray by a northerly course, but he was foiled in the attempt, after destroying many of his horses and losing some of his men by desertion. He was at length compelled to retrace his steps, and after much suffering he reached Mitchell's Bridge, on the Yarrayne, about three months after he first saw that watercourse. Weakened as he was by the loss of horses and the desertion of some of his men, he persevered on his journey, and following on our tracks, arrived at the settlement in Adelaide free from further troubles."

I must state that Hawden and Bonney brought in their cattle and horses in fine condition, but Mr. Eyre and his party, men and stock, arrived in a weakened state. I had good reason to know this, for I had the charge and sale of the cattle, which were purchased from Mr. Eyre on account of a Sydney firm, whose agent I was. Although I was able to put these cattle on splendid feed, it took many months before they recovered from the hardships they had undergone. At the same time I must admit they were cattle of a much inferior description and breed to the fine herd which Mr. Bonney conducted for Mr. Hawden, which, although the first introduced overland, have never been surpassed by any large draft brought from the adjoining colonies.

CHAPTER XI.

ON the 12th of October, 1838, the news spread that our new Governor, Colonel Gawler, was on board the ship just arrived.

No regular arrangements were made as to any public reception or demonstration on his landing, but it was bruited about that he would be coming up on horseback about midday. A few mounted men mustered and straggled down the track towards Holdfast Bay, where the *Pestonjee Bomanjee* had anchored. We gradually formed a troop of about twenty horsemen. On arriving a little below where Hilton now stands, on what was then open ground, we were met by a one-horse vehicle of unpretending appearance, with a lady and some children and one female servant, all in ship array, with no escort or other servants. We continued at a slow pace, utterly ignorant that we had passed the Governor's lady and children. Soon afterwards we perceived in the distance a considerable dust approaching us on the track ; this was the old and lower track, before roads were formed. We soon became conscious that the Governor was coming with a small escort, at a hand gallop. His Excellency shot past us on old Black Jack, a blood entire, usually ridden by the Commissioner, Mr. J. H. Fisher. We followed after they had passed, according to the speed of our horses, and remarked to one another, "This will be a fast Governor," and so he proved ; but not too fast for the new country he had to carry forward towards a successful development of its great resources (*i.e.*, if he had been supplied with sufficient means). On arrival at Government House, humble as it was then, a concourse of settlers soon formed, as well as a muster of aboriginals, with their interpreter, Cronk. His Excellency did not keep us long before he appeared, and went through the formal proceedings required on such occasions. These concluded, he gave us a very suitable address, and one also to his black brethren, as he called them. Before he turned to them he asked the Protector (Dr. Wyatt) if he was competent to interpret what he should say to them. The answer was, " Yes, your Excellency." His address to them was rapidly delivered. He told the blacks he came from their great Queen, that she loved her black people, and they must also love her white people, &c. &c. The interpreter kept on gabble, gabble, doing his best to interpret a discourse so rapidly delivered and translated ; it was like parson and clerk racing ! but not a word do I believe most of the black brethren understood of the address.

On the Governor concluding his oration, he waved his cocked hat with its white feather, when a knowing native up a crooked overhanging tree shouted out: " Plenty tucker ; berry good

Cockatoo Gubbernor." His Excellency's last words to the Protector were—" I shall order for them a supply of food," which the cunning fellow understood as "plenty tucker," adding by way of compliment, and as if impressed by the motion of the white feather, the title "berry good Cockatoo Gubbernor."

The Governor soon got to work on his official duties, and much energy was thrown into the service. He found only a small organisation as to police. The first governor's marine guard, such as it was, had left with Captain Hindmarsh, and there was no military force. Captain Hindmarsh had appointed Mr. Inman as Superintendent of Police, who had a small number of raw policemen under him. Shortly after the arrival of Governor Gawler he appointed Major O'Halloran Commissioner of Police and Police Magistrate, with an increased number of men. He also called for volunteers to form a semi-military force. In answer to this appeal, gentlemen willing to serve as officers abounded, but rank and file were scarce, and only a few at first came forward to be enrolled. Major O'Halloran was gazetted Colonel, and among the officers appointed were Alex. Tolmer, captain and adjutant of cavalry, and Mr. Litchfield, captain and adjutant of infantry. An early muster was ordered, and uniforms, it was announced, could be obtained at the Government Store. I had allowed a man in my employment to enrol; he was driver of the mail to Glenelg or Port Adelaide (I was the first mail contractor), and I had arranged to put a substitute on the box when his services were required as a volunteer. As I was anxious to see how things went on at the muster in front of Government House, I started in that direction, and as I approached I saw F. G., my driver, on his way, in some sort of a military uniform. On nearing me he halted with a military salute (he had served in a yeomanry regiment at home). I said to him : " Well, G., what an extraordinary figure you cut !" " I am aware of it, sir," was the reply, " but it is not my fault; we were ordered to apply for and to appear in slop uniform. I turned over a lot of the clothing, and have taken the nearest I could find to fit me. This shell-jacket and the pants will not meet, as you see, and I have adopted a large red comforter to fill up the gap." Of course I had a hearty laugh, but could not risk the chance of indulging in indecorous manners before His Excellency, and so turned back. I received a report of the miserable failure of the first attempt to muster a force, at which were present nine officers, as I was informed, and six rank and file. I must add that after some little time a respectable regiment was organised.

Governor Gawler brought with him extended powers, which were generally ample. His appointment embraced also the office of Commissioner of Crown Lands, from which Mr. J. H. Fisher retired. The Governor was supreme, and only trammelled by a limit on his powers to draw (except in extreme emergency) on the Board of Commissioners in London, or on Her Majesty's Treasury.

On Colonel Light resigning, as mentioned in a previous chapter, Mr. G. S. Kingston (afterwards knighted) assumed the position of Acting Surveyor-General, as empowered by his original instructions from the Commissioners, bearing date 9th March, 1836. Mr. G. S. Kingston did not long occupy the position of acting-head of the department, and soon after his retirement Captain Frome arrived, with a few sappers and miners as a staff of surveyors. I am not aware if any essential or beneficial changes were made in the work of the survey department after Colonel Light left the office, where a very insufficient staff remained for his "acting" successor to rely on. Colonel Gawler reported on the state of the survey staff in one of his first despatches, from which I shall quote hereafter.

After the arrival of Captain Frome, of the Royal Engineers, to fill the post, the surveys were rapidly proceeded with. Whether greater accuracy obtained or not I am unable to say; but I was informed by one of the sappers when engaged in my neighbourhood, that in off-working on to previously surveyed sections, to fill up unsurveyed pieces of country, it was a difficult task to *thumb* in his own work. I had no occasion to complain of the old surveys, as I had an excess of quantity in a section I then held. One of the works executed by the sappers and miners under Captain Frome was to erect a small mud or sod fort on North-terrace, with embrasures and carronades mounted therein pointing to the city. So, if the citizens had become rebellious, they could have been slaughtered there with ease if they had chosen to place themselves within the range.

Captain Frome was energetic in his office, and most gentlemanly in his deportment to all who had to apply to him for information, or on any business connected with the Survey and Land Office. He fulfilled the duties also of Engineer-in-Chief without any additional pay. Two bridges over the Torrens within the city bounds, which he erected, were, by unusual floods, swept away; succeeding floods have not been so heavy, nor have such large trees been brought down since, which were the cause of the destruction of those first erections.

I am bound to mention that Mrs. Gawler with commendable zeal aided the Governor in every good work. As became them, they exhibited great interest in the welfare of the natives. One of their early steps in encouraging them was to call them together to display their prowess in throwing the war spear, boomerang, and waddy, on which occasion the settlers were invited to a lunch, and the blacks to a feed, after the trial of their skill. And here they completely out-generalled Colonel Gawler, as I shall show.

Archery targets of the full size were placed near Government House at suitable and fair distances, according to the directions of those who knew something about their habits.

The warriors of the tribe were marshalled up with their spears, boomerangs, &c., King John at their head, with his cutlass by his side, in addition to his native arms. The cutlass was presented to him in a formal manner on board the *Buffalo*. King John first made a grave and dignified inspection of the target at the farther end, and returning half-way towards the attacking position paused, measuring the distance with his eyes, and returned, shaking his head, to the starting-point where his men and the company were standing. He then said : "No, no, too much long way." The distance was not 100 yards. On this protest the outer target was brought in some 15 or 20 yards. He then poised his spear, and brought it to the recover, saying : " Blackfellow no throw big one spear that long way." Then at or about sixty yards he consented to try their skill, though he with admirable acting expressed his doubts. Now fixing his womera (a casting agent for long distances), amidst the objecting grunts of his tribe, he discharged his spear so as to strike the rim of the target with the middle of the spear instead of the point, and then came the ejaculations of his men, implying, "Ah ! ah ! we told you so !"

Then came up in turn the warriors of the tribe, but with well-expressed reluctance, some just missing the target, others following the example of King John; and now they pretended shame under the derisive cheers of the lubras. The boomerangs were then thrown high, and so as, in their eccentric flight, to return towards those who cast them, and appeared more calculated to endanger the thrower than an opponent. On this many of the ladies exclaimed, "Poor fellows, you see they cannot hit anybody even at that short distance," and many of the spectators were convinced of the harmless character of the warriors amongst whom we had arrived. In accordance with their customs, they had been brought on to the field in their war costume, i.e., their faces and breasts decorated with white war paint in bars, but with an addition of European costume as far as pants went, which the Governor had ordered to be given them, thereby hiding their natural spindleshanks. The exhibition ended, they retired to their feast, and we to a plentiful luncheon. If they laughed at us on the sly before us, it was internally and well disguised. No doubt the joke circulated far and wide amongst the surrounding tribes, and most likely formed the subject of one of their corroborees, their custom being to rehearse with musical accompaniment any striking occurrence, the accompaniment being performed by women beating sticks together, and uttering "Ah, ah, ah, ah," continually during the dancing of the males. I once, on the Murray, was highly delighted to witness the performance of a corroboree of the first steamboat that passed them on that river; at the same time one of them commenced an exhibition of the first passage down the river of Captain Sturt with his boats. The actor was engaged, as I was afterwards informed, in snaring wild fowl up to his chin in the water, amidst the reeds, with a cap of green leaves on his head, when to his surprise and alarm he saw in the middle of the stream "a great beast with plenty of heads and legs." He dropped his rod and remained quiet, and, as quick as he dared, darted out of the water and secreted himself in the scrub. I have been frequently amused at their singular performances.

I may here relate a surprise which Mrs. Gawler got on one of her visits to the residences of the colonists (not intended for the upper classes), in distributing tracts to the inhabitants of tents and shanties. I have mentioned the small miserable hut where our first postmaster carried on his duties. At the door of this Mrs. Gawler knocked, and on the door being opened she was greatly surprised when the name of the Postmaster-General was given, in answer to her question as to the name of the occupant. "I was not aware that Government officials occupied such strange places," said the lady, and feeling she could not leave a tract with so high an official, she walked on, and soon found herself in Emigration-square, to which she had started to make a special visit, as it was then filled with freshly-arrived emigrants. The good lady here found an ample field for her pious works. This necessary establishment has vanished long ago, and has not been replaced. It was situated on the flat beyond the north-west corner of the city, and was built of weatherboards, which answered a temporary purpose. These huts were pulled down after the stagnation and stoppage of emigration from England.

In December, 1839, Judge Cooper arrived. Of him it must be recorded that a more upright and just judge never occupied the highly responsible seat of judgment in this or any other country. His conscientious dread of erring in judgment caused him, through the invariable caution he exercised before giving his decisions, to subject himself on some occasions to impatient remarks from the advocates who pleaded in the courts. He was for some time the only judge in all three courts, the Civil, Criminal, and Insolvent Courts, and he fulfilled his onerous duties in an unexceptionable manner. In private life he set a bright example as a consistent and liberal Christian.

Judge Cooper retired on a liberal pension, which he has lived long to enjoy. To show the pure and unsophisticated mind of the judge, it is only necessary to relate two cases amongst the first he heard when on the Bench in Adelaide. In one a storekeeper sued for the amount of a debt owing to him, and in his evidence to support the correctness of his claim, informed the Court that he kept his books by double entry, when the judge interrupted him in a hasty and surprised manner by asking the witness : "Do you admit on oath that you enter an article twice?" In another case, an action to recover for damage to a cargo of wheat shipped to the Cape of Good Hope, a witness (the supercargo, who had held the rank of chief mate) swore that the cargo was damaged by salt water let in through open seams in the deck. In cross-examination he admitted he had consented to the captain's putting in to the Mauritius, and that on leaving he himself had made an affidavit that the ship was well found, taut, &c. His manner in giving such a contradiction was most trifling. Judge Cooper hastily exclaimed : "You deserve to be prosecuted for perjury," to which the witness replied : "Oh, your Honour, it is only a matter of form to get clearance, and done every day to get into good company."

The judge showed he was much shocked by such levity, and ordered him to leave the witness box.

CHAPTER XII.

IN the months of November and December in the year 1838, the ship *Zebra*, Captain Hahn, and the *Prince George* arrived from Hamburg with German families, under the pastoral care of the Rev. Mr. Kavel, who was truly a shepherd over them, not only administering to their spiritual wants, but also acting as overlooker to a great extent to their temporal affairs. The community of useful colonists whom he brought out had been assisted to a great extent by Mr. G. F. Angas, formerly of London, and late of Lindsay House, Angaston.

Of this action I may remark, without fear of contradiction, that this wealthy and beneficent gentleman never made a better use of his money than by affording to this body of Lutherans the means to migrate to this colony. Without being guilty of an intrusion on the quiet and unostentatious actions of Mr. Angas, I think, as a public benefactor to a much greater extent to the colony of South Australia than any other of its founders, some record should be made of the obligations we owe to him. He was not only one of the committee who struggled to obtain our charter; but when his funds and presence in the colony were so much needed he further made large investments, and a few years later took up his residence among us, and spent the remainder of his valuable life here, and thus set an example which has not been always followed by those who have made their fortunes here; too large a proportion of such fortunate individuals being now absentees, who draw their incomes to be spent in other countries, untaxed by us.

Shortly after the arrival of Pastor Kavel he called upon me and explained the circumstances under which this large body of immigrants had arrived, viz. : that they were generally poor but industrious and honest ; that they had been, by the assistance of a loan, enabled to make the passage, and that they required cattle and other things, including land, which they must to a great extent procure on credit, and asked me if I could oblige them with cattle. Some few amongst them had money, and might pay with cash; some could pay part of the purchase-money, and those who required full credit would pay instalments at certain fixed periods. I did not hesitate to comply, and was soon visited by a number of his people.

First came a small capitalist who wanted a pair of oxen, and exhibited his small bag of sovereigns with some pride. At the time, the stockyard was full of cattle brought in for sale. He pointed out to me on the outside of the yard a hand-truck to which he had fixed a long slight pole, and gave me to understand that he wanted a pair of oxen to attach to that vehicle to take his luggage, with which it was loaded, over the hills, pointing to Mount Lofty. He had a companion with him who could speak a few words of English. I knew nothing of German. He showed me a rope, and gave me to understand he intended to guide or drive the oxen according to his country fashion. As I was much puzzled what to do with him, I shook my head to imply that his system would not answer with our cattle. On this he again produced his money-bag, to which I nodded and said "Yes," which gave him and his family much pleasure, and caused them to exclaim "Yah, yah;" and then they climbed on the fence of the large stockyard, in which were a number of wild cattle brought in for the butchers. Now I had to shake my head again and say "No, no;" but it was no use, my customer kept repeating "Yah, yah," and his friend said "How much?" pointing out two bullocks. He was told £42 the pair. One was the wildest and wickedest beast in the yard, and the other a good match for him. As I could not make him understand me, I was leaving the party, when my stockkeeper called my attention to a quiet pair of small leaders in another yard in which were a number of quiet milking cows, which I told the German he could have for £42 the pair in yoke, but he declined with contempt, as I had mentioned the same price for the larger bullocks in the other yard. Finding I could not make myself understood, and that the intended buyer had worked himself into a violent passion, implying, as I thought, a charge that I wanted to cheat him, I walked away to my house, leaving him violently gesticulating to my men.

I had not been long away when I heard a great noise of roaring bullocks and men's voices, and returned to see what was the matter. It appeared after I left he had tendered to my foreman the money named, which was the price fixed for

the pick of unbroken bullocks in the yard. My men wished
for no better fun, so they complied with his wishes, and roped
up one of the beasts he had chosen, which went quietly into
the strong bail used to yoke up steers in, and on roping the
other brute, which he was so determined to have, the bullock
became quite furious, and was roaring and dashing about in
such a manner that the German was frightened enough, and
met me, begging for his money which my man had received. I
ordered the rope to be cut, when the beast rushed at and
cleared the fence, and made off. A man on horseback was
sent after him, and the bullock was found on the banks of the
Torrens, where he had tossed a constable and seriously injured
him, and was quickly shot by one of the troopers. As the
German had been so obstinate and had caused so much trouble
I refused to return his money, but desired him to call on me
with his pastor. Before he could leave, the man returned with
the news of the damage done. The German's whole family
were now present. His wife had in the meantime been handling the quiet milking cows in the milking yard, and now they
petitioned me to let them have two quiet cows in place of the
bullocks, with which I complied, and the whole family went off
with their newly-acquired live stock highly pleased, especially
as I made a return of the difference in the price, as the wife
had not chosen two of the highest priced ones but the quietest,
and I was willing to submit to some loss on the bullock to get
clear of the party. Some of the family yoked themselves to
the truck, which was such a one as two large goats might have
drawn; and after making several journeys, I was told in the
same manner by hand, they managed to get the whole of their
goods over the hills. It must not be forgotten that at the time
this was done no road had been cut or formed, and the greater
part of the goods of the community was carried on backs and
shoulders to the village named by them Hahndorf in honour of
Captain Hahn.

 I have given the above account of my first transaction with
these people to show how little they were acquainted with colonial matters. I had subsequently many dealings with them,
and invariably found them punctual and honest. I continue
to relate what difficulties this community had to experience
and overcome in acquiring land on which to found their settlements. One they formed at Klemzig, where Pastor Kavel
lived for years.

Owing to our land system not then admitting of purchase on credit from the Government, the Germans who arrived in the early days, instead of paying £1 to the State paid long credit prices and heavy interest to private speculators. For the Hahndorf land they had to pay £7 an acre. I do not know what interest they were charged, but I daresay 10 per cent. Now this land was part of the first special survey taken up by Messrs. Dutton, Finniss, and McFarlane, at a cost to them of £1 an acre, and was not by any means the pick of their land; so no favour was shown in this essential arrangement with the strangers, who, I think I may say, were taken in. They had to pay off the principal by annual instalments. The quantity of land was 240 acres, which cost them £1,680. Then, through the pastor, they obtained credit for provisions, &c., to the amount of £1,500, until their own crops were realised on. Their seed wheat had cost them £1 a bushel, and they had to procure working cattle at no less than £40 a pair. Up to the time of their arrival the inhabitants of Adelaide had been insufficiently supplied with vegetables and dairy produce, and these at an exorbitant price—butter at 2s. 6d. a lb., and eggs 2s. 6d. a dozen. The Germans very soon began to carry into the city for sale small supplies of butter, and, within a few months, vegetables, generally on the backs of the females, and in the same manner taking back their supplies of rations. After a time a string of matrons and girls would be seen wending their way to the capital in their German costume. Before the end of their first year of residence amongst us they furnished the townspeople with a good supply of vegetables, &c., realising to themselves a good profit. At their first harvest their little handmills were set a-going; and they soon cleared off all their debts, and purchased from the Government 240 acres of land for cash, at £1 an acre, contiguous to their township.

Their implements were of their own construction, and primitive enough, after the forms which had been in use in their native country for hundreds of years. For some time after their arrival we would see funny rigs attached to one of their small ploughs or wooden harrows—say a woman with a strap over her shoulder with a rope to a swingletree, a necessary advantage given to her in length, and at the other shorter end a small bullock, cow, or a pony, the husband or father holding with one hand the one-handled plough and with the other a long pipe, which he was deliberately smoking—the wooden plough light enough to be carried on a man's shoulder.

It was not long before we saw them in better circumstances, with their pairs of fine and fat horses, kept and treated in a manner which set an example to the settlers amongst whom they had come.

At an early period old Lubasch (who was a sergeant in the Prussian artillery at the battle of Waterloo) opened in the village of Hahndorf first a coffee-shop, and soon afterwards a licensed house, and ran a pony mail-cart, much to the accommodation of the small population then settled in the district. Many a hard battle of words have I fought with the old sergeant, but never succeeded in convincing him that the battle of Waterloo was won before the arrival of old Blucher. Lubasch claimed to have been with the advanced detachment of guns which unlimbered and fired the first volley, and saved, as he maintained, the English army.

At the first shearing of sheep after their arrival at their village, the community at Hahndorf contracted to shear a flock for Mr. D. Macfarlane; and as I witnessed their peculiar mode of performing the work, I will relate what I saw. The shearers were principally young women, who were waited on by men of the village, who, when called on, caught and carried the sheep to the shearer who was ready. The sheep was carefully laid down on its side; the young woman, without shoes and stockings, had a piece of thick soft string tied to one of her great toes, the other end was then tied to the hind foot of the sheep; the girl's leg was then stretched out to extend the legs of the sheep; her knee or left hand was pressed on the neck or shoulder of the animal, which was then left to her charge, and she commenced her clipping work, most carefully avoiding any snips of the skin. The number shorn by one never exceeded thirty a day. At first I was inclined to laugh, but I was soon pleased to see how tenderly the sheep were handled. The wool was not taken off very close. The whole party worked with a will, and the amount they earned went towards the payment for their land, as Mr. D. Macfarlane, the owner of the sheep, was one of the original proprietors who sold the land to them.

This first and successful experiment in the introduction of German immigrants was followed by several other shiploads, some, as I am informed, assisted also by Mr. Angas, and many others who have been aided by their friends who had preceded them and been successful. The influence of Pastor Kavel was very great, his personal exertions on behalf of his countrymen were untiring, and with a perfect forgetfulness of self, so that he could not fail in establishing a community remarkable for probity and respect for our laws. Mr. Kavel was universally beloved. He had married a wife of an alien nation, viz. English, shortly before his arrival, and in this respect departed from the general actions of his people, amongst whom a certain degree of jealousy was from the first displayed against becoming amalgamated with the English population amongst whom they had settled. It has been objected to these German immigrants that the colonists do not derive any direct benefit from their labour, but this is not a liberal view to take, as they rent a good deal of land from English proprietors, and when not engaged on their own holdings gladly take work from the adjoining settlers. By the untiring industry and rigid frugality of the inhabitants of Hahndorf they soon paid off all their debts; and although most of those who arrived here and are still alive, remain in their original location, many of the younger branches have taken up land on their own account, and are becoming amalgamated with the English population. At all events, they all, young and old, prove themselves 'good and loyal subjects of our gracious Queen. On some occasions I attended the services of the Rev. Mr. Kavel, and, without notice, on his observing English hearers present he would address us in our own language, apparently to the gratification of his own people. He early suffered the loss of his wife, who was buried at Klemzig, and the good man seemed for a time almost bowed down with grief.

He procured the publication of a neat pamphlet, containing statistical accounts of the colony, with a lithographic print of the city and a map of the colony, with letters from German settlers containing glowing descriptions of the success they had met with. This little work was extensively circulated in Germany, and no doubt has led numbers who have left their own nation to join us in this antipodal region.

The following German villages were early formed, viz. :—Klemzig, Hahndorf, Lobethal (in which our first woollen factory has been established), Bethanien, Langmiel, as well as several other smaller settlements, and now as fresh arrivals come they are more dispersed abroad than when the first communities arrived. From the Hartz Mountains and Saxony we have not had the number of miners and smelters that could be desired, such workers being specially adapted to obtain and smelt our minerals.

CHAPTER XIII.

IN this chapter will be related the erroneous impressions published by experienced explorers on their first and hasty inspections of the new colony.

Such errors have, however, been common in other colonies. Captain Sturt, shortly after his arrival in August, 1838, invited settlers to meet him, offering to deliver a lecture on the prospects of agriculture and horticulture in South Australia. About twelve persons attended, all being interested in the subject, and who had come out with the intention of embarking in country pursuits. I was one of the company, having brought out two land orders on my own account, with power also to exercise selection for a non-resident. The lecture was very interesting. Captain Sturt's description of the country he passed over, after leaving the River Murray, was most favourable; but when he came to give us his opinion of the plains of Adelaide, and of the country to the west of the extensive ranges running north from Cape Jervis to a then unknown distance, his expressed anticipations were most discouraging. He said: "You, gentlemen, who have taken so long a voyage to form agricultural farms, I caution you, from my own experience of the climate of Australia, after residing in the province of New South Wales, not to attempt to break up land on the western plains, or you will meet with sad disappointment. You must not expect to get crops of grain or fruit on this side of the ranges; but I advise you to go to the beautiful hills, valleys, and flats between the ranges, and on the eastern slopes; there you will find excellent soil and plenty of good water. If you attempt to cultivate land around Adelaide you will be grievously disappointed," &c. &c. Three practical men in the company, two of them now dead and the other myself, ventured to express different opinions, and said from their examination of the alluvial soils on the condemned plains, they were convinced that with sufficient rainfall good crops would reward the farmer. To this Captain Sturt replied : "The frequent droughts to which this continent is subject, as I have experienced, is the ground upon which I base my remarks."

Within three years after the delivery of this lecture sections on all sides of the city were smiling with crops of wheat, which yielded from 30 to 40 bushels an acre, and in successive years only diminishing in quantity of yield through *exhaustion and bad management*. Such prolific yields have never been exceeded in any district in the colony, even when favoured in respect to elevation and rainfall.

Captain Sturt, however, was not the only experienced explorer who erred in his opinions of the capabilities of the country, as will appear from the report of Mr. Eyre on his exploring journey north, when he discovered the lake, which he named Lake Torrens. In his account published in the papers he gave such a deplorable description of the country north, that several intending settlers who had just arrived passed on to Melbourne. It must be explained that in this trip Mr. Eyre's course was generally in sight of one or other of the gulfs, and on that course he did not meet with good land, and so was led to condemn the northern country as useless, not having tried the nature of the land to the east of his line. This country, a few miles east of Mr. Eyre's tracks, was seen by the Author, an account of which he now gives. It so happened that he made a short excursion north, and returned a few days after Mr. Eyre published a report of his first trip. The Author left Adelaide on a horse, fresh and fit for a long journey, to endeavour to meet a large herd of cattle which were expected to be near the north-west bend of the River Murray, and so started by way of Mount Barker. In that district he met a man who gave the information that the herd had left the river at the bend and had gone north ; on this he altered his course west, and passed to the west of Mount Torrens. In following down on a native track through high grass and herbage, something was seen to glisten in the narrow path. The horse suddenly made a violent start, when a large black snake was seen gliding away. The horse commenced to tremble violently, and on dismounting him it was apparent that he had been bitten by the snake, probably on the breast. The poor brute soon broke out in a copious sweat. The only course to be pursued was to hasten on to the nearest encampment, which was known to be a few miles ahead. Before reaching this place, where a temporary station had been formed, the poor horse began to show by the swelling of the breast that little hopes could be entertained of saving his life, as the vital organs were so near the bites, and on reaching the camp it was plainly to be seen that death would soon occur.

The long grass nearly meeting across the path must have prevented the horse seeing the snake, which if trodden on would, as is its custom, throw itself back and bite. The horse was left at the camp, and a small and weak horse was borrowed from the owner of the herd of cattle, which was encamped near Mount Crawford. Information was afterwards obtained that the poor brute died the following day.

Leaving Mount Crawford on the east, beautiful hills and gullies were passed through, now known as Pewsey Vale, where the residence of the late Joseph Gilbert, Esq., and his celebrated vineyard, are now to be seen; from thence the rider descended by a rich spur of the western range, having ridden continuously through miles of country covered with high grass. Arriving at a small dairy station he received hospitality for the night; on the following day he headed north, and met no one, nor found the tracks of the herd he wished to meet with. On crossing the River Light he found large water holes, in which some cattle had been drowned; the banks of the holes were either steep or overhanging, and the poor beasts had swum round and round, unable to get out. At these ponds there were no tracks of a large herd, so a more northerly course was followed, but the horse ridden was too low and weak to be pushed; the Dirty Light (which was the early name of this branch) was followed up and was camped on, a saddle had been crossed, and the Black Springs were seen; from high ground farther north, a fine green looking country was seen, and on all sides as far as the eye could reach, high topped hills were visible in the far north. In the nearer distance was discovered a large camp of blacks, so a return was decided on. The writer was particularly struck and pleased by the appearance of the distant ranges of high hills, and regretted that he was not horsed or supplied with necessaries for pursuing a further examination of the northern country. He camped for the night with only dry biscuits and no water fit to drink; on following down the Dirty Light a few miles the next morning, he came to a pond of good water, and pushed for home, driving his exhausted horse before him ; before reaching half way to Gawler town he met with a friend who lent him a horse and took charge of the one he had previously borrowed, home being reached after five days' absence. He was then greatly surprised on reading in the papers Mr. Eyre's unfavourable report of his trip north, skirting the coast only, and he lost no time in giving a very different report of the country he had ridden over, on a line east of the tracks of Mr. Eyre, and of the promising appearance of the hills farther north, to his friends Messrs. Horrocks, Hill, Hancock and others, some of whom took advantage of the information, and within a few days went out to judge for themselves. His report was discredited at the time by some parties, who, however, followed the example of those who went out first, and speedily several runs were taken up on lease, and special surveys were applied for from the Government on the favourable country he had passed over and among the promising ranges he viewed to the north. Mr. John Horrocks (a purchaser of land) obtained a camel, which was the first landed in the colony, and with a few horses started to explore still farther north than the country just taken up. After passing Mount Remarkable some miles a halt was made to camp for the night. Here Mr. Horrocks met with a fatal accident ; the camel was not under good command, and when Mr. Horrocks, with some help, was endeavouring to unload the beast, in taking down a loaded rifle, it was unfortunately discharged, and the contents were received in a vital part, the effects of which he did not survive many days. The pass in the Flinders Range at the entrance of which Mr. Horrocks received his fatal wound, is now known as Horrocks' Pass.

On June 18th, 1840, Mr. Eyre started from Adelaide on his second northern exploring trip. This expedition may be said to have been fitted out by private contributions, £100 only having been furnished by the Governor, Colonel Gawler. On the return of the party the total costs incurred amounted to £1,391 0s. 7d.

	£	s.	d.
Amount contributed by Mr. Eyre	680	15	10
Do. do. by Government	100	0	0
Sale of part of equipment	28	0	0
Subscriptions by colonists	582	4	9
	£1,391	0	7

FRAMEWORK OF PUNT IN WHICH McKINLAY AND PARTY RETURNED FROM THEIR EXPLORING TRIP.

This account is given to show the cost of this first expedition, which returned without accomplishing the object for which it was undertaken. A brief account of Mr. Eyre's experiences before he returned from the most distant point he reached, is all which is deemed necessary to be given. He started with fourteen horses and three drays. The party consisted of Mr. Eyre, Mr. Scott, assistant, four white men, and two black boys. Before starting a lunch was given to the party by the Governor, and a flag (the Union Jack) was presented to Mr. Eyre by Captain Sturt, to be planted in the centre of the continent. Mr. Eyre adopted the same line of country as in his first journey north. July 8th. He made Lake Torrens and found the lake completely girded by a steep sandy ridge. On descending to its basin found the dry bed to be completely coated over with a crust of salt, glittering brilliantly in the sun : in his diary he says : " On putting my foot upon the crust I found it yield, and that below was a soft black mud, so could not proceed to ascertain if there were water farther west or not. The extraordinary deception caused by the mirage made it almost impossible to believe one's eyesight."

On July 12th he arrived back at Mount Deception. In the meantime he had entered in his diary most distressing accounts of the plains he passed over, his course being to the west of Flinders Range, and described the appearance of the range as high, rugged, and very barren. From the top of the mount, which he ascended with great difficulty, the view was extensive and unsatisfactory, Lake Torrens appearing as large and mysterious as ever.

On July 16th, having endeavoured to get a view of the east from a rugged ironstone range, he writes : " It now became a matter of serious consideration whether I should pursue my researches any further. I was about 120 miles from my party." He rejoined his party after being absent 15 days. Provisions of all kinds had been obtained by his men during his absence from the Water Witch at Port Augusta.

August 14th Mr. Eyre continued on a bearing N.W., and was pulled up by what he calls "a winding arm of the Main Lake ; found the waters to be salt as the sea, the bed near the shore was dry. On ascending a high bank the lake was seen to be stretching away to the N.E."

On August 29th, with Mr. Scott and a native boy, Mr. Eyre ascended a very high hill, not less than 3000 feet, which he named Mount Searle. " From the summit," he says, "our view was extensive and final. At one glance I saw the realisation of my worst forebodings, and the termination of the expedition of which I had command. Lake Torrens (now known as Lake Frome) faced us to the east, whilst on every side we are hemmed in by a barrier which we could never hope to pass." From this spot he returned to Adelaide, his report entirely confirming that given of his first trip as to the barren land he passed over.

Mr. John Chambers with his brother William were the next who passed on northwards to look for runs, and they found the Pekina Run, which they took up. They then engaged Mr. Holland to go to New Wales to purchase a herd of cattle, which, on arrival, were placed on Pekina Run. No rain having fallen in that locality for 17 months, it was feared the failing waters would not hold out, and the cattle were removed to a run on the River Murray, in Lake Bonney district, and the lease of Pekina Run was sold to Mr. Price Maurice for a small sum. This run, in Mr. Maurice's possession, afterwards turned out one of the most profitable sheep runs in the province, until (under the reserved rights in the lease) it was resumed by the Government, and surveyed into agricultural blocks, and sold under leases with agreements of rights of purchase. Mount Brown, in the Flinders Range, was named after the three brothers Brown, who near that Mount formed a sheep station, and here the youngest of the brothers was killed while he was minding lambs near the hut. His grave can now be seen near where the old hut stood.

Captain Chase was the next to go farther north to investigate the country, and he did this on foot, in some measure living with the blacks. He was taken by them to many permanent waters; a range he visited is known as Chase's Range. In this locality the following runs were taken up: Arkaba, Wilpena, and Arroona. These runs were stocked severally by Dr. Browne, Mr. H. F. Price, and Mr. Haywood.

Mr. Haywood had, not long after stocking Aroona, two of his shepherds killed by the blacks. The flocks of sheep were seized by the natives. Mr. Haywood soon mustered a party of his neighbours, and found the enemy with the sheep in a gorge with precipitous sides, forming a pound, and here a more equal fight took place, on St. Patrick's Day, in 1852, which resulted in the death of several of the blacks and the recovery of the greater part of the sheep.

The next move north was made by Mr. John McKinlay and John Rose, who discovered several permanent waters and good feeding country, and stations named the Mount Samuel, Moolooloo, Mundy Creek, Mount Stuart, Mount Chambers, Howannigan Gap, extending on to Mount McKinlay, and Mount Rose.

Mr. John Chambers stocked Moolooloo; Howannigan Gap was stocked by Dr. McKinlay, Mr. John McKinlay's brother, who lived on and managed the run until it was sold to Messrs. Chambers Brothers, who held leases including 1400 square miles. At this time these were the most northerly runs stocked.

The Honourable John Baker subsequently took up country farther north and stocked it with cattle—Perrana, Angipena, and Blanchewater. The natives here became aggressive in killing cattle, although farther south they had received such a severe lesson.

In the year 1856 Mr. Baker's hutkeeper was killed in his hut at Angipena, in the absence of the stockkeeper. On this outrage Mr. Baker applied for police protection, and obtained his request. Inspector H. Holroyd was sent out with a body of police, and a police station was established in the neighbourhood, over 400 miles from Adelaide. No further outrages have occurred.

CHAPTER XIV.

IN May, 1844, Governor Grey received a letter from Lord Stanley, informing him that he had previously sent a despatch authorising him to engage Captain Sturt, to equip and take in charge a party to explore and, if possible, reach the centre of New Holland. This despatch was not received till the end of June, when no time was lost, and the following party was organised and the outfit quickly provided. The party was thus constituted: Captain Sturt, leader; Mr. James Poole, assistant; Mr. John Harris Browne, surgeon; Mr. McDougal Stuart, draughtsman; Mr. Louis Piesse, storekeeper; Daniel Brock, collector; Robert Flood, stockman; David Morgan, with horses; George Davenport, Joseph Cowley, servants; Henry Foulkes, John Jones, Turpin, William Lewis (sailor), John Mack, bullock drivers; John Kirby, with sheep; 11

horses; 30 bullocks; 1 boat and boat-carriage; 1 horse-dray; 1 spring-cart; 3 drays; 200 sheep; 4 kangaroo dogs; 2 sheep dogs.

It may be well in this place to give the nature of the correspondence between Captain Sturt and Lord Stanley, Secretary of State. Captain Sturt, in his communication, proposed to the Home Ministry to take charge of an exploring party to reach the centre of the continent, and that such party should take a course east. up the River Murray to the Darling Junction, and then to follow the course of the latter upwards north to about the latitude of 28°, and from thereabouts change his course to the west and north-west, to arrive to the north of and clear of Mr. Eyre's Horse-shoe lake (Lake Torrens). This proposal was submitted by the Secretary of State to Sir John Barrow, who gave his opinion against that circuitous course, and advised a direct course north from Mount Arden, giving his opinion that any range met with would be trending down from north-east to south-west. On giving his instructions, the Secretary of State wished Captain Sturt to understand that he was not absolutely prohibited from pursuing his proposed course. Unfortunately Captain Sturt adhered to his own opinion, based on Mr. Eyre's published experiences. The party left Adelaide August 10th, 1844, after being entertained at a public breakfast given by the inhabitants, and arrived at Gawler Town. Next day proceeded east, to camp at Moorundi, where Mr. Eyre was stationed, having received the appointment of Protector of Aborigines. From thence the party started and kept a course on the north bank of the River Murray, about one degree east to the Junction of the River Darling, and then followed that river up about one degree north, leaving the river when its course led off easterly, and striking in a westerly direction.

On Sir John Barrow's opinion, Captain Sturt remarks in his narrative: "I presume by the tenor of Sir John Barrow's memorandum that he was not fully aware of the insurmountable difficulties the course that he recommended presented." He continued his course up the Darling to the Junction of the Williorara with the Darling (Laidley Ponds). Major Mitchell retreated in 1836 from this place, through the natives, on his exploring trip from Sydney. Captain Sturt continues: "As I understood my instructions from the Secretary of State, I had to keep on the 138th meridian (that of Mount Arden) until I should reach a supposed chain of mountains, the existence and position of which Lord Stanley wished to ascertain—Lake Torrens being due north of Mount Arden."

From Laidley Ponds Mr. Browne was sent forward, on October 12th, to look out in the west for grass and water. Mr. Browne returned and reported good feed and water. The Darling was left on the 19th, Captain Sturt proceeding generally westerly till the 20th November, when he despatched Mr. Poole in advance, Dr. Browne accompanying him.

On their return they reported they had been turned by brackish lakes, extending north, without any visible termination. It was evident to Captain Sturt, from the result of this excursion, that they had struck the lower part of the basin of Lake Torrens, or some similar feature, and that the country in that direction was not favourable for any attempt to penetrate it, since there was no surface (fresh) water. The heat was excessive, the thermometer from 112° to 120° in the shade, and all horn handles and combs split, and the lead fell out of pencils, and scurvy attacked the men. The quantity of water required could not have been less than 1000 gallons per day for the party. Flood had been sent out and returned, stating that he had found a small creek, in which there were long deep waterholes, shaded by gum trees. This creek was about 40 miles in advance, but no water between, but with an abundance of grass. On the 9th, the whole party moved forward to Flood's Creek : Mr. Poole was still ahead, with instructions to keep east of north. Up to this time the party had been exceedingly fortunate; after this, troubles commenced. In endeavouring to reach Flood's Creek, after the party had struggled through many miles of a sandy pine forest, at length, on the 30th, one bullock fell, and shortly after another, when the drays were left and the bullocks unyoked, and with the sheep driven on, until they were saved by reaching the water, from whence water was sent back to the men and the fallen bullocks, one of which was found dead. On the 27th January, a depot was fixed on a rocky glen (Flood's Creek), where there were successive pools in stony basins, wherein it was considered there was an inexhaustible supply. At this depot the party were imprisoned from the above date till the 17th July following. Captain Sturt remarks : "This ruinous detention paralyzed the efforts and enervated the strength of the expedition. It was not till they had run down every creek in the neighbourhood that it became evident that we were locked up in the dewlate and heated region into which we had penetrated, as effectually as if we had wintered at the North Pole."

On the 27th June was completed the fifth month of detention at the depot. During the imprisonment of the party numerous expeditions were undertaken, many of them by Captain Sturt himself, the remainder by Dr. Browne, Mr. Poole, and Mr. J. McDougal Stuart, with each one or two of the men, or by Flood himself alone, proceeding as far as each party could carry water enough for their return to the depot. Various courses were taken, west, north, and east, with no discovered line for escape from the depot. And until men and horses were exhausted, Mr. Poole was brought to a total collapse of strength. These searches were continued until their rocky ponds were well-nigh spent. On the 12th July a most providential rain fell during the night, bringing down the gorge a flow of water. Captain Sturt writes: "As morning dawned, the rippling sound of water close to our tents was a sweeter and more soothing sound than the softest melody; how thankful was I for this change, and how earnestly did I pray that the Almighty would still further extend his mercy to us!" Mr. Poole had experienced, at the end of June, a severe attack of inflammation, which was subdued by Dr. Browne with great difficulty; the day before the saving change of weather came he was very restless, and expressed a desire to be removed into the underground room, into which as the men were tenderly carrying him the first few drops of rain fell.

Preparations had previously been made for his removal home; a dray had been prepared, into which, on the 15th, he was lifted on his stretcher. The parting with him was a painful scene. He shed tears, and expressed to Captain Sturt his wishes that he would still succeed. Dr. Browne was spared to accompany the sufferer, but to return the next day.

On the morning of the 16th the tents were struck, and a start of the whole party was made, but one of the drays soon stuck in the softened ground, and a halt was occasioned at 4 miles.

In the evening the main party were surprised by the return of Joseph from the home-returning party, with the sad news that poor Poole had breathed his last.

On the 17th of July the officers and men were present, when his remains were buried under a grevilla tree; his initials and the year were cut in the bark.

On the 18th the expedition pushed on to the north-west;

through the rainfall the ground was soft and almost impassable.

"On the 5th of August the position was lat. 29° 15′ 14″, and the boiling point of water $212\frac{95}{100}$. We were on a sandhill 100 feet above the level of a large depressed basin of country, which made the same to be considerably below the sea level."

Here Captain Sturt formed a depot and left the bulk of the party, and started with Dr. Browne, Flood, Lewis, and Joseph, with 15 weeks' provisions. On the 14th August, after beating about on a course of 45° west of north, over sand ridges, barren flats, and meeting with stony desert, the most important water he struck was a fine creek, in latitude 27° 44′, longitude 27° 56′, which he named Cooper's Creek (after Judge Cooper). This fine succession of fresh-water pools is now so well known, in connection with the fate of the gallant explorer Burke, who here some time after, by want of food and exhaustion, terminated his career. It is not necessary to follow Captain Sturt farther through the details of his wearying and disappointing journeying, than to close the history by the account of the date of his return to the Darling, viz. 21st December, where he spent Christmas Day, and of his subsequent arrival at Moorundi.

On the 15th January, 1846, Captain Sturt arrived at Moorundi, and found Mr. Eyre had gone to England on leave of absence, and Mr. Nation was filling the appointment. On the 17th he mounted his horse, the first time since he was taken ill in November. On the way to town he was met by Mr. Charles Campbell and Mr. A. Hardy, in a carriage, and by them conveyed to Adelaide.

Thus ended the expedition on which so much hard work and suffering of officers and men had been experienced, without accomplishing the main object for which it was despatched. Before Captain Sturt turned back and abandoned further trials, he called a meeting of his officers and men, and gave them to consider the question of abandoning further attempts to reach the centre of the continent. "He had reached," he said, "within one hundred and fifty miles of the centre of the continent."

He writes as follows: "I should be doing an injustice to Mr. Stuart and the men if I did not mention that I told them the position we were placed in, and the chance on which our safety would depend, if we went on. They might well have been excused if they had expressed an opinion contrary to such a course, but the only reply they made me was that they were ready and willing to follow me to the last."

CHAPTER XV.

IN giving a connected but brief history of the Methodist Church in the Colony, it has been necessary to concentrate the same within this chapter, in which will be related the most thrilling incidents which that Church encountered in opening the work in Australia. At the end of the month of June, 1838, the brig *Fanny*, from Hobart Town, bound to Western Australia, was wrecked on the sandy beach to the east of the mouth of the River Murray. At that time the number of the inhabitants of South Australia did not exceed six thousand, and to supply the spiritual wants of such a population we had two ministers of religion, viz., the Rev. C. B. Howard (Episcopalian) and the Rev. T. Q. Stow (Congregational). At that time the Wesleyan Methodists had only a small staff of class-leaders and local preachers, appointed at a small meeting of members, so that with the rapid increase of population from the frequent arrivals of shiploads of passengers, assisted emigrants, and well-to-do settlers, there was ample room for additional authorised clerical workers. One more worker in God's vineyard was, however, unexpectedly provided. The Rev. Mr. Longbottom and his family being despatched by the authorities of the Wesleyan body in Tasmania to fill a post in Western Australia, on his way there, on board the *Fanny*, was landed on our southern coast by the wreck of that vessel, and so placed, by an act of Providence, overriding man's designs, to work in a field of usefulness in our province. He and his family, with the crew, were most mercifully saved from the raging billows, and on the wild beach were kindly received and succoured by the untamed blacks, on or within a short distance of the spot where the passengers and captain of the *Maria* were subsequently slaughtered. As no whites survived from the *Maria* to give any account which might explain the cause of the different conduct of the natives towards them, it must remain a mystery to all time. It has been communicated to me that in the case of the *Fanny* the Rev. Mr. Longbottom and the captain exercised a sufficient influence—not only on the natives, but also on the sailors—to restrain them in their conduct.

I will now give Captain Gill's statement, as published in the *Register* of September 8th, 1838, in which he gives a report of the accident which befel his ship, and a description of the means by which he safely conveyed his passengers and crew across the outer channel of the Murray, and delivered them at the whaling station at Encounter Bay, and his flattering opinion of the natives, as he found them so marvellously different from their subsequent conduct. Captain Gill relates:—

"The *Fanny* left Van Dieman's Land on the 9th June, 1838, and when off Kangaroo Island, on the 16th, encountered a succession of heavy gales from W.S.W., which drove her to leeward. On the 21st the gale increased, and the squalls with rain became more violent. About half-past 1 A.M. the sea broke on board in all directions. We had now shoaled in about four hours from 30 to 7 fathoms water, and all attempts to sail were ineffectual. Every sea threw the vessel's head round off; sometimes she was above water, and at other times it may be said she was below. When the soundings decreased to 3¼ fathoms the lead was laid in. Now a heavy breaker hove her into the trough of the sea, and we were up to our waists in water. She now struck the ground forward, the following sea made a passage over her fore-and-aft, and we were up to our necks in water. I ascended the forerigging, and for the first time saw land, which appeared a low dark ridge. As soon as the vessel was broadside on, which was shortly after striking, I endeavoured to swim ashore with the end of the lead-line; but it being too short I was obliged to slip and swim ashore clear, though not until the line had drawn me two or three times under water. In a few minutes two of the men came on shore with a line, when by that I returned to the ship, and conveyed through the surf the little boy, son of our passengers. Mrs. Longbottom was unfortunately put over the side the very moment I told the people to hold on, and so was some time under water, from which we were able to recover her, but not until she was greatly exhausted. In about half an hour all hands were on shore."

This was about sundown, and the only shelter which the shipwrecked people had was such as the sandhills afforded, and there they had to pass their miserable first night on shore, at the coldest time of the year, in saturated garments, without fire or food." Captain Gill's narrative continues:—

"On the following morning at daybreak we returned to the vessel, and got on shore such of our clothing and provisions as were at hand. Shortly afterwards the gale freshened, and the surf beat over the vessel with increased violence. In surveying the coast around us I was much surprised to observe an expanse of water inland; a series of lagoons extended east and west as far as the eye could reach, separated from the sea by a sort of peninsula, about three-quarters of a mile in breadth, the lagoons appearing from three to four miles across, and, as far as I could judge, about six feet deep. In the course of the morning we were visited by nine natives, who brought us a firestick, and showed us their fresh waterholes, and were every way well disposed during our stay amongst them, which was about seven weeks, and also showed us the greatest friendship. They were decidedly the most inoffensive race I ever met with."

After the failure of several attempts to reach the whaling station at Encounter Bay, they were joined by Captain Tindal, master of the *Elizabeth*, which had been wrecked in Rivoli Bay, over fifty miles to the eastward, and who walked overland with part of his crew to Adelaide, and reported the two wrecks as having occurred. The dingy, which Captain Gill had recovered, after being repaired and lengthened about six feet, was launched upon the lagoons (*i.e.* the Coorong). In this boat, with two men, Captain Gill sailed westward to the sea entrance of Lake Alexandrina (the Murray mouth). Here they were joined by four men who had walked along the sea beach. They all crossed the estuary in the boat, and arrived at the fishery. Captain Gill's account goes on to say:—

"My object was now to procure a whaleboat, to bring up from the wreck Mr. and Mrs. Longbottom and child, whom we had left behind with three men. I did not wish to risk them in the small boat, which was leaky, and then the passage out was unknown to me. On these accounts I deemed it desirable that they should remain behind until a better boat could be procured, and the nature of the passage could be ascertained. After considerable trouble I succeeded in getting a whaleboat and prepared to start with three men, including a native, whom I found very useful. In the meantime I despatched the small boat back with two men, to inform Mr. and Mrs. Longbottom of our success, and to instruct them to be in readiness for their departure. I must now remark that the passage we had crossed was the same where Sir John Jeffcott and Captain Blenkinsop, with part of their boat's crew, were lost from the swamping of their boat in attempting to go out last year. The information I received about this estuary was that there was a long succession of long rollers, that never failed to roll heavily, even after a continuance of easterly weather; that they had a perpendicular fall of five or six feet; that a number of sealers and whalers, all good boatmen, had made several ineffectual attempts to get in; that one gentleman had waited three weeks off the entrance, with a cutter of about 20 tons, endeavouring to effect an entrance, but failed; that the current was always running out, and other reports equally absurd and vague. In our most recent and best charts we are informed that the passage from Lake Alexandrina to Encounter Bay is impracticable even for boats. I now give the result of my own observation and experience."

When this report was published Mr. Pullen had not passed in and out. He entered in a whaleboat, on the 26th of September, 1840. "The first time I crossed this passage was during a fresh gale from the eastward, and the flood tide was running in strong, perhaps at the rate of three knots an hour. After leaving our luggage I returned to the eastern side, and brought over the remainder of our small party of men, the boat being too small to venture with all in one trip. On this second trip in the small boat we experienced a squall, with hail and rain, which so darkened the air that, although the distance is only half a mile, for about twenty minutes we could not see the land, and those on shore could not see the boat."

Captain Gill having procured a whaleboat determined to proceed along the coast, to be nearer the sea mouth, and then by the use of a pair of bullocks, which he procured from Mr. Harper at the Bay, proceeded to drag the boat over the sandhills, and launch it into the western outlet (*i.e.* into the Goolwa). After encountering many difficulties in attempting to track the boat, he at last succeeded. The party now proceeded along the lagoons (the Coorong), but when a few miles east of the estuary he met the little boat, with Mr. and Mrs. Longbottom and son, and two of the crew.

Captain Gill continues: "The little dingy was despatched back to the camping-place, and I returned with the passengers across the estuary, and put up for a day or two at the native huts, where we had spent the preceding night. In the morning sailed to the estuary, and found the wind and tide both strong out, and it was therefore necessary to wait until low water slack, which enabled me to survey the harbour's mouth from the high eastern head. About midday, being low water, we sailed out under a close-reefed sail, the wind being N.N.W., and there was not a single breaker in the channel, nor did I perceive any bar. The lead I had made for the purpose of sounding proved to be too light to be depended on with the boat's rapid sailing. Although our boat was considerably lumbered, she did not ship a spoonful of water. It would have been to me wonderful if I had not succeeded in getting out with ease and safety."

Yes, it may be added, under such favourable and providential circumstances as have been seldom experienced in the same passage. To Captain Gill belongs the credit of being the first man who either sailed or rowed safely through the Murray mouth outwards in any kind of craft.

A vessel from Sydney (the *Lady Wellington*, Captain Develin), which had met with adverse weather, and after much knocking about, did not reach her destination, Port Adelaide, until she had expended eight weeks and two days on the passage, had called in at Encounter Bay, after visiting sundry ports of refuge on her way. In this ship the Rev. Mr. Longbottom and his family obtained a passage to Adelaide, and on this short sea trip further accidents might not have been anticipated; but they were again called on to suffer inconvenience, as Captain Develin, on endeavouring to cross the outer bar at Port Adelaide entrance, stuck fast, and there had to discharge his passengers and goods, as the ship's back was broken. Amongst the passengers was Mr. Emanuel Solomon and members of his family, to whom the greater part of the cargo belonged.

Mr. Solomon had arrived to establish a house of business in connection with his brother, Mr. V. Solomon, of Sydney. Mr. E. Solomon remained to the last a determined supporter of the young colony he had joined, and lived long enough among us to witness the high position we have attained by the untiring energy exercised by him and other old colonists, sticking to their adopted land through good and evil report, adversity and prosperity, as thorough colonists.

The Rev. Mr. Longbottom was received in Adelaide with enthusiasm by the inhabitants; he was, with his family, hospitably accommodated by Mr. E. Stephens, the manager of the

South Australian Bank, in his small wooden residence on the first camping ground, now occupied by the Railway Station, until a temporary residence could be provided. Subscriptions were raised to replace some of Mr. L.'s losses, but his library and papers could not be restored to him. The small number of the Church to which he belonged gladly availed themselves of his services, and looked upon his arrival as a godsend. He arrived among them about the 1st September, 1838.

On the 25th May, the previous year, a meeting had been held in the house of Mr. S. Stephens, at which a Society was formed called the Wesleyan Methodist Society. Fifteen persons gave in their names (a small beginning this); two class-leaders were appointed, and two local preachers received on trial for three months. On September 31st a local preacher was appointed—not one of those who had officiated on trial, but still one of the original fifteen, of whom eight were men. Out of these, including the Secretary, six officers were appointed. Services were first performed in a small reed hut on the banks of the Torrens; afterwards the kitchen of Mr. E. Stephens was used. In March, 1838, the foundation-stone of a substantial chapel, was laid in Hindley-street. Since May, 1837, the church had increased to six local preachers, seven class-leaders, fifty members, and about one hundred school children. Officers still out of proportion to members. "They did not cease to pray that God would send them a good shepherd: of this, however, there seemed little or no likelihood." The history of churches, as well as of individuals, will often furnish illustrations of the truth that God accomplishes His designs by unlikely means. While the infant Church in Adelaide was praying that a minister might be sent to them, and when they saw no likelihood of their desires being granted, a series of circumstances were transpiring which resulted in the settlement of a minister among them, and that, too, in a manner remarkable and unexpected. I make an extract from the life of the Rev. D. J. Draper: "No one will be surprised to learn that the Wesleyan Methodists of Adelaide regarded the accident which landed the Rev. Mr. Longbottom as a special providence, as it has been before pronounced in this chapter—saved as they were from the raging sea. The hearts of savage blacks softened to receive and succour the distressed people, on or within a short distance of the ensanguined spot where at a subsequent period the most shocking murders took place, as it must have been by part of the same tribe, if not by some of the same wild and benighted natives."

Such was the beginning of the Wesleyan Methodist Church in this colony, and from such a small start they can now with commendable pride point to their imposing buildings, not only in the city, but throughout the whole colony. Their churches, schools, and college are fully attended, and greatly assist in dispelling ignorance and vice, and in exhibiting to the Christian world a population where peace and harmony prevail amongst all those who call themselves Christians, under whatever denomination. It is to be hoped they will help greatly to bring about the promised day when will be forgotten all those distinctive names which, in fact, have arisen and are kept up by the present weakness and selfishness of human nature.

Having given a description of the arrival of the Rev. W. Longbottom, and his reception with open arms by the small number of Wesleyans then in the colony, I now propose to give a brief account of his actions after he accepted the post of first preacher of that communion; also of the work of his successor, the Rev. D. J. Draper, in building up what Mr. Longbottom commenced. I shall also give some extracts from the published life of the Rev. Mr. Draper, presenting a heartrending picture of the last moments of that good man, when he spent his latest breath in comforting the crew and passengers before they were engulfed with him by the foundering of the steamship *London*.

Before the arrival of Mr. Longbottom, in 1838, an organisation of members of his denomination had been made, starting with fifteen persons. Shortly after this, a small chapel was built in Hindley-street. In this building Mr. Longbottom was able to officiate on his arrival; and, in this respect, he found himself placed in much more favourable circumstances than were the two ministers of religion who preceded him when they arrived; for they had to gather their flocks, and assist with their own hands in the erection of mere temporary coverings in which to hold worship. In the natural order of things, Mr. Longbottom would feel some embarrassment at finding such a large proportion of officers to members, and would have some anxiety as to future means and management.

The founder of the Wesleyan Church, the Rev. John Wesley, in the organisation he prescribed, did not adopt any approach to a democratic form of government for the management of this section of the Christian Church, nor has any such principle, as far as I know, been admitted since his time. It appears to me, as an outsider, from a perusal of the Rev. J. C. Symons's work, from which I shall now quote pretty freely, that in the early steps which were taken to appoint office-bearers out of so small a number of members, more zeal than discretion was displayed, and I am under the impression that the difficulties which occurred in the early days to this Church may be attributed to the proceedings of a democratic character which were necessarily adopted, in electing officers from so small a number as then presented themselves, which almost amounted to self-election. It is not necessary to enlarge upon this state of things further than to say that when the first difficulties were got over, the Church rose to its present strength and state of harmony.

"In about eight years from the commencement of the Rev. Mr. Longbottom's services, and including his second appointment, five preachers in succession occupied the post. Not long after the ministrations of Mr. Longbottom commenced, necessity for enlarged church accommodation was felt, and the foundation of a large and handsome chapel was laid in Gawler-place, which was completed at a cost of over £2000, exclusive of the land, which was given by Mr. E. Stephens. When completed a debt remained on the building of £1300. Mr. Longbottom's health had been greatly enfeebled by his residence in India, where he had laboured as a missionary; his shipwreck and subsequent privations had completed what the climate of India had begun; and to this must be added the anxieties he was subjected to, without the aid of a colleague to strengthen his hands, and under the peculiar circumstances in which he was placed in this colony. Nor must it be forgotten that he and his family, for the greater part of his time, had no better accommodation as a residence than a small pine cottage. It thus soon became apparent that he was unequal to the heavy work which pressed upon him; in the increasing demands of his church he sought for aid, and no colleague could be sent. He was at length compelled to depart, which was painful indeed to himself and the Church. He had won the esteem of his own flock and all who knew him, and the people had drawn forth his deepest sympathies and energies. Seldom have pastor and people parted with more regret. Mr. Longbottom removed to Tasmania, and was appointed to New

Norfolk, the healthful and bracing air of which it was hoped would restore his health. He was succeeded by the Rev. John Eggleston, who reached Adelaide in March, 1840. He remained less than two years; the heat of the climate, the unsuitable house, but chiefly what he described as a series of afflictions, induced in the first instance by excessive exertions, compelled him to seek a removal. His brief period of service had been signally owned of God; many were added to the Church, and great was the sorrow of all classes of the community at his departure.

"The Rev. J. C. Weatherstone, Mr. Eggleston's successor, remained in Adelaide about two years. Commencing well, and even prosperously, it was not long before dissatisfaction, financial embarrassment, and all but ruin—at least temporary—came upon the Church. The colony had scarcely recovered from the crushing crisis which terminated Colonel Gawler's term of administration, which crisis tended to produce the break-up of the unity of the Church to a great extent. In Mr. Weatherstone's time, in September, 1843, a petition of the Wesleyan Methodists of South Australia was presented to Governor Sir G. Grey, praying 'that the Government would grant them monetary aid to pay off the debt of £1300 on their chapel in Gawler-place, and in supporting the ordinances of religion.' From a complication of difficulties, Mr. Weatherstone had to retire, and it was asked, who would come in his stead? None were willing, and for the year 1844 Adelaide does not appear as a station in the minutes of Conference.

"Meanwhile, Mr. Longbottom had been directed to remove from Tasmania to Sydney. He reached there just when the Adelaide difficulties were under discussion. Such was the unfavourable impression produced, that no minister would come here. Deeply moved by the scattered and all but destroyed Church, he offered to return to his former field of labour. His offer was instantaneously and gladly accepted. He was a true soldier, ready to do his Master's work at whatever inconvenience to himself. He arrived the second time, with Mrs. L. and his son, in April, 1844. Mr. Longbottom's health soon again proved totally inadequate to the toils and responsibilities of so extensive a circuit. The society in general were a warm-hearted, earnest, and generous people, who only wanted a leader, and this post Mr. L., with his failing health, could not fulfil, while his genial spirit and entire devotion to the spiritual requirements of his flock still created the warmest respect and gratitude towards him. This was exhibited not by mere sentiment, but in making such provision when he retired as supernumerary in 1846, as enabled him to pass his declining years in somewhat more of comfort than his allowance as a supernumerary would have enabled him to do. I must here add that members of other communions also assisted in this becoming action, and so displayed their feelings of love and respect towards him."

The place of Mr. Longbottom was ably filled by the Rev. Mr. Draper, who at this time was engaged in the Sydney first circuit, and would gladly have spent more years in New South Wales, but who, feeling deeply for the connexion in the colony of South Australia, volunteered his services to occupy the post. Results have shown this arrangement to have been most happy and successful, as witness the position the Wesleyan connexion holds in South Australia at this time.

Postscript.—Mr. Draper, some time after a return to duties in Victoria, required rest and change, and after several attempts to procure leave of absence to visit England he was at length spared. He embarked with Mrs. Draper on board the *Great Britain* on March 16, 1865. After an unusually pleasant voyage they arrived in Liverpool 20th May. The number of souls on board was 787. Three days after their arrival they left Liverpool for London. On the following Sunday Mr. Draper preached in Great Queen-street Chapel. Having visited the place of his birth he, with Mrs. Draper, made a tour through Wales, Ireland, and Scotland, preaching and delivering addresses in the various places he visited. He also made a hasty continental trip, and in Paris preached to the small flock of Wesleyans in their nice chapel there. In one of his letters to his friend Mr. Symons, dated 18th August, he mentions "we have travelled 2450 miles by rail since we landed. I guess another 1000 will do. Thank God we have not had a day's sickness since we left you. Our thoughts are beginning to turn homeward." His purpose was to remain absent a year, and though many efforts were made by friends in England to prolong his stay, they were unavailing. September 19, he writes: "I see the *London* is advertised to sail on the 20th December, but I expect it will be a fortnight later. If cholera, &c., should prevent our going via Egypt, we may go in her. I hope we shall be in Melbourne in March. Mr. Boyce and others are trying to get me to stay another year, but I do not think of doing so." In a letter dated 18th December, he subsequently wrote : "The time of our leaving is now definitely fixed. The *London* will leave the East India Docks on the 20th inst., and finally leave Plymouth at 6 P.M." In bidding adieu to Mr. and Mrs. Powell both Mr. and Mrs. Draper appeared to be unusually depressed, and expressed themselves in terms very different from their usual buoyant character, so much so, indeed, that it led the Powells to remark on it before any calamity had occurred. Mr. and Mrs. Draper embarked at Plymouth, on 5th January, 1866. "There was nothing at this time to indicate the severe weather which was to come on ; the barometer was unsteady, but not low. It was almost calm when the ship started ; she steamed along against a head wind. On Sunday, the 7th, the wind freshened somewhat. Dr. Woolley, President of the Sydney University, and Mr. Draper united in conducting Divine service. The same night it blew a gale, with heavy squalls and a high sea. On Monday, the 8th, the sea was so heavy that the engines were stopped, and the ship was put under easy canvas. About midday the wind lessened, and steam was again used. Tuesday morning the wind greatly increased ; the flying jibboom, foretopmast, topgallantmast, and royalmast were carried away ; the gale had become so violent that all the wreck could not be cleared, the spars swinging to and fro, doing much damage. In the afternoon the wind increased to a hurricane, with fearful cross seas, which broke over the ship and carried away the port lifeboat, and did other damage. At 3 P.M., of the 10th, the ship was put about under full steam for Plymouth. She immediately began to ship green seas all over, which swept her decks and carried away the starboard lifeboat, and destroyed one of the cutters. At half-past 10 o'clock, on Wednesday night, a mountain of water broke on board and swept away the main engine skylight ; the engine-room was filled, and in three minutes the fires were out. Sails, mattresses, tarpaulins, spars, and all available means were used to stop the opening and prevent the water from rushing into the ship. All efforts were futile. Pumps and the donkey-engine were kept at work, even when the ship went down. Long and gallant was the struggle continued between man and the furious elements. At last, when the issue was no longer doubtful, Captain Martin said to his men : 'Boys, you may say your prayers.' All earthly hope had gone, and unless wind and waves were hushed and stilled by the power of their Creator, it was a mere question of time when the *London* should go down. The gale increased in fury. At midnight the Rev. Mr. Draper commenced that memorable prayer meeting, which lasted till the ship sank on the next day, at two o'clock. With one impulse, passengers and crew gathered in the saloon, distinction of class forgotten. One of the rescued tells that there were no cries or shrieking of men or women, no frantic behaviour. Mothers were weeping over their children, and the children pitifully asking the cause of the tears. During the intervals of prayer, Mr. Draper earnestly besought, as he moved among the crowd, the people to come to Christ for salvation. When the captain had lowered the starboard pinnace, which was immediately upset and lost, he entered the cabin, and said: 'Ladies, there is no hope for us; nothing short of a miracle can save us.' To this Mr. Draper calmly replied: 'Then let us pray,' and used these memorably words—'Well, my friends, the captain informs us that our ship is doomed, and that there is no hope of our getting into port; but the Great Captain tells us there is hope, and that we may all get safe to heaven.' At two P.M., the ship appeared to be sinking. The captain then directed the second engineer, that as the port cutter was ready to be lowered, he had better get into her, saying: 'There is not much chance for the boat, there is none for the ship; your duty is done, mine is to remain here with the passengers; I wish you God speed, and safe to land.' The number who escaped in the boat, out of 180 on board, was nineteen. In about five minutes after pushing off those in the boat saw the *London* go down by the stern. The boat drifted before the wind about twenty hours, when she fell in with the Italian brig *Marianople*, and they were ultimately landed at Falmouth, on January 17."

I have felt it appropriate to conclude this chapter with a republication of the thrilling picture of a devoted missionary finishing the work assigned to him on earth in a manner so grand as he did; as well as to record the last act of Captain Martin, whose death was that of a true hero. I had given the account of a merciful dispensation of Providence when a missionary was saved from a wreck and granted to open the services of the Wesleyan Church in South Australia, and thought it well to conclude with an account of the loss of another missionary of the same communion by wreck, after he had built up what the previous one had commenced. I have introduced the latter wreck, although it does not belong to "Early Experiences of South Australia," as both occurrences have such deep interest for the Wesleyans of the colony of South Australia. The latter is conspicuously marked by the Draper Memorial Church, which was erected to the memory of the good man after whom it is named, a characteristic building and one of which the Wesleyan Methodists are justly proud.

CHAPTER XVI.

IN Chapter IX. was recorded the spearing of Captain Barker by the Milmertura tribe, which occurred some years before this colony was founded. It will be seen that that tribe were at one time relentlessly murderous, and at another kind and compassionate. In this chapter an account will be given of the return of the tribe to actions of extreme ferocity, and no doubt to cannibalism, when the brigantine *Maria* was wrecked on their coast, and the whole of those on board were slaughtered, not one being left to relate the horrid tale.

From the trial and execution of two of the tribe, given up by the assembled tribe, it may be fairly concluded that the good or bad actions related may be attributed to the presence or absence of the more savage members.

On Saturday, July 25, 1840, the inhabitants of Adelaide were thrown into the greatest state of excitement by the arrival of an express from Encounter Bay with the alarming news that there had been a wreck on the south coast, to the east of that station, and that part or the whole of those on board, after reaching land, had been murdered by the natives. In a letter from Mr. H. Nixon to Major O'Halloran, commissioner of police, the following account was given, which he received through a native of the Bay tribe, known as Encounter Bay Bob, who reported that two of the Big Murray tribe had arrived, and he gave an interpretation of their statement as follows: " They found ten white men, and five women and some children, who had been killed ; one of them said 'all killed in one place.' It took them three days after leaving the dead bodies to make the mouth of the Murray."

On the arrival of this information, Mr. Pullen, who was employed in surveying the lower part of the River Murray, started with Dr. Penny from Goolwa to search for the wreck, and to ascertain news of the people. It will be seen in the course of the narrative that although the statements of the two blacks were only too true as to the fearful massacre of the party, in minor particulars their information was incorrect. All were not killed in one place, and the distance was also wrongly stated. In the *Gazette* of August 13 the letter from Mr. Pullen was published, of which I avail myself: "I started from Goolwa in a boat, with the following parties, viz., Dr. Penny, five sailors, one policeman, and three blacks—Encounter Bay Bob, Peter, and Charley. Made twenty miles up the Coorong the first day. Next day started at 8 A.M.; at 10.30 Peter said some of the whites were killed on the mainland to the north of where we had arrived. Hauled in, landed, and searched, but found nothing. Pushed off, and at 12.30 Peter pointed to the spot where he said the murders had been committed on the coast.

"We now landed and crossed the neck of land between Goolwa and the seashore, not being far from the part of the coast where the *Fanny* had been wrecked some time before. I now divided the party into three. I and Dr. Penny kept the coast line, directing one party to travel along the neck of land, and the third to push forward with the boat down the Coorong, and arranged signals to be used on any discovery being made. We had not proceeded far when we were hailed by the centre party, and on joining them the sight we witnessed was truly horrible. There were legs, arms, and portions of bodies visible, partially covered with sand. In one place by itself was a body with the flesh completely cut off the bones, except the hands and feet. Horror sat on every countenance. Sad and sorrowful was the task, but we determined to bury the bodies in something like decency. The boat was stopped and a spade procured; when, after digging a deep grave, we uncovered the whole of the mangled bodies. From one spot we took four bodies—two males, one young woman, and a child about ten years old. The skeleton spoken of was a female. Two male children, one fifteen and the other ten, we found in separate holes, and at a little distance alone, a female infant with very light hair. Both the women had wedding rings on, and one of the men handed me their rings. The bodies were in a complete state of nudity, and dreadfully bruised about the faces and heads. The whole of the bodies were placed in the deep grave we had prepared. We were occupied on this sorrowful business until four o'clock. Friday, 31, pulled down two miles to be opposite the wrecked *Fanny*. On reaching the spot saw natives ahead of us, but they escaped. In crossing the strip of land dividing the sea from the Coorong, we came suddenly on two black women, who screamed violently, but Peter managed to pacify them. They said they knew of no other wreck, but that some of the people we were asking about *died* farther down; that three of the party—one woman and two men—had crossed over to the land by the islands, and there were killed at the spot we had searched unsuccessfully, and that the other bodies we had found and buried had been killed by a tribe not far from us. On reaching the boat a small party of men showed themselves, and at our camping-place many more natives appeared, but kept at a distance. On the following morning crossed the sandhills and saw many groups of natives with blankets and sundry wearing apparel about them. It was some time before they would come near us, and then they threw off the clothing they had on.

"From the silence of this party, when questioned through Peter about the murders, and their apparent uneasiness at our searching the pockets of the coats, and in examining a woman's bonnet, I was convinced we were among the guilty parties, especially on looking at two men of the most ferocious and forbidding aspect, such as I never saw before. On returning to the boat we were followed by several old men, who showed no fear, one of whom had a woman's shawl on. Peter, who could speak his language, obtained from him that he had brought the whole of the party along the coast to a short distance from the spot we were on, and caught fish for them, for which they gave him the shawl. He knew of no fresh wreck. The number he gave was fourteen, not agreeing with another account we obtained. Finding I could not take the boat farther up the shallow channel, I decided to continue along the beach on foot, and at intervals found several spars and planks stuck on end. On the beach found a whaleboat. By one of the natives we were told that the boat was left there by five men who had gone across the mainland." (These must have been the sailors, but they were not subsequently heard of.)

Mr. Pullen returned, and made his report to his Excellency

the Governor, who appended to the same the following note :—
"In reference to Mr. Pullen's report, I consider it important to remark that the tribe of natives by which the murders described by Mr. Pullen appear to have been committed is not connected with the tribes with which the colonists are in familiar intercourse. From the first discovery of the province this tribe, inhabiting to the south-eastward of Goolwa and the sea mouth of the Murray, has been little known, and when known has been remarkable for its ferocity."

Governor Gawler, with most commendable promptitude, organised and despatched a strong party under the Commissioner of Police (Major O'Halloran), accompanied by Mr. C. Bonney, and Captain H. Nixon, with a number of mounted police, and arranged that the party should be joined and strengthened by Mr. Pullen and his boats' crews, to follow up the Coorong arm, as it was first called, a narrow lake, running east, parallel to the seacoast, and extending within a few miles of Lacepede Bay (at that time an almost unknown district). This channel was found navigable for boats nearly to its eastern end, but partially obstructed by a few limestone bars. The strip of land between it and the seacoast is very narrow in its widest part, the western end forming the eastern side of the sea mouth of the river. Major O'Halloran having crossed the channel at the mouth of the Murray on the 21st of August, 1840, with the aid of Mr. Pullen's boats, the horses swimming behind the boats, made a start the following day as described in his official report. I continue in Major O'Halloran's own words :—

"I started at an early hour on Saturday morning, the 22nd instant, with the main body along the seacoast, having detached Captain Nixon and Mr. Bonney, with an orderly, to keep up communication between me and Mr. Pullen in the boats, who were to notify to me if any natives were seen, as we were now in the country of the hostile Big Murray tribe. About 12 o'clock we discovered a number of natives at a great distance ahead of us, running from us. We followed in pursuit, and in two miles approached them, when they took to the scrub and the sandhills. After a long chase we contrived, without injury to any of them, to capture thirteen men, two lads, and about fifty women and children. Some of the natives took to the Lake (or Coorong), but some of them were captured by Mr. Pullen's party. Upon the persons of almost every man and woman, and in almost every wurley (and they were numerous), were found various articles of European clothing belonging to males, females, and children—many of them stained with blood; also were found an excellent silver watch, and some silver spoons marked with JEV. The men were secured and guarded during the night; the women and children set at liberty. On the morning of the 24th the party mounted before daybreak to scour the country ahead of us, and where Pullen on his previous trip saw a number of ferocious blacks with European clothing on them. We beat the country a long way between the Coorong and the sea beach, and in some wurlies captured women with a quantity of European clothing, male and female, several articles of which, especially a woman's under garment, were covered with blood.

"Close to these wurlies we saw two men, who escaped by swimming across the Lake (or Coorong), and at the water's edge Mr. Pullen picked up a sailor's cap, which he recognised as worn by one of the worst-looking of the men he had seen in his former trip, and whom the friendly natives he had with him pointed out as belonging to the party who had committed the murders. Finding these fellows would escape, I ordered the police to fire upon them, and they were both wounded; they nevertheless swam to an island, on which Inspector Tolmer, having cast off the principal part of his clothes, and hanging his naked sword behind his back, swam after and overtook them, but before the boat arrived to his aid they escaped. At another spot in the same neighbourhood, in native huts, we found newspapers, receipted bills in the name of Captain Smith, mail letters from Adelaide opened, and the torn leaves of a Bible, another book, and part of the log of the brigantine *Maria*. These facts prove clearly that the crew and passengers left the ship deliberately, and were making their way to Adelaide. It appears strange that we found no arms. The captives on our return to camp were much alarmed, and pointed out one of the number as the murderer of Roach and his mate, who came down here some time before to the wreck of the *Fanny*, and were both killed. Pieces of the wreck were still lying on the beach opposite the camp. The captives also pointed to the mainland across the Coorong, and said one of the murderers of the people who had escaped from the *Maria* was there, and could easily be caught, and two of them, on the suggestion of Mr. Bonney, volunteered to bring the man over and give him up to us. I sent Encounter Bay Peter with them, and they returned with the culprit."

A formal and deliberate investigation into every particular, relative to the two separate cases of murder, was gone into, and full particulars of the trial by court-martial, under the authority and instructions given by his Excellency the Governor, are here given.

COURT MARTIAL.

MONDAY, 24*th* *August*, 4.30 P.M.

Major O'Halloran assembled the blacks, the officers and gentlemen, some of the police and sailors, when the following proceedings took place. Bob and Peter, Encounter Bay blacks, were engaged as interpreters.

The native Mongarawata, who was brought in by Peter and two volunteer natives, was now arraigned.

Major O'Halloran asked of the members of the tribe present—Is this the murderer of the white men?

Answer—(Unanimously, by the tribe)—Yes.

Q.—Whom did he kill?
A.—Only one white man.
Q.—How did he kill him, and when?
A.—With a waddie, and in the day-time.
Q.—Can any of these people show where the body is?
A.—No.
Q.—How many white men, women, and children were killed?
A.—Three women, two men, and four children.
Q.—Are there any white people still alive? If you tell me I will reward you.
A.—None.
Q.—Where is the wreck?
A.—They came along the coast.
Q.—Where are the graves of the people killed—are they all in one place?
A.—All in one place.
Q.—Had the people any guns with them?
A.—No.
Q.—Did the men fight?
A.—No.
Q.—Did they kill them by night or day?
A.—Day-time, with waddies.

Q.—Had the white man any sword or gun?
A.—None.
Q.—How long ago?
A.—A short time.
Q.—Where are the men who killed the rest?
A.—More that way (pointing south-east).
Q.—Who killed the women and children?
A.—The same men.
Q.—Where did the prisoner bury the man he killed?
A.—At the place we are going to to-morrow.

Major O'Halloran—Bob, tell the men of the tribe that as they have given up the prisoner as one of the murderers we will not hurt them; that the great Governor has sent me to catch and punish the black men who killed the wrecked people; that the next time a white man is killed by this tribe the Governor will send me here again with a greater number of police, and then more blacks will be killed. That if the black men are kind to white men when in distress, the great Governor and white men will be friends, and give rewards to such black men. I will take Peter and the two men (pointing to them) who went with Peter and brought in the prisoners, to the Governor, who will reward them.

The murderer of Roach, Pilgarie, was now arraigned.

Major O'Halloran—Bob, ask these men of the tribe if this man killed white man.

Answer by the tribe (unanimously).—Yes.

Q.—When?
A.—Last year.
Q.—Who was the man, and where did he come from?
A.—Encounter Bay.
Q.—What was he doing?
A.—He was coming with another white man to the wreck *Fanny*.
Q.—How did he kill him?
A.—With a waddie.
Q.—In the day, or night?
A.—The day-time.
Q.—Was he asleep or awake?
A.—He was sitting down.
Q.—Did the blacks kill the other man?
A.—Yes.
Q.—Had the white man any weapon?
A.—None.

Q.—Did the white man resist?
A.—No.
Q.—Where is the body of the white man?
A.—Where the wreck is.
Q.—Did a great many men attack them?
A.—Yes.

Peter, ask the prisoner Mongarawata if he is guilty of killing the whites.

Peter answered—He will not tell.

Ask the prisoner Pilgaric if he is guilty of killing Roach.

A.—He will not tell.

Q.—Peter, ask both the prisoners if any of the blacks present have killed any white people.

A. (by both prisoners)—No.

Now, Bob, tell these natives present who are under guard that they will not be hurt, but they must remain quiet to-night, for I want them to be present to-morrow. Tell them that if a white man kills a native the Governor will hang the white man.

The Major now turned towards the officers present, and said: Gentlemen—By virtue of the authority vested in me by his Excellency the Governor, I declare in the presence of Almighty God, and of those assembled round me, that I believe these two men who have been given over to us by their own tribe, to be guilty of murder, and to merit death. This I declare according to my conscience, so help me God.

Captain Nixon, I now request of you to give your deliberate opinion whether you consider these men guilty of murder and deserving of death.

Captain Nixon—I do, so help me God.

Mr. Bonney, yours?—I do, so help me God.

Mr. Pullen, yours?—I do, so help me God.

Mr. Tolmer, yours?—I do, so help me God.

Major O'Halloran—

Encounter Bay Bob, do you say these men have killed white men and ought to die?

Encounter Bay Bob—Yes.

Charley, do you?—Yes.

Peter, do you?—Yes.

Major O'Halloran then pronounced the following sentence on the prisoners:—

I now, by virtue of the authority I have from the Governor of this Province, whose representative I am, pronounce the sentence of death upon the prisoners Mongarawata and Pilgaric, that they be conveyed to-morrow to the grave of our unfortunate countrymen, and there be hanged by the neck, and may God have mercy on their souls.

[Certificate.]

I declare the above is a true statement of the questions and answers, declaration, and sentence, and that the whole ceremony was carried on in an impressive and proper manner.

(Signed) H. NIXON,
Captain and Brigade Major, South Australian Volunteers.

We declare the above to be perfectly correct.

(Signed) { W. J. L. PULLEN.
C. BONNEY.
ALEXR. TOLMER.

August 25th.—A wet and miserable morning; ordered the camp to remain here in charge of a sergeant and three men; Mr. Pullen with his crew in the whaleboat, and the mounted party on horseback, to proceed with the condemned men and the other natives of whom we had kept charge, back about fifteen miles to Palcarra, the place where our unfortunate fellow subjects were slaughtered, and reburied by Mr. Pullen, where the party arrived at 2 P.M. through incessant rain. The gallows was erected a little before 3 P.M., and the murderers were then executed in the presence of sixteen natives, to whom I made the following address:—

"Black men, this is the whites' punishment for murder; the next time white men are killed in this country more punishment will be given. Let none of you take these bodies down; they must hang till they fall in pieces. We are now all friends, and will remain so unless more white people are killed, when the Governor will send me and plenty more policemen, and punish much more severely. All are forgiven except those who actually killed the wrecked people, who, if caught, will also be hung. You may go now, but remember this day, and tell what you have seen to your old men, women, and children."

"The above was interpreted by Peter, and the natives, whose hands had been unbound by my orders before the execution, bolted, with an amazing amount of agility. They trembled much before, and after the men were swung off. They died almost instantly, and both showed extraordinary nerve and courage to the last. The one given up by his tribe had the most ferocious and demon-like countenance I ever beheld.

"I (the writer) was informed, after they had hung the usual time some of the men of the tribe were required to touch and speak to their dead countrymen, and told to leave the bodies hanging. It need hardly to be mentioned that for a long time they avoided that neighbourhood.

"The names of the passengers were reported to be Mr. and Mrs. Denham, three boys and two girls, Geo. Green, his wife, T. Daniel and wife, Mrs. York and infant, Mrs. Smith (wife of the captain), Jas. Strut, Captain Smith, and mate, and crew, said to be eight men and boys, but none of the bodies were ever found."

Major O'Halloran's report continued—"All the clothing, &c. I have carefully preserved, in the hopes that they may be identified.

"On the morning of Thursday, 27th August, we started south-east along the coast, in search of the wreck of the *Maria*, with six days' provisions for each man. Leaving Mr. Pullen at the camp, we found fresh huts, with European clothing and a watch; but as we could not carry the clothing, I ordered the huts to be fired. The watch dial and the outer part were stained with blood. On Friday we moved on at an early hour, and soon met Captain Nixon and Mr. Bonney, who had preceded the main body; they reported they had fallen in with two men, Thompson and Walker (Kangaroo Islanders), from whom I received the following statement, taken down by Captain Nixon. They had passed up the Coorong before we arrived at the Goolwa.

"Thompson's statement :—'After leaving the mouth of the Murray we passed up the Coorong, and hauled the boat up where we now are, and supposed we had made about 100 miles, when we divided our party, two to keep the beach, and two the south shore of the Coorong. On Sunday evening we fell in with the longboat belonging to the *Maria*, having in her two oars and a mast, but no sail. We hauled her up above high water mark. At about six miles farther east we fell in with part of the quarterdeck and skylight of the vessel; at another six miles from the wreck we found the companion, and then walked on to Captain Wright's camp at Lacepede Bay, where he was engaged with a party of his men in endeavouring to get afloat a schooner which had been driven ashore during a storm.'

"'On our return we found sundry other parts of the wreck, which we suppose came to grief on Bundin's Reef. Major O'Halloran on his return met a native of the Big Murray tribe, named Tom, who said that three males and one female belonging to the wrecked party had been waddied by some of his tribe, not far from where we now stood, being clasped round their bodies by some of the tribe while others waddied them. Tom offered to show us the spot, and point out the wurlies of the murderers, and identify them. He gave the names of two of them as brothers (Polaraynaka and Porielpeepool). As these murderers were distinct from the others, both as to locality and the persons by whom committed, we considered the duty we had undertaken would not be complete until we searched further.'"

After an interview with his Excellency, who came down and met Major O'Halloran and his party before they had left the Coorong district, and in obedience to fresh orders from him, Inspector Tolmer with half the number of police returned to scour the country inland, with Mr. Pullen and the boats to keep abreast of them. Major O'Halloran, with remainder of police, searching along the banks of the Coorong.

Major O'Halloran's report continued: "The several parties returned on Wednesday, September 2. Between 11 and 12 o'clock my party discovered the mangled remains of two Europeans, a male and a female, the skulls of both frightfully fractured, particularly that of the female, whose lower jawbone was broken. On asking Tom if he knew of these two likewise being killed, he said no. No more bodies were found, but a large man's shoe and some books. On reaching the spot where the four men were said to have been murdered, we could not find their bodies. I find these seventeen murders—fifteen from the *Maria*, and two whalers—have all been committed by the Milmenura or Big Murray tribe, who are notorious among the other tribes as most brutal and ferocious. The neighbouring tribes evince confidence in us, and abhorrence of the atrocities that have been lately committed."

There is no record of any other murders committed in the lower Murray district until some years after, when one white man was killed several miles to the north of the Coorong. It will be my duty to give in future chapters accounts of attacks by numerous natives on the Rufus, and at some miles farther to the east of the great bend of the Murray, on parties coming down with sheep, as well as a number of separate murders of white settlers by various detached tribes in the Port Lincoln district, at a later period—such bitter experiences having been endured in the course of settling this province. At present I am confining myself to the time Colonel Gawler occupied the seat of Government, from which it will be seen what an anxious time he had in protecting and saving the lives of the whites, and at the same time the peculiar duty he had to perform in adopting such a policy as would discourage indiscriminate and unauthorised measures of retaliation against the aboriginal race.

Severe censure was visited on the Governor by a certain party at home, and by a small section in the colony in opposition to Colonel Gawler, who made this a handle against him, but were not in the habit of exposing their own precious bodies to dangers of any kind in the bush. I cannot help thinking that the treatment Colonel Gawler met with at home after his recall, may be attributed, in a great measure, to the mistaken decision arrived at by the party alluded to acting on the Government at home, which assumes to be especially the protector of the aboriginal races, who could not see and would not believe that there were peculiar circumstances to justify the irregular but humane mode of action which was ordered by the Governor, and carried out by Major O'Halloran, in inflicting the punishment then put in force for such crimes. I am not writing as the apologist of the officials, but have taken on myself the duty of truthfully recording early experiences in founding and settling South Australia. I call upon readers to form their own conclusions after reading the particulars of these Milmenura murders, and what I propose to record in future chapters of subsequent attacks by other Murray tribes on parties coming down from Sydney with stock. A much heavier punishment in those cases was ultimately given, which resulted in a number of the blacks being killed; and there was no public agitation respecting them. As to the Milmenura case, it must be admitted that if such speedy and severe action had not been adopted by Colonel Gawler, the settlers would have taken the law into their own hands, and then who can tell what sad consequences would have ensued? I at the time became acquainted with the excited feelings of the parties under Mr. Pullen and Major O'Halloran, and know it must have called for the exercise of all the influence possessed by the leaders to have kept the men from acts of retaliation on their own private account. I conceive it becoming all old colonists, in justice to the memories of the gallant men who were the chief actors in the performance of the retribution visited on the barbarous murderers, to give their decided opinion that the punishment inflicted was fully justified by the peculiar circumstances surrounding the case, and with the object of preventing a repetition of such horrors, which object has been successfully attained.

I conclude this chapter with an extract from a letter published in the *Register* of the 5th September, 1840, after the two reports had reached the Government.

Of the writer, Captain G. Hall, then acting Colonial Secretary, it may be said a more humane and Christian man has never occupied a position in office in South Australia. His letter followed Major O'Halloran's report of his expedition. We who have lived in the colony during the succeeding period of forty-two years can certify that his predictions of the effects of the exceptional action taken have been fully realised. Captain Hall said as to the report—"Upon this statement of facts I would only remark that there is great reason to believe that prompt execution of the guilty parties on the spot where their crime was perpetrated, and in the presence of their tribe, who were fully aware of their guilt, will have a very beneficial effect in deterring the natives of that district from making wanton and unprovoked attacks on persons or property of Europeans who are about to settle in that neighbourhood. If the offenders had been brought up to Adelaide to be tried and punished under the English criminal law, the effect of the example would have been lost to the other members of the tribe, who would have been more irritated by the removal of their comrades than awed or impressed by any account which they might hear of the punishment of the offenders."

The full report of the trial by court-martial of the guilty members of this murderous tribe is given, as much blame was at the time heaped on Governor Gawler and Major O'Halloran for punishing by the extreme penalty of the law two of the savages who were, it may be said, chosen by the tribe, and admitted to be guilty, and as most worthy of death. The fact generally believed by out-settlers was that the tribe were glad to be relieved of their presence, as troublesome members of the tribe.

Postscript.—The following copy of a letter from Dr. Moorhouse, Protector of Aborigines, is added, addressed to Major O'Halloran, Commissioner of Police, March 12th, 1841 : " Dear Sir, -During my recent visit to the Coorong, I inquired particularly after the two natives who were shot at when crossing the channel (by the police). Peter and Charley did not know their names. They said that neither of them died, as their wounds were very slight. All the natives with whom I conversed agreed that both took part in the murders committed upon the Europeans.—M. MOORHOUSE, *Protector.*"

BOOK II.

CHAPTER I.

AMONGST the early experiences of the colonists during Colonel Gawler's administration must be counted the destruction by fire of several of our first temporary public buildings, as well as some of the residences of Government officials, the fire-king seeming to mark such structures (composed of inflammable material, chiefly wooden, and mostly thatched with reeds or grass) as temptations thrown in his way. The first fire occurred in 1840-41, shortly after midday, resulting in the total destruction of two wooden buildings which were situated to the west of the small Post-office, and near where now may be seen the sheep-market, on North Terrace. These were Government offices. One was occupied by the Resident Commissioner and his staff; the other was used for the Land and Surveyor-General's Offices. The flames spread so rapidly that the officers and clerks were unable to save much, and many books, papers, and maps were lost. On the day of the fire I was driving on my way to visit sections about halfway to the old Port, and passed near these offices, where business was going on as usual. On my return, when about five miles from town, I saw smoke spring up, and although I drove at a quick pace, when I reached the scene of the fire the two buildings were reduced to smoking heaps. Great inconvenience was experienced by the loss of books and public documents. The Resident Commissioner was Mr. (afterwards Sir James) Fisher, and the dwelling which contained his office was also his private residence. Colonel Light, the Surveyor-General, had also lived in the other dwelling, and the devouring element did its work so rapidly that he saved nothing of the cases he had left there for safety when he retired from the office, containing his journal to date, and records of his experiences in Turkey, Egypt, the Mediterranean, and on the battle-fields of Spain, where he served on the staff of Wellington. Colonel Light felt the loss of his journal very deeply, and stated that he would not have parted with it for several thousand pounds.

The next building which met a similar fate was Government House, a temporary erection of one storey, with a thatched roof, the timbers principally of native pine, procured from what was then called the Pine Forest, now known as Nailsworth. The fire commenced a short time before midnight, on the outside of the roof, and was supposed, and with good reason, to have been ignited by an insane gentleman, whom, I may mention, I met under that roof at a Government ball in Captain Hindmarsh's time. This fire was also almost like a flash of gunpowder, and very little of Colonel Gawler's property was saved. The police were on the spot in a very few minutes, and Inspector Tolmer, after breaking in the window of his Excellency's private office, had succeeded in dragging a small safe or tin deed-box to the window, and had himself passed out again, when the roof fell in before the safe could be lifted out. A loss of most important papers and documents was thus sustained by Colonel Gawler. At the time the roof fell in, and as the inspector was at the window, the fire reached a loaded musket, and the ball passed those who were leaving the window. The Governor and his son were present ready to receive the box if it could have been saved; and to do which the inspector risked his life, as the blazing thatch fell on him, but he escaped with singes only. These two fires forced upon the Governor the task of erecting a substantial Government house, and Government offices. Part only of the present modest palace was erected in his time, as well as a very small part of the present public offices. This necessity was a further calamity, as thereby labour was absorbed by the Government which was required by the colonists, and, in consequence, wages rose to an inconvenient extent, and private works were hindered.

I think the next fire was the destruction of the residence of Mr. John Brown, emigration agent, &c.—a wooden building also, from which very little was saved.

Sometime afterwards occurred the burning of a structure called the Octagon Cottage, the first residence of the Colonial Treasurer, Osmond Gilles, Esq., one of the London-built frame houses, constructed of deal, which he had given, with the land on which it stood, as a parsonage for St. John's Church. At the time of this fire the cottage was occupied by the widow of our first Colonial chaplain, with whom was her sister. The fire broke out after the ladies had retired to rest, and they had only time to save their lives.

After a time, substantial stone buildings having been erected, the colony has had a low average of visits from the fire-king, except when he has come and travelled in his bush invasions, of which, unfortunately for myself, I have had considerable experience and heavy losses.

I was once met by a grand conflagration in the Tiers, or stringy-bark forest—which I fortunately escaped with singes only—when coming towards town with a mob of fat cattle on a hot day, a strong north wind blowing. After crossing the Onkaparinga by the Echunga road I met clouds of smoke, indicating a fire at some distance ahead of my course, but as I mounted the first hill it seemed to be raging to the south of my line, and so I kept on. The cattle were travelling at a good pace. On attaining the next summit I found the fire had crossed the road at some distance ahead, and was rushing down a gully to the right of me, carried at a flying rate by the north wind. In my endeavour to head the cattle they rushed off to the right, towards the approaching fire, and charged a thick course or belt of green cherry tree, which, being dense and high, somewhat obscured the flames. Before the cattle reached this shelter, as they expected to find it, the fire had overtaken it, and the green foliage was soon burning and crackling about them and over their heads. They could not, however, stop or turn in their impetuous rush, but dashed through the flaming hedge. As I was close upon them, I followed over burning brushwood which had been a good deal trampled out by the bullocks, and passed on, over smouldering grass and bushes, at full gallop after the cattle, trees on all sides being on fire to their tops, and falling branches crashing in all directions, but was soon safe on the track again, on to which the cattle had turned; and soon after safely yarded them at Crafers. This was the only time I ever met and charged an approaching fire. I have on other occasions retreated, and started a fire to meet and contend with the one approaching when such an occurrence was met with clear of a stringy-bark forest; and also have had many a struggle in beating out bush fires, when, with sufficient beaters, it is a good plan to run a line of fire, although I, as well as many others, may have on some occasions been outflanked. I was once called upon to suffer a severe loss from a bush fire, as many old colonists have been, after an unavailing contest.

In a former chapter it was mentioned that Mr. Emanuel Solomon arrived in the *Lady Wellington*, the back of which vessel was broken on the bar at the entrance of Light's Passage. The wreck was bought on account of a Sydney firm, and was got off and towed up towards the Old Port. I afterwards, as agent for that firm, sold her to the Governor, Colonel Gawler, for £800. As she was quite taut above and below, she was for a short time used as a Government store ship. At the time of the sale, some doubt being thrown on the Government transactions, by the refusal of the first Treasurer to sign the bills drawn by the Governor, I required cash, not feeling justified, as an agent, to risk any inconvenience to the parties for whom I was acting. On this unfortunate vessel a great loss was sustained by the Government when she was sold and broken up, the retrenchment orders being put in force by Captain Grey, when the cruel crisis came, and the sacrifice of much public property was made, as well as of the property of the pioneers. Sheep which cost 38s. a head were sold first for 5s. and resold a few months afterwards for 2s. 6d. Cattle which I had purchased at £13 10s. a head, on a forced sale realised only £4 10s., after being kept twelve months, and when in prime condition.

An early circumstance in the transactions of Mr. E. Solomon may be mentioned, who, seeing the great influx of population, and that nothing was being done to produce the staff of life, made a good speculation in purchasing a cargo of flour, immediately on its arrival, from a Mr. Russel, then a merchant here, part of which he shipped to his brother in Sydney, and offered the remainder of the same to the Government here at £30 a ton, well aware of a scarcity in New South Wales and Tasmania. The Government refused to buy the flour, and to prevent reshipment of any of the small stocks in the colony of flour and rice an export duty of £100 a ton was immediately put on breadstuffs. The flour Mr. Solomon had shipped to Sydney realised to him £50 a ton, and the price in this colony soon reached £100 a ton, under the *protection* of the prohibitory export duty. The highest price the writer paid was £8 a bag, but for some time the price was £10 a bag. The plough in a short time gave relief, and before the end of five years, wheat was delivered in Adelaide at 2s. 6d. a bushel.

Mr. Solomon and his firm suffered heavily in the crisis, and during the period in which the colony was recovering from the severe depression, which was so severely felt by all when the Government stopped payment, but more especially by those of the early settlers, who had expended their means and energies in first settling in the land of their adoption. It must with justice be recorded of Mr. Emanuel Solomon that he has left his mark upon our now progressive and beautiful city. At a very early period he erected our first and capacious theatre in Gilles Arcade, so named when no arcade existed, or has since appeared. But the previous existence of a theatre must be mentioned; it was a small wooden structure at the back of the Black Swan public-house, on North-terrace, where some who are now alive and moving in more exalted positions exhibited themselves. In justice I must declare that I was never within its paling walls, either as a spectator or a performer, but I remember being told that a man named Bartlett was one of the performers—a bullock-driver, whose deep bass voice was often heard in our timber ranges, and afterwards on his section at Balhannah. The inhabitants of the young city were promised by the first manager that the tragedies of the immortal Shakespeare would be exhibited in this building. I do not know what characters Bartlett attempted, but his deep sepulchral tones were peculiarly adapted to give effect to the part of the ghost in Hamlet. This performer is introduced by name, not because he long ago departed this life, and so cannot be annoyed by a reference to his ambitious appearance on the stage with some of our earlier inhabitants, but that in truth nothing worse can be said of him than his appearance on the boards of our first humble theatre as a tragedian. I am quite sure all old colonists who heard his extraordinary voice will agree with me, that it was one calculated to make a deep and lasting impression on any human audience as well as on his team of bullocks.

Some considerable gatherings, in proportion to the number of the inhabitants then in the city, used to occur in the neighbourhood of the Gilles Arcade. Mr. Solomon there had his first wooden store, and there were wooden cottages occupied as offices by the Treasurer, the Resident Magistrate, and one was the dwelling of Judge Jickling. On the other side of Currie-street was the Southern Cross Hotel—a wooden structure brought out in frame from London—kept by F. Allen, where generally in a morning would be seen a number of people. It was a sort of exchange or place of meeting, and when no Court or other business occupied the time or thoughts of those present, idlers would indulge in practical jokes. On one occasion, after a heavy downpour of rain, which had left a number of ponds in various directions in the city, and when a large company had gathered for shelter and for refreshment, little dapper K——, then clerk of the Local Court, civil side, which was not sitting that day, walked in, attired most suitably to take a direct course in any bearing across the city. No streets were then formed or channels to carry off surface water. K——, on entering, exhibited with pride his nether limbs encased in a brand-new pair of, for him, exceptionally long patent-leather boots, saying: "There, I can defy the deepest pond of water within the city." A wag offered to bet him he would point out a pond through which he would not be able to cross without getting out of his depth. The bet was made. Rain had ceased to fall, and so the company followed the betting parties. K—— was to walk in a straight course from where he was placed by his opponent, to him, on a signal he would give from the opposite side of the pond, which was known, as far as to the natural surface of the ground, not to have a greater depth of water than would reach K——'s knees. At the signal, off started K——, setting at defiance the advice of jokers to take off his coat, etc. etc.; but to his sorrow, on reaching about halfway across the temporary pond, he suddenly popped out of sight, but was soon out on the other side of a sawpit, of the existence of which he was not aware, and of course he had an uproarious laugh against him; and on a return of the amused company to host Allen's, he had the consolation of partaking of refreshment ordered by the winner of his money, the landlord, as usual on such occasions, being the chief winner.

This brings to remembrance a scene which occurred at the opening of the town of Glenelg, on which occasion a splendid lunch was provided for a numerous invited company, to take place under a large tent, or rather collection of tents. On the same day it was proposed to launch a cutter, to be named the O.G., which was built on the banks of the Pattawalonga Creek, by Henning and Fenden. To add to the calamities, the tide in the creek did not rise so high as to float the first vessel built in the colony. The lunch was given by the proprietors of the township, viz., the Treasurer, O. H. Gilles, Esq.; the

Resident Magistrate, W. R. Wigley, Esq.; Matthew Smith and W. Finke, Esquires. The morning was fine, the company as numerous as the tables would accommodate, the provisions abundant, if not exhibiting any great variety of viands, but as to the supply of drinkables, that was as choice, abundant, and various as was ever seen on any table of the same picnic character even in the Old Country. Mrs. Gawler having honoured the occasion with her presence, the entertainment was graced and enlivened by a large number of ladies in most elegant attire. Every available vehicle the settlement afforded was pressed for the occasion, but few covered ones, unfortunately, being obtainable. It should be mentioned that the road between the city and Glenelg was then not formed, and very few of the sections between the two places were fenced; mere tracks over the natural surface of the ground were used. At the Bay were a few huts, two of which were licensed public-houses—one kept by Henning and Fenden. This building was formed of pines, thatched with reeds, and was, as far as the author recollects, about 30 feet long by 10 feet wide, and 8 feet high to the eaves. I give this description as a specimen of the first houses to which licences used to be granted, and to explain the position the numerous company were placed in by the heavy storm of wind and rain which overtook the party, and through which they had to hasten home in the absence of adequate shelter. I had driven my wife, and two male friends with their wives, down in an open waggonette. The morning being so fine umbrellas had, in too many instances, been left at home.

When the arranged toasts had been nearly exhausted the downpour of rain became very heavy. Before this it had been sufficient to prevent the retirement of the ladies, who were perforce compelled to remain during the carrying out of the programme, and as there seemed to be no abatement, the sitting was considerably extended, and the consumption of drinkables also, the water pouring in from various swags in the canvas. At length, as no cessation of the heavy rain appeared likely soon to occur, the ladies determined to defy the elements. Mrs. Gawler's carriage was first at the opening of the tent, and she was conducted and sheltered to the door of her carriage by Mr. McLaren, the Manager of the South Australian Company. The ground had become so slippery that this polite gentleman fell down at the feet of the Governor's lady.

I should have mentioned that, on the orders to bring up the carriages being given to the servants, who were taking shelter in a small framed building where the stock of drinkables had been kept, word was brought to Mr. McLaren that his coachman had imbibed too freely, and could not be depended on, and that it was on Mr. McLaren's rushing back from a lecture he had given the erring coachman, to assist Mrs. Gawler, that he slipped and fell. However, it was for a long time a standing joke that his coachman was summarily discharged for taking too much, on the same occasion when the master could not keep his own legs. I galloped my horses back, leaving the track along which so many were moving as fast as their animals could travel. The storm of wind and rain was fortunately at our backs. I did not hear of any more serious mishap than the fall of one or two horsemen in the muddy track, and the destruction of feathers, ribbons, bonnets, etc. Whatever complaints were given way to among the ladies they kept to themselves, as the pockets of the paterfamilias had chiefly to suffer in restorations.

I should mention, in closing this chapter, that the cutter O.G. was, immediately after this unpropitious day, privately christened and launched, and was for a long time usefully employed as a coasting vessel.

CHAPTER II.

THE earliest mineral discovery made in the colony was the Glen Osmond silver-lead lodes, the first indications of which were found almost immediately after Preliminary Section 295 was taken up by Mr. Osmond Gilles, in 1838, situated on the slope and foot of the first tier of hills, four miles south-east of Adelaide. As an incident and experience in my own career, I think I may fairly explain my first connection with this valuable section, although to do this a return must be made to a past date. Shortly after I arrived in the colony my attention was called to this section, by Mr. G. S. Kingston, then acting Surveyor-General. I had visited the original Survey Office, and was examining the second map of District A. Mr. Kingston pointed to the east corner of the surveyed sections, and informed me that the map was a copy of the one from which the preliminary sections had been selected by holders of land orders or their agents, on which original map their selections had been marked off. He, at my request, ordered this original map to be produced for my inspection, and I then saw on that map a section (No. 295), unselected, which did not appear on the copy, and in the situation he pointed out to me, and I at once rode out and found the western corner pegs, and perceived near the south-western corner of the same an appearance of a surface spring ; on which important find I returned at once to my camp on South-terrace, and took two 80-acre land orders, and tendered them for Section 295 and the additional quantity required, and the tender was accepted. Subsequently, on the same day, when spending an hour with Mr. Osmond Gilles, near whose residence I had encamped, he asked me if I had found any land to suit me. I replied : " I have this day exercised two land orders, and I can see the spot from your windows ;" and on pointing out the locality to him, he said : "What! those dimples?" I said : " Yes ; if you call the spurs and the indents between them dimples." My wife and another lady were present, and enjoyed a laugh ; and as Mr. Gilles seemed a good deal interested by what I told him about the non-accordance of the maps, I proposed the party should take an evening ride and view my selection. Mr. Gilles at once assented, and his gig and two of my saddle-horses were ordered out—one lady in the gig and the other with myself on horseback—and we passed joyously over the open plain, covered with long kangaroo grass and flowery herbage. On arriving at the " dimples " we dismounted under the shade of trees, and I alone climbed the hill to find the back pegs of the section, and found a large part of the same was on the hillside, stony and unsuitable for agriculture, and perceived that the lower part was thickly covered with trees ; the view across the plains with the young forest city in the centre and the gulf in the distance, formed a most delightful picture, with which I was sufficiently enraptured. We returned and spent the evening with Mr. Gilles, and I and my host enjoyed some of his splendid hock, over which we had a long chat. Mr. Gilles regretted his bad luck in drawing for his numerous choices for preliminary sections, by which he had not been able to obtain for himself even one section near enough the city on which to erect a suburban residence, and expressed his annoyance that his attention had not been called earlier to Section 295. He then asked me if I had any particular desire to retain the section, and proposed to me to withdraw my application, as it might be some time before I could obtain the additional quantity of land and in a manner to suit me. After some consideration, I did not hesitate to comply with his expressed desire, for I had seen that the back and hilly part of the section was not suitable for the plough, and the lower part was thick with trees, which would be expensive to clear. The following day I accompanied the Treasurer to the Land Office and withdrew my land orders, and Mr. Gilles exercised one of his preliminary orders, which he had been under the necessity to reserve for one of the southern reserved districts; the Commissioner (Mr. J. H. Fisher), and the acting Surveyor-General (Mr. G. S. Kingston), threw no difficulty in the way of the transfer, and the section was marked off and registered to Mr. Gilles, and he and I put our initials on the map, which now seldom sees daylight, but which initials I saw not long ago, on the map being produced in the Supreme Court, on a trial about the boundaries of sections. Some few weeks after this arrangement was effected I formed one of a small picnic party to the "Dimples," as the ladies continued to call the hollows. On the spurs some whitish quartzy-looking stones were picked up, which showed small bright specks of lead, not thought much of at the time. In the following year, 1839, large projecting blocks of what appeared to be limestone, on being broken on the hillside, were found to be internally pure galena; and now great excitement was caused. A few men were put on by the proprietor at first, under his chief clerk, Mr. Finke. Some of the Adelaide speculators endeavoured to come to terms with Mr. Gilles as to purchase, but he met them by saying that he would not part with the property even if £30,000 was offered for it. Ultimately six or seven distinct veins or lodes were discovered, and some 20 tons of good lead ore were soon raised, which parcel on reaching home was represented to give seventy-five per cent. of lead with eighteen ounces of silver to the ton. The average published value given was £13 a ton of 21 cwt. On this a London Company was formed, called the Glen Osmond Union Mining Company, with a paid-up capital of £30,000. At a very high royalty a mining lease was granted to the Company by the proprietor. A captain with a strong body of good miners was soon despatched, under engagements to work a certain time, which engagements were not in all cases fulfilled. Operations were for a few years carried on in a miner-like manner. The spring indication, which I had seen at surface, was tapped at a shallow depth, and found to be strong enough for washing such of the ore as required to be dressed. Large quantities of ore were raised and shipped, until a smelting establishment was built by the Messrs. Penny, on adjoining land; but unfortunately the Adelaide management got into litigation with the proprietor, which, together with the heavy expenses of management, shortly led to the lease being abandoned by the Company. At the same time sufficient ore had been raised to cover first expenses of sinking two main shafts, driving two principal adits into the hill, and erecting the necessary buildings, machinery, etc., but the stoppage took place before the adits reached the main lodes, and so a promising mine was knocked, as the miners say.

Subsequent to the opening of the first lead mine an extraordinary bunch of galena was discovered on an adjoining section, known afterwards as the Wheal Watkin's Mine, and many tons of rich lead, rich also in silver, were raised; but the workings were abandoned when at about forty or fifty fathoms below surface, when the lode became pinched and the ground harder. On other adjoining sections lead lodes were worked a short time; one, the Wheal Gawler, and a lode near to it, and one in Hardy's Quarry. All these prospects stand over for a future day, if ever wages and expenses permit the workings to be resumed. The sum realised on the Glen Osmond mine, as I was informed at the time, amounted to over £13,000—this fully covered all costs under extravagant management. No doubt the royalty was much too high, which might have been the primary cause of the stoppage.

In 1842 the Kapunda Copper Mine was discovered. I extract particulars of this from Dutton's work. "The first discovery of the ore was by the youngest son of Captain Bagot whilst gathering wild flowers on the plain. Shortly afterwards, not far from the same spot, I ascended the top of a small hill to view the surrounding country. One of our flocks of sheep had been dispersed during a thunderstorm, and I had been out nearly the whole of the day in drenching rain in search of them. The spot where I pulled up my horse was beside a protruding mass of clay slate. My first impression was that the rock was covered with a beautiful green moss; but on dismounting and breaking off a piece, it proved to be green carbonate of copper. To my neighbour, Captain Bagot, I confided my discovery; the place was on his sheep-run. He also produced a similar specimen, which was found by his son, as related. The two spots were in close proximity: the discoveries were of course kept secret. We applied for a survey of eight acres, in conformity to regulation: the section was advertised, as required, in the *Gazette* for one month, and we became the purchasers of the same at the upset price of one pound an acre. At one time there were a number of eighty-acre land orders unexercised, and any one of them might have been tendered, and have gained the section for the owner of it. We quietly waited for the expiration of the month, and then lodged the money, having trusted to the general depression of the times as preventing any competitors, and we were not mistaken. Having secured the land, the next step was to ascertain the value of the ore, and we sent samples to England, and from Mr. Percival Johnston obtained a return of an assay of the average of twenty-three per cent. of copper. We then lost no time in beginning working with a small party of men, and with three miners and a party of friends, ladies included, started in a bullock-dray with a tarpaulin hood, Mr. Menge being in the party. Proceedings were opened by an interesting address on mining in general by him, and the ground was broken by the men. At this time a few Cornish miners were quietly following other pursuits, who gladly resumed mining tools, and commenced to raise ore on tribute of 3s. 6d. in the pound, to set the interest a-going. They did very well, and raised a quantity of rich ore. The place was a complete wilderness; the nearest water was half a mile away, and brackish; we soon succeeded in finding a good spring, and erected a row of stone cottages for the workmen, and they quickly had their families with them. The mine was about forty-two miles from Port Adelaide, and at first no track even had been made between the places. Captain Bagot undertook to select and mark out a line, which he did in a primitive manner by fastening a plough behind the first dray, and by that striking a furrow for succeeding drays to follow. On the plough breaking he had a crooked forked branch cut from a hardwood tree, and with that produced a sufficient scratch to be followed, and so the line was made and adopted, and for a long time used, being worn to a hard surface, and remained a good road until road-makers were set to work.

"In justice I have to record a most popular act of Governor

Grey in declaring, in July, 1845 (at the time when copper and lead ores were promising to be raised in large quantities), all South Australian ports open free of all port charges to ships of all nations without exception. At this time, from recently opened mines, ores had arrived for shipment from Port Adelaide. This free grant was made after the revenue had attained a comparatively flourishing condition, from the successful occupation of country lands, by an industrious population lifting the colony from its deep depression to such a state of prosperity as to justify the Governor in establishing such a wise, liberal, and well-timed policy, and which drew freight-seeking ships to our colony. The previous year's revenue, derived from port dues and charges, had amounted to about £2000. The loss of that amount of revenue was correctly anticipated to be made up in other branches under increasing prosperity. Contracts for the first cartage of ores from Kapunda were fulfilled at 22s. 6d. a ton of 21 cwt.—probably as cheap as it could be carted for the same distance in England. After the richness of the mines became publicly known applicants came forward for a section of one hundred acres of adjoining land, and the section, on being put up for public competition, reached the amount of £2210, which was purchased on joint account by Messrs. Bagot and Dutton." From this additional purchase, before the end of the year, ores were raised sufficient to repay the first cost and expenses.

" In the year 1840 three miners were employed in the colony ; in the last month of the year twelve men were at work. The gross produce from sales at Swansea amounted to £6225.

" In the year 1845 Mr. Dutton sold his one-fourth interest in the mine, and subsequently Captain Bagot parted with the remainder to an English company, by which company the mine has since been carried on. The fame of South Australian mines soon spread through the neighbouring settlements, and when once it became known that everyone who went there found immediate and profitable employment, we began shortly to receive a large accession to our population, by voluntary free emigration from New Zealand, New South Wales, Port Phillip, and Van Dieman's Land. Tables for 1844 show increase from arrivals, 973 ; first quarter 1845, 616 ; one month, August same year, 500 arrived at Adelaide."

Amongst early experiences I cannot properly give the subsequent transactions of the Kapunda Mining Company.

The Burra Mine is the next important discovery to be mentioned, which so largely aided in placing South Australia in the position she now holds. This mine was discovered in the year 1845, after the previous mines mentioned had got well at work, by a shepherd of the name of Pickett. A rumour of a discovery of a monster mine in the Far North, as it was then called, had been for some time rife in Adelaide. Reports were current that this discovery was of such an extent as to eclipse everything which had been seen or heard of, but the locality was wrapped in mystery, and by many was considered to be a hoax. At length it was proved to be a fact. The excitement this discovery caused was unprecedented; the richness of the ores and the extent of the outcroppings were soon placed beyond a doubt. The tide having turned in favour of prosperity, arrivals from England were daily expected; with a large amount of capital; and if so the prize would be lost to those first interested, so it was made manifest that nothing short of a special survey of 20,000 acres quickly demanded would secure the prize. The strivings and rivalries and exciting articles and communications in the papers were unexampled for some weeks. At length two Associations were formed. They could not agree to coalesce further than to club their money together to form the necessary fund of £20,000, required to be deposited to secure the claim, to be after survey subdivided.

The two parties of gentlemen between them acquired this splendid property of 20,000 acres, on which was subsequently opened one of the richest copper mines ever worked in the world. Out of the first struggles to form a party with sufficient cash at command, two associations were formed, which by some wag were named "The Nobs and the Snobs;" not that the men of each party were not, as colonists, equally respectable, but amongst the Snobs were a few retail storekeepers and humble people, with whom the Nobs would not further combine. The survey of the special block being quickly made, and in length lying northerly and southerly, it was divided into two equal parts by an east and westerly line. On the northern half the first great surface block of ore existed—afterwards the Burra Mine. On the southern half had been discovered indications of large copper lodes—afterwards named the Princess Royal Mine. Well, on the fortune of the two great speculating parties being decided by lot, the rich Burra fell to the Snobs; and, as it afterwards proved, the deceitful Princess Royal to the Nobs.

In the successful Burra Company were a large number of small contributors. In the Princess Royal party were fewer individuals, and amongst them Captain Bagot, Mr. F. S. Dutton, and other proprietors of the Kapunda mines, together with a few outsiders; so part of the unsuccessful Association had their own valuable previously-acquired mineral property to fall back on, and the public generally, who had no direct interest, were satisfied with the action of Dame Fortune. The Princess Royal property was for a time worked as a mine, but though large copper lodes were found to exist, and to carry every usual symptom of permanency, the ores proving what the miners call "dredgy," it was ultimately abandoned as a mine and sold as a sheep-run, and fell into the hands of a fortunate sheep-farmer, Mr. A. McCulloch.

Postscript.—The Glen Osmond Silver Lead Mine has not been worked for many years, but may again be reopened after the decease of the present holder, a very old man, who is the surviving brother of the original owner, the late Osmond Gilles, Esq.

To show the almost unbounded mineral wealth of South Australia, it is only necessary to give the number of the mineral properties which have been opened and partially worked only, from want of capital and the high price of labour, in distinction from such self-paying mines as the Moonta and the Wallaroo, the dividends from which paid to the fortunate shareholders have been almost unexampled; these mines, as well as most of the numbers given below, are Government property. Number of silver-lead partially-opened mines, ten. Number of copper mines, over ninety. Some of the latter class are still held on lease; others are open to application.

Nearly all these idle mines have been opened and found to contain absolute lodes of rich silver-lead and copper ores. Most of them are now available to be worked with profit, from the railway lines recently opened, and others will be shortly placed in equally favourable conditions, by lines now in progress.

CHAPTER III.

THE Resident Commissioner and the Surveyor-General, in opening the work of the new colony, had first to order and arrange the survey of the City of Adelaide and the preliminary districts, extending from the city down to Cape Jervis, in which the preliminary land orders (mostly held by absentees) might be first exercised. No other country land was open for selection until near the end of the first quarter of the year 1838, which was over two years after the colony was proclaimed. The size of all sections surveyed up to this time was to suit the preliminary land orders, viz.—134 acres. After the best sections had been chosen, the rejected ones had to be cut up into 80-acre sections, and green slips as they were called; and then the 80-acre land orders might be exercised. As was natural, all the best sections as to quality of land, supply of water, or locality, had been absorbed by the representatives of the preliminary land-order holders. The authorities had no power to place *bonâ fide* farmers, or others having 80-acre land orders, on sections, although purchased and paid for in England, until after preliminary selections had been made. A further great evil shortly arose, viz., the commencement of land speculation in South Australia, by applications for special surveys of 15,000 acres, out of each of which after survey 4,000 acres could be selected and obtained at £1 an acre; and thus the number of absentee proprietors was further increased, and the surveying and opening free districts for selection to *bonâ fide* applicants for land for immediate agricultural operations was further hindered.

I may here also mention that the new colony at first was entirely dependent for supplies of sheep and cattle for consumption on such as arrived by sea, nor was there any other introduction of horned stock until the arrival of Mr. Bonney, who brought Mr. Hawden's herd of cattle down the Murray, early in the year 1838. Previous to their arrival fresh meat at one time was 2s. 6d. a pound, even for mutton not of the best quality. Captain Sturt subsequently arrived in August in the same year with stock overland. The mode of landing sheep from ships at anchor was generally to pack them on end as close as possible in the ship's long-boat, and when that grounded some distance from the sand hills to cast them into the sea. Many through drinking salt water died on their road to town; some were drowned, and both accidents were said to be corrected by muttonising the carcasses. At all events the arrivals were generally grievously affected by scab, so our choice of fresh mutton was very doubtful; but then we had occasionally fish and game, the latter consisting principally of kangaroo and opossum. But under all these preliminary trials we were not a discontented community. Energy in action, and patience under unavoidable trials, were the order of the day. A few discontented mortals quickly retreated, and left to those possessing more pluck and perseverance the glory of successfully establishing one of the finest colonies under the British Crown.

Importations of flour and grain were made principally from Van Diemen's Land, at one time at a cost of from £80 to £100 a ton. The Parliament and Government of the mother country must be justly blamed for the short-sighted and parsimonious policy they adopted in launching the colony, thereby leading to the most serious of our first troubles. When the Act of Incorporation was granted, it was stipulated that it should not be in force until the sum of £35,000 was realised by the sale of land, and an additional sum of £20,000 by the issue and sale of South Australian bonds, that amount to be invested in the British funds " as a guarantee that the colony would at no time be a charge on the mother country." The negotiation of these bonds at such a time was, as a matter of course, a losing transaction. The above treatment may justly be termed step-motherly. For such hard terms the gentlemen on the Committee for establishing the colony worked hard for three years, and at last accepted them on finding there was no prospect of obtaining more liberal treatment. Thus arose the necessity for the forced sales of land in London, and at a reduced price. The South Australian Company and a few fortunate private individuals took advantage of the preliminary sale in England, and thus was created an absentee proprietory. These preliminary sections near the capital cost only 12s. an acre with one town acre thrown in to each, as I have already stated. I do not desire to cast blame on these fortunate purchasers who came forward to invest their cash in a speculation which was treated by the authorities as a wild scheme, but to explain the primary mistakes which resulted in the unfortunate crisis of 1839-40. The early settlers who had invested their capital in legitimate pursuits suffered great losses. The delays I have recounted which took place in obtaining suitable land for agricultural purposes caused many who had come out to embark in farming to adopt other pursuits, but when the crisis approached, and after flour had obtained the unheard-of and famine price of £8 and £10 a bag, many of those who had any means left, returned to the occupation they joined the colony to embark in, although in most instances with greatly diminished means. I myself closed my town business in 1839 at a great sacrifice, and made arrangements to occupy and reside on my sections, only recently selected, which were situated about twenty miles to the east of the city. I had the first choice in the first special survey after the 4,000 acres had been selected. It may be as well here to give a description of our first experiences in this line.

Having sent on men to prepare timber for building and fencing, I followed as soon as temporary shelter was provided. I give an account of our journey as a fair specimen of what early settlers had to experience. I first despatched two bullock teams with our furniture and fixings as early in the day as possible, and followed some hours afterwards with my family in a roomy waggonette, to which were harnessed three horses, one in the lead and two wheelers—a dangerous rig for the rough and hilly track we had to pursue. In the trap, I being the driver, I had my wife, sister, two sons (three and four years old), one female servant, and our youngest boy in arms : also a man to assist me on the road in procuring timber drags, and in fixing them on to the hind axle of the carriage before I ventured to drive down the steep hills which we had to pass—in those days screw skids had not been invented. This great improvement in skids over all other plans which had been previously used in easing loaded vehicles down hills was shortly after invented by one of our earliest colonists, viz., Mr. Stephen Hack. The first one which was constructed on his suggestion was made by J. Adamson. To pass over the Mount Lofty Range at that time was no easy task. The first ascent to be made was by either of the spurs between Beaumont and Glen Osmond. I fixed on the one nearest Greenhill, as being most used and having more space for making tacks. I had a staunch team, and with many zigzags I surmounted this first difficulty, my man following behind with chocks to stop the hind wheels when necessary to ease the horses. On the top of the brow, to my surprise and annoyance, I overtook the drays. The day being very hot one of my best leading bullocks dropped, and could not be got up again. I had in consequence to leave my man to assist in yoking up one of the body-bullocks as a makeshift leader in the place of the fallen one, and to continue with the drays to assist the disarranged team ; and I had no alternative but to go on the best way I could, without help or the use of drags. My next serious difficulty was Breakneck Hill, rightly named, as I can speak from experience of broken-necked bullocks in descending, but on this occasion I had to surmount it. I afterwards got on pretty well, down moderate and short pinches, having an excellent leader who would turn to the right or left as sharp as required with slack traces. When I came to the steep and longer descent at Cox's Creek, on which spur trees had been felled and split into palings and shingles, the stumps of course left standing, and sundry rejected bad splitting pieces of timber lying about, I felt I had arrived at my worst trouble. I pulled up and looked on each side hoping to find at hand a suitable timber drag, but was disappointed, and with much trepidation I started the team at a foot's pace, but when, without skid, the pressure came too heavy on my wheelers they began to trot in spite of all my efforts to hold them back, and at length they broke into full gallop. By the sagacity and obedience of my leader I was able to clear the stumps and logs without an accident. The females and children fortunately did not scream or utter a word. At the foot of the hill, on pulling up, I found two men on horseback, who had paused in astonishment at seeing us make such a flying descent. Before I could gain my breath or speak to my family they addressed me most abruptly (I could see they were fresh arrivals). They said, "We wish we could hand you over to the police for driving down such a dangerous hill in such a reckless manner to the risk of your passengers' lives, &c., &c." I replied, "I must excuse your ignorance, gentlemen ; the passengers I am driving are my wife and family. I have scarcely recovered from my fright. You have interrupted me and all of us in returning silent thanks for our deliverance from so great a danger. Look at my hands, black with the force I have used." We continued on the track over the natural surface, now steep sideling, now sharp rise or fall, and reached the Onkaparinga River without accident. The crossing was too rough, and here one of our back springs gave way, after having stood all the heavy jolts and jars we had previously encountered. A cross-bar cut and fixed, we again passed on, and reached the station at sundown. After a picnic supper we turned in on beds of dry grass, as the drays with bedding and food did not arrive till next morning, when we had a sumptuous breakfast. Poultry and dairy cows had been sent up some time before with a small flock of sheep.

The kitchen and dairy being finished we soon had our usual comforts. And now the work of fencing was continued, and grubbing trees, and preparing land for corn. An orchard and garden were trenched, to be ready at the right season for planting. I had purchased seed wheat at 15s. a bushel, and having to pay that price for seed, and so much to do in clearing, fencing, and erecting farm buildings, I did not crop more land this first season than what I thought might yield me seed for the following year and enough for domestic use.

At this time, 1840, on the first farms established, the proprietors, some of them quite unused to manual labour, might be seen undergoing the heaviest work their powers would admit of; their wives and children engaged in unaccustomed employments totally unsuited to their strength—a boy of eight or ten years of age driving bullocks at harrow, occasionally a young girl driving bullocks for her father at plough, or with a sister cross-cutting logs for fencing; then all had to help at odd times of the day, early and late, at log burning. All this toil was necessary, because labour was scarce and wages high, or money wanting; and so a variety of hard shifts had to be adopted to accomplish indispensable work. Before I arrived at the farm with my family some preparatory work had been done in fencing and building. For some time an overlander—*i.e.*, a lag of the name of Tom Fuller—with his mate, had been employed in sawing timber for buildings and in splitting posts and rails for fencing, and his work went on until late in December. I am about to give some account of this man, as he was, as I believe, the last of his class in my employment. I had a final settlement with him on Saturday night a few days before Christmas Day. He left my service apparently well satisfied, as he received a lump of money. On the following morning, Sunday, I turned out early. On my walk round the premises I observed one favourite goose was missing. On walking forward to the edge of a small gully, on the opposite side of which Tom's hut stood, at about three hundred yards up the rise, I observed Tom coming out carrying a bundle. I hailed him, but instead of waiting he dropped the bundle and ran to the top of the heavily-wooded range at his best speed, and I after him. On reaching the summit I could see him rushing through the bushes on a slant, to reach the main gully. This gave me a little compensating advantage, as I could take a line to head him. I soon found he was blown, and that I was gaining on him rapidly. I was still alone, although at starting I had called aloud to arouse my people. On coming near him at a great pace, my course being down hill, and charging him on his left flank, he suddenly stopped, and taking out of his pocket a large clasp-knife, he said in a loud voice—" Now your life or mine, you b——." My hand was quickly at his throat, and between that and his handkerchief, and down he went, and I on the top of him. In the fall the knife was lost by him, and after a short struggle a labourer whom I had aroused, and who had followed in haste, came up, and shortly after him my old shepherd Miles, who, as usual, had his pocket-pistols with him. So Tom was allowed to get up, and I soon decided to take him to the next magistrate's house, about two miles off. I sent the labourer back for the slaughtered goose, with instructions to meet us at the justice's residence. I had heard that this gentleman had been appointed and gazetted the previous week, and that one of his men had been sworn in as a special constable. On my laying the charge before him, he decided to commit the thief to my custody. I declined such a trust, stating I had risked my life in taking him, and I thought it was his duty, as he had a constable in his establishment, to keep him in charge. He then turned to my shepherd, Miles, and charged him in the Queen's name to keep the prisoner secure until he could be handed over to the police, and made out a *mittimus* accordingly; to which poor trembling Miles said, "Your worship, what am I to do if he will run away? I am sure I cannot hold him, but I have got my pistols in my pocket; may I shoot him?" With the utmost gravity the justice replied, "Certainly." After this Tom walked back with us to my residence, and was placed with his guard in the stone kitchen. I took Miles on one side and asked, "Are your pistols loaded?" He replied, "Yes, master; am I to shoot him if he offers to escape?" I said, "If you do except in defence of your life my opinion is you may be hung. To prevent accidents we will withdraw the bullets." In doing this I had more fear for Miles than for Tom Fuller. I added, "Tom must still think they are fully loaded. Keep him safe and give him food." On the way home I had a conversation with our prisoner. On his asking me to forgive him this time, declaring he had not lifted anything of mine while he was working for me,

I declined his request, as his conduct was so bad after my liberal treatment of him. He had the impudence to explain that he and his mates had agreed to have a spree at a public-house some miles away, and now he was very sorry he had robbed me. After dark I heard a commotion in the kitchen, and then a shot fired, and the voice of Miles calling out, " Tom has bolted." I could hear him running, and his little dog yelping with joy; but presently heard the dying yells of the poor faithful animal, which had lain at the kitchen door. Its carcase was found by us in the morning on the track with its throat cut, killed to keep the fugitive's course secret. So much for Tom at present. I ordered the men not to follow him, as that would be useless. A trooper in due time came out, but Tom was not again captured, as he had plenty of money and was wary enough to resist drink, and so cleared, as I supposed, out of the colony. His taking credit for respecting my goods did not say much for him, as, he being on contract work, I had always money of his in hand, so his conscience could not be credited, but his prudence might. He was not seen again in the colony for some years.

As an occurrence of some interest, I have to relate that in the month of September, 1841, I went in company with a Mr. S—— (a new arrival) and the late Mr. John Emery, to a cattle station on the Light, of which he was the manager, to select a small dairy of cows from the herd of cattle under his charge. We started on horseback from Adelaide late in the afternoon, intending to remain at Gawler Town for the night. On our arrival there we found that the house at which we put up our horses was full, with no beds for us. Accommodation in those days was very scanty, so we had no choice but to sup, bait our horses, and push on by moonlight. About the time the house was closing, we started under the guidance of Mr. Emery, and made the station a little before sunrise. On rousing the people in the hut, we found them a long time in turning out, and then very unusual excitement was exhibited, especially by the stockkeeper, Roach, who pretended that he thought we were blackfellows, and produced a gun with a broken stock, the barrel being severed from the stock, and complained to Mr. Emery that the blacks had been killing calves, and he was now without firearms. He was aware we were coming out, and by orders had mustered the cattle on the previous day, and a large number were in the yards for our inspection. After an early breakfast the stock-keeper said there was a special mob he wished to get in, and which he had missed the day before, and he hastily mounted his horse and started with the ostensible purpose of bringing them in to give us a larger choice. I saw him start off in an easterly direction from the hut. A large patch of scrub was in sight from the station to the west. The country for some miles was flat; to the east and north a jumble of hills shut in the prospect, so he was soon out of sight. Having nothing to do until his return, I wandered alone to higher ground to obtain a good view of the country. We had passed through a corner of the western scrub in approaching the station, and I desired to see the extent of it. Looking steadily in that direction, I saw a horseman ride into it as if he came from a north-east direction, and not long afterwards a great smoke arose in the part of the scrub where I had seen the horseman enter. This, at the time, I did not think singular, but as connected with what I have to relate, might have been an important link in bringing to punishment a cruel murderer. But I must mention I did not see the horseman leave the scrub, and when Roach was seen returning, his approach appeared to be from a different quarter, and the distance of the man on horseback, as seen by me, was too great for me to have sworn to his identity. When Roach returned he had no cattle with him, and those already in the yard were sufficient in number and in quality to enable us to select such a draft as was required. Having obtained our quantity we started, after a station dinner, for Gawler Town, leaving the cattle to follow, to be delivered in Adelaide. That night we stopped at Robertson's Hotel, in Gawler Town, and had a comfortable night's rest. At the breakfast table next morning we met Dr. Moorhouse, the Protector of Aborigines, and before we had concluded our meal the kind landlady brought in a little native girl of about twelve years of age, who, before the company, in a mixture of broken English and native words, told a pitiful tale to Mr. Moorhouse. She said that she and her grandfather were sitting down in a scrub eating kangaroo which blackfellows had killed, and had then gone away, leaving her and the old man to follow. Whilst they were " sitting down in scrub a white man on horse, with a gun, said, 'You have killed a calf.' We said, 'No, no spear—eating kangaroo.' White man plenty growl, and then he shoot old man grandfather. I ran and hid in scrub, and then came on to Gawler Town, where white woman gave me tucker last night and let me stop for night, and then she tell me Mr. Moorhouse in Gawler, and me come to tell him all about white man shoot grandfather." We did not then understand the locality where the murder had been committed. Mr. Moorhouse lost no time in taking police with him and the poor native child, believing her distressing tale, which he found perfectly correct, as I was made aware of some time afterwards. She charged the stock-keeper, Roach, with the crime, and guided the Protector and the police to the place in the scrub, where they found the body of the murdered old man, partly burned, and Roach was at once taken into custody. This man was from one of the convict colonies. I should have mentioned that we found in the hut two strangers, who said they were out looking for country, and had been at the station the whole of the previous day. The evidence of the child was unsupported. Roach brought forward the two men, who swore that they had been with him the whole of the day, and that he was never out of their company or in that scrub on the day the child swore to: and so the prisoner was discharged, to appear when called upon, although the child positively and without hesitation said he was the man who shot her grandfather.

After his discharge Roach mounted his horse to return to the North, but before he had well passed North Adelaide his horse reared with him and fell back on his rider, and in the fall his neck was broken, and so he died, and met with a punishment he richly deserved, as I have no doubt on my mind he committed a cruel and cold-blooded murder upon a poor, unoffending, helpless old man. This is the case of a barbarous murder of an old man, a native, by a white, which I previously alluded to.

My first experience in giving employment to the natives in a regular way was after I left Adelaide and commenced farming in the Mount Barker district. They picked up and bagged potatoes and did other farming jobs. On one of these occasions, after work was finished, I was talking to them at their camp in the dusk of the evening, on the side of the hill above my premises, when a large meteor appeared (the largest I ever saw), which came from the east at an apparent slow pace, showing larger and larger as it approached. I supposed it fell to the ground at or on the east side of Mount Lofty proper, but I was informed it had been seen crossing the plains of Adelaide. At the camp were a large number of blacks, many of them employed by neighbouring settlers. They no sooner saw the meteor than they cast themselves with their faces on the ground, uttering one combined and long-continued hideous yell. When the meteor had vanished all I could say did not pacify or relieve them of their fright; they persisted in saying it was devil-devil, come to kill blackfellows. On rising early the following morning I was greatly surprised to find the camp entirely deserted, nor did I see any of them till months afterwards, when some of them again visited me. They told me in distressing tones that many of the tribe had died through the coming of the big one fire. They undoubtedly had been suffering from some kind of fever, for those who had survived came in a most pitiable state of emaciation. They had suffered far away from the help of white men. I may mention that I have often given them medicine, which they were always eager to take, and so made excellent patients; the more nauseous the taste, the more they approved of it.

This tribe belonged to a piece of country on the banks of the Murray, called by them Wall. We called their chief King John, and the name of his chief lubra was Monarta, which was considered so pretty a name the whites never changed it. King John and Monarta often paid me a visit, and I set apart a small hut for them. He was a very good workman, and kept good order when I had a number of them employed. On one occasion John appeared anxious to tell me something. At last he pointed to Monarta at a distance, and said—"You see Monarta?" "Yes, what then you mean?" "Well, by-and-by a piccaninnie come." I then found what had filled his heart with joy. This was Monarta's first promise, and all other children by his other lubras had died. He was doatingly fond of children. I introduce the above particulars to lead to what follows.

After they left this time I did not see them for some months, when one day I saw two wretched black women slowly approaching. They did not as usual first visit the kitchen, but passed on at once to John's hut. I sent a female to see what was the matter. On her return she said Monarta was crying, and would not speak; that her hair was cut short, and there were large gashes on her head. I now went myself and questioned them, asking for John. At last Monarta blurted out— "John no more stop along of me; he say he kill me;" and then she put her hands up to inform me who had battered her

head, and burst into a lamentable cry. After a pause I asked,
"Where piccaninnie?" I had now touched on the cause of
all this distress. I got no answer from Monarta, but the old
woman said, "Piccaninnie dead; tumble down in scrub."
After much trouble I got out of them that "Monarta walk
walking through big one scrub, plenty hot day, no water, child
and blanket on her back. John gone long way, child plenty
cry, cry all same as wild dog, so she put him down and left
him." On my expressing horror at her action, she justified
herself by saying, "You see, master, he all same as wild dog."
It appeared from the state she was in that John did not accept
such a justification of her conduct, but beat her almost to
death. It was many months before John became reconciled
to her. He and the wreck of his tribe subsequently fell on my
hands to procure for them the annual dole of blankets and a
few necessaries. The tribe is now extinct, the few remaining
alive having joined another diminished tribe. The last time I
saw poor John, I was walking along one of our most crowded
streets, when I saw two young black men leading an old and
blind native, when one of them, on seeing me, must have
mentioned my name, for the old fellow cried out, "Where's my
master? Oh, my master, Mr. B——! where is he?" Now
all eyes were on me; but I could not resist the impulse to go
to my old friend, although several gentlemen standing at the
door of an hotel were greatly amused as he called out my name
loudly. On my approaching him he cried out, "Oh, my
master! my master!" and, throwing his arms round me, he
kept patting me on the back in a most loving manner. I did
not heed the laughter of some of the many spectators. I was
rather proud of being the cause of the exhibition of so much
affection from a poor benighted black fellow-creature.

CHAPTER IV.

IN this chapter I shall describe the progress in farming
operations and the successive annual yields of grain as
estimated from the number of acres cropped. By this record
it will be proved how soon a small band of agriculturists
changed the condition of the colony from one of importation

to that of exportation of breadstuffs, after suitable land was procurable. In the year 1838-9 a crop from about 20 acres was gathered, grown within the city, yield nominal. Harvest 1839-40, about 120 acres were cropped, yield say, 25 bushels to the acre, nearly all in Adelaide or in the district. Harvest 1840-1, the breadth under wheat 1,059 acres, estimated yield 21,180 bushels; in barley, 388 acres, yielding 7,760 bushels; in oats, 424 acres, yielding 12,720 bushels; under maize, 192 acres, yielding 2,880 bushels. Total acreage, 2,503 acres.

At the 1839-40 harvest, I had good crops on my small patches of wheat and potatoes; my seed wheat, which had been raised on town acres, had cost me 15s. a bushel. I had a few bushels of this, my first harvest, beyond what I required for domestic use and seed, for which I got 9s. a bushel. We now obtained our flour by the use at home of a handmill, which some neighbours had also used, and so commenced independence as to bread-food against imported flour. To turn this mill was a change of work, either before or after ordinary long hours of daily labour.

I will give an account of my own experiences in the harvest of 1842-3, and in the conveyance of the crop to market. Prices had fallen considerably and buyers were scarce. My crop was in condition for hand-reaping before the end of December, but I could not procure reapers before the 24th, as men had been earning large wages on the plains. Harvesting hands had been so scarce that the soldiers had been allowed to lay down their arms and take up sickles, and many soft-handed gentlemen had also turned out to give their doubtful but well-intended assistance in the emergency. On the 24th December, 1842, I was able to induce five men to accompany me, and I conveyed them to the farm. I did not allow them to work on Christmas Day, but they had Christmas fare. I engaged to give them 15s. and one bottle of rum an acre, with rations, for hand-reaping. The crop was dead ripe, the heads drooping with the weight of the plump grain. On the 25th a fiery hot wind was blowing, and continued on the following day, when I expected the reapers to start work, but they were missing. I found them at the nearest grog-shop. After some trouble I got them away to start work on the following morning. Before a sickle was put into the crop, the loss in shed wheat was over one bushel to the acre, and a further loss necessarily followed in harvesting.

Immediately on my return I took one of the men, the most

sober of the lot, to see the over-ripeness of the crop, and by what transpired it will be seen how providentially, out of the difficulties of my situation, the idea flashed upon me as to the possibility of thrashing a standing crop of wheat, and which idea, on being worked out, has since wrought such a beneficial result for the colony at large.

On taking this man into the crop and pointing out to him its over-ripeness, and how careful they would have to be in performing their work in handling the standing crop and in binding, calling his attention to the shed grain on the ground (I was standing a short distance within the crop), and to show how tender the heads were, with the full grain staring us in the face out of the gaping chaff, I passed my left hand with my fingers spread, under, and just below the ears, allowing the straws to pass between my fingers, the ears being close to the palm of my hand. I then struck the heads with a sweep of the edge of my right hand, and held out my open hand for the man to see the clean thrashed wheat in the hollow of it, most of the chaff having been carried away. (I must here mention that before this occurred I had for many weeks been pondering over plans for applying machinery to a standing crop, and had passed many sleepless hours in bed, and had been remonstrated with by my good wife, who said I should lose my senses.) Before I moved from my position in the standing corn, I stood in a sort of amazement, and looked along and across the fine even crop of wheat. The ideas I had in vain sought for now suddenly occurred to me, and I felt an almost overwhelming thankfulness. I did not move, but sent the man for a reap-hook, and caused him to cut me a small sheaf of wheat, which I took into the barn. There, holding a bunch of it in a perpendicular position, I struck the ears with a circular sweeping blow upwards, using a flat and narrow piece of wood, and found the thrashed grain to fly upwards and across the floor; and thus I satisfied myself that the grain would bodily fly at a tangent up an inclined plain. when struck by beaters, and that a drum, as in a thrashing-machine, would not be required to complete the thrashing, and so felt I had gained the correct idea for a field thrasher, and that a segment below the beaters would be apt to cause the wheat to be carried round, and so be lost. All this occurred in 1842.

I afterwards lost no time in exhibiting a rough drawing to many of my neighbours (some of whose certificates I hold, see appendix), but I got no encouragement, but from my oft recurrence to the subject was sometimes told I had lost my senses.

The crop was reaped, and the reapers were settled with, and allowed to return home.

Before carrying and stacking was undertaken, I had to consider how I could get over the thrashing, as a thrashing-machine was not procurable, and the price asked for hand-thrashing was a shilling a bushel, cleaning and bagging extra.

Many months before this harvest I had anticipated a great fall in price, as well as the other troubles I have described, and had procured a large number of store and breeding pigs. I decided to have the grain beaten out of the heads of the sheaves only, without unbinding them, and engaged several German women from Hahndorf, with their curious flails, and a number of blacks to supply the thrashers with the sheaves, to remove them as so partly thrashed, and to place them on frames around a large contiguous pig-yard, to be ready to be thrown to the pigs in fattening them. The sheaves were left out in shocks in the field, and were carted into the unskilled thrashers as required, and so the expense of stacking was saved. I counted the cost by this novel process of thrashing, cleaning and bagging, to be about 6*d*. a bushel. In the absence of a winnowing machine I had the assistance of natives, and got up a good sample by casting the wheat against the wind.

Next came the carting the wheat to town over the hills on the natural surface, with very little improvement from the hand of man. Now, bullockdrivers demanded ten shillings a day and expenses, so I undertook to drive one team myself, and started with a driver to conduct a second team. This was my first attempt to pilot a team of eight bullocks over such a chain of hills. I could comfortably handle a four-in-hand team of horses, but I was not up to the skilful management of a team of eight bullocks, although I had, as a matter of course, the handiest cattle for myself. The first rises accomplished successfully, in going down a steep pinch my polers fell, and Larry, a favourite beast, sticking his horns into the ground, went heels and body over head, and his neck was broken. The next job I and my man had to do was to prepare and dress the carcase, to avoid a total loss, and then to seek purchasers amongst the nearest splitters, to whom I had to dispose of the beef at a nominal price, although the bullock was in prime condition. He cost me twenty pounds, so my loss was considerable. With this delay we were unable to reach Adelaide that day. In making other trips that season I had sundry other accidents, but shortly afterwards improvements in the roads were made.

Immediately the thrashing was over, the fattening of the pigs on the partly thrashed sheaves commenced, and so the preparation for the knife and salting trough began. The pigs had water at hand, and whilst feeding themselves were doing good work in treading their bedding into a macerated bulk, as a valuable return to the land for crop taken off. Here is presented a striking change from famine prices for consumers to unremunerative prices for growers, with the ruinous rates of wages necessitating the introduction of machinery, about which I shall have something to say before I conclude this chapter.

I sold my wheat of this harvest, part at four shillings, and remainder at three shillings and sixpence a bushel. I estimated that about one-third was left in the sheaves and given to the pigs.

It was not long before I commenced to kill and cure hams and bacon, and used a smoking-house. When I had about three tons ready for the market, I carted the same to Adelaide, where, on going wearily about from store to store, I found I could get no offer for the whole lot, and less than fourpence per pound for small quantities, and to take part out in stores. I declined these conditions, and when at a loss what to do I met Mr. A. L. Elder, who, on hearing of my unsuccessful attempts to obtain a customer, ordered me to take the lot to his small warehouse, then in Hindley Street, and gave me fourpence a pound, cash, for the lot, which he shipped to the Mauritius. I was glad to hear from him some time afterwards that the shipment met with a good market.

I may here mention that at this time prime beef and mutton were procurable at from one penny to three pence a pound.

After harvest work was done and I had time to visit Adelaide, I met with the same lack of encouragement wherever I spoke of my discovery for a locomotive thrasher, except from one individual at that time.

A sort of club had been formed of town gentlemen, who, with farmers, used to dine together at an ordinary at Payne's Hotel (now known as the Exchange Hotel, in Hindley Street), and here discussions on agricultural subjects used to be introduced. Out of this gathering a committee was formed, called the "Corn Exchange Committee." I can remember some of the names :—Messrs. Alderman Peacock, Bentham Neales, Joseph Johnson (of the Reedbeds), Hamilton, and his partner Henderson, corn merchants, their managing clerk, Thornber, G. Stevenson, Weaver, Southam, Herbert, Robert Smith, Hogarth, and others. The necessity of some contrivance to aid farmers in harvesting having been made so apparent at the previous harvest, the committeemen who had been appointed took the matter up with zeal, and gave notice in the papers that they would be prepared to give a reward for the best invention to be exhibited to the committee, and advertised a day for the first meeting to be in the month of September following (1843), so as to allow time for the construction of machines before the coming harvest. At this time more than one machinist was engaged in constructing *ordinary fixed thrashing machines*, and, in consequence, of all those who were setting their wits at work to bring out a field-machine none gave their energies and thoughts to the principle of a mower or cutter, except myself. I did not waver; I had placed my ideas and plan before the late Mr. Thomas Hudson Beare, and he was the person to whom I have alluded as the only one who saw the correctness of my plan, and he set to work to oblige me, and constructed for me a *working model* entirely on my own principle, and was with me when it was exhibited before the Corn Exchange Committee on the appointed day, when a number of models and plans were also presented, but mine was the only one which proposed to deal with the heads only, as reported in the *Observer* and *Register* papers. At this meeting Alderman Peacock was in the chair, and the committee passed the resolution at the end of this paper. But there was one person present at the exhibition, neither on the committee nor an exhibitor (Mr. John Ridley), who approved of my principle and afterwards adopted it, and a short time before the next harvest (1843) constructed one machine which embraced my ideas of a horizontal projecting comb, and revolving beaters driven by belts from the carriage wheels. Old colonists will remember that this first reaper was propelled by a pair of horses working behind the machine, harnessed to a long pole; but even with this awkward rig, the principle of taking the grain and leaving the straw standing was proved to be the right thing for the country and climate.

Harvest 1843-44. I give the estimated yield of this season to have been 280,000 bushels. I had a fine crop of over thirty bushels an acre. A few standing crops were gathered by Mr. Ridley's first machine, the only one constructed that season. Mr. Ridley after employing it on a few of the standing crops he had purchased, as well as some of his own near Adelaide, was kind enough to send me a man with horses and machine, and by this means my crop was gathered. Prices fell materially after the first field-machine sample reached the market. Several fixed thrashing machines had been constructed, and were at work at the stacks. I may here mention that one of the arguments against the stripper, and which was much dwelt on, was that the crop having to remain until fully ripe, and being harvested and bagged in such a dry state, became flinty. Well, as soon as the way of shipping to England was found to answer, the dryness of our grain became an advantage, as it arrived in such good condition as to maintain the top price in London, as it has always done against the world. It has also been said the land by the use of this system of harvesting is both exhausted and rendered foul. To these complaints it is answered that the fault is in growing wheat crop after wheat crop, which is neither necessary nor wise, and was only adopted as a necessity when the farms were small, and which process now, under more liberal land laws, is *inexcusable*.

December, 1843.—As I have mentioned, I had been favoured by Mr. Ridley with the use of the first machine which was constructed to thrash a standing crop. I explain I had a large yield, and sold part of it at 3s. 6d. a bushel, but could not dispose of more than a few loads, and was advised to ship the remainder of the crop I had for sale by a vessel about to start to New Zealand; and I hurried the stock down and consigned the same through an Adelaide firm to a house in New Zealand. After patiently waiting for the return, which, to my great inconvenience, proved a blank, the report came that the whole cargo was condemned as unsound. A large quantity of smutty wheat being placed on board above mine, the whole was condemned and sold as a damaged cargo, and I got no return, and had only to console myself that the proceeds of the sale were admitted to have covered freight and charges; and so the bulk of my crop was a total loss of as fine a sample of wheat as was ever shipped. Before the following harvest Mr. Marshal constructed my first machine, and Mr. Ridley built more than one machine. Other colonists also took advantage of my public gift of the invention, which I made the day after the Committee gave their decision on the merits of the plans presented. (*See* Appendix.) To Mr. Thornber, the Honorary Secretary of the Corn Exchange Committee, I entrusted my model, with the expression that it was at the service of the public, and so it has remained. The machine built for me by Mr. Marshal differed from all others at first built, as I dispensed with a drum, and had a long inclined plane, which was in accordance with my first ideas, and has since been generally approached.

COPY OF REPORT EXTRACTED FROM *Register*, *September* 23, 1842 :—

"At a meeting of the Corn Exchange Committee, held at Payne's Hotel on Tuesday, Wednesday, and Thursday evenings, when thirteen drawings and plans (models) were exhibited, it was resolved that this meeting, having carefully examined the models and plans submitted to it, is of opinion that no machine has been exhibited which the Committee feel justified in recommending for general adoption ; but the plan of Mr. Swingler presenting some ideas which the Committee are desirous of seeing developed in a working model, they have awarded him the sum of three pounds to place one at their disposal.

"(Signed) WM. PEACOCK,
"*Chairman of Committee.*"

Note.—No notice of any action as to the plan they considered worthy of support was ever made public. A few of the exhibitors shortly after the meeting constructed cutting machines, which were never successfully used. The one designed to gather the grain only, as has been shown, was adopted by Mr. Ridley in the first instance, and its value proved by him. The inventor of it and Mr. Ridley (who constructed the first machine on the principle) have been spared to rejoice in the yearly-increasing benefit the same has conferred on the inhabitants of South Australia.

In this chapter, I would wish to contrast 1839-40, 120 acres, yield 25 bushels each acre=3,000 at 15$s.$ a bushel, £2,250, with 1874-75, 839,638 acres, yield 11 bushels 45 lbs.=9,862,693, at 5$s.$ 5$d.$ a bushel, £2,670,729. It must not be forgotten that the first of these crops was from good virgin soil. The second from a large proportion of second and third-rate land,

and much of it reduced in productiveness after years of the usual colonial exhausting courses of wheat after wheat, as long as a fractional yield can be got. Remember also that this result was not obtained until after Mr. Strangways succeeded in carrying his Land Reform Bill, with the principle of credit to agriculturists, by which the land sharks were baffled, and farmers enabled to obtain larger quantities of land direct from the Government, prices per acre also ruling higher, to the benefit of the land fund.

I think it proper here to mention that in the session of 1882 the Parliament, during the ministry of the Honourable J. C. Bray, passed a vote for the sum of £250 on my behalf, as a reward for the improvements I had introduced in harvesting machinery. This recognition of my claim I here gratefully acknowledge.

CHAPTER V.

IN this chapter I propose to relate the doings of three gangs of desperadoes who, after alternate intervals of hard work and deep drinking bouts, thought to adopt with impunity a course of plunder on the scattered stations newly settled, when there was only a small and recently established police force, whom they lightly esteemed as being inexperienced. They were also emboldened by the deplorable state of disunion amongst the Government officials, which had been notorious for some time previous. I must first remark that after Magee had been punished with death, and his mates with transportation for life, it in a short time became apparent that such severe examples had lost their effect, especially on the following parties :—First, Green and Wilson, who commenced their career by stealing horses; then Curran, Hughes, and Fox started, in the most foolhardy manner, on their short course of bushranging. All these men found to their sorrow that an efficient police force had been established.

The career of Curran, Hughes, and Fox, who started on their expedition in the neighbourhood of Gawler Town, in which part of the country they had been at work, was as follows : —The first action in their new or renewed pursuit was a visit to the hut of a Mr. Pfender, five miles from Gawler Town, and finding only the wife at home they stuck her up, as they said, for a drink. This establishment was a sly grog shop. After supplying themselves to their hearts' content, they next demanded money of her. To this she demurred most resolutely, and as she managed to escape and get outside the hut, they fired at her, but did not wound her. They then departed after taking what they chose. Information was quickly given to a policeman in the infant settlement, then at Gawler Town; accordingly a mounted trooper started during the night to warn people on the few detached stations in the neighbourhood, to put them on their guard. Amongst others he called at Captain Walker's sheep station, not more than three miles from Pfender's residence. Mr. M—— was then in charge as manager, and from him I obtained the following particulars:—

"About 4 A.M. I and the three men, all of them ex-convicts, were aroused by a trooper calling us up to inform us that armed bushrangers were in the neighbourhood, who had, the previous evening, attacked and robbed Pfender's hut, and had fired at his wife. They desired us to be on our guard. I accordingly set a watch until daylight, and made myself as easy as possible. At sunrise the two flocks were sent out, the bullock driver (the third man) also left the hut on his duties, and I was left alone, but I was not favoured with any visitors during their absence. At 10 o'clock, or thereabouts, the three men returned as usual to breakfast, the sheep being left coiling. I observed three other men also with them, named Curran, Hughes, and Fox. I did not take much notice of them, as they had frequently called as they passed to their work, but I observed they had guns in their hands. Even this did not strike me as anything unusual. Shortly after their arrival one of them, Curran, walked into my apartment and seated himself without ceremony. He had still his piece in his hand. He commenced the conversation by asking me if they could have tucker, to which I replied they could when the men's breakfast was ready. He said, 'Oh! but we must have something for the road as well.' I now perceived the other men, one at the door of my room and the other at a window, and that they also had their firearms in their hands: and now my eyes were opened as to their character and business, and I felt my position as stuck up in a civil sort of way, so I asked Curran, in answer to his demand, if they had taken to the bush. He answered, 'Yes,' in a very cool and indifferent manner. I then said, 'Why have you done this?' He answered, 'It is all through the cursed drink.' Then

I asked, 'Well, what do you want of me? I will give you nothing; what you get here you must take yourself.' 'Well, we do not want much; to begin with, where is the damper?' I pointed to a large one on the shelf, which he took down and said, 'Is that all you have got?' I said, 'All that is ready baked.' 'Well, I won't take it all,' and then he cut it in half, and put one part in a bag. Then he demanded tea and sugar, and took part of my stock, and asked for meat. I said, 'There was none cooked, but some in the pot boiling.' 'Well, we will wait till it is done.' During this time they took caps, powder, and shot, half of what I possessed; so that, under the circumstances, forbearance and generosity marked their conduct. Their conduct was the more surprising as to their coolness, and the little haste they showed, as my men must have told them of the visit of the police, and that a hue and cry had been raised some hours before their arrival. However, they patiently waited till the meat was ready for them, and then they produced a bottle of brandy, and insisted on all hands taking a drain as a parting compliment, and in this manner departed; before which I said to Curran, ' You have told me that drink has brought you to this, and why do you carry it about with you, as your continued indulgence will be likely to bring you into the hands of the police, and to punishment?' Curran then threw the empty bottle away, saying, ' There, that is the last b—— drop we will get,' and then broke out in violent threats against several settlers, especially against Captain Hall, who had a station near us. Before this I had noticed Fox to be quiet, soft-looking, and half-hearted in the work. I spoke to him aside, and urged him to give his bad companions the slip as soon as possible. This he promised me he would do. They left peaceably, and wished me good morning.

"When they had disappeared I called the men in, and asked how it happened these fellows came in with them. They excused themselves by saying, 'They joined us while we were out in the bush as we were about to return to breakfast, and admitted to us that they had turned out. On which we exacted from them promises that they would not take more than what they wanted to carry them on with, nor injure any one on the station, or do any mischief, but confine themselves to what they required for the road.' They must have been surprised at my manner towards them on their first arrival, as they would naturally think I would be down on them, as they term it, from the warning I had received from the police. After they had left I sent as quickly as possible to Gawler Town information how I had been interviewed; but then this was by the hands of a man who, although in our employment, was one of the same class as the bushrangers; or, as they say, one who had 'been in trouble,' so that he would not be likely to hurry himself."

It will be seen in the course of this narrative how exactly and speedily Mr. M——'s warning prediction to these men came to pass, and how soon two of them suffered the extreme penalty of the law. The picture this chapter gives is without exaggeration, and conveys to readers who have followed us in settling in the colony, and to others, some idea of what risks and trying circumstances those of us had to endure who had undertaken to form out-settlements, and what cool courage and tact were often required to be exhibited by pioneers. It may be asserted that if Mr. M—— had not commanded the respect and goodwill of the men under him how extremely probable it would have been that they would have merely absented themselves, and have left the depredators at liberty to sack the hut and to maltreat their overseer. Many may disapprove of their conduct in acting as neutrals on such an occasion, and it may be only those who have been placed in similar difficulties who will be able to appreciate such half-and-half protection as these men adopted towards their overseer; but it must be remembered that had they behaved in a more decided manner they would have been "bailed-up" themselves, *i.e.*, tied up to trees, and the manager would then have been at the mercy of desperate men excited by resistance, and left without the presence of even friendly neutrals. From my own experience of such characters, I believe that human beings, however low they may have descended in sin and crime, have yet a soft spot in their hearts, however small, which may be worked upon when reason has not been lost by drink.

As I was the last person who fell into the hands of these our first bushrangers, and was to some extent the means of their arrest, I will continue the narrative with my own experience in their short detention of me. Their career was a brief one. Some hours after leaving Captain Walker's sheep station four mounted policemen were sent in pursuit of them, but did not succeed in capturing them, although so close on their heels. They next appeared in the neighbourhood of Mount Crawford at a temporary station, where a Mr. Crawford with cattle overland had settled. It so happened that I started from Adelaide a day or two after the bushrangers commenced this tour. On calling at Mr. Crawford's hut I found a man in charge—an old soldier—who surprised me with the information that the night before his hut had been stuck up by three armed men, that they took firearms, ammunition, and rations, and had greatly alarmed him, as he was all alone ; that they stopped for the night, and he pointed out the direction they had taken in leaving that morning. As I had not heard of their doings in the neighbourhood of Gawler Town, I did not know what to make of this information. He pointed to a large gum tree about one hundred yards from the hut, and told me they practised their pieces on it, attempting to hit that mark ; but, said he, " They were poor shots, making more misses than hits." The following morning, on riding a few miles towards Woodside as it is now called, I came upon a party of troopers who were camped there. From them I understood they were after two horse-stealers, and that a reward of two hundred pounds was offered for their apprehension. They were much surprised at my information when I told them what I had heard only a few miles away at Mount Crawford about the bushrangers. I also told them that by what the old soldier told me, I thought they had taken to the overland track, *i.e.*, gone easterly. To this they replied that they were acting under orders, and must confine themselves to the course pointed out to them. At this time the officer in command of them, Alford, had left them to obtain fresh orders from head-quarters.

I then continued on my own course south through the Mount Barker district to my cattle station, and remained one night there, and was busy in mustering cattle. I afterwards returned towards Adelaide, and about 3 P.M. reached Crafer's old bush pub., intending to refresh myself and feed my horse, as I had been riding him three days, and had travelled many hours a day. As I approached the slab hut I saw a great bustle about the place ; but this was not unusual, as a number of splitters and sawyers employed in this part of the Tiers were in the habit of frequenting that place to knock down, as they called it, their hard-earned cheques—working like horses, and spending like asses. I alighted at the stable door, close to the hut, and drove my tired cob into the stable, calling for the ostler. As no ostler appeared, I pushed my way through the crowded tap-room and bar, all in one, and with some trouble entered the private room. On turning round to give my orders, I saw standing at the door of the room a big fellow with a horse pistol in his hand, which he presented at me and said, " Here's another b—— jimmy ; I'll walk into him." I then heard a voice, which I knew to be Black Dick's, a well-known splitter, from whom I had bought much timber, say, " Let him alone ; he's all right. He carries no blunt with him ; he's just in from the bush."

I now found I had stepped into a lion's den, and that these were the veritable bushrangers, whose path I had crossed two days before, now drawn back by the temptation of drink to what proved to be their last carouse. I, however, put the best face I could on the position I found myself in, and said in as jolly a manner as I could command, " None of your gammon, young man ; Mrs. Crafer, send me in bread and cheese and brandy and water, and send Hardyman, the ostler, to feed my horse." I could now see one of the men (Hughes) breaking open a brandy case, and that the landlady and ostler were bailed up behind the counter. I shall never forget the terror-stricken faces of these two persons, both as pale as death. Now a scuffle occurred, and I saw a man bolt out and run past the window and heard a shot fired. Curran, who had bailed up and threatened me, had another prisoner bailed up in the corner of the tap-room out of my sight, who, observing Curran's attention taken off himself, took advantage to make a rush out of the door with Curran after him. I have since been told that one of the tiersmen pushed Curran's arm on one side, thereby probably saving the escaping man's life, as they were so few yards apart. I now saw my chance, and pushed my way through the half-drunken crowd, who were enjoying the treat the bushrangers were affording them with stolen goods. On reaching the stable-door I fortunately found my cob coming out ready for me, as he had found no provender. I sprang on his back, and had not time to recover my stirrups, but stuck my spurs into his sides, when Curran, returning from the chase, met me and grabbed, intending to unhorse me. I struck him on the head with the heavy loaded handle of my stockwhip and felled him to the ground. His horse-pistol having been discharged, I think he must have cast it away when he missed his man, or he would have struck me with it if he had kept it, and our positions would probably have been reversed. At this time he, as well as all hands, was about half drunk. I then pushed my horse as fast up the hill as he could carry me towards town, feeling as I mounted the rise that a shot might follow me at any moment. When I had ridden about half-way I met Crafer, the landlord, on a fast horse. I told him what was going on, and that the bushrangers were treating themselves and the houseful of tiersmen to the best in his house, and that his wife and servants were bailed up. I urged him to return for the police, and that he was welcome to the reward, as I was sufficiently thankful I had escaped out of their hands unharmed, except by the loss of my lunch. He took my advice and said to me, "What good can I do unarmed against armed men and all their friends, whom they have been treating with my stuff?" My pace was necessarily slow, and he was mounted on a remarkably fast horse, so before I reached town I met Crafer with a party of mounted police at full gallop, who found the bushrangers helplessly drunk, and the handcuffs were put on them without a struggle. On the following morning they were conveyed to Adelaide and by the Police Magistrate committed on a capital charge for trial to the Supreme Court. Here I may mention that on meeting the police I renewed my declaration that I should not put in any claim on the reward, and stipulated that I should not be called on to give evidence against them, unless such should be absolutely required. Prudence dictated this course, as in the pursuit of my business I was so much exposed to danger from that class of men. I was present at their trial, but was not called as a witness.

After sentence had been passed on the bushrangers they were first confined in the insecure gaol of which jolly old Ashton was governor. He had a number of short-sentenced prisoners under his charge, who were marched out daily to work on the roads, and were locked up at night in a wooden building. In a small stone building, called by the prisoners "the stone jug," Curran, Hughes, and Fox were confined. Whilst these men were under the charge of Mr. Ashton he was informed one night by one of the guards, named Kennedy, that he had reason to believe by the riotous conduct of the prisoners after they were locked in for the night that they meditated an outbreak, and that he feared they were filing the rivets of their irons. Mr. Ashton immediately on hearing this report sent to the horse-police barracks for a file of men with loaded carbines. Inspector Tolmer was quickly on the spot with his men. After these were placed around the building, the door was opened by himself and the turnkey. The prisoners being cautioned by him (he had at all times a marvellous influence over them) and also in dread of the carbines in the hands of the police, they allowed their irons to be examined and the cut rivets renewed, without any resistance, but they were left for the night with extra guards over them. In the morning Mr. Ashton waited upon the Governor, and requested that Curran, Hughes, and Fox, and two other prisoners who had received heavy sentences, might be removed and placed at the horse-police barracks, in charge of the police. This request was complied with, and the five prisoners were removed accordingly, and confined in the sergeants' day-room, to enter which it was necessary to pass through the guard-room. On one side of the day-room temporary beds were made up on the floor for the five prisoners, who were all ironed. They were under the especial charge of Sergeant-major Alford, who had a mattress on the table in the same room, on which he rested at night. In the outer or guard-room, in bunks, slept three or more men with loaded carbines ready, a sentinel also pacing backwards and forwards between the rooms. In the first instance the window of the day-room was not guarded by iron bars. This insecurity, on the report of the inspector, was ordered by the authorities to be rectified, and a smith was sent to do the work. Shortly after this was done, the prisoners were ordered to turn in, and while the sergeant-major was reclining on his mattress, the guard aroused him by touching his leg and whispered to him that the prisoners were filing their irons; on which he got up quietly and passed into the guard-room, and said to the men, "I will take a drink of water," in a loud voice, to blind the prisoners, so that they should not suspect their actions to have been detected. He then charged the men in a whisper to have their pieces in their hands, and on his making a signal, to rush into the day-room and present their carbines, and on his giving the order, to fire if the prisoners did not surrender. He gave them to understand that he would return to his mattress and lie down as if all was right, and allow the prisoners to continue their work until he gave the signal, which he shortly did, by stripping off their blankets by a pull from the ends at their feet. They had, in order to effect their object, covered their heads with their blankets, and drawn up their knees so as to reach the rivets, and to disguise the working of the files kept up a loud snoring, feigning sleep. Five loaded pieces being presented at them, they obeyed the order to rise and pass across the room, and seat themselves on a form, where they were kept till morning. Inspector Tolmer had been called in, and in the morning communicated to Mr. Ashton the attempt to escape made by the prisoners. Mr. Ashton arrived with a smith and heavy irons; the prisoners' lighter irons were taken off, and several of the rivets were found to have the heads filed off, when the heavier were substituted for the light ones. On the beds being searched, the tools they had used were found, and some screws to be put in place of the rivets intended to be removed. The smith who had been previously employed to fix the iron bars on the windows was afterwards charged with dropping the implements and screws, the latter being the size of those used by him in fixing the bars. He stoutly denied the charge, but was not believed. The prisoners were well known to have friends and confederates outside who would render them any assistance in their power.

The prisoners, up to the night on which they made this attempt, had conducted themselves in a most quiet and orderly manner, in order to allay suspicion; but now they commenced to behave in a most disgusting and riotous style. Fox and two other prisoners were removed, and Curran and Hughes only were left, who continued their reckless behaviour to the last.

The sentence of death was in the case of Fox commuted to transportation for life, but Hughes and Curran were left to suffer the extreme penalty of the law. The Colonial Chaplain (Mr. Howard) visited them in their cell, but for some unaccountable whim they took a dislike to this amiable clergyman, and wished to see the late Rev. T. Q. Stow, who attended them in the barracks and on the gallows, and was on the platform when the bolt was drawn. His efforts to arouse them to a proper sense of the awful position in which they stood were wholly fruitless.

On the fatal morning, on the executioner entering to pinion them, Hughes refused to submit to him, and addressed him in unmentionable language, calling on him to pull off his mask, and finished by knocking him down, when Mr. Ashton had to interfere. After being pinioned Hughes required a lighted pipe to be furnished him, and continued to smoke until he reached the gallows, which was erected in the police yard to guard against a rescue. At the gallows, Hughes bent himself so as to catch his pipe, which he cast away, saying "No b—— man shall smoke my pipe." At length Curran, who in action had always taken a leading part, now called on Hughes to be quiet, and die like a man. To the last this most reckless mortal continued his mad career, for at the sound of the withdrawing of the bolt setting free the scaffold-flap he made a spring, and caught with his feet on the sides of the opening, and it was necessary for the hangman to seize his legs to pull him through the opened space; thus, by resisting his inevitable fate, he lengthened his last sufferings.

It is necessary to step a little out of the course of events in order to give Mr. Alford's account of the time I met with his party. He had been hastily despatched with three troopers to catch Green and Wilson, who had first stolen from Mr. John Hallett a quantity of rations. With the stolen rations they crossed the Mount Lofty Range, and visiting Mrs. Murdoch, robbed her of two horses. Mr. Alford and his party had returned from the Wellington Crossing on hearing that the men they were pursuing had crossed, as he deemed it necessary to have the horses shod, and to be well found in rations and outfit for a stern chase through such a desert and unsettled country as they would have to travel. He therefore decided to leave his men where I saw them, and report himself at head-quarters. The day after I saw his men, on his way to town with led horses, he called at a settler's place on the Onkaparinga River, Mr. Richardson's, and there had a drink of milk; at the same time a young man, a stranger, was supplied with a drink. In that neighbourhood Mr. Alford saw a shepherd, who told him that on his round the day previous he saw three men firing at a gum tree.

Mr. Alford continued towards town at a slow pace, and passed Crafer's public-house without calling, nor did he see anything remarkable in passing. Before he reached Adelaide he met Inspector Edwards with a party of police, and from him he received information of the outbreak of Curran, Hughes, and Fox, and that there was a reward of £100 for the arrest of each of those men, and that he was after them. Mr. A., on seeing their description. declared at once he had seen one of them drinking milk at Mr. Richardson's, and now supposed the whole of them must have been on the road he had followed, and that two might have been before him at Crafer's, and the one he saw, whom he pronounced to the inspector to be Fox, would be behind him. Having given to the inspector a report of what he had ascertained of the men he had been after—that they had crossed the Murray—he was ordered to continue on and report himself. This report made at head-quarters, he was instructed to go back the next day to bring in his men, as it was considered Green and Wilson, on fresh horses, had got too long a start to be overtaken.

These men having made good their escape from this colony, the Government took the first opportunity by ship to forward to Melbourne information as to the crimes of Green and Wilson, a description of them, and the reward offered for their apprehension, and they were arrested by two of our officers on their way from Sydney. These policemen, namely Corporal Wilkie and Private Higgins, having landed some prisoners who had been transported to Sydney, had to take their passage back to Adelaide viâ Melbourne. As the vessel was stopping a few days there, these men spent their time on shore, and soon got wind of the reward out for Green and Wilson, and were not long in finding them and taking them before the Police Magistrate, who remanded them to Adelaide. On their being charged at the Police Court in Adelaide with stealing Mrs. Murdoch's horses, evidence was wanting to connect them with the stolen animals, and so they were remanded from time to time that the horses might be procured. Nevertheless, Corporal Wilkie and Private Higgins received the reward for their arrest.

An intelligent and active officer, Sergeant N——, was selected, and sent to Victoria to collect evidence and obtain the horses, to complete the case against the criminals, and make perfect the work his predecessors had left undone. He had ample powers given him, and a letter from our Governor to the Officer Administering the Government of Victoria (or Port Phillip, as that settlement was then called), requesting that every assistance might be rendered to him. Sergeant N—— was accompanied on the expedition by Mr. Lorrimer, then manager of the station from which the horses had been stolen, that he might identify and claim them when found. The sergeant and his companion started for Melbourne in a small vessel, and the passage was most boisterous throughout. On arriving off Port Phillip Heads the tempestuous weather and heavy sea obliged the captain to bear up for Sydney, his final destination, and there our passengers had to land and take their passage back to Melbourne by the first sailing ship bound thither. On arriving at Melbourne the sergeant presented his credentials, on which a mounted trooper was placed at his service. He soon discovered the public-house at which Green and Wilson put up, and where they disposed of the horses, and was informed that three men were engaged in the sale of them, two answering to the description of Green and Wilson, and a third, a man who represented himself to be their master.

As to the acting gentleman-master, our officer got a particular description of him, and concluded that he was Morgan, who, having been transported for life from our colony, was reported to have escaped from Van Diemen's Land, and was supposed to have landed at or near Portland Bay. In coming to this conclusion Sergeant N—— was not supported by the Melbourne police, who held a contrary opinion; but he acted on his own judgment, founded on the description gained as to the extreme tallness of the man, his pleasant countenance, the colour of his eyes and hair, and the great probability of his having been picked up by his old comrades, Green and Wilson, as they passed through the Portland Bay district. As will be seen in the sequel, the sergeant was correct in his assumption. It now became doubly important that this third man should be secured. From the landlord spoken of he obtained much information, also from the police, and on following this up step by step, he heard that a horse answering the description of one of the stolen ones had been seen in the possession of a sporting innkeeper, well known in all the colonies. On him he waited, and on the question being put to him, "Do you know anything of such and such a horse?" he answered, "I neither know nor care." "Then you may expect to hear from me again," replied Sergeant N——. After this our active officer, on a visit to the horse police barracks, seeing the horses brought in from the paddock to be fed, on casting his eyes over them, saw a horse which he thought answered to the description of one of the stolen ones, and asked if that was a police horse? The answer was, "No, that horse belongs to an hotel-keeper, and is sent here to be under treatment by our farrier. His owner is Mr. ——." Now, this being the individual from whom he had received such an unsatisfactory answer to his question, he felt the scent was getting hot. The horse was immediately caught, and on the water brush being applied to his long coat, at the place where Mrs. Murdoch's station brand should be, it was visible. On the following morning the overseer confirmed the claim, and the case was taken before the Police Magistrate, and on the razor being employed, the part was shaved and the brand shown perfect.

A decision in favour of the claimant was made, and an order given to remove the horse to Adelaide, much to the annoyance of the sporting landlord. This first step successfully gained, and also some information of the probable whereabouts of the other horse, arrangements for a bush trip were made, on which our officer was accompanied by a mounted trooper. The scent being closely followed, the second horse was found in the possession of a sheep farmer, at a station on the river Plenty, and was given up. To make the case complete it was now only necessary to secure the third man, but very slight traces had yet been found of him. After riding many miles and visiting many stations the officers made a station on the Rocky River, at about one hundred miles from Melbourne. To this station the scent had been followed up, however slight and contradictory the evidence appeared. On entering the men's hut, amongst a number of assigned men, Sergeant N—— discovered him whom he was seeking. On challenging him by the name of Morgan, he denied that was his name, and said he had never been in South Australia. He was now seen with only one arm. Nevertheless, although the sergeant had not heard that he had been so maimed, he took him into custody. It may be mentioned here that it was afterwards reported to our officer that the Melbourne police had some months previously made an attack on a party of bushrangers, and after an exchange of shots the bushrangers had escaped with one of their number wounded. This was now found to be Morgan. At a subsequent period he confessed that he was the man whom the police wounded, and said that a shepherd had cut off the shattered part of his arm and bound it up. It was still a green, unhealed wound at the time of his arrest. He had adopted the quiet life of a shepherd in the hopes of recruiting himself and of getting his arm healed.

Morgan had to walk to Melbourne, a hundred miles, as Sergeant N—— was unable to procure any conveyance. In this shattered state, this iron man, as I have before called him, walked the whole distance, and with apparent ease.

With this complete array of evidence our officer returned to Adelaide, and arrived at the port early enough to prevent the release of the prisoners. Ill luck fell against them, for on this day only an order had been obtained for their release on small bail. They thus were soon presented again before the Police Magistrate, and committed for trial at the next Criminal Sittings for horse-stealing, where also Morgan was present to be used as a witness.

They were in due course tried by Judge Cooper. On the day of their trial I was at the court before the business commenced. In the absence of any public court-house, the judge had fitted up a large outer room, now part of the Bushmen's Club House. Here, before the doors were opened, I saw the prisoner Morgan in charge of the police, pacing backwards and forwards under a verandah, like a wild beast in a den; and here an instance of his extraordinary character and hardihood was manifested, for on his perceiving an officer of police in uniform approaching, on recognising him he called out, " Ah, Alford ! " in a jocular manner, holding up the stump of his shattered and unhealed arm, " you cannot handcuff me round a gum tree now, as I have been winged since I saw you," alluding in this joking manner to the horrid position in which he was left—four days and four nights without food or water—after being arrested by Mr. Alford at Encounter Bay. Morgan was at this time still under age, and was at that place and time to appear before the judge, with the probability present to him of return to imprisonment for life. That he should under such circumstances call attention to two such dreadful occurrences in his short life in this jocular manner is unparalleled. I had it from good authority that after his arrival in Adelaide, when the colonial surgeon examined his arm and found he could not do anything for him, he himself gave the information that, after the bone was shattered, a shepherd cut off with a knife the part of the limb hanging by the sinews. Perhaps the most striking feature in his conduct was that he exhibited no malice in his manner to Serjeant-major Alford, who had been the agent in fastening on him his grievous punishments. Many other circumstances have been related of him ; one I had from good authority, viz., that when at Encounter Bay, engaged at fishery, he was said to have been crossing between the mainland and Granite Island with a whaler, both the worse for drink wading along the ridge of connection, when they both staggered into deep water. Morgan released himself from the grip of his comrade and was saved, but his mate was drowned. Before this occurrence something similar happened at Adelaide to a man of the same name, and some say it was this Morgan, but for that I have no certain authority ; but there is no doubt that two men crossing the River Torrens when in flood, by a fallen tree, at mid stream wrangled, and both fell in, and here the man of the name of Morgan escaped, and the other was carried away by the flood and perished.

It has been supposed, but I think without foundation, that Morgan was a relation of the notorious bushranger Morgan, who so long and with such impunity defied the police of the neighbouring colonies, and was at length shot down in a treacherous manner, as men of his class would say, but a man who outlaws himself must take the consequences.

At the Criminal Sittings on the 7th November, 1840, Green and Wilson were brought up for trial as before mentioned, and on the overwhelming evidence produced against them were found guilty of horse-stealing, and sentenced to transportation for life.

Morgan was produced as a witness to prove the sale of the horses, but his evidence was not admitted or required. He was subsequently transported as an escaped convict, and it is to be hoped that he fell into good hands, for there was little hope that he would recover from his wound or long survive it. No information has been met with as to what happened to him after he was banished from this colony the second time.

CHAPTER VI.

I HAVE already mentioned the suspicious and mysterious arrival of Foley, Stone, and Stanley. I propose continuing their histories, in which will be narrated a few more instances of the exciting work which such visitors created for the police as well as for the settlers. In the confession from Foley and Stone, they explained that in coming to this settlement they followed the coast between the Coorong and the sea, and reached the whaling stations at Encounter Bay. Here Foley separated from his travelling companions and went into business on his own account; the others made their way to Adelaide, and there cut the throat of one of the horses, as previously related. It was afterwards proved that Foley rode his own horse—at any rate that horse was not successfully claimed; the other two men stole the horses they rode from Mr. Henty, of Portland Bay. Foley continued in the neighbourhood of the fisheries, and obtained rations and other supplies in exchange for kangaroos and game. He was not in the habit of making his visits there except when fully armed with a double-barrelled gun, and two brace of pistols. On this and other accounts he was looked upon with suspicion and some dread, and there was a desire on the part of the officers at the fishery to get rid of him; so a communication was forwarded to the authorities in Adelaide that he was a suspicious character, and would arrive on a certain day in town. The horse he was riding was suspected to be a stolen one. To entrap him and induce him to carry a despatch to Adelaide, he was offered a good reward on his delivering a packet to the manager of the South Australian Bank, Mr. E. Stephens. He started without hesitation and in good faith, and arrived late in the evening of the day appointed. He was fully armed as usual. On entering the Bank-yard gate, he dismounted, and unslung his gun from his back, in which manner he was accustomed to carry it, and fastened his horse to the fence, unconscious of the arrangements which had been made for his reception and capture. On knocking at the back door of the manager's residence a servant appeared, of whom he asked if "Mr. Stephens was at home;" and, on being answered "Yes," he delivered his missive. He was asked in to take tea; the invitation was accepted; he was shown into a room and took a seat, placing his gun near him. In a short time his suspicions were aroused on hearing several persons whispering, and he at once rose, slung his gun, walked out into the yard, and, seizing the bridle of his horse, prepared to mount. At the same moment the reins were grasped by a policeman on the opposite side of the horse, but he threw himself into the saddle, drew a pistol, and presenting it at the man who was detaining him, threatened to shoot him. The pistol was seized by his assailant, and in the struggle it did not explode, but the hammer flew off, and before Foley could draw a second pistol he received a blow from a weapon on the back of his head, which felled him to the ground. Inspector Inman, who was in the house expecting Foley's arrival, on hearing cries of murder rushed out and struck the blow. Foley was taken to prison and his wound was dressed. Mr. J. B. Hack was also present in the yard, as he had come by appointment to examine the horse, suspected to be one he had lost. Foley was detained in prison on a remand on the charge of horse-stealing, and suspected to be a runaway convict from Sydney. His conduct, however, in prison was so good that he was engaged by the Government to assist the police in seeking for two men who were suspected to have stolen horses from Mr. Hack, and to have broken into a store, and supplied themselves with rations, and were heard of near the Lake. The men who were supposed to have committed these crimes were Stone and Stanley, who had done so to escape from the province, as they were aware they were enquired after on account of the horses they had stolen to reach this colony, and so wanted similar conveniences to take their departure. I may mention that the man who had the struggle with Foley was an ex-prisoner, and had been appointed acting-gaoler, and afterwards, with Foley, consented to assist in taking his former associates; but then it was explained that Foley had a private "down" on them, as having stolen from him a favourite kangaroo dog. So it is seen there had been a breach of "honour among thieves," and to assist the police "a thief was set to catch a thief," carrying out the old proverb.

To take these horse-stealers a strong party was formed, consisting of Superintendent Inman, Sergeant Alford, Mr. Stephen Hack, and three policemen, all well mounted and armed, with Foley also on horseback as tracker. The country they were going to scour was the then densely thick scrubby country skirting Lake Alexandrina, where the police would frequently by necessity be separated, and so a strong muster was called for. They were led by Foley to a creek which since the time of their visit has been named the Inman, after the commander of the party. Arrived at this place, Foley gave the information that they were in the neighbourhood of the camping grounds he frequented before he was taken, and that his tent was within a mile or so from them. He made a request to Mr. Inman to be allowed to go with one man to the place to procure his blankets and other things, to which request Mr. Inman replied, "If Sergeant Alford chooses to go with you I will allow him to do so." Mr. Alford did not hesitate. But Foley was told by the Superintendent that he would instruct the Sergeant to shoot him if he attempted to escape, and handed to Mr. Alford an additional brace of pistols. They accordingly started, the remainder of the party waiting till they returned. On their way Foley said to Mr. Alford, "Now I will show you how I foiled those who sought to find out my retreat." On their arriving at a patch of close-growing dwarf teatree scrub, such as was often in that day found in rich bottoms and at the mouth of gullies, Foley pulled up and said, "There in the middle of that clump is my small tent;" but though they were in the saddle Mr. Alford could see nothing but the deep green of the close-growing teatree, with no opening or passage visible; and so addressed Foley—" Now understand, if you attempt any game on me to escape, I shall obey orders and shoot you. Are there any of your companions here—Stanley, or any other man? for if anyone appears I shall shoot you first." No, Sergeant," was the reply; " I am acting honest, as I have promised the Superintendent. Never fear. We must dismount, and I will show you how to reach my tent." On this he was ordered to dismount and show the tent. This he did by spreading the teatree, which reached in height to their shoulders, with each hand, as in swimming, and then stepped forward on one foot, and then advanced in the same manner on the other foot in an exact line, calling on Mr. A. to follow, and act in the same way, the plants rising unruffled behind them, not being trodden down, and showing no track. In about 100 yards so passed over, they reached a round place where the plant had been cut and cleared away; and now appeared a small tent, constructed in the gipsy fashion—a piece of canvas stretched over bent sticks, large enough to allow one man to lie down in, and to hold his necessary traps, which were found safe, the retreat having escaped the eyes of his previous mates. Before these things were rolled up in his blankets he gave to Mr. Alford a Jew's harp, with which, he said, he amused himself during his lonely nights. Foley explained that he never entered or left over the same ground, and, laughing at the Sergeant, said— "You policemen would never have discovered my hiding-place, for I could have shot any one approaching."

On their return Mr. Inman continued the search for the horse-stealers, and after some time they found wurlies, which had been recently used, and other traces which led them to be wary. From the life he had led for so many years, Foley's vision and hearing had become so acute and keen that he was able to hear sounds and distinguish objects at almost fabulous distances, as

exemplified by what follows. He shortly after rejoining Mr.
Inman called the attention of the party to sounds of dogs
yelping at a distance, but which none of them but himself could
hear. He soon, however, led the way in such a direction as
brought them to some kangaroo dogs tied up in a thick part of
the scrub, and from that spot pointed out footprints leading
away, from the appearances of which he felt confident, he said,
that those they sought were not far off, and proposed that
Sergeant Alford and he should hasten on foot to a sudden rise
of ground near, being the commencement of a spur leading to
the ranges, and there to look out over the scrub, the others to
wait for signals from them. They had no sooner gained the
elevation than Foley pointed out the men at a great distance
skirting the scrub; but Mr. A. could not for some time see
them. They then returned as fast as possible to the waiting
party, who had, during their absence, relieved their horses of
all the swags to be ready for a gallop, as they supposed the men
were off to mount the stolen horses. On Mr. Inman receiving
the Sergeant's report he ordered him to mount instantly, and,
with one man, to ride in the direction where he had seen the
men, first letting loose the dogs. Mr. Alford followed by choice
a young dog, which, after sniffing about, at last took a line
which ultimately led them into a thick scrub, and then made a
pause, and after creeping into it for a short distance, was seen
to stop and wag his tail, and so betrayed the hiding place of
his master, who was found lying down under the thick bushes.
The Sergeant instantly dismounted, and presenting a pistol at
Stone's head, called on him to surrender, and rise without
touching his gun, on which he was lying. Stone complied, and
submitted quietly to be handcuffed. On the Sergeant returning
with his prisoner to the officer in command, he was ordered to
return with him and one of the policemen to town. Stone was
then attached by a chain to his guard's stirrup-iron, the other
end locked to his handcuffs, and so marched to town and placed
in gaol.

The Superintendent of Police with the rest of the party
remained to follow up the pursuit of the other man, but were
not successful, after several days' search. Stone subsequently
made his escape from gaol.

Not long after their return to town information was brought
to the police that Stanley had been bold enough to pay a visit
to Adelaide, where, in a low public house, he was captured by

Sergeant Alford, and safely lodged in gaol, where Mr. Alford did not leave him until he saw him shackled to the iron bar in what was called by the prisoners the "stone jug," being a small stone cell or room, the only substantial one in that insecure establishment. The prisoner thus secured, the Sergeant left, to make his report to the Superintendent, who, highly pleased at the capture of such a troublesome customer, returned with the Sergeant to pay a visit to the prison and see all safe, but on arriving there they found the bird had already flown. He had, with some assistance from his fellow-prisoners, managed to break the lock, which enabled him to clear himself from the bar, and had escaped by jumping the low paling fence; and although every effort was made to recover him, he was not again taken, and the colony was relieved of his presence. The Acting-Gaoler for his neglect was dismissed, and his office was permanently filled by Mr. Ashton, who had been in the police force in London, and a better appointment was never made.

To return to Foley. The Messrs. Hack were so pleased with the action of Foley in the successful expedition in capturing Stone, that they obtained from the Governor his discharge, on a verbal pledge they gave as to his future good behaviour.

He was first employed by them to accompany a party to Portland Bay, which was dispatched to bring a herd of cattle from thence, and on that occasion he was so useful, and conducted himself so much to the satisfaction of the gentlemen in charge of the party, that the brothers Hack engaged him as their stockkeeper on their special survey of the "Three Brothers." In this employment he continued about two years, until Mr. Stephen Hack paid a visit to England, and took Foley with him as his servant in the year 1840.

As connected with his residence in the Australian colonies, it will be in place here to relate some of the accounts that he gave of himself, which I received from the party to whom in a confiding moment he unbosomed himself, and have reason to believe to be generally true. He said his proper name was Lovett; that he had been brought up as a gipsy; that he was transported to Sydney for horse-stealing (he was always fond of a horse); that he escaped, and after he had procured a mount, he spent seven years as a solitary bushranger in a small way, occasionally assisting settlers in recovering stock. He then led a lonely life, and only lifted necessaries for his daily wants until he joined Stone and Stanley in their journey to this colony; but he soon separated from these men, and was at deadly enmity with them, and kept a sharp look out, that they might not come upon him unawares and shoot him. He had no intention, he said, of doing anything wrong in this colony. So far as to his own account of himself, which is certainly rendered probable in its main features by his conduct here. I obtained from Mr. J. B. Hack the following character of him—" Foley was a good and efficient hand." Then as to his habits. He had a decided objection to sleep in a hut, but preferred to lie under a few palings or boards, placed against the end of the hut provided for him. He did not much associate with men of the prison class, but seemed to have a great dread of them, especially after it became notorious that he had assisted the police in making captures of such characters, and in doing so had acted on the principle of "dog eat dog."

After Foley returned to the old country, we first heard of him exhibiting himself in the costume and character of an Australian stockman, in the horse market in the town of Chichester, in the presence and to the astonishment of the Duke of Richmond, and a large number of county gentlemen and townsmen. Mounted on a suitable horse, he turned and stopped suddenly, as he galloped about, with yells, and with the swinging and cracking of an exaggerated long stock whip, the sounds of which, to English hearers, more resembled the reports of a pistol than the cracks of a whip. He would at one time be galloping as if to head a mob of cattle, then suddenly turning, and with his whip alternately used in the right and left hands, successfully force, as it were, a refractory bullock into an imaginary stockyard; all this to the great amusement of the Duke and other spectators, many of whom probably considered him out of his senses.

The information received of this remarkable man, after Mr. Stephen Hack's return to South Australia, was at first, and for some time, of a favourable character. He was left at home (as I cannot help calling the dear old country) by his Australian employer, in respectable employment, but probably under police supervision. In the colony it was some time before anything further was heard of him, and then a rumour reached us that he had been hung; but on enquiry it was ascertained that in a brawl he had drawn a knife and stabbed a man, for which he had been tried, found guilty, and sentenced to penal servitude in the mother country; in which state of durance he probably will end, or has ended, his days, as his fondness for freedom and the open air was so predominant that I think confinement within walls would be more than he could long exist under. From the known actions of Foley, it must appear that in his character there were many good points, such as under moral and religious training in his youth might have produced a useful and superior member of society. We must now look upon him as a social waif, to be pitied, and yet to be classed as superior to too many of his fellow-creatures more favoured as to the advantages which had been afforded them. He exhibited fidelity when trusted, and showed gratitude for kindnesses conferred upon him.

I must here mention an encounter I had with Stone previous to his capture by Sergeant Alford. About twelve months after my arrival I expected a herd of cattle overland from New South Wales, and made an excursion to find a good fattening run as near as possible to the River Murray. After beating about between the hills and the river and not finding anything to suit me, and having gone through a hard day's ride, I turned towards the hills, after skirting part of the shores of Lake Alexandrina, and followed up a creek towards the close of the day, when I arrived in a bend of the same, and decided to camp for the night. I had no sooner made up my mind to do so than I saw on one side of me, about 100 yards off in a small opening in the scrub, a man in the act of covering me with his gun. I immediately held up my hand, and dismounted, and commenced to walk towards the man. He was still on his guard, although he did not further threaten me. I was to all appearances unarmed. On his grounding his piece I addressed him in a most unguarded manner by name, supposing him to be Stone. I say unguarded, as if I had reflected, I most likely would have considered it prudent to have avoided anything like a recognition of him, but the decided tone in which I was enabled to speak disarmed him, and caused him to think he could trust me. The words I used were, "Well, Stone, I am out hunting for a piece of country for a cattle run; I do not come to disturb you; have you got any tucker?" His countenance at once became friendly, and he replied, "No; only a piece of kangaroo." "Well, I have ship biscuits and German sausage, with tea and sugar, in my saddle bags. Shall I camp with you?" "All right, mate." I next asked him to go with me to the horse to help me, wishing him to see I had no arms there. The horse hobbled, we returned to his wurlie ; he carried my saddle, and I the rest of my swag, *i.e.*, blankets, bridle, and saddle bags. While he replenished his fire, I fetched the water from a clear water-hole. The camp was on the creek where Strathalbyn has replaced the then wild bush. We had soon a quart pot of tea boiling, and supped together, and I slept by his side comfortably on a bed of dry fern leaves under the shelter of a few boughs rather artistically put together. The following morning after breakfast, I gave him all my supply of food. He accepted what I willingly gave, and asked for nothing. He told me he should get the blacks to take him across the river in one of their bark canoes. I promised him I would keep secret the course he was taking, and would not divulge the fact that I had seen him until I was satisfied he was safe. I did not then know of any charge against him in this colony, except that he was suspected to have cut the throat of a supposed stolen horse, and also believed to be a runaway lifer, as was afterwards proved. He was evidently in great fear of being enquired after. He was not communicative to me about his antecedents, and I prudently asked him no questions. His conduct in this respect differed much from that of other men of his class with whom I have been brought into contact. I must mention that, unknown to him, I had a brace of small pocket pistols, which I always carried in the bush on such expeditions at that time. I cannot help a remark or two on his remarkable forbearance and self-control. Now, this was a desperate, hunted man, escaping as it might be for his life, and he had only to demand of me my horse and all I had about me ; had I refused there would probably have been a death struggle between us ; but such reflections did not occur to me at that time, as I placed entire confidence in him. Knowing what I was looking for, he directed me to follow up a certain spur of the ranges, and to continue south on the saddle of the ranges, and I would find a good grassy and well-watered extensive gully, well adapted for a fattening run for cattle. I travelled according to his directions, and found what proved to be one of the richest spots I have ever occupied in this colony, now known as Bull's Creek, but I was soon displaced by a special survey.

CHAPTER VII.

I MUST relate some circumstances which occurred on this cattle run, pointed out by Stone, during the short time I was allowed to use it. On the arrival of the herd of cattle which I expected from New South Wales, they were placed on this run. Mr. Huon, from whom I purchased the cattle, advised me to engage a man named Hart, whom I found to fulfil all Mr. H. had promised. He, however, told me he knew nothing of his antecedents prior to his overtaking and joining his party on the Murray; that he was on foot, and was most probably a runaway, but that he never had a more active and trustworthy man of his class in his employment, and he had always under him a number of assigned or freed men at work for him. I can with perfect truth say that Hart was a good servant, and for one of his class remarkably civil and well-behaved, besides being well up to his business, so I soon placed a confidence in him which I never found abused. My custom was to visit the station at least once a month, and to remain generally a few days. These visits I found to be quite a treat. At first there was also a hutkeeper who had charge of the stores, but after a time Hart proposed to dispense with the hut-keeper, *i.e.*, when there was a vacancy on the man leaving, and offered to perform the double duties for a small advance in his wages, which I agreed to give him. He explained to me he preferred to cook for himself, and I never regretted the change; the establishment became much more pleasant, and I always found everything in perfect order, the cattle and horses well attended to, my room clean and comfortable, and the cooking and change of food excellent; then the man was always so *cheerful* and *good tempered* that I could not avoid liking him well. I mention these details as remarkable, as compared with what I have to relate concerning his antecedents immediately before he joined the party coming down the river, and the horrid crime he had committed a few days previous. How little I could have imagined such an occurrence to have taken place may be felt when I explain that for a treat I took my wife out to spend a few days on the station, Hart being the only person within three or four miles. His clever management and invariably mild and respectful manners were such as to have qualified him for filling a situation as domestic servant, even at home. Well, such a

man as he appeared to be naturally led me to hear from him
revelations of his previous life as a prisoner, which he always
seemed most anxious to impart. How much of truth he gave
me I know not, but the narrative, unquestionably, if believed,
was such as to produce a favourable impression. He was
about thirty years of age, rather slightly built, and active in his
movements. As a youth, he stated, he and one of his master's
sons ran away and enlisted in the Royal Artillery, then stationed
in Dumbarton Castle, and after undergoing all the hardships of
drill, &c., they were guilty of some breach of discipline and
deserted, and to escape took away two horses, not intending to
steal them, but to aid in escaping. They succeeded in reaching
a ship at Greenock, and having exchanged their clothing (for
Hart's companion had plenty of money) they managed to
secure a passage, but were pursued and taken out of the ship,
and handed over to the civil powers, tried, and sentenced to
transportation for life. On arriving in Sydney in a transport-
ship with a number of prisoners, his comrade, through interest
made by his family, soon got assigned to a favourable master,
and he saw no more of him. Hart was sent to Norfolk Island,
where he was soon selected by the Superintendent, and employed as a domestic servant, and here he became expert, as I
found him. He was now very happy, and soon by good conduct became a favoured man, and promoted to be coxswain in
the Superintendent's boat. After some time he was placed in
one of the boats employed in receiving supplies from a brig
standing off and on. The boat was eight-oared; he was steering; one guard (armed) was only in the boat, as the men were
picked, and some confidence was placed in them. The brig
having taken a long tack as they approached her, the day being
calm, advantage was taken of this condition of things. The
men were resting on their oars, when the guard was suddenly
seized and thrown overboard, and Hart followed, as he was a
favourite of the Superintendent, and they would not trust him.
The transaction was seen on board the brig, and all way possible
was made, and both men were saved.

The shore was signalled, and although chase was given to
the boat, they adopted such a course as did not suit the brig,
and so for that time escaped. Amongst the boat's crew was an
ex-captain of the Royal Navy, who knew how to adopt all measures calculated to complete their escape; but ultimately they
were taken. Thus far, Hart's tale goes; but it cannot be all

true, as the ex-captain (whose name I suppress, out of regard to his high connections) would certainly have been hung, which event did not take place. That such a man did escape from Norfolk Island is doubtless a fact, and that he afterwards finished his infamous career on the scaffold at Sydney is true— but for a different crime from that recorded by Hart; also that by the great interest of his family he had been long spared is well known. Hart, however, had introduced him into his own history, I believe, simply to give as much interest to his recital as possible.

Hart got away from this colony, and had provided for his escape in more ways than one. I have mentioned what care he took of the horses I had given him to use in his work. I now add other particulars showing how well he laid his plans. His habit was to draw his pay from me monthly, and from the first he returned the greater part to me to deposit the same in a bank for him, but desired me to lodge it in my own name. To this I at first objected, but at length gave way. After a time he asked me to supply him with a stout double-barrelled gun and ammunition, so that he might shoot game. There was already in the hut a rifle, &c., used in shooting cattle for slaughter. He was very successful in bringing in stray cattle for the neighbours as well as my own, and frequently got rewards, which he gave to me to be added to his savings; and so he continued to act until he had been with me about eight months. As a further proof how careful and thrifty he remained, although he had frequent occasions to visit town on my business, he was at all times sober and respectable in his conduct, as far as I had the means of judging from observation or report. And such uniform, steady, and sober conduct in one of his class was the more remarkable as public houses at that early time were in greater proportion to population than they are at present, and the working population were more generally addicted to intemperance. I mention these matters, trifling as some may think them, to show how much self-denial and restraint were exercised by Hart in carrying out his plans to get away before he was sought for. The wonder to me is how he waited so long with such a heavy reckoning to pay if caught. It is also a marvel how arrangements for his capture were so long delayed on the part of the Sydney Government and the friends of his previous master, whom he had murdered. At the time above-mentioned, on one of his attendances in town, he came and informed me he had found at the post-office a letter from an uncle of his in good circumstances at the Cape of Good Hope, who had written to him in answer to one he had sent him, and had pressed him to come without delay and live with him. As at that time there was a vessel in Port Adelaide from that colony, I believed his tale. He made a most pressing application for me to excuse him the remainder of his engagement, that he might get to a colony where he would be far away from a prison population, so I consented to his request on the condition that he found a good man to take his place, and asked him if he could name such a one, on which he gave me the name of Bob Moorhead, whom I knew to be a first-class bushman and a good stockkeeper. I accepted him as a substitute, so the two men went out to muster the cattle, and I followed. The cattle being found all right, were handed over to the charge of Moorhead, whose previous history I knew so far as that he had gained a conditional pardon and freedom, for his general good conduct as a prisoner, and for the exemplary services he had rendered when accompanying Major Mitchell, Surveyor-General, in his explorations in the Province of New South Wales; but he was not at liberty to leave the Australian Colonies.

Shortly after my return to town after handing over the cattle to the new stockkeeper, Hart waited on me with great glee, to tell me he had succeeded in obtaining the situation of steward on board the ship which had brought his letter from the Cape, to return with her to that port. He was dressed smartly in ship costume, and appeared no more as a bushman. He now received from me his money in sovereigns, about eighty pounds, with the most grateful expressions, not at all called for. After this he frequently managed to meet me, and took every opportunity of addressing himself to me in public places, especially if any policeman was in sight; but he kept on board ship some days before the ship sailed, and I saw him no more. Within a month after this a herd of cattle arrived for me, down the Murray, which I had ordered from the same stockholder who had brought down Hart on his previous trip, and who had recommended me to employ him. From him, to my amazement, I heard the following account of the crime Hart had committed immediately before he joined him. Hart's previous employment had been with a squatter on a cattle station on one of the upper branches of the Murray, who engaged him, knowing him to be a runaway convict. With this employer he had remained about two years, when a herd of cattle were heard of, as going down the main stream of the river. At this time, on his obeying the order to bring his master's horse ready for him to mount, and after he had fastened the horse to the rail in front of the "government house," as the hut used by the owner or manager is called, he entered the room where his employer was sitting after his breakfast, and petitioned him, in return for his services, to give him an old stock-horse with saddle, &c., to enable him to overtake the party with cattle going down the river to the new colony. To this his master replied, "No, you rascal, I will send you in to the Government." On this Hart made a jump to a corner where stood a loaded rifle, and shot his employer dead. He then immediately rushed out and mounted the tied-up horse, and rode for his life, but there was no fear of his being immediately pursued, as the assigned and freed men sympathised with him. He had served this employer for nearly two years, and had only received in return rations and bush clothing. One mounted man from the station started immediately to report the circumstance to the nearest police—some miles to the east—while Hart was escaping to the west. These particulars I heard from my friend, who brought me the cattle; also that Hart on overtaking him on his previous trip, when he came within one day's journey of his party, destroyed the horse on which he escaped in a thick clump of bush, and joined him on foot. I felt greatly shocked on receiving such news of a murder committed by a man who exhibited such a different character whilst in my service, and who had been so faithful and true to me; but I had now the key to explain his action in leaving his money in my hands, and his great care of the horses, especially one of them; also in his obtaining from me a valuable gun, which he left in the hut, where also were found capacious saddle-bags which he had made, a leather cover for a gun, and other articles useful on a long journey. So I concluded his original intention was to have gone away overland, if the chance of the Cape voyage had not presented itself, which if he had carried out, his conscience would have been clear as to any injury done me in what he would have taken away, viz., the horse, gun, &c., as the money I held would about cover their value. I may mention he had frequently offered to buy from me the best of the two horses, but I would not sell him.

I must now give an account of Moorhead and his fatal end. I have to relate circumstances of a most shocking nature, for he also had committed murder. I have shown that at the muster of the cattle I was alone with these two men, who had been guilty of such heavy crimes, but I must say that from their conduct and language, such actions as I afterwards learned they had been guilty of I could not have imagined to have been perpetrated by either of them. I do not think Hart had made a confidant of Moorhead as to the crime of killing his master when he rode away from the station, or that he told any of the men in the party with whom he came down, as most of them returned to New South Wales to bring down the second mob, as there is no doubt that one or other of them if they had known of the murder he had committed would have jumped at the reward which they would well know would be offered ; for although I have found some honour among men of his class, it is the exception and not the rule.

For some time Moorhead went about his work to my satisfaction, but I found him getting more and more morose and melancholy, and, to tell the truth, I myself became somewhat uncomfortable by being alone with him, and in consequence engaged a hutkeeper. But I did not find the stockkeeper to get better in his mind even with company, and fortunately for myself I proposed to him to go into town for a few days, after he had got the cattle together, and see if a change would improve him. The news of the crime his friend had committed having been made public, appeared to have stirred up reminiscences of his own crime, and the two things together had preyed on his mind. Well, he carried out my instructions, and left the station for the town, and put up at an hotel in Grenfell Street, and there remained only a few days, when, as he did not appear at the breakfast-table one morning, a servant was ordered to go to his room, and as no answer was obtained to a summons given to him, and his door was found fast, a forced entry was made, and he was found dead, with his throat cut by his own hand.

Recitals of the miserable careers of fellow creatures of the prison class are always painful to give, but in relating occurrences of the first days of the colony, some of these sad tales should be given, in the hope that the young, by reading these examples taken from *real life*, may be deterred from deviating, by a first step, from the paths of rectitude. They serve to prove how next to impossible it appears to be to return, and to get rid of evil habits thus acquired.

I had found Moorhead apparently in a most uncomfortable state of mind, commencing from the time the news came down the river from New South Wales, which was soon followed by confirmation by ship, with the notice of the reward of £500 offered by the Governor of New South Wales for the arrest of Hart, for the murder of his master. An officer also arrived with a warrant for his arrest. Before this news came down, Moorhead had shown me the conditional pardon on parchment he had gained, granted him by Governor Darling, setting out that he had been sentenced to death in India for the crime of ——(here was an erasure), which had been commuted to transportation for life to Sydney in consideration of circumstances, &c., and on account of his good conduct as a soldier, &c., &c. Moorhead explained that the word had been worn out by being in a fold of the parchment, and confessed he had killed a Lascar in a quarrel about a native woman, and that the man had attempted to stab him, but he wrested the knife out of his hand, and with it inflicted a death wound. He made the above confession to me a few days before he left the station. He also showed me high testimonials from Sydney Government Officials.

CHAPTER VIII.

OLD colonists well remember the difficulties encountered by parties on their way down our great system of water communication from New South Wales with sheep and cattle to stock our newly-established colony. The account given in even a condensed form will necessarily occupy considerable space, and present a succession of thrilling pictures of the sufferings endured by pioneers, and, sad to relate, the necessary slaughter of blacks—banded together in large numbers—in their attacks on travelling Europeans with stock.

As an introduction to this subject I will take advantage of Captain Sturt's description of his first contact with natives on the Murray. Immediately after entering the Murray country he found that the natives were much more numerous than on the Murrumbidgee, and it was with great difficulty that they were enabled to pursue their way without coming into collision with them. Captain Sturt's admirable tact, coolness, and presence of mind alone saved the party from actual conflict; but they were at one time upon the very point of an affray, which must have resulted in the destruction of the whole party. I will give the circumstances in Captain Sturt's own words :—

"As we sailed down the stream we observed a vast number of natives under the trees, and on a nearer approach we not only heard their war-song, but remarked they were painted and armed as they generally are prior to their engaging in a deadly conflict. Notwithstanding their outward signs of hostility, and fancying friendly natives who had been met with higher up were with them, I continued to steer directly for the bank on which they were collected. I found, however, when it was almost too late to turn into the succeeding reach to the left, that an attempt to land would only be attended with loss of life. The natives seemed determined to resist it. We approached so near that they held their spears quivering in their grasp ready to hurl. They were painted in various ways. Some who had marked their ribs, thighs, and faces with a white pigment in stripes looked like skeletons; others were daubed with red and yellow ochre, and their bodies shone with the grease with which they had besmeared themselves. A dead silence prevailed among the front ranks, but those in the background, as well as women, who carried supplies of spears. and who appeared to have had a bucket of whitewash capsized over their heads, were extremely clamorous. As I did not wish a conflict with the people, I lowered my sail, and putting the helm to starboard, we passed quickly down the stream in mid-channel. Disappointed in their anticipations, the natives ran along the bank of the river endeavouring to secure an aim at us; but unable to throw with certainty in consequence of the onward motion of the boat, they flung themselves into the most extravagant attitudes, and worked themselves into a frenzy by loud and vehement shouting. It was with considerable apprehension that I observed the river to be shoaling fast, more especially as a huge sandbank, a little below us, and on the same side on which the natives had gathered, projected nearly a third of the way across the channel. To this sandbank they ran with tumultuous uproar, and covered it over in a dense mass. Some of the chiefs advanced into the water to be nearer their victims, and turned from time to time to direct their followers. With every pacific disposition, and an extreme reluctance to take away life, I foresaw that it would be

impossible any longer to avoid an engagement; yet with such
fearful numbers against us, I was doubtful of the result. The
spectacle we had witnessed had been one of the most appalling
kind, and sufficient to shake the firmness of most men ; but at
that trying moment my little band preserved their usual
coolness, and if anything could be gleaned from their countenances, it was that they had determined on an obstinate
resistance. I now explained to my men that their only chance
of escape depended or would depend upon their firmness. I
desired that after the first volley had been fired, McLeay and
three of the men would attend to the defence of the boats,
with bayonets only, while I, Hopkinson, and Harris, would
keep up the fire as being more used to it. I ordered, however,
that no shot was to be fired, until after I had discharged both
my barrels. I then delivered their arms to the men, which
had as yet been kept in the place appropriated for them, and
at the same time some rounds of loose cartridges. The men
assured me they would follow my instructions, and thus
prepared, having already lowered the sail, we drifted onwards
with the current. As we neared the sandbank, I stood up and
made signs to the natives to desist, but without success. I
took up my gun, therefore, and cocking it, had already brought
it down to a level. A few seconds more would have closed
the life of the nearest of the savages. The distance was too
trifling for me to doubt the fatal effects of the discharge, for I was
determined to take deadly aim, in the hope that the fall of one
man might save the lives of many. But at the moment when
my hand was on the trigger and my eye was along the barrels
my purpose was checked by McLeay, who called to me that
another party of blacks had made their appearance upon the
left or opposite bank of the river. Turning, I observed four
men at the top of their speed. The foremost of them, as
soon as he got ahead of the boat, threw himself from a considerable height into the water. He struggled across the
channel to the sandbank, and in an incredibly short space of
time stood in front of the savage against whom my aim had
been directed. Seizing him by the throat, he pushed him
backwards, and forcing all who were in the water on to the
bank, he trod its margin with a vehemence and agitation that
were exceedingly striking. At one moment pointing to the
boat, at another shaking his clenched hand in the faces of the
most forward, and stamping with passion on the sand; his

voice, which was at first distinct and clear, was lost after a time in hoarse murmurs. Two of the four natives remained on the left bank of the river, the third followed his leader who proved to be the remarkable savage I had previously noticed before we arrived at the scene of action. The reader will imagine my feelings on this occasion. We were so wholly lost in the interesting scene that was passing, that the boat was allowed to drift at pleasure. For my own part I was overwhelmed with astonishment and in fact confused, so singular, so unexpected, so providential had been our escape." Captain Sturt continued his course down the river, and although he met with many more blacks than he did on the Murrumbidgee they showed no indications of hostility.

I commence the experiences of parties coming down the river with flocks of sheep with the attack on Messrs. Field and Inman as the most serious, though not the first. This was the first encounter, however, of the natives of that particular locality with white men, and their assaults for a time assumed the proportions of regular combats.

On Wednesday evening, April 21, 1841, information was received in Adelaide that an overland party conducting a large flock of sheep, under the charge of Mr. H. Inman, previously superintendent of police in Adelaide, and Mr. Field (that gentleman being part owner) had been attacked by natives to the east of the great elbow of the River Murray, and that one or more of the persons employed had been wounded, the whole of the whites dispersed, and the sheep, bullocks, dray, and stores had been taken by the natives. It was stated that on the sheep entering the Rufus country a numerous body of blacks made their appearance, and in a most impudent manner commenced disturbing the sheep, and attempting to drive them away. The men of the party, ten in number, were armed, but on the natives presenting an hostile appearance they all fled, leaving the two leaders of the party alone to defend their property. Mr. Inman had previously been wounded when in the Murrumbidgee country, and in that disabled state was unable to assist Mr. Field, who had to abandon the sheep and make the best of his way to the nearest station, that of Mr. Dutton, at Mount Dispersion, and from thence forward information to Adelaide.

Fuller particulars arrived as follows :—At the Darling, and after leaving it, the blacks became troublesome to the party.

On one occasion Mr. Inman seeing a few blacks ahead of the sheep and approaching, rode forward and had a friendly parley with them. On turning to ride back to join his company three spears were thrown, one taking effect in his shoulder, one in his arm, and the other fetching him out of his saddle. This was a jagged spear, and entering near the backbone, went in a slanting direction through his body, the point appearing below his ribs on the same side. One of the sharp jags had hitched into his backbone, and was so fast that the spear could not be withdrawn, and it became necessary to cut the head from the shaft with a saw close to his body. A sling was stretched across the dray from the side rails, on which he was laid, not one of the company expecting him to survive for any length of time after such a wound, and it was out of the question to delay the journey onwards. After enduring the jolts of the dray in passing over a rough country for two weeks in a recumbent position, he seemed more easy, and on the morning of the day when the successful attack was made on the party, the jag became detached from his spine, the head was extracted, and the wound dressed as his comrades were best able to do it. Vast numbers of the blacks had been about for some days, and were evidently increasing. They were now in the Rufus country. I now quote from Mr. Inman's report :—

"On the morning of April 16th ult., when about forty miles on the other side of Lake Bonney, having encamped on the bank of an exceedingly brackish creek, we broke up the camp and pushed on about three miles to breakfast, during which meal the natives presented themselves, in number appearing to be about thirty or forty. They had, since we left the Darling, speared several of our sheep. By what occurred afterwards we found that considerable numbers were in the scrub close behind those who first presented themselves, although unseen by us. They were armed, and evidently meant mischief from their endeavours to conceal their weapons from us in the long grass. They essayed to make friends with us, but we did not like their movements, and warned them off with our hands. Not the slightest violence was offered by us. The natives seeing they were not allowed to enter our camp on pretence of friendship, soon exhibited their determination to gain their object by force, when treachery could not be employed. After breakfast, and before we made a start, the blacks resumed their spears, and making signs

with their hands that they would meet us again on the road
or track, immediately made off at a quick pace with an apparent intent to cut us off. Our suspicions being thus aroused,
the men were ordered to examine their firearms and renew
the priming, when the party moved on. We had not proceeded above three miles when we saw the natives ahead of
us in the scrub in great numbers. Mr. Field, from the time
I was speared on the Murrumbidgee, had altogether conducted
the party. The spear-head having been removed, although I
was very weak, I mounted my horse. Mr. Field with two horsemen advanced in front of the party, and although very weak I
found them, and kept them company. None of the party were
aware of the numbers they had to encounter. On our approach
to the position occupied by the blacks, they shouted and struck
their waddies, and from their movements we soon found out
that their object was to oppose our passage. On this Mr. Field
ordered the driver of the dray to stop and wait for the sheep.
On their coming up the shepherds rounded the sheep, to support the men at the dray. One of the horsemen of the name of
George Crow, and the best armed man of the party, was now
found to have absented himself, and did not make his appearance at all during the fight. This weakened the party considerably, as I could not be accounted as a combatant; the spear-
head which I had carried in my body for nearly three weeks
was upwards of seven inches in length, so I could be of no use
to Mr. Field. The natives, in number about three or four
hundred, commenced the attack by issuing boldly from the cover,
and waddies flew in all directions. A slow but ineffectual fire
from two or three pieces was returned by the men at the dray,
the remainder of the fire-arms being so inferior that they would
not go off. We were now surrounded. Two shepherds were
speared at the dray; one an old soldier, when defending himself by clubbing his gun, was carried off, and several spears were
run through him. He had the presence of mind to cross his
arms over his chest, and was left by them for dead. They first
stripped him of almost all his clothing. He, however, managed
to travel during seven days, living on roots and on part of a
carcase of a wild dog, which he found in a deserted native
camp. After this man was carried away, the remainder of the
party, after struggling for some time against overwhelming
numbers, and finding their firearms all but useless, retreated
through the scrub, Mr. Field behind them, who had done his

utmost to save the property, and at length was compelled to abandon all to the natives, who took full possession. He then conducted the retreating men through the scrub until he hit the Murray at some distance from the scene of action, and proceeded onwards alone to procure assistance from the nearest out-stations.

"On leaving the place of strife I proceeded alone and shortly picked up the other horseman, and after a week's privation and bodily suffering managed to reach the station of Mr. Hallack, where I was hospitably received; the shepherds also managed to get as far as the Narcoota Springs, where they were met by Messrs. Hawker and Bagot, who had come out in search of the party and to bring them food. After being refreshed they were conveyed into the station. The shepherd who was carried off and speared had managed to reach the Springs before the shepherds left. He had seven wounds in the body."

Thus all escaped with their lives, and the wounded afterwards recovered. Mr. Inman continues—

"I beg leave to say that on no occasion during the journey had any act of violence been committed by my men; on the contrary, they universally treated them with kindness, but still with that caution which was necessary for the safety of the party."

I have, through the favour of Mr. T. J. S. O'Halloran, S.M., the use of his respected father's diary, from which I give the account of the proceedings of the first police party under Major O'Halloran, which was despatched by His Excellency Colonel Gawler on the day after the distressing news was published. His Excellency, however, from his embarrassed position, found himself compelled to recall them when within two days' journey of their destination—that is, from the spot where the greater part of the sheep were supposed still to be alive, and might have been recovered. Major O'Halloran in his diary records :—

"On the 22nd of April I started with a police force consisting of Inspector Tolmer, Dr. Weston, and thirteen men, sub-officers, and privates.

"On the 23rd arrived at Dutton's station, and found Messrs. Bagot, G. C. and J. C. Hawker, Jacob, Hart, and others. Inman and his party had arrived only two hours before us, in a very weak and exhausted state, Inman and two of his men severely wounded, he having three spear wounds, and one of the men seven. They are now all doing well, although Inman is greatly emaciated, having travelled seven weeks in his wounded state.

"*Saturday*, 24.—Dr. Weston returned to town, having dressed the wounds of the patients. Moved off at 11.30 a.m., guided by the native boy Tommy, for the Nicota Springs. Arrived at 5.30 p.m. Here met Messrs. Jacob and Field, jun. Found the course we took quite dangerous for carts or drays. Detained waiting for cart with supplies from Gawler. Police-constable McLean arrived, and reported cart coming up drawn by bullocks, horses having been refused. At 1.30 p.m. Corporal Prewett arrived with two police-constables, one native, "Sambo," and two of Inman's shepherds, with a cart and three bullocks with provisions from Gawler. After dinner, at 3 p.m., leaving Mr. Jacob, jun., started with Inspector Tolmer, eighteen police-constables, Lieut. Field, jun., two shepherds, two natives, a bullock-driver, twenty-three horses, three bullocks, and two carts. At 5.30 p.m. camped at margin of scrub. Scrubby feed ; no water.

"*Monday, April* 26.—Moved off at 8 a.m. Made the 'Pound' on the Murray at 4 p.m.

"*Tuesday*, 27.—At 8.30 marched for the North-west Bend. Ordered the Inspectors on the march to drill the men in carbine and sword exercises, and in the formation of threes charging. Explained to the party my orders from His Excellency in presence of Lieutenant Field and Inspector Tolmer. At 4.30 camped about the west end of the bend, and just past a lagoon, where we disturbed some natives who were cooking.

"*Wednesday*, 28.—As I find our flour likely to run short, and our progress is slow, waiting for the dray, I have ordered two of our troopers to return, and by this arrangement our flour may last ten days. Marched at 8.30 a.m.; encamped at 5.15 p.m. Made nineteen miles ; road very heavy ; cart horses knocked up. Encamped at a spot where several parties have been attacked by the natives, and where one European was killed by them, and lies buried between two trees, with ' F ' cut upon one of them. From what I can gather from some of the men who came overland, several blacks had been killed here. Mr. Tooth was attacked and nearly killed. Mr. Eyre was turned back, and obliged to get further strength before he could pass. This night, and for the future, good positions for camping will be selected, and double sentries posted.

"*Thursday*, 29.—Left 'Dead Man's Flat,' so named by me, at 8 a.m. Found roads dreadfully heavy. Changed draught horses at midday, hoping to make better progress, but will scarcely make twenty miles. At 9.30 a.m. saw a vast number of native feet-marks along the track. Had to pass a flat seven miles long, which I named the 'Great Flat.' When about half way across saw natives on the opposite bank, who gave us the 'Cooee.' Others, I think, were hiding behind trees, as the voices seemed to be numerous. Encamped for the night on another flat not far from the former, at 4.30 p.m. Distance nineteen miles. I called this 'Pine Flat.'

"*Friday*, 30.—Marched at 8 a.m. About midday a despatch arrived from the Private Secretary by a trooper, ordering me to return with the party to town. (The Major was reported to have said—under the disappointment he felt on receiving this order—to the trooper who brought the despatch, aside, 'Why did not you lose yourself?') Proceeded onwards, however, expecting to find a flat to feed the horses and refresh the party, and despatched Inspector Tolmer in advance to see if he could fine a good flat. On his return he reported that we must proceed several miles further ere we could be suited. At fourteen miles a halt was ordered. At 2.30 p.m. made a movement homeward. Our advance from Adelaide was at our return 161 miles. Lieut. Field proposes to return to-morrow morning to Mount Dispersion, and in that neighbourhood to beat up for volunteers to accompany him back to endeavour to recover the sheep. I will give him, as escort till he gets to his destination, two troopers. It is with extreme pain that I have been obliged to return back to Adelaide when within fifty miles of the place where Inman and Field were attacked; but I have no alternative, as an old soldier, than to obey His Excellency's orders, who, of course, has his own just reasons for ordering me back, and which it is my duty not to question, but obey. Ordered Police-constables Stuart and Rose to be ready in the morning to accompany Lieut. Field back, and to take sufficient rations for the journey.

"*Saturday*, *May* 1.—Lieut. Field and the two men left the camp at daybreak. On the 29th as we got to the extreme western end of this long flat we surprised a party of natives, who had a canoe with a fire in it, and a duck, which I suppose they were about to cook. They had also a fishing net, and on seeing us they dashed off in great alarm, and remained in the centre of the stream till we departed. At 4.30 P.M. halted for the night in a good reed flat.

"*Sunday*, *May* 2.—Started at 7.30 A.M. Delayed at a steep hill up which the horses refused to pull, and the cart was drawn up by the men. Some time after this, when riding on ahead of the party a considerable distance, I saw about fifty natives on the opposite bank, who began chattering loudly when they saw me. At the extreme end of Dead Man's Flat the horses again refused to draw the cart up that very steep hill, and the men had to do it. At thirteen miles the horses in the cart were done up, and with a change of horses reached the Bend at 5.30 P.M.

"*Monday*, 3.—Reached the Pound at 11.30 A.M., doing seventeen miles in four hours. Soon after our arrival some natives came over from the opposite side with fish, and were very quiet and well-behaved. At 3.30 P.M., to our astonishment, we saw a whaleboat approaching, rowing up the river, and shortly after Mr. Scott and his crew came on shore. He left Pullen's party that day week with supplies for us, and has made his way from the river mouth in seven days. I now gave Inspector Tolmer orders relative to marching into town, and to leave on his way one man at Dutton's Station, and one at Gawler Town, to be ready to convey any orders from His Excellency to Mr. Scott, whom I requested to wait at the Bend to receive instructions from head-quarters. The march through the scrub to the Nicota Springs being a long and fatiguing journey without feed or water I decided, as the heat was now extreme during the day and the moon was about full, to march about sundown, and we left the Pound at 7.30 P.M. I pushed on ahead of the party for Adelaide, accompanied by Police-constable Cusack.

"*May* 5.—Having slept at Robertson's like a top left at 8 A.M., arrived at home at 4.30 same day."

The only benefit of this toilsome and expensive expedition was the good done to Mr. Inman and his men by the attendance of Dr. Weston. It appears that when His Excellency the Governor (Colonel Gawler), received Major O'Halloran's first despatch, which gave the information that the whole of the party had survived the attack, and that Mr. Inman and his wounded men were doing well, after being treated by Dr. Weston, he did not consider himself called upon to allow the police to come into collision with the natives, when the rescue of the sheep was the only object to be gained.

Immediately on the recall of the police party becoming known, a meeting of settlers was held, when it was resolved that a party of volunteers should offer their services to Inman and Field, to go out and endeavour to recover some of the property seized by the blacks. Lieut. Field lost no time in collecting and organising the party of volunteers offered at the public meeting.

"*May* 5, 1841.—The following volunteer party started from Adelaide (the same day as the return of Major O'Halloran), to endeavour to recover some of the 5,000 sheep, the bullocks, dray, and other property of which the blacks had taken possession when they defeated the party of Messrs. Inman and Field:—Lieutenant Field, R.N. (in command), Messrs. G. C. Hawker, John Allan, James Kinchela, Kenneth Campbell, S. Samuel, J. Jacob, and H. Field; also some shepherds. Five mounted and two foot police were ordered by the Governor to accompany the party to the supposed boundary of the colony, to protect the volunteers, but not to proceed or act beyond the boundary of the province; also Turner and Ross, Mr. Allan's overseers, in all twenty men."

The following narrative is from Mr. James Hawker's diary:—

"*May* 7.—On arriving at the Pound on the Murray we found Mr. Scott with the surveying boat. He was in charge of a survey party. Lieutenant Field delivered to him a letter from His Excellency Colonel Gawler, instructing him to keep with the force as far as the police were ordered to go, and to render assistance to the party.

"*May* 8.—Left the Pound at 8.30 A.M. Camped at 7.30. Made twenty-two miles. Two blackfellows joined us here. Scott with the boat did not arrive. Having no tents we lit large fires, and cut bushes for screens, huddling together for warmth.

"*May* 9, *Sunday.*—Off at 7 A.M. Track very sandy. Passed Dead Man's Flat. Found the approach to the river to be so steep that we had to lower the cart down with ropes. Distance travelled, twenty-five miles. As our supporting police force, by orders, had to remain here, it was decided to leave the cart, and each man to take on his horse rations for five days, consisting of flour, tea, sugar, taking no meat to avoid overloading our horses. Lieut. Field left a note for Mr. Scott with the non-commissioned officer in charge of the police, instructing him to supply them with rations, and to push on after him.

"*May* 10.—Left at 8 A.M. Our party consisted of ten volunteers. Three mounted and two men on foot, employed as paid assistants, were left with our dray. We passed through eighteen miles of dense gum scrub; total distance, thirty-three miles to camp. Two natives in a canoe made a visit of inspection, but on seeing the watch which had been set, dropped down the river, and remained on the opposite side, where we could see two large native fires.

"*May* 11.—Started at 7.30. Came upon natives fishing. The women, alarmed, swam the river with children on their backs. Camped at twenty-six miles. A large signal-fire to the north-west of us.

"*May* 12.—Off at 7.30. Crossed a salt-water creek and pushed on, hoping to reach the place before dark where the attack on the sheep party was made. Had to camp on a brackish creek. Mr. Field, who had come down with the sheep, considered we were not far from the place, and rode on with his brother—Lieutenant Field—and myself, and at two miles arrived at the spot where the sheep had been taken from him. We then returned to the camp. The distance from last camp twenty-eight miles, and from Adelaide 230 miles.

"*May* 13.—This day will decide whether our expedition is to be successful or not. Our only hope is that they will stand, in order that we may show them the use of good firearms. Reached the place of attack about 8 A.M., where the sheep were taken from Messrs. Inman and Field. Found the abandoned dray. On the ground were scattered in all directions tea, flour, fragments of casks and chests. As the tea was not much damaged we secured some part of it, and some tobacco. One wheel was off the dray, and some of the ironwork had been cut away. A little farther back on the overland track, on the bank of a large lagoon, we found two of the bullocks lying dead, and two more on the further bank of the same lagoon.

"By forced marches, and after a hurried preparation, we had reached the supposed boundary of the colony in seven days, from thence the volunteer party started carrying only tea, sugar, and flour, camping at night under bushes, our only meat a few wallaby which we succeeded in shooting. The police, in obedience to orders, remained here, and we proceeded onwards unsupported. On the evening of the 12th we camped on the creek where the attack had been made on Messrs. Field and Inman. We first found Mr. Field's trunk empty on the track.

The natives had chosen a most favourable spot on which to make the onslaught. It was on a little flat, through the centre of which a gully ran, and was surrounded by a thick scrub. It was when the dray was crossing the gully that the rush was made. The providential release of the spear-head from Mr. Inman's back enabled him to mount his horse, and to this he owed his life. From the hasty departure of the rescuing party we were badly provided with arms. Most of them were rifles, and we had only one powder-flask to three men. Many of the balls fitted very tight, so that speedy or convenient loading was out of the question. The barrels also had become rusty after the damp nights to which they had been exposed. At the first discharge two of the pieces became useless, one hammer breaking, and in another a ball stuck fast when half home. The natives when met were in their war paint, with white bars on their bodies and limbs, giving them the appearance of skeletons. It was found that the horses would not steadily face them, the blacks also yelling in the most hideous manner."

I now follow with extracts from Lieutenant Field's official report, which was published in the papers:—"We first found sheep tracks, and on following them down observed natives running through the trees. We soon came to a large body of them concealed in the scrub, waiting our approach. We then formed in line, and rode towards them; they at the same time boldly approached us to within forty yards, well within spear range, when one of the chiefs gave the signal to attack by sticking a spear in the ground, and with a wave of his hand, they then gave vent to a loud war-cry, and commenced a discharge of spears. The first man who threw a spear I shot through the head, and gave the order to fire, hoping when they saw two or three fall they would retreat, but they still advanced in the form of a crescent, in number at least 200, while many more were seen through the scrub behind. At this time Mr. Hawker called out to me that they were encircling us, and seeing they were advancing both wings while the centre were attacking us, a large lagoon lying in our rear, I ordered the party to follow me and outflank them on the right. While effecting this movement, Mr. Hawker's horse fell across a tree and he was dismounted, at the same time Mr. Jacob's horse received a second spear and was soon unable to carry him farther. He dismounted, and we were all engaged in covering his retreat." [One of the party informed me that before they lost sight of

Mr. Jacob's abandoned horse he was like a porcupine from the number of spears sticking in his carcase.] "We succeeded in reaching a rising ground, where we formed line while Mr. Jacob mounted behind Mr. Bagot. The affray had now lasted more than half-an-hour, a very few shots were fired without effect, and the last man shot was one of their chiefs. I must here remark that had not the gentlemen displayed much steadiness and coolness Mr. Jacob must have fallen, as it was by frequently coming to the present, but reserving our fire, that we kept the headmost men back, as on those occasions they doubled themselves up into the smallest possible compass, holding shields before their heads. In covering Mr. Jacob I was struck with a spear in the fore part of the head, but as it passed through a thick tarpaulin hat the wound was but slight; but the mare I rode was severely speared in the shoulder. When I was struck the natives gave a loud yell, as they did on every occasion when they appeared to gain an advantage. Having retreated a mile we had to halt to sew up the wound in the mare's shoulder, or she must have soon dropped from loss of blood. Then, choosing the clearest line to retreat upon, we continued our retreat, and found our cart and the police the following day. I feel convinced that the remainder of the sheep were not far distant, and the natives had assembled to defend them and resist their recovery. I further remark that a very strong party would be required to subdue them without loss of life to the attacking force, as their activity and courage, combined with their numbers and the necessity to attack them in a country unfavourable for horse movements, render them a much more formidable enemy than the colonists have generally any idea of."

Having given Lieut. Field's report of the fight and retreat, I will only add a little more here from Mr. J. C. Hawker's diary:—"On the retreat a number of blacks followed behind their fighting men, and continued to hand them spears. I consider the total number of them to have been over 300. One native with a white band round his head carried no arms, evidently the chief or leader giving orders. In addition to the number who opposed us were many who were not immediately engaged. They were not in the least intimidated by the number who fell, which could not be less than eight. When the ground was clear for us to gallop they kept on after us, and did not seem the least winded. The wish I had written down in the morning was thus disagreeably realised to our discomfort. Had not Mr. Jacob's horse been speared many more might have been shot; but still it was the opinion of all of us that it would have been impossible to recover the sheep with our small party, as we had only eight effective men, two of the pieces having become useless early in the fight; and after rallying the third time, by the loss of Mr. Jacob's horse we were again reduced, and subsequently also by the spearing of Lieut. Field's horse. The ground the encounter took place on was covered with polygnum and scrub, and intersected with creeks. The place had been rightly named by Captain Sturt on his way down the river—'The Islands.' We rallied three times, and kept our adversaries in check. On our arrival in Adelaide we found that Captain Grey, formerly of the 83rd regiment, had arrived to displace Colonel Gawler." It will be only bare justice to Colonel Gawler to remark that the indecisive measures adopted by him at this crisis, and so unusual in him, are fully accounted for by the weakened position he felt himself to occupy after the severe censures heaped on him for his vigorous actions in punishing the Milmenura tribes for their murders.

A numerous meeting of the inhabitants was quickly held in the Auction Mart, when it was resolved that a respectful memorial should be prepared and presented to His Excellency the new Governor, particulars of which will be given in a subsequent chapter.

CHAPTER IX.

BEFORE continuing the account of the affrays with the Rufus River natives, I have deemed it expedient to devote a chapter to the relation of the events which led to deposition of Governor Gawler by Captain Grey, which took place on the 10th May, 1841. At that date the volunteer party under Lieut. Field was vainly endeavouring to recover the stolen property of Messrs. Inman and Field.

By his early actions Governor Gawler threw life into the service, which soon affected favourably the general business of the colony. The various staffs were strengthened, and the place became much more lively.

It was soon after the arrival of Colonel Gawler that the erection of substantial public buildings was commenced from the designs and under the superintendence of Captain Frome; one of the first being the present gaol. Then two bridges were commenced to span the Torrens, substantial, as they ought to have been, but which heavy floods soon carried away. Among other energetic actions of the Governor were the various explorations on which he went to judge for himself the capacity of the colony for settlement. After he had seen as much and had travelled as far as he deemed requisite, he published interesting and encouraging reports of what he had seen. He expressed his belief that the portion of the colony he had inspected would carry a large population. I forget exactly the number he ventured to give, but I think it was 200,000. He pronounced it to be a decided mineral country, and rich in argentiferous and auriferous promises. For publishing these opinions he was laughed at by the croakers; but what has been proved? His anticipations have been very far exceeded, in spite of many errors and adverse circumstances.

In the midst of his active career he received a serious and unlooked-for check before he could carry out his policy to success, which unfortunately "pulled him up by the round turn," as the sailors say. He had exceeded his general powers by overdrafts on the authorities at home, but in an amount only of about £300,000, small indeed, when compared with the annual interest now being paid on our loans. His drafts were dishonoured, he was recalled, and the colonists were ruined. Ultimately, after a fatal delay, the claims were met by a loan and debentures guaranteed by the Imperial Government. All such advances were recouped in a very short time, but the management of the colony was taken out of the hands of the Board of Commissioners in London and transferred to the Colonial Office, Downing Street. The constitution provided under the original founding Act, and to be granted to the colony on the population reaching the number of 50,000, was also forfeited.

A greater commercial crash never fell on any painstaking and industrious community than we were called upon to endure when the Governor's drafts were dishonoured. The ruin reached every class, and most of those who had invested the whole of their capital in legitimate pursuits never afterward recovered their lost position or property. The stagnation continued over many months. Some few amongst the recent arrivals were fortunate enough to acquire stock and land at nominal prices, the unfortunate sellers having locked up all their capital.

During the time Colonel Gawler administered the government of South Australia many special surveys were taken up, which were found useful in providing funds at that time, but which exercised a mal-influence in placing so much of the best and well-watered land in the hands of absentees. Amongst others, two special surveys were applied for on Yorke's Peninsula, which were afterwards abandoned, worse luck for the speculators, as one of them would have embraced Kadina and Wallaroo, and the other the mineral land fronting Spencer's Gulf, including harbours—one in each gulf. I may here mention that the late Mr. Osmond Gilles was one of the subscribers to the Association organised to take up the special surveys on Yorke's Peninsula, and also acted for some of his friends in England, and that he read to me one of his enthusiastic letters to them, in which he predicted that there would be included in the properties a port on each side of the Peninsula with a railroad connecting them (which latter work has since been accomplished). I also remember his angry remarks when the speculations were given up. Some year or two later I heard another remarkable prediction as to the future of Yorke's Peninsula from that eminent mineralogist and geologist, the late Mr. Menge. We were resting on one of the hills at the entrance to Glen Osmond, when he pointed across the gulf and said, "Before many years are over, rich copper mines will be worked there, and ships will be in harbours on both sides of the Peninsula to convey the ores away." To which I replied, "How do you know, you have not visited that part, I believe?" "No, I have not, but I pronounce the Flinders Range to be a rich copper-bearing vein of country from the part of it I have examined in the north; that range in past ages extended to the southern end of Yorke's Peninsula, and a mighty sea-wash long continued, has carried away the same and reduced it to the present level, and copper will be found near the surface."

At the time this prediction was made we were still suffering under our first crisis. By the working of mines in fulfilment of his predictions, and by the untiring energy of a small population engaged also in other pursuits, the colony has been

ARRIVAL OF McKINLAY AND PARTY AT ESCAPE CLIFF, NORTHERN TERRITORY.

raised from that crushing depression, which ought never to have been allowed to occur, to its present proud position. We have received accommodation on the most favourable terms to develop those great resources which Colonel Gawler and Professor Menge rightly perceived the country promised, and yet the first-named was allowed to pass his latter days in obscurity, and die a disappointed man, as many great and good men, benefactors to their fellow-creatures, have done before him.

A sad event occurred on the occasion of the Governor's flying visit to the North-West Bend of the River Murray. Some time before he started he purchased from me three horses, the price of which was £320. On one he rode himself, on another he mounted a young gentleman, a Mr. Bryan, and on the third one of his staff. On their arrival at the North-West Bend, a camp was formed, from which he started with his visitor, Mr. Bryan, and one attendant, on a flying trip in a northerly direction. He expected to find water on the course he took, but after pushing on many miles without coming to water, he endeavoured to return. Shortly before sunset one of the horses gave up, and they were unable to proceed. After a rest he left Mr. Bryan with the knocked-up horse, and pushed south to reach the Murray River for water to send to the relief of horse and man. The weather was fearfully hot. His Excellency and his attendant, unused to bush deprivations, before they could reach the river were so exhausted that one of the horses was killed and his blood drank. On reaching the camp men and horses were sent on their return tracks, with all that was necessary to save man and horse. On the relief party reaching the place where the unfortunate young gentleman was left, it was found that he had gone. The track of his horse was followed by the mark of his tether rope, which he had dragged, and a long-continued search was made of the scrub for miles in every direction, but no traces of Mr. Bryan were found, and his remains have not been discovered to this day. Some years afterwards, several miles from the place where he was left, the horse was discovered alive, with his hoofs turned up like skates. On Colonel Gawler's return from this unfortunate expedition his distress of mind may be imagined, as this young gentleman was a visitor at Government House, and was not lost in the execution of a public duty.

Our first Resident Commissioner, Mr. Jas. Hurtle Fisher, held office until the arrival of our second Governor, Colonel

Gawler. One great mistake made during his management of the Crown lands was the sale of the whole of the town acres at a time when so few colonists had arrived. This was done in obedience to instructions emanating from the Commissioners in London. Thus a great sacrifice of public property was made to the advantage of a small number of mere land speculators, and to the disappointment of settlers immediately following.

Mr. Fisher was not only head of the Land Department, but also of the Commissariat; and this brings to my recollection a transaction I had with that department shortly after my arrival. I had purchased stock which arrived in two ships from Twofold Bay, and I was applied to by the Commissioner for some dairy cows for the Government, and was also informed by Mr. Fisher that he had purchased in Tasmania a quantity of breeding and store pigs which he wished to dispose of. As I had purchased a large stock of damaged flour and ship biscuit, a double transaction was carried out by the Commissioner, and an exchange made between milking cows and grunters. To take charge of the cattle and sheep which I had purchased I engaged two young Scotchmen, one of whom was a cousin of an eminent Scotch baronet. Mention is made of these particulars to give a correct account of the diverse materials out of which our community has sprung. The pigs had to be let out and driven to water daily to the river, a distance of about one mile, from whence water for domestic use had to be carted. As I had given employment to the two respectable young Scotchmen, a third, a shipmate of theirs, continued daily to apply for work. He had been clerk in a bank in Scotland, and would take no denial that the establishment would not be likely to have any opening for one of his class. On one occasion he was present when the pigs were let out, and was told there was only the office of pig-minder open, on which he immediately applied for and accepted the appointment, and continued to mind and feed the pigs, and do all such work, chasing them to water and back, and performing all the other uncongenial parts of his duties to his employer's satisfaction, if not to his own; but no time was lost in procuring more suitable work for him. On a party being organised to go to Sydney to purchase and conduct sheep overland, he was recommended to be employed as a drover, and was engaged. The party was successful in the purchase of sheep, and in the return with them down the Murray River. The young Scotchman succeeded in obtaining, on

favourable terms, sheep for himself, and was most fortunate in placing them on a good run about one hundred miles to the north of Adelaide, which he took up, where he remained perseveringly for about seven years, and then sold out, realising, as it was said, the large sum of £25,000, with which he retired from the colony.

To return to Mr. Fisher. On losing his office of Commissioner he resumed his profession, and became the leader of our bar, moving many juries by his sensational and touching appeals, and soon had a leading practice.

Mr. Fisher was spared in life to enjoy several of the highest appointments obtainable in the colony. Under the first Corporation of the City of Adelaide he was chosen to fill the office of Mayor under the Bill of Incorporation established by the Act of Council 4th Victoria, No. 4, the officers being the Mayor, three Aldermen, thirteen Councillors, a Treasurer, Town Clerk, Town Surveyor, and sundry subordinate officers. The allowance to the Mayor provided under the Act was £300 per annum. Powers were given under the Act to levy rates on the citizens, not to be *more* frequent than once in each quarter. The inhabitants were hardly numerous enough to bear the pressure of this unwieldy establishment at so early a period. Town offices, Council Chamber, &c., &c., had been rented, and well furnished. The corporate body having had several sittings, a rent day came in due course, and at last, when the Treasurer had not sufficient funds, the landlord walked in and saved the Mayor, Aldermen, and Councillors, &c., from vacating their seats by seizing all the chairs and other furniture for arrears of rent, and shortly after this climax the ponderous body collapsed. The landlord, in accordance with the old saying, finding nobody to kick nor soul to be blessed, consoled himself by the sale of the movables. So ended, after a very brief existence, our first grand Corporation, cut out and constructed on the ancient patterns of the old country. On looking over the names of the civic dignitaries forming that body, it must be admitted that it would be a difficult matter to select more respectable or suitable men to fill such offices now that the city has attained its present importance.

On the passing of the Imperial Act granting the colony two elective houses, Mr. Fisher was chosen President of the Legislative Council, which high office he filled with dignity and success for some years, and had the honour to receive from Her Majesty the dignity of knighthood. Sir Jas. Hurtle Fisher remained in the colony until his decease at a ripe old age, universally respected.

In justice to the memory of Colonel Gawler it is right to give, in considering his sudden recall, the following explanation of the financial difficulties he encountered on his assumption of office as Governor of South Australia, quoted from one of his first despatches to the Secretary of State for the Colonies.

The despatch is dated January 23, 1839. Colonel Gawler says:—

"On arriving here about three months ago I found the public offices with little pretension to system. There were scarcely any records of past proceedings, or of public accounts, or issue of stores. The non-fulfilment of one of the leading principles of the regulations made for the disposal of land, that the surveys should be in advance of the demand, had produced a number of complicated questions which the letter of the law as it stood could not rectify. Sections were only laid out in the plain about Adelaide. Seven other districts remained to be marked out for the choice of preliminary purchasers, who will occupy the greater part of the good land in them. The survey department reduced to the Deputy-Surveyor, Mr. G. S. Kingston, with one draftsman and one assistant. The population shut up in Adelaide, capital flowing out for the necessaries of life almost as fast as it was brought in from England. The colonial finances in a state of thorough confusion and defalcation. Almost all I have been able to discover definitely of the finances of this period is that the whole of the regulated expenditure for the year was drawn and expended in the first quarter."

It is natural to suppose that a copy of this despatch would be supplied to the Board of Commissioners, who were then responsible for the management of the finances of the colony; but it is scarcely probable that Lord Glenelg ever read this despatch. Colonel Gawler held his appointment as Governor from the Crown, but his office of Commissioner from the Board of Commissioners sitting in London.

The despatch proves that the home authorities were at an early period made aware of the embarrassed position of their representative on his arrival in the colony, viz., that three-quarters of arrears of liabilities were incurred prior to his assumption of his double office. Then, notwithstanding the information so promptly sent, ship-loads of passengers and immigrants continued to arrive, to complicate and add to the Governor's embarrassments. Thus it is evident that the Governor was compelled to stretch his powers to draw on home authorities, who must have been kept posted up from time to time of such drafts. We know that the influx of population was not arrested; and we are not informed that Colonel Gawler received any special instructions in answer to the information he sent as to how he was to meet the emergency of arrears which could not be laid to his door. It appears clear enough to the writer that the Commissioners at home were bound either to have met the difficulties which had occurred through the mistaken opening arrangements, and by their accepting a trust tied down by conditions which could not be carried out, or at once, if unable to do so, to have thrown up the work they had undertaken into the hands of the Imperial Government, as they had ultimately to do.

The real requirement was a loan of, say, half a million, guaranteed by the Government, to meet arrears and to provide for necessary works.

It is, indeed, a wonder to me how the Board of Commissioners, good men of business as they were, could have expected successfully to launch and build up a large colony, at such a distance from the mother country, without sufficient capital within reach of their working representative. The fact of the appointment of officers, with the exception of Governor, resting with them, left them solely responsible for the first errors. In reviewing the material losses as well as the loss of time, in respect to public interests, we now see that subsequent prosperity has recovered such wastes ; but the sacrifice of the small capitals of the pioneer settlers they have had themselves to bear without compensation.

By the Act of 15th August, 1834, the Home Government appointed a Governor, and the Board of Commissioners in London had the appointment of a Resident Commissioner in the colony under whose control the Land Fund was placed. By a clause in the Act a most unfortunate blunder was made, which provided that the whole of the proceeds of the land sales were to be devoted to immigration, without power to apply any portion to defray the expenses of surveys, or for the erection of indispensable public buildings and other works, to meet which imperative demands a debt had to be incurred, at a ruinous rate of interest, at the same time that the forced capital which had been raised at a great sacrifice was lodged, at a low rate of interest, in the British funds. The first mistake was a divided Government in the colony : the second, the Governor having to serve two masters, viz., the Home Ministry with the Imperial Parliament, and the Board of Commissioners, no sympathy being felt between the two powers, but on the contrary, the Commissioners were held in no respect by the Government as to the principles on which the colony under their management was to be carried out.

In this unfavourable state of the affairs of the colony it is quite clear that Colonel Gawler was compelled, in accepting the position, to take upon himself a responsibility, the absolute necessity of which I consider is amply proved by his despatch to Lord Glenelg, from which I have quoted. To make matters worse, Captain Grey was afterwards hastily sent out with inadequate means and unworkable instructions.

Foster, in his History of South Australia, says :—" Captain Grey's duty was not an agreeable one. He had to commence immediately to bring the expenditure of the Government into something like agreement with its *income;* on this subject his instructions were specific and stringent.

" He had also to stave off as well as he could the creditors of the Government, who held many thousand pounds of dishonoured Government bills, besides a considerable amount of unsettled claims, until arrangements could be made with the home authorities for satisfying them."

Answers from home could not be expected to reach the colony under twelve months, if immediately attended to, the only means of communication being then by sailing ships of the old stamp.

In this state of things Captain Grey arrived to displace Colonel Gawler, on the 10th of May, 1841, without notice, and walked into Government House without ceremony, having on the front steps read his commission in the hearing of a very small audience there assembled, and received by them with no marks of approval. Not many months before he had been hospitably received and entertained by Colonel Gawler when he visited the colony after he had accomplished his difficult but successful exploring trip in Western Australia, and spent sufficient time here to become acquainted with the value of the country and its requirements. Of him it might reasonably have been expected, from his experiences of the causes which had kept back the elder colony of Swan River, and from his subsequent visit to our younger one, that he would have been looked up to by the authorities at home as a traveller of experience, competent to advise the Ministry of Her Majesty as to the capacity and requirements of South Australia; and in any case, if he came out to accept the government without first giving his opinion, founded on his experience as to the truth of Colonel Gawler's report of the intrinsic value of the undeveloped country of South Australia, or had thrown discredit upon those reports, he is much to blame for the crowning ruin he assisted in bringing on the first inhabitants of the infant colony.

I feel I shall be doing right, before I conclude the brief history of Colonel Gawler, to republish the following notice from the *Australian Mail* of the 15th of June, 1869 :—

" George Gawler, born in 1796, was destined for the military service. He joined at an early age the 52nd Light Infantry Regiment, in November, 1811, and served to the end of the Peninsular War. He was present at the storming of Badajoz, where he led the ladder party of the 52nd stormers, and received a wound below his right knee, and at St. Munos a wound in the neck. He was present at the battles of Vera, Vittoria, Nivelle, Orthes, and Toulouse, besides various minor affairs. At Waterloo he commanded the right company of his regiment. He received the war medal, with seven clasps, as a reward for his services. After the restoration of peace he continued with the regiment, performing his duties with that zeal and intelligence which so largely distinguished the officers of the 52nd, and assisted in making the regiment one of the best in the service. His military career soon closed, but he continued on half-pay until 1850, when he sold his commission with no ordinary feelings of pain. As a civil officer his career commenced under the auspices of his illustrious commander-in-chief, the Duke of Wellington, who interested himself in his advancement, urging that ' Gawler could not act otherwise than wisely, for he never did a foolish thing in his career.' His merits were recognised in 1838 by the appointment of Governor of South Australia, when the Imperial authorities and the ruling classes did not hold in favour the principle on which the colony was founded, not recognising it to be a means to provide homes for the toil-worn sons of England, of those unsoiled by crime, and as establishing another market for its exports.

"On entering his important, and to him novel duties, he found serious obstacles to be overcome, of sufficient weight to deter an ordinary man, but which Colonel Gawler grappled with with firm determination. It should always be looked upon as a turning point in the history of South Australia in acknowledging the influence he had upon its early struggles. What, then, did he accomplish? He had no light task to bring order out of the chaotic materials of the early expeditions. There was little or no authority amongst those who attempted a settlement between 1836 and 1838. The settlers, disappointed as they were at the delay they experienced in getting their land, were yet without a protecting force, either police or military. The administrative officers were for months disagreeing about their duties and responsibilities, and not only was the Government destitute of public offices and buildings, but the small population at the time of the Governor's arrival may be described as nomadic rather than as having houses and homes such as could be acceptable to English settlers. Colonel Gawler, by his own confession, admitted that he entered on his government hastily, and without being able to make minute calculations. He accepted his instructions under a strong conviction that the emergency clause in them would always protect him, and that expenses of a special or extraordinary nature might be incurred without previous authority, when justifiable on the ground that delay would be productive of serious injury to the public service.

"It is worth while, now that the colony is an established success, to inquire in what state it would have been if these emergency powers had not been liberally given and extensively acted upon. The home authorities did not approve of his actions in the extent to which he relied upon such emergency clauses, although he had in his despatches given full notices of his actions, and the grounds by which he had been influenced. It does not appear that they believed his reports of the value of the country and its prospective importance, although such reports were based on his own personal toilsome excursions, in exploring an extent of country not even yet fully occupied, after a lapse of time exceeding a third of a century since they were made.

"Colonel Gawler left the province on the 22nd June, 1841.

He was presented on his departure with unanimous addresses and a purse containing £500, contributed by the colonists out of their diminished means, which sum he left to be invested in land on his account, as a connecting link between himself and the colony. The amount raised, considering the depressed state of the inhabitants, was respectable, and was made up by many small contributions from persons who had been greatly reduced by the policy forced on the Home Government by a niggardly Parliament, who could not look into the future and see that the Australian colonies were to become the best customers for British goods, and so great a safety-valve to relieve the mother country of her teeming population. Following immediately after his recall, a committee of the House of Commons investigated the consequence of his large but not lavish expenditure. The result was a loan from the Consolidated Fund of £155,000 towards the temporary relief of the colony. Mr. G. Wakefield had remarked, 'I cannot imagine the possibility of founding a colony without obtaining money for its first expenses from some other source than itself. At first it has no existence at all, and one might as well propose to manufacture cotton goods without the outlay for the building, machinery, and the raw materials, &c.' The consequences, not only of the temporary relief granted by the British Government, but also from the carrying out the early policy of Colonel Gawler, have proved all that could have been desired. The land has yielded its increase, not only in rich and abundant crops, but the mines also in silver, lead, and copper ores.

"Colonel Gawler, after appeals to Parliament and to successive Governments in vain, wearied and disgusted with routine and red tape, exercised the right of petition to Her Majesty, but received no other response than a bare acknowledgment through the Secretary of State. When he afterwards applied for some honorary title in reward for his long and faithful services, he was absolutely refused, and the grand old soldier had but little to wrap himself in but his martial cloak and a conscience void of offence. Sincerity, earnestness, and devotion marked his career. His last appearance in public in London was at the dinner to Sir James Fergusson, previous to his proceeding to occupy the Governorship of South Australia. He spoke more than once with a vigour which charmed those present, and with an enthusiasm fresh and youthful, of the substantial progress since his time. At this dinner, in honour of the newly-appointed Governor, Colonel Gawler quoted the following lines :—

> ' What constitutes a State?
> Not high raised battlements or laboured mound,
> Thick wall or mounted gate;
> Not cities proud with spires and turrets crowned ;
> Not bays and broad-armed ports,
> Where, laughing at the storm, rich navies ride ;
> Not starred and spangled Courts,
> Where low-browed baseness wafts perfumes to pride :
>
> ' No ! men, high-minded men,
> Who know their rights, and knowing dare maintain,
> Prevent the low-aimed blow
> And crush the tyrant while they rend the chain —
> These constitute a state,
> And sovereign Law, that State's collected will,
> O'er thrones and globes elate,
> Sits Empress—crowning good, repressing ill.'

" A standard not less high was ever present to his mind, and although his true worth was not recognised largely and publicly, it is through such sons that England has reared her Empire, and that her influence the wide world over is regarded as just, wise, and beneficent."

I quote a speech which Colonel Gawler addressed to a sorrowing audience of colonists in Adelaide the day before he departed from the colony. He said :—" Gentlemen, it gives me very deep regret, very great pain, to leave the colony with so many accounts, which have arisen under my administration, unsettled ; but I have the fullest confidence that not one account will remain unpaid, because such accounts have been drawn upon my authorities. It has been difficult to explain to you such authorities, which are scattered through the whole of my correspondence during that period. Parties in England have judged of the effect which ought to have been given to these instructions by the standard of what they *supposed* the colony to be, but I have judged of those instructions from what I have *known* the colony to be, and from what I knew of its requirements; and from their imperfect knowledge of the colony in England, as opposed to my knowledge of it, these unfortunate difficulties have arisen."

" On May the 7th, 1869, at Southsea," says the *Australian Mail*, " Colonel Gawler died, and his most enduring monument will be the colony of South Australia, which he lived to witness a permanent success." I am happy to be able to add, that on a recent occasion the city of Adelaide received, as a present from Colonel Palmer, an excellent oil painting of this good and gallant man, which has been placed in our splendid Town Hall.

CHAPTER X.

SHORTLY after Governor Grey's arrival, a numerous meeting of the inhabitants was held in Adelaide, and a committee appointed to present a respectful memorial to His Excellency, urging him to take the promptest measures to protect parties on their way overland with stock. The committee consisted of Messrs. Inman, Kinchela, James Fisher, Captain Ferguson, and Mr. Giles, as chairman. The deputation was politely received by Governor Grey, who expressed his readiness to promote the objects in view, so far as the means at his disposal would permit. He promised to lay the matter before a meeting of his council, and communicate with the chairman of the committee. In his answer he stated that it would be necessary to communicate with the Governor of New South Wales. He was willing to accept the services of the volunteers offered to assist the police, but he could not admit the idea that a military expedition should take place against the natives; but the services of the volunteers would be accepted as special constables. That positive instructions had been issued by Her Majesty's Government to treat the aboriginals of all parts of the continent as subjects of the Queen within Her Majesty's allegiance. However, orders were immediately given to the Commissioner of Police to prepare for an expedition to the disturbed district, and a large number of colonists were sworn in as special constables—peace officers to meet victorious blacks with spears in their hands!

Major O'Halloran, Commissioner of Police, was appointed to command this second party, with special orders to protect the lives and properties of the settlers, but was not to levy war or to exercise *belligerent actions* against the aborigines of Australia. The Major was supreme in command of the combined party of police and volunteers, but to be accompanied by the

Protector of Aborigines, Dr. Moorhouse, with some native interpreters. Subscriptions of money and stores were raised by the inhabitants towards the expenses of the expedition.

The following gentlemen were sworn in :—Mounted : Captains Beevor, Inman, and Ferguson; Messrs. Berry, J. C. Hawker, Langhorne, H. Field, Jas. Fisher, Barber, Brown, Whitpine, Tooth, S. K. Langhorne, Daniel, and Oliver. Foot : Messrs. Martin, Gatwood, Dennis, Pavlin, Head, Day, Deprose, Daverell, Taylor, and three men as bullock-drivers. Volunteers, mounted and on foot, 27 ; mounted police, officers and men, 26 ; foot ditto, including four drivers, 11 ; in all, 64. Volunteer officers : Mr. J. Beevor, senior officer ; Mr. R. Ferguson, junior do. Commissaries : Mr. J. C. Hawker, senior officer; Mr. G. Daniel, junior do.

On the 29th May the drays were despatched, containing camp requirements from Captain Ferguson's store. On the 31st, the greater part of the volunteers, desirous of showing their respect to Colonel Gawler before his departure, mustered and waited on him in a body to bid him farewell.

On the 5th June the expedition arrived at the Pound, on the Murray. On the 6th the Major read the Governor's instructions to his command. Mr. Moorhouse, with three natives, who were to be employed as interpreters, had joined, and was present. Some additions to the force having arrived, the total muster amounted to sixty-eight. Two boats, under Mr. Kiffin, were ordered to join the party from Lake Alexandria, in case they required to cross the Murray.

I now take advantage of the Commissioner's diary.

"*June 8th, Tuesday.*—Morning bitter cold ; our native interpreters returned by moonlight from their visit to the tribe in whose country we are now encamped, and state that the natives have promised to come and see us in the morning, and are very anxious that we shall kill all the blacks of the tribe who have got the sheep, that tribe being their enemies (as they pretended). Three of the natives from the river came into the camp at 7.30 A.M. Two of them offered to go with us as interpreters to the tribe who have the sheep.

"*June 9th, Wednesday.*—Three natives, who joined us yesterday, have promised that no injury shall be done to the dray sunk in the river. Mr. Moorhouse and myself put them through an examination after breakfast.

"These men commenced their statements by falsely declaring

that the sheep were near. On being detected they said they meant that the first sheep tracks were near. Now, this was a still grosser falsehood, for the fight occurred more than 100 miles from this camp. Much falsehood is apparent throughout their answers.

"*June 10th, Thursday.*—Several more natives have crossed over to our camp this morning. Feed bad here; struck camp at 10.30 A.M., and moved on nine miles on account of better feed. One of the volunteers' bullocks lost.

"*June 11th.*—Halted here. Passed a bitter cold night. Foot drill and sword exercise from 11 till 12.30. The drilling gets on admirably. The boats have not arrived. They ought to have been here.

"*June 12th, Saturday.*—Another cold and frosty night. Halted for the day, most anxiously looking out for the boats. Sword and carbine exercise. During the afternoon some more natives joined, but could not get more satisfactory information from them than from the previous examination of the men of their tribe.

"*June 13th, Sunday.*—Halted for the day. The two blacks whom we examined, and who promised to accompany us to the hostile tribe, have disappeared, and told our natives previous to departure, one of them that he was lame, and the other that his children would cry, so that all hope of their usefulness as interpreters has vanished, and their desertion will I fear prove a most serious disadvantage to us.

"*June 14th.*—Blazed three trees close to the river, and wrote largely upon them—'Boats to follow on.' I have named this camp Wallaby Flat. Some natives joined us on the march, and one of them said he had seen the sheep three days ago, and that they were numerous, but were afraid of the blacks, who could not manage them. He also stated that the blacks were aware of our approach, and were going up the river, and would not fight us. This blackfellow offered to go with us and show us where the sheep are. The drays did not come up till 6.15 P.M.

"*15th, Tuesday.*—For the last three days the wind has been fresh and fair for the boats, and yet they have not arrived, though we have halted at various times, in all six days, to enable them to come up. I must now calculate the distance we may have yet to advance, and push on for our destination with all speed possible, to prevent the chance of our provisions falling short. We are now sixteen days from Adelaide. If the boats do not come up the day after to-morrow, I shall blaze the trees, and order the boats to remain after their arrival at the blazed trees until our return. Two of our Adelaide natives refused to go further, and have remained behind with some of the river blacks. Their loss to us will be great, for the third black is lazy and stupid, and he was not engaged, but allowed to accompany us as a supernumerary.

"*June 16th, Wednesday.*—Moved off at daybreak. Marched through a seventeen-mile scrub, and encamped in a very long polygnum flat, with a long pole stuck up in the centre by natives, at 2.15 P.M.; distance, twenty miles. Drays up at 4.45.

"*17th.*—Heavy rain about 4 this morning. Yesterday the Governor's servant, Binstead, was assaulted by one of the river blacks who had joined us. The tents wet through, and as the camp is in low ground, we are surrounded by water.

"*18th.*—The morning fine and clear. Examined Binstead's charge against the blackfellow and ordered him out of the camp. At 10.45 started. On the march fell in with thirty-one blacks; saw also others in various directions, and fourteen on the opposite side of the river. All the blacks we have seen are small and by no means powerful. Blazed three trees close to the river, and wrote largely on them, 'Boats return to Bend. Dig underneath.' Buried a bottle containing instructions and information to look out, as natives are numerous and not trustworthy. Established an alarm post, and ordered extra sentries, five in all, to be placed around the camp during the night.

"*June 19th, Saturday.*—Struck camp an hour before daybreak. Moved off with the drays at 8.30 A.M. Passed Lake Bonney at 10 A.M. About 150 natives are in our rear who say they want to see us fight and kill their enemies, with whom they will also fight. I do not allow them to come near us. We are marching in fighting order with an advance and rear guard; the drays in the centre. I keep these rascals off, for if we beat the natives they will take their wives, and if we are beaten they will fall upon us. Crossed Lake Bonney and got to the north side of it, and upon a ridge of scrub, the commencement of the country of the hostile tribe, at 11 A.M. On looking to the rear we saw a large signal fire just lit by the vagabond blacks behind to give notice to those ahead of our approach."

I now continue with extracts from Mr. James C. Hawker's diary:—

"*20th, Sunday.*—Off at 9.40. The mounted men had to halt at about every three miles to allow the drays to come up, the country being boggy. Passed a great many tracks of wild cattle. Large numbers of natives showed themselves on both sides of the river. Efforts were made to induce some of them to come to us, but they remained shy.

"*June* 21*st.*—Off at 9 A.M. Track better. At 3.30 arrived at a creek running into the river, on the opposite bank of which many natives were assembled ; with them some of the blacks who had been with us and had bolted. They told us that the sheep were still alive, and they would give them up to us ; they also said a party with cattle coming down the river were a few days' journey from us. Camped on the lagoon.

"*22nd.*—The men in bringing in the working bullocks reported they had seen recent footmarks of a number of sheep. Off at 8.30, as the Major desired to recover the sheep without delay. The natives here left us, saying they would join us when we reached the place at which we would find the sheep alive, as they would take a shorter cut than we could travel on. At 12 camped, distance eight miles, on a creek which crossed the small flat where Messrs. Inman and Field were attacked, the creek now running good water. After an hour's rest the Major proceeded on with the mounted men."

Mr. J. C. Hawker, having charge of the drays, did not accompany the advance party. In addition to Major O'Halloran's diary I am indebted to information furnished me by Inspector Tolmer, Sergeant-Major Alford, and Sergeant Naughton, for the following particulars and remarks :—

The Major with the mounted men pushed on, hoping to come up to the travelling cattle party as well as the remains of the sheep. After riding five miles they met a white man in a deplorable state, naked, except a blue shirt which he had converted into trousers hanging from his waist, with a pair of Wellington boots on his feet, but with no other clothing. He reported an attack of the blacks, and that some of the party had been killed. A little further on we met the drays with the survivors of the party, one of them named Miller, the conductor, lying in a dray with five spear wounds in his body.

The Major was told that at the time of the attack some of the drovers had been sent back by Mr. Miller to recover and bring up part of the cattle which had gone back, and the weakened advanced party were attacked ; the men being overpowered, and seeing three of their mates killed, and their overseer seriously wounded, took to the river, and after remaining some time in the water, finding the blacks had retired from some (to them) unknown cause, came out of the river, and finding three of the bodies of their dead comrades, they rolled them over the bank, as much out of sight as possible, and hastened forward on the track.

As Major O'Halloran subsequently found one of these bodies shockingly mangled, it must appear that the cause of their suddenly abandoning the ground on which they had defeated the overlanders was, that they had received in the midst of their work the first news from a flying scout of the large number of armed whites who were approaching; and that afterwards getting further information from the lying spies that the police were still some distance off, they had returned to effect the mangling of the bodies, and, perhaps, at the same time slaughtered the remainder of the sheep.

Such weak tampering with aboriginals, when combined and with arms in hand, and after murderous conduct, is anything but a policy of mercy, either to the natives or to the settlers, as no grounds ought to be given to the latter to take the law into their own hands. It is a remarkable circumstance that immediately after the arrival of Captain Grey to displace Colonel Gawler, he should have to report to the Imperial Government the non-success of the weak policy he had undertaken to carry out as to the treatment of the natives. He had himself experienced in his explorations in Western Australia something of the dangerous character of untamed blacks.

I feel it a fair remark to make that as it was taken for granted in his instructions that the aboriginals of all parts of Australia were "subjects of Her Majesty and within her allegiance," that it should have followed that subjects of whatever colour found in arms, and after committing such crimes as these had, should have been promptly treated as subjects in revolt, and have been dealt with accordingly, constables' staves being left at home.

I continue this account of Major O'Halloran's expedition, from information given by Mr. Miller, the wounded overseer of Mr. Langhorne's cattle party, and from the diaries and reports of officers.

When the attack was made, the overseer had despatched some of the men to the rear to bring up a part of the herd which had separated from the main body. These drovers did not come on to the ground where lay their slaughtered mates until the survivors had passed on, but overtook them shortly before they met the relief force. The cattle were then got together with the aid of the relief party, and with the loss of only seventy-three out of the original number of seven hundred, so that Mr. Langhorne had great cause for thankfulness that the police and volunteers arrived in time to save so large a proportion of his cattle, and probably the lives of the whole of his men. When the rear party overtook those who had survived the attack, it was resolved to push on with all speed to reach the nearest stations, as they had no idea of an approaching party. Their firearms were mostly useless, and they had only a few charges of ammunition left; the blacks had taken from the drays everything except part of their flour, and this was all the party had to depend on for the remainder of the journey. I now return to Mr. J. C. Hawker's diary, and continue with the further occurrences of the 23rd of June.

"At about 9.30 all the mounted men, and as many of the men on foot as could be spared from the camp, started to scour the country, to see if any of Inman's sheep were still alive, but nothing was found but the stinking carcases of about two thousand sheep, wantonly speared. A camp of about thirty natives was come upon, but the blacks bolted and took to the river, laughing and defying the party to shoot, and remaining within shooting distance, evidently aware of the orders under which the men carried their useless arms—with strict injunctions not to fire unless attacked. Amongst this insulting mob was identified one of the natives who had left the party the previous day, promising to procure a conference. The natives who had promised to give up the sheep were amongst the swimming niggers, thus proving their treachery. On the return of the force to the camp, Major O'Halloran took the depositions of Mr. Langhorne, jun., who was with the party when attacked, as well as of the overseer and men, and decided to start the next day to Lake Victoria, and endeavour to make prisoners.

"24*th*.—At 7.30 the party started for the lake—leaving Messrs. Inman, J. C. Hawker, and Field, in charge of the fortified camp—with the men on foot and all Mr. Langhorne's party except three."

The Major's diary continues—

"On the 26th the mounted force returned. They had divided into two parties at the lake, one party crossing the Rufus, keeping the easterly side, and the other continuing on the near side, in order to intercept the natives, but they had been on the alert, and had reached the farther side of the lake, and eight canoes were seen on the lake crossing the remainder, and so they accomplished their escape. When the party arrived at the junction of the Rufus with the Murray, they found, to their unspeakable horror, the mangled body of a man named Martin, one of the four murdered men who had been placed over the bank by their escaping mates. One of the bodies (the one found) had been brought up by the blacks, and placed on the upper bank, stripped naked; the skull had been battered with waddies, and exhibited masses of mangled bone, brains, and congealed blood; the bones of the arms and thighs had been removed; the sides had been opened, and the vital organs, with the kidney fat, had been extracted. In the hands small green boughs had been placed. All this had been done in derision after the men had been killed with spears, to accomplish which diabolical act the savages had returned to the spot. By the side of the body of Martin was seen a faithful bulldog named Blucher, which appeared to be wounded. The poor brute, alarmed at the approach of the police, took to the water, giving vent to a most piteous howl, which none of the hearers would be likely to forget. The rescued men said the dog had fought the blacks nobly, and was supposed to have been killed. The metaphorical fiendish display the blacks had time to indulge in may be read to mean that the whites when they intruded on their country had not bodily arms to fight with, or to defend themselves, and had not legs to escape from them, nor brains to cope with them; and to complete the unheard-of picture, they placed in the powerless hands small branches of green boughs as an emblem of their unarmed helplessness."

One of my informants, a very kind-hearted and genuine Englishman, thus expressed himself to me respecting the effect the shocking spectacle had upon him on seeing the derisively mangled body of his countryman. "Before this I never knew what it was to feel bloodthirsty or to desire to take the life of a fellow creature, but this sight caused my blood to run cold; and I then felt as if my brain was on fire, and that no command would restrain me from wreaking vengeance on such barbarous murderers. I do not know what the Major felt, but I could guess by his distorted countenance, silent as he was, how he felt his false position. I was with him in his raid against the

Milmenura tribes of natives after the Maria murders, but then his hands were not tied by instructions from the Home Government, and he there carried out what proved to be a humane policy, under the orders of Governor Gawler."

After a pause, to allow the feelings of the party to quieten, "the Major ordered a grave to be dug, and he performed funeral service over the body. Then a large fire was made and kept over the spot to disguise the grave. A watch belonging to one of the slaughtered men and a few other articles were found lying about, with broken spears, and here fifty-three head more of cattle were recovered."

Lake Victoria is twenty miles from the last strong camp, Lake Bonney being fifty-six, and the grave is 233 miles from Adelaide.

Continued from the Major's diary :—

"The place where Langhorne's overland cattle party were attacked was called Langhorne's Ferry by Major O'Halloran, as he here prepared the body of a dray by covering the bottom, back, front, and sides, with a tarpaulin; and in that makeshift crossed a party of eighteen men, under Inspector Tolmer, swimming their horses over to the opposite side. He gave the Inspector strict orders to make prisoners, if possible without bloodshed; to carry out the commands issued by His Excellency Governor Grey to the letter. The inspector, with his party, was directed to proceed a little inland, where some natives were known to frequent, and to force them, if found, towards the junction of the Rufus with Lake Victoria, towards the Major and his party of fourteen, who would be there ready to intercept them; after which, if time permitted, he would order both sides of the lake to be scoured. The drays and party in charge of them (thirteen in all) were to remain at Langhorne's Ferry till the scouring parties returned. The parties on both sides of the channel (known as the river Rufus, being the connection between the Lake and the Murray) mounted, and commenced operations at about mid-day. The Major's party had not proceeded far in extended order, when one of his scouts gave him notice that about thirty blacks were crossing the lake. Orders were given to pursue. The channel or junction of the lake being waded, the party passed to the New South Wales side, and with speed skirted the lake, when to their regret they found they were too late. They found at the bank of the lake eight canoes, which the blacks had left and vanished in the scrub. The Major, being thus foiled, turned back and recrossed the channel, which near the junction was found to be fordable. He now extended his men along the banks of the Rufus, in hopes to intercept any blacks that the inspector's party might drive before him. At 2.30 P.M. the inspector came in with his detachment, and reported he had met with no success. The country around was now seen to be in a blaze with signal fires, and finding it would be useless to make any further attempt to secure prisoners, the whole party returned to Langhorne's Ferry, and all hands were carefully employed in searching along the banks of the Rufus towards the lake in hopes of finding the other three bodies of the murdered men, which might have been carried by the current then passing from the river to fill up the lake. No more bodies were found, but a musket, uninjured, a morocco cigar case, and other scattered articles, with many broken spears. Trees here were blazed, and on them written, 'Beware of blacks,' to warn the next party of their danger on arriving in the country of these bloodthirsty tribes. The flour and other property of the previous sufferers had been found distributed in all directions on the Murray, Rufus, and lake, thus proving these vagabonds participated in the late dreadful and cruel murders.

"The party were ordered to return to the morning camp. Mr. Langhorne this day recovered four more of his cattle, having with the assistance of the relief party ultimately regained all but sixteen head of his number of seven hundred."

The party were now 260 miles from Adelaide and (the Major in his diary says) they could not expect to arrive there under three weeks, which in all would make an absence of nearly seven weeks. He felt much disheartened, after so much anxiety and exertion, that no prisoners had been taken, but he still hoped to be able to do so at or on arriving at Lake Bonney. One great source of consolation to him was that his party had been, under Providence, the happy means of saving the lives of twelve white men, as also the bulk of the cattle for the owner and the colony. He could not speak too highly of the admirable conduct of the entire detachment since they left town, every duty having been performed with a prompt cheerfulness; the gentlemen volunteers deserving especially his warm thanks for their gentlemanly conduct and strict obedience to orders; and their admirable example and quickness in learning their military duties had both surprised and greatly pleased him. The party returned to the fortified camp, and to the regret of the Major and the party the faithful dog Blucher did not again show himself.

On the 28th of June the whole party left the camp, which the Major named the Hornet's Nest, but the volunteers called it Fort O'Halloran. Their next camp was on the ground where the famous "Blue Beard" was shot some 18 months previously. Sturt mentioned him in his work. He was a very old man, and had a long white beard. It was reported that he was shot in the act of some treachery towards Miller's first party. The Major named this spot "Blue Beard's Den."

"*July 1st, Thursday.*—Marched seventeen miles, crossing Lake Bonney. Now out of country of hostile blacks. Captured a number of women and children, who, however, through a misunderstanding of orders by the men in charge, were released, and they escaped. One of them bit a policeman in the leg, and taking his sword about the middle snapped it in two. I was in hopes, by the capture of these women, and by releasing one of them with a message to her tribe, that we might, on promising to release the rest, have secured the three men who joined us in this neighbourhood with the promise of acting as interpreters with the hostile blacks, and who afterwards acted so false and treacherous a part. Looked for and found the bottle buried at this camp for the boats, from which I conclude that the boats have been counter-ordered. Just before dark six blacks fearlessly came to our camp. They were asked if they were not afraid to come near us; but they said no—they had done us no wrong, and they knew we would not hurt them. They knew we had caught their women and children and had released them. The men who had deceived us were ahead, and we should see them. I could not find in my heart to make prisoners of them after thus confiding in us. The point of a spear came out of Mr. Miller's groin this evening.

"The faithful bulldog Blucher, that we found at Langhorne's Creek guarding the dead body of poor Martin, to our astonishment came into camp this evening with the cattle. He is very thin and emaciated; had a spear wound through his body, and another in the hind leg, on which he is very lame. He has followed us in this state upwards of seventy miles, and appears at present very shy and timid.

"*July 5th.*—Dead Man's Flat.—A board on a tree, and on it 'Boats left for the Bend June 25th.' Some hours after arrival at camping-ground caught one of the blacks who had so grossly deceived us by acting as spy to the hostile tribe; notified to him in presence of other blacks that he should be taken as prisoner to Adelaide for the future good conduct of his tribe, for it seems that this fellow and five other men of his tribe were about to attack our cart on the line of our march homeward, and were only prevented by Sergeant Naughton presenting his carbine at them. He was in the cart sick, with Mr. Miller. The blacks doubtless coveted the rugs and blankets that were laid in numbers in the cart to form a soft bed for the wounded overseer.

"*July 6th.*—Left for town, giving over the command to Inspector Gordon."

Extract from Major O'Halloran's report, published in the *Register* of July 10, 1841 :—" Unfortunately, after great anxiety, we have failed in making any prisoners, but this has been owing solely to the boats not joining, and for which I cannot account. In a country such as I have gone over, intersected by rivers, lagoons, and creeks, and thick with polygnum scrub and high weeds. it is next to impossible to surprise any blacks, who all know (by scouts and signal fires) of the approach of any party from the time the same makes the river, into which the natives are ready to plunge, and are there secure from all danger. The cruel tribe we are now surrounded by are very numerous, and have doubtless become emboldened by having defeated three successive parties of Europeans, and having also escaped punishment from any detachment. Mr. Inman was attacked three miles from this, and Mr. Langhorne's party fifteen miles east of us; and this clearly proves that this tribe in the last three instances are the murderers of our countrymen, and the plunderers of their property."

I make the two following extracts from the *Register* :—

July 17th.—" The whole of the police party, we understand, returned from the Murray expedition on Wednesday, bringing in custody a native, though with what crime charged we have not heard. It is said the man was fastened to and obliged to follow the dray. He was tied up on his arrival in the Police Barracks, but during the night he contrived to escape, and no tidings of him have been gained."

July 24th.—" It will be recollected that one of the objects of the late expedition to the Murray was to protect the party of Mr. Langhorne (reported by him to the Governor), and known to be on the road with a large herd of cattle. The Mr. Langhorne who was with the party is indebted as well for his life as for the property to Major O'Halloran's party of police and volunteer gentlemen on the occasion. In knowledge of these facts it was with some surprise we heard it stated on the return of the party that the Mr. Langhorne who was with the cattle had refused to supply the expedition with more than one bullock, out of nearly seven hundred saved. We received last week a statement from Mr. J. C. Hawker, who took the trouble to act as commissary to the volunteer force, which we publish without comment. 'One beast only was killed for the police and volunteers. As commissary I represented to Captain Beevor that our rations of salt meat would not last us out if we supplied Mr. Langhorne's men with meat. On which Captain Beevor asked Mr. Langhorne when he would be killing a beast, as some of our men were suffering from scurvy. Mr. Langhorne's answer was, that if we thought we had come out to eat fresh meat all the way in we were very much mistaken, as it would cost him twenty head to last us into Adelaide. Mr. Beevor then asked if he would sell some to him, but he refused to sell any, making several paltry excuses.' The following is the account of the expenses incurred by the volunteer party:— 'To Messrs. August and Cook, flour, rice, &c., £42; hire of two teams at £8 a week, £55; bullock driver, &c., £8; total, £105. None of this amount was defrayed by Mr. Langhorne.'"

After the return of Major O'Halloran on the 8th of May, 1841, from his second expedition, Governor Grey being informed that other parties were on their way down, and made alive to the increased danger they would be likely to encounter from the same murderous blacks who had hitherto had it so nearly all their own way, felt it incumbent on him to send a third party under Sub-Inspector Shaw, and with him Mr. M. Moorhouse as Protector. (Qy.—Of the whites from unjust censures?)

In the *Register* of September 11, 1841, was published a report of that expedition from the Protector of the Aborigines; also a letter from Mr. Robinson, who was met by the Government force at the Rufus Junction, where a conflict took place, when the natives placed themselves between the two parties, and advancing to attack at length met with their deserts. I give an account of this affair from the public records of the time:—

"Yesterday morning Mr. Robinson arrived in Adelaide overland in advance of his party with stock from New South Wales under their charge, and has furnished accounts of two desperate affrays before reaching the Rufus, from which they safely escaped. We are enabled to present to our readers with full extracts from the official report of Mr. Moorhouse, the Protector of Aborigines, to His Excellency the Governor. The painfully interesting details which these documents furnish render comment for this week at least unnecessary, as an investigation has been ordered by the Governor to be made by the Bench of Magistrates. It is clear, however, on the surface that no party can for the present pass safely from New South Wales territory into South Australia unless sufficiently numerous and well armed.

"THE PROTECTOR'S REPORT.

"Lake Bonney, *September* 4, 1841.

"SIR,—I have the honour to inform His Excellency the Governor that the expedition consisting of twenty-nine Europeans with three Aborigines, which left Adelaide on the 31st July to meet Mr. Robinson and others on their route from Sydney, is now on its return, having been effectual in rendering all the assistance that was necessary to the parties. I joined the detachment fifty miles from Adelaide on the 4th of August, and with it reached the Pound on the 7th. I had all the party mustered, and read and explained my instructions to them. Several natives were within a mile of the camp, but did not visit us. Our blacks went to them, and returned with some curious reports, that in consequence of a black scout coming down the river, the bulk of the active natives had gone upwards on being called on 'to congregate and attack a party coming down the river with bullocks, sheep, and clothing.' I received the report with doubts, but as we travelled along the Murray I noticed an unusual absence of native camps, which soon led me to believe the story. In passing over a distance of over ninety miles we only saw natives on one place, the number being twenty-four—emaciated old men and women unable to travel.

"On the 18th of August we halted for the night, three miles to the south of Lake Bonney. Our Adelaide natives took three of our party—myself, Sub-Inspector Shaw, and a volunteer gentleman—to a creek two miles distant from our camp, where we saw 105 blacks, who seemed frightened at our approach, and several women took their children on their backs and ran into the water. Some of the men seized their spears and stood firmly by their wurlies. Two of them came to me, whom I had seen on my previous visit, and asked if I did not know them. They showed great anxiety to be on friendly terms with us, and said they could prove that they had not speared white man's property. They said there are three horses near our camp, and we could spear them at any time, but we have not done so, as we wish to be friends with white man. They then took us through a belt of scrub and showed us the horses within 400 yards of a wurlie.

"19th.—When about to march, forty of the natives we had seen last night came up to us, and urged us strongly not to go on, as there was a great number of blacks congregated two days' march ahead, at work preparing spears and other weapons, and they would be sure to attack us. They were 'turla butta' (full of wrath), and would take our clothing and provisions. I desired one of them to go with us, but he declined. This interview produced a bad effect on the blacks we brought from town. Two of them on the following day turned aside from the track, pretending to hunt, but did not return. Fortunately we had the other fellow on the dray, whom we did not suffer to escape.

"20th.—Halted to rest the cattle, now in the country of the hostile natives, and here had the first instance of aggression I witnessed on the river. The party were all at drill; the sheep we had with us for food were allowed to graze without a shepherd. When drill was over, and the shepherd went after his sheep, he found one with a spear in its side, and saw the aggressor, but he escaped. We now had some difficulty in keeping our interpreter. As we passed along the river he made many inquiries from natives on the opposite side, and frequently asked me how many sleeps we were from Lake Victoria, because he was told we would be attacked there. He induced three of these blacks to join us, whom we supplied abundantly with kangaroo, and allowed them to sleep at our camp, but charging them not to move about during the night lest one of the four guards might shoot them. Pangi Pangi, our Adelaide black, urged us to keep up drill that the strangers might see the superiority of white men's arms.

"On the 25th Sub-Inspector Shaw had a tree marked at a distance of fifty yards, and ordered the men to fire at the mark, allowing three seconds between each shot. Pangi Pangi said, 'I am glad, and no more frightened.' The three blacks who had been with us several days were terrified and wished to go before us to the lake 'to tell tribe what white man can do with mucketty.' I was glad to let them go.

"*27th.*—Now only five miles from the lake I mustered the party and repeated my instructions. Each man was told that no firing could be allowed until the inspector gave the command. I advised them, in case of attack from the natives, to use every exertion to protect the drays. At 9 A.M. we marched, and in an hour we saw two mounted men on the opposite side of the Rufus, whom we found to be Mr. Robinson and Mr. Levi, at one mile from Langhorne's Ferry towards the lake. We saluted them heartily, and asked if their party were all safe. They answered 'Yes, both persons and property,' although they had been attacked on the preceding day by a body of 300 blacks, who were repulsed after receiving eight rounds from the overlanders. At the time of the attack they were about two miles from the Rufus, and marched on and encamped at Langhorne's Ferry. They asked of us where the herds and drays could cross, as they were then looking out for an easy place to cross, and wished to do so immediately. They had found the junction of the Rufus with the lake too wide and deep, and now would take the ferry. We now left them and rode along the Rufus towards Lake Victoria, and greatly to our surprise discovered a large mob of natives running towards us, each carrying his implements of war. We hastily returned to our party. The drays were drawn up on the banks of the river; the men were formed in a line of two deep to protect the drays. In half an hour the natives were seen in the scrub at about half a mile distant, evidently prepared to commence an attack. I, seeing this, gave the command of the party to Sub-Inspector Shaw, and said he was at liberty to issue such orders as he thought necessary for our safety and of the overland party whom we had been sent out to protect, desiring him not to commence firing until I had spoken to the hostile natives. I ordered Pangi to accompany me in advance. After we had proceeded about three hundred yards, the three blacks who had gone forward at their own request to confer with the advancing tribe left the mob and came to us. I asked them what message they brought. They said the lake people would not listen to them; they knew the whites had tomahawks, blankets, and food, and they would have them at all risks. I took these fellows back and told them to sit down out of the way of the strife. The police party were on the western bank of the Rufus, and Mr. Robinson and his men on the eastern bank, who advanced towards the closing natives and commenced to fire on them; Mr. Shaw also ordered firing to commence. The natives were almost immediately thrown into confusion, the greater part running into the scrub, and about fifty running into the water to conceal themselves in the thick reeds. Both parties closed on to those in the water. The firing lasted about fifteen minutes, and the result to the natives was, according to my estimate, about thirty killed, ten wounded, and four prisoners taken (one adult male, one boy, and two lubras). Mr. Robinson was speared in the left arm. As soon as there was the least probability of taking prisoners firing ceased. More prisoners might have been taken if an alarm at the drays had not been given which called the party off from searching the reeds, and in the meantime the natives escaped.

"At 11 A.M. the following day the whole of Mr. Robinson's party were safely crossed. The police fully armed, being drawn up, the prisoners were placed in the centre, whom I addressed through the interpreters. I told them they had been advised by their allies not to attack the whites, whose arms were so superior to their own; that we had not any desire to kill black men, or their lives would have been taken; that I was empowered to allow the two who were wounded to go to their friends (that was a boy and a woman); that the other woman, whose husband had been killed, and who was rescued by the Adelaide black, having consented to become his wife, might go with him to Adelaide; that I should take the black man, the other prisoner, to Adelaide, and he would be there kept as a hostage, and if the tribe attacked any other party coming down the river, he might be put to death. I then gave the woman and the boy their liberty, and one day's supply of provisions, telling them we wished to be friends with their tribe, and that the prisoner was taken as a pledge of their future good conduct, &c."

Mr. Robinson's statement :—

"On July 1st, in company with Mr. Warriner (a crack shot with a rifle) and Mr. Barker, I left Gundaguy, on the Murrumbidgee, with 6,000 ewes, 14 horses, 500 mixed head of cattle, 3 drays, and 26 in party. We were well armed, and had heard of the attacks on the previous parties. We saw blacks all the way down, but did not allow them to come near us. On approaching the Rufus I had remained a day's march behind looking for strayed cattle, and saw thirty or forty natives fully armed on the track towards the lake. The blacks on seeing me crossed the Murray. The day following I had gone on ahead to look for a crossing-place. On my return towards the party I saw about 300 blacks, who, perceiving me, formed themselves into a half-circle to oppose the advance of the party. I immediately got all the sheep and cattle together, left nine men with the drays, and with the remainder of the party went to the blacks, who by this time had approached near to the sheep, yelling most hideously, and by their gestures evidently intent on an attack on us. They met our approach, on which we commenced firing. After receiving eight rounds the blacks gave way, and we drove them to the bush. During this affair about fifteen were killed or seriously wounded. We then proceeded on and camped. The following morning we were met by the party from Adelaide sent to protect us. We were told by them that they expected an attack that day. I said I thought not, as we had the previous day encountered a large number of blacks, and had beaten them. As we were preparing to cross at Langhorne's Ferry one of the Adelaide party came and informed us that the natives in force were approaching through the scrub. The three blacks who had preceded Mr. Moorhouse also told us that the hostile blacks were close at hand, determined to fight and plunder us. We met their advance and fired on them, &c. (as stated by Mr. Moorhouse). The prisoner on a subsequent day attempted to escape, and was not retaken until he had received three gunshot wounds."

Register, September 18th—Remarks of the Editor :—

"The Bench of Magistrates are to assemble on Monday to inquire into the late deplorable *rencontre* with the natives. The investigation is to be public. As the matter stands at present it is very plain Mr. Moorhouse cannot act as Protector, for it was under his protection they were shot down by dozens, and by his own showing, before they had thrown a spear or committed a single offensive act in his presence."

I have quoted the above, as the remarks of the editor will be so completely answered by the unanimous resolution of the Bench in justification of Mr. Moorhouse, after an examination of himself and others during three days; extracts from the published reports of which follow:—

On Monday, at midday, the Bench of Magistrates sat at the Court-House to investigate the circumstances under which about fifty natives were shot on the Murray by Mr. Robinson's overland party and by that under Mr. Sub-Inspector Shaw, despatched by His Excellency Governor Grey.

The Chairman of the Bench addressed Mr. Moorhouse, and informed him that in order to satisfy the public mind in the colony and at home, the Governor had thought it necessary to have an official investigation into the circumstances of the late engagement on the Murray, and requested Mr. Moorhouse to state to the Bench the facts of the case. Mr. Moorhouse's published report was read by Mr. Richman. Mr. Smillie asked Mr. Moorhouse if he adhered to that statement and confirmed it, and that gentleman replied that he did.

In answer to other questions Mr. Moorhouse stated—No spears were thrown before the firing commenced. The blacks were approaching in line with spears quivering in their hands poised ready for throwing. A message of defiance had been previously brought by three blacks (allies of the hostile assailants) that they were determined to have our property.

Captain Sturt—What was the conviction in your mind when you gave over the command of the party?—My conviction was that we were to be attacked; that if we had allowed them to approach within spear's throw we should all have been cut off. Firing was the only advantage we had to compensate for our small numbers, the muskets being able to kill at a greater distance than their spears. I calculated that one hundred and fifty fighting men who were in front had at least four hundred spears with them, each spear being equal to one gun if within their range.

Major O'Halloran—You think their object was to make a rush?—I think so, and so we all thought. I made signals to them not to approach, but they paid no attention.

Dr. Kent—What were your instructions?—They were, in case the natives manifested any hostile intention, to give over the command to Mr. Shaw that he might issue such orders as he deemed necessary for our safety.

Captain Sturt—You did not give up the command to Sub-Inspector Shaw till you saw all hopes of an amicable understanding were at an end?—I did not.

Captain Sturt—Can you venture an opinion as to whether Mr. Robinson's party would have driven them off without the assistance of the police?—I think they would have taken his drays and sheep from him.

Mr. Moorhouse further stated that about two days afterwards he saw about one hundred blacks with their arms, going down the river, but they offered no further annoyance.

Mr. Robinson also underwent a long examination, as also the native interpreter, and confirmed Mr. Moorhouse.

The prisoner, Pul Kanta, was examined, and admitted it was their intention to take the sheep, &c. To other questions he would not answer, and was silent when asked if he had fought the whites on the same spot before.

Mr. Moorhouse said he did not fire on natives; he never carried arms when among the natives.

It was moved by Major O'Halloran, and seconded by Mr. Eyre, "That the bench of Magistrates, after full and careful examination of all the evidence brought before them relating to the late affray with the natives on the Rufus, and the police and Mr. Robinson's party, are unanimously of opinion that the conduct of Mr. Moorhouse and his party was justifiable, and indeed unavoidable, and that much praise is due to him and the combined party for the great forbearance the force evinced when placed under circumstances of the most trying nature."

It must be here noticed that no subsequent censures were uttered or published of this much to be deplored heavy slaughter of natives, rendered necessary after the weak, vacillating policy had been so unsuccessful.

A resolution was also passed that His Excellency be respectfully solicited, under the circumstances then elicited, that an armed party should be stationed in the vicinity of Langhorne's Ferry, and also that the native prisoner, Pul Kanta, be placed forthwith under the charge of the Protector of Aborigines, and after receiving from him such instructions as at his command, be set at liberty to return to his tribe.

Register, October 2nd, 1841.—"Yesterday Mr. Eyre left town on his road to the Murray, where he is to be stationed as Police Magistrate of the district. Mr. Eyre takes with him the native captured in the late affray on the Rufus, and he trusts through his means to be enabled to open up a friendly communication with the hostile blacks."

The following is from Mr. Dutton's *South Australian*, published 1846 :—" Mr. Eyre held this appointment at Moorundee, 85 miles from Adelaide. Governor Grey made this appointment after many Europeans had been from time to time killed and their property destroyed or plundered; whilst, on the other hand, whenever the parties of whites had been in sufficient force, great slaughter of the blacks had been committed. The Governor, therefore, had apparently sufficient grounds for going to the expense of the above establishment, even at a time when colonial finances were at the lowest possible ebb."

As to this appointment I have no adverse remarks to make, and only desire to bring such an incomplete plan into contrast with the infinitely superior system inaugurated by Archdeacon Hale, and commenced in a great measure with his own private funds, which has since attained a decided success, viz., the Aboriginal Mission at Poonindie, Port Lincoln, founded after the grievous murders committed in that district on different white settlers and their servants by the natives.

I may here mention that the Government, after the Milmenura outbreak, applied the same principle of overawing the natives as they did afterwards in the Rufus affair, having appointed a sort of deputy protector of the lake tribes, who was ordered to reside at Wellington, to keep those tribes in order with carbine, sword, &c., but no attempt was made by Government to instruct or form any establishment or home in which to train the wandering human beings in habits of industry and civilisation even, not to mention religious training. Of Corporal Mason, the Sub-Protector, it is admitted he fulfilled his limited duties to the best of his ability, his chief influence arising from the miserable dole at distant stated times of blankets and rations, and here the duty of Government was allowed to end. It is a pleasure to me to record that in this portion of the colony also private benevolence afterwards stepped in to establish an institution and home for the dispossessed aboriginal tribes in the Point Macleay Mission, which, as far as its means extend, is effecting good work, placed as it is on very inferior and unprofitable land. Strangers will naturally ask how is it that a Government composed of professing Christian people has not appropriated and set apart suitable blocks of land of sufficient extent in the several districts for such establishments? Well, if such an appropriation of what may be called their own land, say five per cent. of the whole, or even infinitely less, in blocks, and encouragement had been given by the Government, many other such establishments as the two I have mentioned might have been formed, and have become self-supporting, as Poonindie has been for some time.

Eyre, Dutton, Forster, and other writers of the history of South Australia have stated their opinions on the native race, *i.e.*, after the first abortive and insufficient means had been adopted for their amelioration by the Colonial Governments under instructions from England.

I first quote from Mr. Dutton :—" The black inhabitant gradually dwindles away before the blighting effects of civilization, and another half century will most probably also see the end of the Australian aboriginal race." Eyre says :—" It has already been stated that in all the colonies we have hitherto established upon the continent the Aborigines are gradually decreasing in numbers, or have already disappeared, in proportion to the time their country has been occupied by Europeans. We are almost, in spite of ourselves, forced to the conviction that the first appearance of the white man in any new country sounds the funeral knell of the children of the soil."

In quoting from writers who record their opinions as to the hopelessness of attempting to ameliorate the condition of the natives, or to save them from certain extinction, I do so to precede the publication of the very different and satisfactory results which I purpose to show have attended the private establishments (as they may be called) now at work in this colony, and so to set up unanswerable arguments with which to force claims on Government to continue and confirm the appropriation of the land now occupied at Poonindie and Point McLeay, and to obtain much larger and more equitable grants in other localities, which cannot be abrogated or interfered with, through or by uncompromising greedy white "subjects of His Majesty." To support this view of our duties I quote from a dispatch of Lord Stanley to Sir Geo. Gipps in 1842 :—

"I cannot conclude this despatch without expressing my sense of the importance of the subject of it. My hope is that your experience may enable you to suggest some general plan by which we may acquit ourselves of the obligations which we owe towards this helpless race of beings. I should not without extreme reluctance admit that nothing could be done ; that with respect to them alone the doctrines of Christianity must be inoperative, and the advantages of civilisation incommunicable. I cannot acquiesce in the theory that they are incapable of improvement, and their extinction before the advance of the white settler is a necessity which it is impossible to control. I recommend them to your protection and favourable consideration with the greatest earnestness, but at the same time with perfect confidence; and I assure you that I shall be willing and anxious to co-operate with you in any arrangement for their civilisation which may hold out a fair prospect of success."

Mr. Dutton speaks thus of the Government post at Moorundee under Mr. Eyre:—

"Mr. Eyre has certainly succeeded in an eminent degree in effecting the object contemplated, as the whole length of the River Murray, from the Great Northern Bend to the coast, is occupied at the present moment with sheep and cattle stations, and no single outrage of a fatal nature has since the establishment of that post been committed by the natives; whilst at the same time a great moral control and influence has been obtained over the more distant and warlike tribes, who were either periodically visited in their own districts by Mr. Eyre, or used to come down to Moorundee to receive the meagre distribution of flour and blankets now and then allowed them by the Government."

As to any of the higher objects, which should have been aimed at through Government posts, Mr. Dutton wrote in 1846:—

"Of the protectorate posts in New South Wales, after costing the large sum of £80,000 since 1821 in keeping up a widely ramified establishment of protectors, that plan has, I believe, been abandoned in despair, as being productive of no good. Had that money been annually dropped into the sea outside the Sydney Heads the loss could not be more regretted than its resultless application in redeeming the savages, and it would have saved both Sir George Gipps and Lord Stanley the trouble of writing the immensity of despatches they did; and, although the experiments in South Australia have been made on a far more moderate scale, no better results can be shown with us than in the neighbouring colonies; but the effects of our civilising influence is shown, as Mr. Eyre says, 'in their diminished numbers;' nor is it in my recollection that throughout the whole length and breadth of New Holland a single real and permanent convert to Christianity has yet been made amongst them."

This as the result of the protectorate system! Forster in his later history says :—

"The aborigines of New Holland are fast disappearing from the face of the earth. The occupation of the country has injuriously affected them in many ways without conferring upon them any compensating advantages. It has broken up their tribal arrangements, by which the land was parcelled out into hunting districts that could only be encroached upon by strangers under such penalties as savages are wont to inflict on one another. Civilisation has in fact impressed its vices, with very few of its virtues, and tended to sink to a still lower depth the already degraded inhabitants of the soil. In saying that no advantages have been bestowed on the natives for the loss of their territory, I do not mean to imply that no attempts have been made to benefit them, or that they have been ruthlessly left to perish by the Government and colonists without protection and without sympathy. It was a special instruction of the Home Government on the establishment of South Australia that they should be *properly cared for;* and for that purpose a Chief Protector of Aborigines was appointed in Adelaide, and Sub-Protectors were sent into the country districts." Yes; and with such results as before set forth!

Then, under what responsibilities do the inhabitants now remain? New systems have been adopted, which are calling aloud as successful experiments for the support of every man and woman according to their means and influence. It is almost past credence that at this time a member of Parliament, at the instance of one or more greedy constituents, should have moved in Parliament to deprive the trustees of the Poonindie institution of the right of occupation of the land on which a large number of civilised and Christianised natives are leading a respectable, useful, and happy life—families permanently residing in a model village, occupying neat cottages, and in all respects conducting themselves as well or better than any white community in the province. In this mission-township at this time the number of native or half-caste inhabitants is eighty-eight. There are forty-four children regularly attending the school, who are clothed and fed. Medical attendance is also provided gratuitously to all who require the same. No public grant of money has been received since 1866, at which time there was a debt owing of over £800, since paid; and under the management of the last appointed trustee, G. W. Hawkes, Esq., the mission has not only become self-supporting, but in addition to contributions from the coloured inhabitants to several charitable objects, grants from the profits of the farm and flocks have for some time been made annually to the Point McLeay Mission. The natives when employed on the farm or station receive regular wages. The following amounts of money wages were paid to coloured labourers:—In the year 1875, £697 7s. 11d.; 1876, £641 13s. 1d.; 1877, £720 5s. 8d. The men when not employed on the station take contract jobs of shearing sheep, grubbing, or any other rural work from settlers, sometimes in amounts of £50 and £70, and employ under them bush blacks from wild tribes.

At this present shearing Mr. A. Tennant has engaged on contract shearers from Poonindie after they had finished their home work; one or two white men joined this party, a pleasing feature. By Mr. Tennant they were sent up to his station on the Middle-back Ranges, to shear, sort, and pack the wool of four thousand sheep, without superintendence, at 30s. a hundred with rations. This work was also done by black men last season from Poonindie, to the perfect satisfaction of the flock-owner.

Tom Adams, one of the men, is allowed to be unsurpassed as a shearer in that district; and although the quantity shorn in a working day by blacks does not average that made by a white party, the work done by them is equal to or superior in quality. Tom Adams turns out in a day from eighty to ninety. The above particulars I acknowledge with thanks to have received from G. W. Hawkes, Esq., that firm friend of the native races as well as of all benevolent institutions.

I conclude this chapter with an appeal to all colonists to exert their influence to procure for the future ample appropriation of land on which to establish native missions where now required.

CHAPTER XI.

THE advent of Captain Grey as third Governor of South Australia has been recorded, and I propose in this chapter to relate a few instances of the cruel wrongs which the pioneers had to endure under the policy which the British Government instructed its representative to carry out with reference to the financial liabilities of the colony. The first instance will give a brief account of the ruin of the firm of Borrow and Goodiar by the action of Captain Grey's Government in cancelling the large contracts under which that firm were bound by the Government of Colonel Gawler. The bills which they had received on the Home Government in part payment for work done having been also dishonoured, they were suddenly brought to a standstill, and had to meet the claims of their numerous workpeople, their merchants, and bankers, with promises. In this crisis they waited on the Governor, and the case was with great force pressed on His Excellency, who treated them with kind consideration, and in answer gave them full and decided assurances that the claims of the firm should be honourably met, and be submitted to arbitration. With this favourable and gracious reception they left Government House, highly pleased and satisfied, and went direct to the Government Offices and had an interview with Mr. Gouger, the Colonial Secretary, and Mr. Jackson, the Treasurer, to whom they detailed the promising result of their interview with Governor Grey, which was received by these officers with the greatest surprise, and they assured their visitors that the Governor had neither the power nor the means to make good such promises, and that there was no chance of an early settlement of their claims on any terms. And so the result proved, to the total ruin of their extensive business. Their engagements extended beyond the building trade, for they had taken leases of suburban sections, which they had fenced in with a view to the cultivation of wheat, and had sunk their capital in legitimate pursuits likely to result in benefit to the country. It was not until a wearied and lengthened contest that their creditors obtained from the Government a dividend by a compromise, and accepted a portion of the just claims of the firm. I may mention here that during the year 1842 no less than 136 writs were passed through the Sheriff's Court, and thirty-seven fiats of insolvency were issued. In one important respect the disastrous consequences of the losses sustained in the colony were made apparent on the non-payment of the Government debts, as out of 1915 houses that had been built in Adelaide, 642 were, in December, 1842, totally deserted, and the people spread out in the country districts.

One of the ruined pioneers of the colony, who has published

a brief history of his early career in the *Methodist Journal*, under the signature "Pioneer," having allowed me to extract therefrom, I take advantage of the privilege, as the ultimate sacrifice of the wreck of his property followed, as in my own case and so many others, when the news was received confirming the second repudiating action of the Home Government. I commence to quote from the termination of "Pioneer's" voyage from home, in order to show how he began from the first, in his colonial career, to go in with all his energies and means as a *bonâ fide* pioneer settler, to assist in stocking and cultivating the new colony :—

"After the inevitable discomforts of a long sea voyage in the ship *Isabella*, which Captain Hart, the commander, endeavoured to make as pleasant as possible, we sighted Van Diemen's Land on the 1st January, 1837, and at once sailed up the river Tamar, and grounded in the mud two or three miles from Launceston. We obtained lodgings, and began to make anxious inquiries respecting the new colony. We found that many shipments of sheep had been made to Port Philip (then a new colony, an offshoot of New South Wales). The *John Pirie* arrived from St. Vincent's Gulf, South Australia, and reported having spoken the *Buffalo*, beating up the Gulf, so that we had arrived in Tasmania nearly as soon as Governor Hindmarsh and his staff arrived at his seat of government. The *Isabella* was laid on for the new colony, our destination, and we proceeded at once to make our purchases of stock (for which purpose we had come round), and all that appeared necessary for the occupation of three preliminary sections purchased in England. We put on board three hundred and fifty ewes, forty-five wethers, six heifers, one Devon bull, ten working bullocks, two mares, one Timor pony, goats, pigs, poultry, dray, waggon, seed wheat, and provisions for twelve months, with the packages brought with us in the ship. I engaged four bush hands, and a female as washerwoman. Three out of the four were convicts, but there was no choice, and the fencing and other work required men of experience in colonial operations. The woman turned out a confirmed drunkard, and was for years known in the colony as Scotch Bella (who had more interviews in her time than any other man or woman, with the resident magistrate).

"We sailed on the 1st of February from the Tamar, and were met by contrary winds and rough weather, during which one bullock died, and many sheep. At length, on the 9th, we reached Backstairs Passage, and when off Rapid Bay a boat was lowered, and the captain, myself, and one or two more went ashore, found no settlers, but only a few huts. The captain said he would run up the Gulf forty miles, when he expected to find the *Buffalo* and the body of settlers. We anchored about midnight, but found in the morning we were two or three miles south of the *Buffalo* at anchor, and the *Coromandel* also, which latter vessel had arrived before us. A strong, hot north wind was blowing, and to save the lives of as many sheep as possible, the captain landed them opposite the ship. No water was near, and as the sheep-netting was not landed according to promise, we could not make a yard. In consequence the sheep broke adrift in the night, and were most of them irrecoverably lost. The other stock were landed in fair order. A heifer calved a day or two after, and I had the pleasure of milking the first cow of the colony. The settlers were camped over the sandhills, at the present site of Glenelg, and were busily rolling their goods over the sand hummocks. My men at once yoked a team of eight bullocks, and brought our goods from the ship's longboat to the camp we formed near a lagoon. It created quite a sensation in the encampment, as most of the people had not seen a colonial team before. Mr. John Hallett had, however, landed two bullocks and a few wethers before we arrived. In a few days, a vessel from the Cape brought some fine Fatherland cows for the Government, several of which I subsequently bought at auction at an average price of £27 each, and subsequently one at £36. We found the colony had been proclaimed over five weeks before we landed, but the survey of Adelaide was not completed. I had brought out two of Manning's cottages. One I first put up at the Bay, and the other I placed at Adelaide, opposite North Terrace. In April I finished the cottage there, and brought up the other from the Bay, and with the two formed a four-roomed habitation. While the *Isabella* lay in Holdfast Bay, Captain Hart said he wished to return in the ship to procure a freight if he could. Not being able to procure land, except at an exorbitant price, I commenced mercantile business, much against my inclination, and purchased goods out of the *Regia*, the *William*, etc. I further agreed to take goods from Captain Hart, and pay freight and ten per cent. on the invoice; also that I would pay for any stock landed in good condition, at specified prices; and we parted, expecting, if Mr. Griffiths, the owner of the *Isabella*, consented, to meet again before long. In April a meeting of holders of preliminary land orders was called, at which a resolution was carried to ballot for the locality in which the sections should be selected, which caused my three to be placed in District D, Yankalilla, the survey of which was not made for some two or three years after, before which we had sold the land orders as useless to us.

"The town acres, after the preliminary ones had been allotted, were offered by public auction, and realised about £4000, after reserving the 437 preliminary (gift) acres belonging to the 134 acres preliminary sections. I became the purchaser of sixty acres of town land for want of other land. I enclosed twelve acres in Lower North Adelaide, and sowed wheat the first season. A sample of the produce was sent home, and excited some notice in Mark Lane. Mr. G. Stevenson also commenced a garden close by, and soon made it one of the show places of the colony. Our bullock-team was fully employed in carting goods from the Port and Bay for the settlers. I have a record of £12 for one day's work, when loaded both ways.

"On the 6th April the brig *William* arrived from Tasmania, and reported that the *Isabella* had sailed the day previous to the *William*; that she had on board 400 sheep and twelve bullocks, and four cows for us, besides a variety of goods selected in Launceston, and consigned to me. I this day dined at Mr. Gouger's, the Colonial Secretary, and met Sir John Jeffcott, who had just arrived. He rode with me to some fine country about ten miles south of Adelaide, where we were putting up yards and huts to receive the stock expected.

"On the 13th of April I rode to the Bay, and on arriving at our camp found Captain Hart there. I was sorry to hear from him that he had lost the *Isabella*, which was totally wrecked on Cape Nelson, near Portland Bay, on her voyage hither. The loss was occasioned by the neglect of the mate, who came out with us in the ship from England. She was uninsured, and the captain said he had lost everything, and his friends had turned their backs on him. He described to a friend that he possessed nothing but what he stood up in. He said, Mr. Hy. Jones, who was a passenger with him, had joined him in the shipment. I invited the captain to remain with us, and at the time thought myself very fortunate in being, as I supposed, free from personal liability. But then there was the disappointment and loss of gain in the stock and goods not coming to hand, all being much wanted." [I may mention here that the captain, who was brought to such a bare position, was the Captain Hart whose after career in this colony was so successful, and who attained a leading political station, and acquired great wealth, whose sons are now carrying on the large export trade in the staff of life, as purchasers and exporters of wheat, which he established.] " In consequence of the difficulty in procuring land and the backwardness of the surveys, a plan was originated called the special survey system by which on £4000 being lodged with the Colonial Treasurer, a block of 15,000 acres might be selected out of which 4000 acres might be chosen."

"After Captain Hart had remained some time with us I entered into an agreement with him to go to Sydney and purchase on our account a schooner to trade between that place and Adelaide, and furnished him with funds for that purpose. Not very long after Mr. Jones arrived in Adelaide, and made a claim on me for the value of the lost cargo, stating they had purchased the goods as my agent. As no authority could be produced in writing, no action could lie against me; but I agreed to an arbitration, and had to pay for the goods, but not the stock. Mr. Jones received about £700 from me, but Captain Hart refused to receive his share, admitting that it was an unjust claim. My brother joined Captain Hart in Sydney, and they agreed for the purchase of about 800 head of cattle, to be delivered at Portland Bay. About half after their arrival were shipped from thence to Adelaide, but arrived in very bad condition. On the safe arrival of the remainder of our cattle, 400 in number, overland from Portland Bay, conducted by Captain Hart, who, taking Major Mitchell's track towards the River Murray, and then following the course down the same and the track to Mount Barker, arrived safe at the spot where the township now stands. We here formed a dairy station, and made arrangements with the Bank, by which we were able to purchase a special survey, of which we were to take 3000 acres, and a Cattle Company, of which I was a director, the balance, 1000 acres. We were, however, forestalled by a few hours by some speculators from Sydney, who obtained the Treasurer's receipt before my money was tendered. Having made ourselves very certain we should be unopposed, the disappointment was great.

"In this emergency we next applied for another survey south of the Mount Barker block, which we obtained. It was afterwards called Echunga, and there we commenced to improve and fence. We soon had two dairies at work, with seventy cows milking in each—one at Echunga and one on a thousand acres we had taken up on the Little Para, part of a special survey—and also established a cattle run at Yankalilla, for dry cattle and breeding.

"In 1839 we built a house at Echunga on the survey, and laid out a garden of twelve acres, to furnish which I sent for a large invoice of trees, &c., from Hobart Town, and it soon became very flourishing and productive. I removed my family there in 1840, and to attend to the business in Adelaide rode in by 10 a.m., returned on the following evening, and remained out one day, and so continued to carry on with the country work and the town business. Experience has shown me that the difficulties in which I ultimately became involved had their rise in carrying out my desire to acquire a large landed property. Early in 1840 I had an apparent balance to the credit of profit and loss of £30,000, but by 1843 all had to be sacrificed. The special survey led the way, but the purchase of the land was only a small matter. A large sum was sunk in making the land acquired produce anything; but these, in common with other heavy business losses, fell on us. Bank assistance was required —very readily granted while the colony flourished, but as summarily called in when the crisis came. I sold my Hindley-street property for £4000, and raised £1500 on the Echunga property, to pay off claims and in part overdrafts. At length, in 1843, the worst of the storm seemed past; the manager expressed himself much gratified with the exertions I had made to reduce my liabilities with them, and I felt secure I should have the continued support of the Bank. Time was all that was required, but this luxury was not obtainable. Almost every merchant and trader in the community had to make arrangements with creditors or to become insolvent. A few days after the satisfactory interview with the manager of my Bank, I was aroused one morning by two men riding into the yard at Echunga, and on asking their business I was informed they were bailiffs come to take possession on behalf of the Bank. At the time there was only one director of the Bank, and an English friend of mine, representing a house in England with whom I had had large dealings, and who held a mortgage (as security for advances) on a portion of the Echunga land, was married to a sister of the Director, and it was determined to obtain my improved property. This could only be done by my being compelled to insolvency, and this was carried out, and the whole of the Echunga estate passed for a small amount over the mortgage to my English friend and schoolfellow. Judge Cooper was sometimes a guest at Echunga, and little thought when he talked over with me the new insolvency law he was preparing that I should be one of its first victims."

So far "Pioneer." In a former chapter I have described my journey with my family over the hills to occupy three sections, which I was glad to take up in the first Mount Barker Special Survey. This was the survey out of which "Pioneer" was choused. Anxious to get into country pursuits in carrying out my original intentions, I lost no time in commencing work on the sections as soon as I got possession, and before I got rid of my town business. As I have described, I had been actively engaged like "Pioneer" in introducing stock into the colony. A few months after I commenced in town, I was induced to enter into partnership with a gentleman who arrived from India, who had left the greater part of his capital there to follow him. Immediately before the crisis arrived I was anxious to withdraw from town business, and was advised by a Bank manager to hand over the partnership, stock, and liabilities to my partner; this was done as suggested. Over 400 head of large cattle were assigned to the manager and a second party whom he named to cover partnership acceptances then current, for the last purchases of cattle made by the firm. Before this was carried out I paid all other partnership claims then due, and lifted one bill for a large amount. I also paid all my private accounts. I agreed to a very low valuation of the cattle, horses, drays, &c. (in a falling market), less than half the cost of the same, with an arrangement that I was to receive out of sales £800. On this matter being concluded a complimentary letter from the Bank manager was received by me. At the time this arrangement was made I was not aware that my partner had obtained large advances from the same Bank (in anticipation of the receipt of funds from India), which he had invested in land, &c., in the colony. He was a large shareholder in an Indian Bank which came to grief. Other heavy losses befell him, and his expected funds did not arrive, but the funds from the assigned partnership stock were taken to clear off his private debt to the Bank. Not long after I had assigned the stock I was surprised at my quiet home on a certain day, by the visit of a bailiff, and was served with writs for the unpaid partnership debts, and held in durance vile until the arrival from Sydney of the drawers of the bills, who immediately on landing discharged me entirely. The first insolvent law having been passed, my late partner became one of the first who had to pass through the court, and in his schedule I appeared as a creditor for the amount of £800, amount of my arranged claim, but I got no dividend, as the insolvent had shortly after again to declare himself.

Not to go into minute details of further bitter "experiences" endured by me, I will only add that advantage at this time was attempted to be taken of my weakened state by a new arrival with whom I had been connected in business transactions, and by whom I would have suffered grievous wrong if I had not been favoured by the support of a strong friend, with whose aid I was enabled to force an arbitration, by which I obtained the greater part of my claims, but only on yielding up my comfortable and well-arranged home; and I had to turn out with a young family to commence again. The above three instances of "Early Experiences of Colonial Life" in South Australia (to which many might be added), are sufficient to prove that the early colonists are not to be blamed for the first crisis under which they suffered ruin. They did not voluntarily confine their operations to town pursuits, as has been represented by some of those who have furnished histories of pioneer work in the colony, and as Governor Grey also stated in his early despatches.

It is only necessary, out of many instances, to give two cases in point to set at rest the cruel and unfounded charges which have been lately made and published, that the ruinous losses the pioneers and others endured arose from their extravagance and want of care. First, Mr. B. G—— arrived from India with his family and a large retinue of Indian servants. He left the greater part of his capital to be realised on and to follow him. He purchased improved sections and a house near Adelaide and joined the Author, as before mentioned, as partner in a business to introduce stock, in the year 1839. Several herds of cattle passed through their hands with good profit, a cattle station was formed on Bull's Creek, on which overland cattle were fattened, and the city of Adelaide supplied with beef, and settlers with stock; several flocks of sheep also were received, chiefly from Tasmania; these were disposed of (store sheep) at an average price of 38s. a head. Mr. B. G—— was anxious to begin a breeding sheep station, but the Author on the fact of the price of store-sheep in the older colonies being so low (3s. to 5s. a head) declined to join in the purchase of sheep at the price then ruling in this colony, and left his partner to invest on his own private account. So two flocks were transferred to Mr. B. G—— at 38s. a head; before the end of two years the crisis in this colony occurred, and the sheep with their increase were sold by the Government auctioneer, the late Bentham Neales, Esq., and realised 5s. a head only.

The continued history of this flock is worth relating, as they had ultimately to be re-sold on the heavy losses of property which befell the purchaser. This gentleman, a retired sea captain, about the beginning of the crisis arrived with a moderate capital, which was to a considerable extent in the hands of an Adelaide merchant. He had purchased sections over the hills to the east of Adelaide, and placed the sheep on his property. Not many months afterwards, when acceptances became waste paper, and houses of business were closed on the repudiation by the Home Commissioners of the engagements of Governor Gawler, the writer while riding over the Mount Lofty Range, met the above flocks of sheep emerging from a cloud of dust, the owner himself (now Sir W. W. Hughes) on foot, assisting to drive the sheep to the same auction mart in Adelaide, where the same auctioneer resold them at 2s. 6d. a head. Now these two gentlemen did not join the Colony as pioneer settlers, but as capitalists, to invest in an established Colony, of which they had heard such flattering accounts. It may be added of these two gentlemen that the first-named never recovered his position, although he strove hard; but of the second, that he was afterwards favoured with a most prosperous career. He realised from his wreck of fortune sufficient to purchase a flock of sheep before a great rise took place, and went north with them, and in course of time took up runs on Yorke's Peninsula. On one of these runs, the rich copper mines, Moonta, Wallaroo, &c., of that district, were discovered by one of his shepherds; mining companies were formed, in which he became a large shareholder; leases were taken up, and he realised a princely fortune, and has since been honoured with knighthood by her Majesty. Sir W. W.

Hughes is now residing in England, and is one of the most munificent contributors to our public institutions and charities. So much for the vicissitudes of Colonial life.

CHAPTER XII.

HAVING related some of the occurrences during Captain Grey's government it should be mentioned that after he assumed the office of Governor of South Australia an Imperial Act was passed which repealed the two former Acts regulating the government of the colony, by which it had been constituted as a separate colony, independent of New South Wales, and its boundaries had been fixed. On the 15th July, 1842, this repealing Act was passed—introduced by Lord Stanley, then Colonial Secretary—entitled "An Act for the better government of South Australia." It abolished the London Board of Commissioners, and in the colony the office of Resident Commissioner, and by the same Act provision was made for the appointment of a Legislative Council for the colony, to consist of the Governor for the time being and not less than seven other persons, to be nominated members by the Queen, or in such a manner as she might direct.

This new Council (of advice, as it was merely) was first established in June, 1843, and the selection of its members being left to the Governor, Captain Grey, he appointed Mr. Mundy (Colonial Secretary), Mr. Smillie (Advocate-General), Captain Sturt (Registrar-General), as official members, together with four gentlemen not holding Government appointments. The following gentlemen were first nominated, and from time to time changes took place, as they retired : Major O'Halloran, John Morphett, Esq., Jacob Hagen, Esq., Captain Charles Harvey Bagot. The repealed Act which constituted the colony had provided that local government should be conceded when its population reached the number of 50,000 souls. At this time the population of the colony fell far short of the number, thus the promised constitution was lost to the infant province, and under the depression, caused as it was by no deficiency of intrinsic value of the country itself or lack of spirit and energy in the pioneers, the increase of the population from without was still kept back by the continued want of action and sympathy on the part of the British Government, as the repeated pressing applications of Governor Grey on Lord Stanley for a resumption of emigration, and a restoration of the amount of £84,697, which had been taken from the Land and Emigration Fund, and otherwise applied without reference to the contributors, were totally disregarded. So the unfortunate first settlers, having suffered the loss of the greater part of their capital by Government repudiations, had afterwards to struggle on in country pursuits, after patiently waiting for their land, with a deficiency of working hands, and with the rate of wages at an unusually high figure. The first relief obtained came from the adjoining colonies, especially from Sydney. Succeeding the first beams of prosperity which arose from successful agricultural operations, the discovery of the mines soon followed, and aided materially in drawing population—people who joined us at their own expense, and at a time when we were denied them from the mother country, teeming then with populations existing on miserably low wages or as a burden on parochial funds.

The large reduction which the Governor made in establishments and works, by cutting off two-thirds of Government expenditure, naturally caused an enormous depreciation in every description of property, and the labouring classes found it more and more difficult to obtain employment from impoverished settlers. At the latter part of 1841 the Governor had the enormous number of nearly two thousand men, women, and children, thrown upon his hands for support as absolute paupers. This state of things was taken advantage of by some few, who made much gain, not always to their credit. The lawyers, of course, reaped a rich harvest.

"The grave question," says Forster, "was forced upon the Governor from whence to obtain the means to support two thousand British subjects, who must either starve or support themselves by rapine and pillage, which they threatened to do in very intelligible language."

Captain Grey reduced the wages of the unemployed emigrants to one shilling and twopence a day, without rations. Great discontent was, as a matter of course, created, and a popular outbreak was more than once anticipated, which the absence of military made serious. The Governor's income was then £1000 per annum, and to his credit it is recorded that in this crisis he contributed over £400 towards charitable purposes. Mr. Dutton, in a note in his "History of South Australia," states "that in the year 1840 the immense sum of £277,000 sterling was sent out of the colony for the purchase of the necessaries of life."

The only way open to the Governor to lower the cost of the police department was to reduce the number as well as pay of the officers and men in the force, and this was done although their work was greatly increased by the outbreak of the natives on the Murray, and through the destitution of the working classes.

In reviving the occurrences of this period in our history after the flight of many years, and comparing the then state of the colony with our present position and prospects, and in recalling the proposal which Captain Grey made in one of his gloomy despatches to Lord Stanley, to dispose of Government House as well as other Government properties to raise funds, in contrast to the favourable opinions so early expressed by Governor Jervois, on his first glance at the country, I can boldly say that history furnishes no parallel to our progress as an infant settlement. At this time our coast-line is the same in extent, and affords only a greater accommodation in the harbours, having been improved since 1841. Our River Murray, a grand natural canal, is without change, except as to the removal of snags. Our land is now, as it was then, unexceptionally the greatest in extent, and of quality equal to that possessed by any Australian community; and to crown all, in spite of much selfish and short-sighted policy on the part of some of our previous legislators, we have arrived at our present position from which to start onwards to attain a state of wealth and influence equal, if not superior, to any other Australian or British colony.

I continue the history of the administration of Captain Grey by an extract from Dutton's history : "In November, 1841, Captain Grey heard from England that Colonel Gawler's bills were in course of payment by means of the parliamentary grant voted as a temporary assistance to the colony. On ascertaining this fact, looking at the justice of the still unsatisfied claims for which Colonel Gawler had not drawn bills, and determined to relieve the distress consequent on the non-payment of these claims, he drew upon the Lords of the Treasury for the amounts which were properly substantiated as due. Governor Grey's despatch announcing his having done so gave in full his motives for incurring responsibility which he was aware at the time had been the cause of his predecessor's recall."

These bills of Captain Grey were also returned protested. The disastrous news did not reach the colony before the arrival of the *Taglione*, in October, 1842, but there was not a single despatch for the Governor on board announcing this fact distinctly. It was on the 24th December following that Governor Grey at length received Lord Stanley's despatch announcing the dishonour of his drafts in the preceding May. "You have," said Lord Stanley, "now drawn bills on the Treasury in discharge of these claims, and the bills have been dishonoured, and will be returned to you chargeable with interest."

Mr. Dutton continues: "Lord Stanley gave no good reason for refusing to pay those bills, beyond that they were drawn without special authority, but the reasons given in Lord Stanley's despatch do not justify the course he pursued in refusing to place those few additional thousands of pounds on the same footing as Colonel Gawler's bills, as an attentive perusal of Governor Grey's despatch clearly shows that these claims were composed of precisely similar ones to those which the British Government had thought it incumbent on themselves to pay to support the credit of the Government." Mr. Dutton in a note comments on the remark made by Lord Stanley, "that the outstanding debts of Colonel Gawler were *created* under the full knowledge of the peremptory orders which Colonel Gawler had received not to draw any further," the fact being "a considerable portion of these claims were for contracts entered upon before the prohibition to draw had arrived, but were not due till after that period; and a large sum was due on account of public buildings in the course of erection, the remainder being for absolute necessaries." Lord Stanley, to meet these dishonoured bills, ordered colonial debentures to be issued, to bear interest at five per cent. To parties in England this may at first sight appear to have been a very satisfactory arrangement, but fresh light will appear on acquaintance with the working of the matter. "In the first place the colonists were kept waiting eighteen months before they got any settlement at all; then they got the Governor's bills on the Lords of the Treasury, to get which cashed they had to pay the banks five per cent. discount. The bills were sent to England and refused acceptance; then the lawyers got hold of them. In addition to noting protest there was a charge of twenty per cent., also charge for re-exchange. Lawyers in the colony were then ordered to call for an early reimbursement from the unfortunate endorsers, which they could not make except by handing over the debentures bearing five per cent. interest, whilst the Bank interest was from ten to twelve. A child might guess the consequences to nine out of ten of the holders of these bills. Half the amount of the bills gone in expenses, and a final settlement gained after an advertisement of the properties of A., B. or C. for peremptory sale." Then properties were mopped up by Bank manager or some of his friends and partners.

The new Governor was forced by his instructions to stop public works, except so far as was necessary to complete them to prevent early dilapidation, for which purpose he obtained a temporary loan from the Government of New South Wales of £3,000. The next downward movement was the stoppage of works of a private nature; the colonists holding large amounts of dishonoured Government bills as well as unsettled Government accounts, as I have stated, for works done and goods supplied, were made bankrupts; thus a large number of labourers fell upon the Governor for work or food. Necessities more compulsory than his stringent instructions, which he had arrived to carry out, were thus created. A number of over 700 immigrants, most of them good working men, were, under compulsion at first, furnished with work at wages reduced to the lowest point at which they were able to subsist, and were marched out daily under inspectors, the majority employed at road-making on a "Government stroke."

In this crisis Captain Grey applied for power and instructions to sell such of the Government properties as might conveniently be disposed of, but he found such a step impossible, as not a fourth part of the value could be obtained for anything offered for sale. He applied to the Bank of South Australia, and was offered £10,000 at twelve per cent. on his personal security! But as such a sum would have been immediately absorbed by liabilities already incurred, and would leave nothing for the legitimate expenses of his own administration, he had ultimately to adopt the same course which led to Colonel Gawler's recall. He drew bills on the Lords of the Treasury, which were also returned dishonoured. After many months of severe suffering for the colonists, and trials and responsibilities for the Governor of no ordinary character, the necessary advances were made by the Imperial Government, and from the time of that assistance, too long delayed, the Colony has continued to rise in importance and wealth. With the appointment of Captain Grey as Governor, the management of the colony was taken out of the hands of the Commissioners in London, and we were passed over to the tender mercies of Lord Stanley. The change in Her Majesty's Ministers at the time of the colonial crisis was no doubt an additional agent in prolonging our difficulties. I think it will be fair in this place to quote from Governor Grey's despatch, of the 31st December, 1842, to Lord Stanley, as being a most unfair comment on the action of his predecessor, and an unjust charge against the then small number of colonists It is the following :—

"The great majority of the community were interested in the maintenance of the lavish Government expenditure. During the twelve months preceding my arrival about £150,000 had been procured by drawing bills, which were ultimately paid by the British Treasury, and had been distributed in the form of salaries, allowances, and lucrative contracts amongst a population of 14,061 people, who only contributed £30,000 towards their own support; that is, the British Treasury paid annually to every man, woman, and child in South Australia, upwards of £10 a head."

Could anything be more monstrous or unjust than to charge the then small population of the young colony with the whole amount of the sum named, which had been principally expended on the substantial public buildings erected, or in course of erection, and which so soon proved to be insufficient in size to afford accommodation in which to carry on the Government business of the rising colony.

Such statements in a despatch to one of the Secretaries of State may cause surprise, but are quite consistent with the remark Captain Grey was, at the time of his arrival, charged with making, that he was prepared to let Government House as a store. In justice to Captain Grey, an extract from a despatch to him from Lord Stanley, of December 24, 1842, must be given, on the liberty he had taken to pay claims.

" The justification which you have urged for the course taken by you is in substance this—that you understand that all the bills drawn by your predecessor were to be accepted at length and paid, and that the *claims*, in satisfaction of which you were about to draw those bills, were similar to those on account of which Governor Gawler drew his bills. It is true that, in order to sustain the credit of the Colonial Government, the Home Government ultimately consented to provide for the payment of all Colonel Gawler's bills; you were warned not to draw any bills without having previously received authority to do so." Astonishment may well be felt and expressed on the extraordinary obtuseness of Lord Stanley in not perceiving that the question was not merely as to Colonel Gawler exceeding his instructions as to drawing bills, but whether the claims were just, and if the liabilities had been incurred principally in erecting necessary public buildings.

However, the severe and unfair censure which Captain Grey received must be accepted as an apology for his strict adherence to orders in other cases, although such a course might withhold justice from struggling colonists.

On October 25, 1845, Captain Grey vacated his office as Governor of this colony. Before the expiration of the usual period of gubernatorial exchanges he was hastily ordered by the Imperial authorities to assume the office of Governor of New Zealand, in consequence of the serious outbreak of the Maories in that dependency. These tribes, as they proved in this contest, were of a higher type than any aboriginal inhabitants Europeans have attempted to subdue in any part of the world during the last three centuries, and were not to be overpowered or treated as the miserable Australian natives might be; nor were they to be deprived of their land without compensation with impunity. Captain Grey found the task which had been assigned to him a most onerous and responsible one, as a war had been drifted into between the British and the Maories—one of the little wars from which it is said England is never free. In this instance the Governor, who was an educated soldier, found these natives worthy to cross weapons with the veterans whom he had to send against them, and that they were hard to beat in their wild country and behind their stockades.

At the time Captain Grey left his seat of government he had witnessed the commencement of renewed and sound prosperity brought about by the indomitable perseverance of the settlers. When called on, the earth had given forth her increase in food for flocks yielding wool for export, and for the sustenance of increasing herds of cattle; also from her bowels had commenced to come yields of silver, lead, and copper ores for export. The colony commenced its career as an exporting community, and has continued in such a course until it has attained in exports the highest average per head of its inhabitants of any community in the world.

During Captain Grey's residence here it was not possible for him to become a popular Governor, as his stringent instructions from the Colonial Office had a most crushing effect on the community, and they were carried out by him with firmness and determination. The Governor also struck upon another rock—taxation; one that Governments frequently meet with, even in countries where representation precedes taxation, but in this case there was not even the semblance of representation. The power of the Governor was unchecked by any influence but such as resided in Downing-street, and no sympathy existed in the person of the Colonial Secretary of State when that post was filled by Lord Stanley.

On the intention of the Governor of imposing heavy and exorbitant port dues becoming publicly known, a public meeting was held, and a deputation waited on him, composed of a body of influential gentlemen, who respectfully remonstrated against the proposed measure, urging, as the subjects of Her Majesty residing in the colony of South Australia, that they had no voice through any form of representation, and they entered their protests on behalf of the inhabitants at large against the proposed impost.

The reply he gave them, as reported in the papers of the day, was that he would enact taxation before any kind of representation was granted.

The deputation left his presence with their feelings considerably ruffled, and great indignation spread throughout the province, but the inhabitants on this, as well as on all occasions since the foundation of the colony, acted with such restraint as becomes good subjects, and in a short time he withdrew the obnoxious tax.

The following short statement will serve to show the condition of the colony in the year 1843 : Over 325,000 acres of land had been alienated from the Crown, of which 28,690 acres were under cultivation; the population of city and country districts was about 17,366; the live-stock numbered about 331,000 sheep, 1,566 horses, and 29,000 head of cattle. The estimated rental of town property for assessment was £50,000. A savings bank had been established. The population was too limited for any extensive undertakings, and other circumstances prevented any rapid accumulation of wealth for the time. The cost of living was, however, very moderate; beef and mutton were procurable at 2d. to 3d. per pound, and the best flour under £10 a ton.

CHAPTER XIII.

ON the 25th October, 1845, Lieutenant-Colonel F. Holt Robe, C.B., entered upon his duties as Governor of the colony. During the short time he filled that office he did not appear to realise his true position, or to feel any necessity to be in accord with the people over whom he was placed as Governor.

His first unpopular action was to carry a measure to grant aid to religious communions, and to grant land for churches, chapels, and glebes. This Act was passed by the Council constituted as explained in the previous chapter, and gave great offence to the majority of dissenters, and naturally to those who belonged to no religious communion—the first class of people conscientiously objecting to all State aid to religion; the latter objecting to be taxed for a cause in which they took no interest. A memorial numerously signed and supported was presented to the Governor. He received the deputation in a curt manner, and merely replied, "I have no remarks to make, gentlemen," and so dismissed them.

A royalty-tax on minerals came next. The Act enforcing this was also passed without any regard to the respectful and urgent protests from the colonists at large. This policy was unjust to those who had purchased land, was bad as affecting further sales of land, and as checking the introduction of capital and emigrants.

It is scarcely necessary to say that, as to the grant in aid, those dissenting bodies who opposed it did not avail themselves of it. The Churches of England and Rome, with some of the outside congregations, did receive their share of the grant for the short time it was obtainable.

The Governor, with his military training, could not approve of the Black Forest, which, in his time, extended from South

Terrace in an unbroken cover, almost to the sea-shore at Holdfast Bay, and, indeed, extended into the city itself. This, in case of an invasion from the Gulf, was a most dangerous cover to leave standing. To avoid such a calamity, or for some other consideration, this military guardian decided to have the South Park Lands cleared. A notice was therefore published calling for tenders to grub all timber and stumps. One offer was made to do the work, to be entitled to all the timber, and to receive the sum of £800. This offer was accepted, the late Mr. Mellor, if I remember right, being the contractor. Now a business man will probably ask the question, "What would be the value of the trees and stumps?" It may be added that a portion of the Black Forest is still standing on the sections belonging to the Messrs. W. and C. Everard, though somewhat thinned.

Mining activity had at this time commenced, as shown by the fact that in the year 1847 the value of ores exported exceeded the value of wool exports, and so from that time was regarded as a leading export. This advance was made although the Act imposing a royalty on minerals was in force.

On September 22nd, 1847, the Savings Bank Act was passed, and on the 5th November the first *over-sea* steamer arrived.

The Right Rev. Augustus Short, D.D., of Christ Church, Oxford, was consecrated Lord Bishop of Adelaide in 1847, and arrived in the colony in the month of December in the same year. He was warmly received by members of his own flock, and by colonists of other denominations. Bishop Short held his appointment from the Crown under letters patent. On his arrival Church matters were in a very primitive state.

Dr. Short was received as any other priest of his Church would be, without pomp or ceremony. Fortunately for his people, he was endowed with just the faculties and habits required in the work he had to perform, viz., to build up the Church in matters material, and to arrange all things in an independent form, separate from the State. His first great work was to prepare the constitution of the synod, a work he completed well.

With the aid of Captain Allen and other liberal men, Dr. Short purchased the fine block of land (52 acres)—most judiciously chosen—adjoining the city, on which to erect St. Peter's College, with a capacious residence for the head master, and accommodation for fifty boarders. A chapel was also built, and school-rooms and every requirement, all of first class order. The Rev. J. P. Wilson, M.A. Oxon., was appointed head master in January, 1848, and was succeeded, on his resignation, by the Rev. G. H. Farr, M.A., Pembroke College, Cambridge, aided by a full staff of under-masters and a bursar.

The institution was under the control of fourteen governors; the Bishop of the Diocese being *ex-officio* a Governor and Visitor. The Rev. G. H. Farr held the appointment of headmaster for many years, and during his term of office St. Peter's College attained a high position. Several scholars have gained respectable positions in the Universities of the mother country. Two gentlemen in the present ministry were educated at St. Peter's College, viz., the Hon. J. C. Bray, M.P., Chief Secretary, and the Hon. J. W. Downer, M.P., Attorney-General. Charles Mann, Esq., Crown Solicitor, who held the office of Treasurer in a previous ministry, was also educated at St. Peter's.

The number of scholars now attending is 150, of whom fifty are boarders. The playgrounds are extensive, and there is also a capacious building used as a gymnasium. The school was opened to receive scholars in February, 1847. The total cost of St. Peter's College, including the chapel, was £29,814 14s. 1d. The foundation-stone was laid on March 24th, 1849, and it was incorporated in the same year. The Rev. F. Williams, M.A., Lincoln College, Oxford, is the present Head Master; Second Master (open); Third Master and Bursar, Rev. J. C. Haynes. The following scholarships and exhibitions are attached to the school :—The Westminster Scholarship, value £10 per annum, tenable for two years; the Christchurch Scholarship, value £10 per annum, tenable for two years; the Allen Scholarship, value £10 per annum, tenable for two years; the Short Scholarship, value £10 per annum, tenable for two years; the Prankerd Scholarship, value £10, awarded annually for modern languages; the Bowman Scholarship, value £10, awarded annually for physical science; the Wyatt Scholarship, value £10, awarded annually for natural science; the May Scholarship, value £10, awarded annually for physical science; the Young Exhibition, value £10, awarded annually for mathematics; the Vansittart Scholarship, value £50 per annum, tenable for three years, to board and educate a boy from the Mount Gambier District; the Farrell Scholarships (4), value £50 each per annum, tenable for three years; two of these are limited to sons of clergymen of the Church of England, the other two are open. Candidates for any scholarship must take first or second class honours at the examination then proceeding. Smith History Prize.—E. T. Smith, Esq., M.P., offers an annual prize, value £5 in books, for examination in a historical subject to be studied out of school hours.

The following donations, from £100 and upwards, were received:—William Allen, £7,084 4s. 7d.; Society for Promoting Christian Knowledge, £2,500; John Ellis, £1,222 10s.; Lord Bishop of Adelaide, £175; ditto from Diocesan Funds, £302 15s. 1d.; the late M. Featherstonhaugh, £200; F. H. Dutton, £135; Price Maurice, £100; the Hon. G. F. Angas, £200; University of Oxford, £150; Joseph Gilbert, £100; John Grainger, £100; J. B. Hughes. £125; Philip Butler, £100; sundry subscriptions from other colonists, £1,299 8s. 1d.; total, £13,593 17s. 9d.

Under the auspices of Dr. Short, St. Barnabas Ecclesiastical College has also been built. In North Adelaide was also erected a residence or palace for the Bishop. All these buildings are monuments of what energy the late Bishop displayed in the building up of a Colonial Church without State aid.

It must also be understood that during that period, in addition to the usual hard struggles attending the opening years of a new colony, the ruin of the pioneers had been accomplished. The real condition of the colonists being thus understood, the enduring and extensive works accomplished by Bishop Short will be properly estimated.

Dr. Short continued his active services as Bishop during thirty-six years. On his arrival there were only five or six churches, six ordained clergymen, and three or four Sunday school-rooms; now, upwards of fifty priests, with churches and Sunday school-houses and commodious parsonages. Before the first Bishop of Adelaide resigned his office, he had raised an amount sufficient to erect the present portion of the beautiful cathedral at a cost of £20,000, the amount required for completion being £14,000.

The foundation stone of the Cathedral of St. Peter was laid on June 29th, 1869, by Sir James Fergusson. The opening of divine services was in 1877, and it was consecrated on the 1st of January, 1878. The cathedral is vested in Dr. Short as trustee during his life, and after his death in the synod upon certain trusts. Constitution of Chapter:—The Right Rev. the Lord Bishop, the Very Rev. the Dean of Adelaide, three Archdeacons; Vicar-Choral, the Rev. Canon Dendy, D.D.

BOOK III.

CHAPTER I.

I NOW return to narrate a continuation of the painful experiences of our early days connected with our contact with the convict element from the older colonies. First I give the career of the cattle-stealers of the Black Forest.

The settlers had for some time missed cattle, of which no traces could be found. Many complaints reaching the Government, Sergeant-Major Alford and another officer were instructed to go out disguised as bushmen and scour the country. After searching the gullies to some distance north of Adelaide, and south as far as the Sturt River, Sergeant-Major Alford, by himself, made a search of the plains south-west of Adelaide. In passing Ashford he saw the late Dr. Everard, and on asking him if he had seen any suspicious-looking people at any time passing with cattle, the doctor replied that he had seen cattle driven down the Forest track, and pointed to it. On this Mr. Alford proceeded in that direction. Although the sergeant-major had not received any leading information from the doctor, he thought it well to make a search, intending, if he found any traces of cattle-slaughtering going on, to return early in the morning, when the cattle stealers might be at work, and when, with a sufficient force, the whole of them might be caught. He proceeded down a slight track, and after going about a mile and a half, came to a fallen tree across the track, of which he took particular notice, and here he made a turn to the north, intending to make a circular course. After creeping through the thick bush for a mile or so, he heard a dog bark, and then took a direction towards the sound, and soon saw through the thick bush and trees a stockyard and cattle, and men.

He then immediately turned away to avoid being seen from the yard, and kept on at a good pace. On clearing the trees he perceived that he was followed and watched by a man on horseback. Without appearing to notice him, Alford kept dodging about as if in search of cattle, and when he saw the coast clear, set off at full speed to the barracks, where he reported himself to Inspector Tolmer, and proposed to go again with one man to lie in wait till daylight, when the suspected persons might be seen at work, and if cattle-slaughtering was going on then to return and obtain a sufficient force to surround the place and capture the lot in the commission of their crime. Having procured a fresh horse, he started from the barracks late at night accompanied by Sergeant N——. They crept down the trodden path and passed the fallen tree, continuing on the track, but not intending to approach too near the yard. The sergeant-major's horse neighed, which was answered by another horse close at hand tied to a tree. It was a starlight night, and on looking about they perceived a pair of bullocks in yoke also fastened to a tree, and near them a dray, with casks and a bag of salt in it. They now saw three or four men in a yard, who appeared to be busy at work—they could hear the noise of steeling the knives. They had unintentionally approached too near to hope to retire without giving an alarm, and then the game would be lost. Mr. Alford decided there was nothing for it but to make a rush in order to effect a capture. He therefore whispered to his comrade that he would quietly dismount and creep to the fence, and on his rushing over, his mate was to gallop round to the opposite side. Accordingly he made the rush, calling out, "Men, surround the yard; shoot down any escaping. Surrender yourselves prisoners or you are dead men!" He caught one before he could clear the stockyard fence, and told him he would blow his brains out if he did not quietly surrender. Not expecting to find the work begun till early morning, they had only gone out as scouts, and had each one small pistol. Alford's man surrendered quietly before the yard could be surrounded by one man, as the Irish soldier did his prisoners. When Alford made his capture, the other three cattle stealers had cleared the fence and bolted. Sergeant N—— followed one, whom he recognised as Dick Fenton; but the timber, standing and fallen, gave a chance to the fugitive, who, after being chased some distance, was lost sight of.

Our sergeant-major now went to work single-handed with his prisoner, who was the owner of the bullocks and dray, and promised him, if he continued to behave well and give him information, he should have favour shown him; he was first asked, "How many beasts have been killed this time?" The answer was, " Four; three cut up, lying on the tarpaulins—one not finished dressing." "Have the brands been cut off the skins?" "No." "Then roll them up and pass them through the fence." This done, he was ordered out of the yard. The horse, belonging to one of the firm, was then tied behind the dray, all ready for a start to the barracks. It would appear that the employment on Sunday had been to salt beef for a shipping order. The sergeant-major having mounted, ordered a start, closely guarding the prisoner, who was driving the bullocks; he, however, tried a dodge before the forest was cleared, by endeavouring to pass down a wrong track leading south, which was no sooner discovered than the pistol was at his ear, with orders to turn. On the party nearing Dr. Everard's residence, Sergeant N—— was met on his return, and the party arrived safely at the barracks. But their duty was not completed. Losing no time, before daylight they visited a grog shanty on South Terrace, which, they had been told, was the resort of Gofton, whom they knew to be one of the three who had escaped from the yard. Arrived at the place, one went at the front and the other behind the hut. On a summons being given to open the door, the wife of Brodrip, the proprietor, answered, and declined to give admission. After being told that they were policemen, and asked where her husband was, she said at Thebarton, where he had gone to a party. She still refusing to open the front door, it was burst open.

On a light being produced, Gofton, the man they were seeking, was found lying on a couch in the tap-room. On being called to sit up, he was asked what he had been at. He said he had been having a spree. "Yes," said the sergeant-major, "I see you have; your moleskins are bloody, so are your shirt-sleeves, and you are without your coat; so get up, you are my prisoner; hold out your hands." The snaps of the handcuffs soon sounded. It should be here mentioned that a coat well known to the police as Gofton's, of a peculiar check, was found hanging on the stockyard fence, and was brought away with the skins. Gofton was also taken to the barracks, and thus two out of the four were secured. Dick Fenton was immediately sought after, but he escaped on board ship, assisted, it was said, by an Adelaide publican. As to the fourth man suspected, viz., Stagg, neither of the officers was able to swear to him, and so he was not had up on this charge. Dick Fenton had come overland with Mr. Huon; though of the prison class, he was a trusted servant of Mr. Huon, and had been placed by him in charge of a preliminary section on the Torrens, which I had sold to his employer, and towards which he had run when escaping from the sergeant. Of course Fenton knew my cattle well, some of which then ran about the Sturt, that is, such as were brought in for sale to the butchers. I had from time to time been losing cattle, which at the time I supposed had strayed, but of which no trace had ever been found, as the skins were, as a rule, destroyed when the cattle were slaughtered by such parties. As Stagg could not be brought up on the cattle stealing charge, there was an inquiry set on foot as to a horse which he was in the habit of riding. Our sergeant-major, pushing his inquiries, found that the South Australian Company had some time previous to this lost a horse somewhat answering to the description of this one, which had escaped immediately on being landed. On this Alford applied for a warrant to arrest Stagg, and waited upon him at a public-house kept by old Anthony Best (who had joined us from Tasmania), where Stagg was known to lodge.

Stagg was found at home with other company of the same class. After conversation on various subjects, Mr. Alford said, "Oh, Stagg, our inspector, Mr. Tolmer, wishes you to call on him—you may as well walk down with me." This message not suiting Mr. Stagg, he declined (smelling a rat), and ordered the landlord to bring round his horse. On the landlord doing this, our officer declared the horse to be a stolen one, and charged Best to take him back to the stable and hold him for the Government. Addressing Stagg, he said, "You are my prisoner on the charge of horse-stealing; and now you must go." On this Stagg drew from his pocket with his right hand a pistol, and also one with his left hand, but before he could cock either of them, as he turned partly round to leave the house, Mr. Alford sprang on his back with his arms round his neck, and after a struggle both came to the ground, and the pistols dropped from Stagg's grasp. The struggle, up and down, lasted for some time. Stagg was much the stronger and heavier man, but he failed to shake off his capturer, who hung on like grim death until assistance came, for the spectators at the commencement of the fray rendered no help to the officer. On the arrival of additional policemen Stagg was escorted to the barracks of the horse police, where the horse was also taken. The horse was claimed by the manager of the company, and Stagg was brought before the police court on the charge of stealing it. As there was some doubt about the identity of the animal, Stagg was released on bail after being committed for trial to the Supreme Court.

Before Gofton could be brought to trial on the charge of cattle-stealing, he managed to escape from custody by jumping over the fence around the temporary gaol (made of palings), the guards placed at the corners of the yard with loaded carbines failing to fire at him.

A fast horse, which I may mention I had some time before sold to a man who was afterwards believed to be one of the gang, was tied to a tree between the gaol and the river bank, and was mounted by Gofton, who thus managed to escape. The country was scoured day after day, and Gofton's haunts visited, from which he continued to move until he was traced to the neighbourhood of the North Arm of Port Adelaide. A considerable number of the mounted police under Inspector Tolmer were out patrolling between Port Gawler and the Dry Creek Junction, and about the North Arm of the port. A black tracker was also with the party. Stagg, on the same horse on which Gofton had escaped, had been seen on several occasions riding between Hindmarsh and Dry Creek before the police had been placed on patrol, but had then to cease his visits in taking supplies of food to his partner in crime; thus Gofton was left to starve. After being brought to a great strait he ventured out, and visited a small dairy station towards the hills belonging to a Mrs. Robertson, to whom he applied for a drink of milk and some bread, and had a quart handed to him, which he took off at one drain, and tendered a sovereign in payment. The woman was much surprised at his actions, and information soon reached the police, when Inspector Tolmer, with the black tracker and Sergeant-Major Alford in close attendance, the bulk of the police also following, were led by the black guide to a salt-water creek connected with the North Arm, to which the black had worked the tracks. He led towards the main or Port Creek. Inspector Tolmer and the sergeant-major were on one side of a back water creek, the tracker was on the other side and somewhat ahead, as the two officers had lost ground in crossing. After a time they observed their skilful assistant beckoning to them rather frantically, on which they hastened along, and on getting opposite the black, to their horror he raised a dead body so as to exhibit the shoulders and bloody head. The officers waded up to their waists through the muddy creek, and found the body to be that of Gofton, who had been shot through the head, the ball entering below the jaw and passing out of the back of the skull. After he was killed he had been dragged by the tails of his overcoat until it had been stripped from the body by the sleeves turning inside out; the coat had been thrown into the creek, and the body rolled over the bank to the mangroves. In the pocket of the coat a newspaper was found in which was an account of the charge laid against Stagg for horse-stealing. This paper was secured by the inspector; a piece had been torn from it. On the person of the murdered man was found some money and a strip of silk pocket-handkerchief—trifles as they might be considered by a non-professional, but which with other clues proved sufficient to convict Stagg of the murder of his partner. Inspector Tolmer on his return to town detached Constable Lomas with a warrant to arrest Stagg, who was accordingly taken.

The body of Gofton was removed to town and an inquest held, at which Stagg was produced and as usual cautioned. The evidence given was deemed sufficient to commit Stagg for trial, as guilty of the murder. Gofton had for some days lived in a wurley, which was discovered about a quarter of a mile from where the body was found. From thence he hoped to escape by being taken off to a departing ship by a boat. Money it was ascertained had been collected by Stagg from some of the persons who purchased beef from the cattle-stealing gang, to be used for his passage and for the expenses of getting him off; and it was supposed when the chances of success vanished his confederates thought it safer to put him out of the way lest he should split on them, as they say, and they could stick to the money, of which, from information that was afterwards gained, there was a good amount, but this never appeared in evidence.

The action of Stagg in taking the life of his friend forms one of the most humiliating pictures of human nature, showing to what depths of iniquity a career of vice may lead, and how one crime leads on to more.

Having brought the history of the first gang of cattle-stealers to the death of Gofton, by the hand of his partner Stagg, before I proceed to give an account of the trial and execution of the latter, I will relate so much of his previous career as came to my knowledge at the time. He was known to have been transported to Tasmania, according to his own account, for sheep-stealing. A large proportion of the ex-prisoners in giving an early account of themselves claimed either to have been transported for poaching or sheep-stealing, crimes which they seemed to consider quite venial; and this brings to my remembrance an incident which I met with on my way to London to embark for this colony, which proved that so long as sheep-stealing was punished with transportation, it was sometimes adopted as a means to get a free passage to Australia.

On the occasion I have alluded to I called on a friend—a gentleman-farmer in Bedfordshire—to bid him farewell, when he surprised me by saying, " Well, you must be going to a wonderful fine country; for a man of this parish, who some time ago returned from New South Wales as an expiree, and who brought some money with him, having spent his money, got tired of working at English wages, and so took it into his head to steal a sheep, and was convicted; but the Government did not indulge him with a second free passage, but sent him to a domestic penal establishment for the term of his sentence."

I give this as one of several instances I met with before I left the old country of individuals committing crimes to obtain transportation, and now proceed with the history and the end of Stagg. I knew him as a stockkeeper, frequently remaining in my neighbourhood, and as doing good work for his employers. He then appeared to me as a quiet and civil man, and a fine specimen of a rough, open-hearted Englishman of a Saxon type, ready to oblige anybody.

I have to thank Mr. Alford for many of the following particulars, as the report of Stagg's trial given in the *Register* is very brief, but of that I also take advantage.

The ball had entered near the victim's ear, and passed out at the back of his skull. He was found with his arms extended. On his person was found a bag containing twelve sovereigns and three half-sovereigns. In the neighbourhood of the body were footmarks of two persons—some Gofton's, and others those of a man who in walking turned his toes out in an unusual manner. The body had the appearance of having been dead about twenty-four hours. The Inspector stated he had observed that Stagg in walking turned out his feet as in the marks left by the man who had been with Gofton at the time of his death, and that about one hundred and fifty yards from the body such tracks led to a tree nearer the wurley where a horse had been tied, and where the rider had previously dismounted.

Sergeant Dean was subsequently sent out from town with boots found in Stagg's house, and compared them with the footprints near the body, which showed the peculiar manner of walking of the wearer as a splay-footed man, and as treading on one side of each foot. He also compared the boots with the marks seen near the wurley, and found there also an exact correspondence. He also identified a strip—part of a pocket-handkerchief—found near the body, which had been torn from a handkerchief found tied on a bag left by Stagg at the house of Peter Rhodes, at Hindmarsh. Peter Rhodes at the trial stated that Stagg came to his house on the Saturday before the body of Gofton was found, and took some bottles of water. He had a gun with him, and asked for a razor. He left and rode from the house towards Port Gawler. He was riding a horse belonging to Tom Oakley (the horse on which Gofton rode when he escaped from gaol). He was at his house again the next day (Sunday). He told him he had left two guns, and would call for them in a day or two. George Henry, servant to Rhodes, saw Stagg on Saturday. The next day he left a bag, in which he said there were two guns, which was afterwards given to the police. Inspector Litchfield said the bag with the guns was brought to the police-station on the 31st. One end of the bag was tied with a handkerchief; the other end tied with a part of a handkerchief. The barrels were dismounted from the stocks. He examined them, and found one loaded and the other empty. E. Strike, gunsmith, said he knew Gofton and Stagg. They were often together. He was shown the guns found in the bag. One belonged to Stagg ; the other had been Dick Fenton's. T. Oakley said he lent Stagg a horse on the Saturday before the body was found, which he returned on Sunday. Further evidence showed that on the charge in the loaded barrel being withdrawn, two bullets were found wrapped in a piece of newspaper, which was proved to have been torn from a *Register* of the same date as the paper found in Gofton's pocket, from which a part had been torn. Thomas Bray, bootmaker, identified the boots said to have been worn by Stagg on the Sunday as the pair he wore on the Monday morning after the body was found, at which time Stagg bought from him a new pair of boots.

Witnesses were called for the defence, endeavouring to prove an *alibi*, but failed. The jury having retired for a short time, returned and gave a verdict of guilty. Judge Cooper was much affected in passing sentence of death, this being the first occasion on which he had performed that painful duty. Stagg was hung at the new gaol, November 18, 1840, being the first criminal who was executed and buried there. He met his death with quiet firmness, but made no confession.

I have given all the material evidence which was produced at the trial, as necessary to precede what I have to relate of Lomas's trumped-up romance, which he some years afterwards volunteered against himself as the murderer, which I propose to give in this chapter, although it took place long after Stagg had been executed for the crime. At the time the sentence was carried out on Stagg, many persons thought there were great reasons to doubt the justice of the sentence, and even the editorial remarks supported such opinions. I had an interview with Stagg after sentence was passed on him, and before he was locked up, which then caused me some uneasiness; but a number of circumstances which have since come to my knowledge have removed from my mind any doubts on the subject. One suggestion I heard was that Gofton took his own life. Now the gun which had been fired was Stagg's, and the one which Gofton may have had with him was brought in by Stagg, and was the one in which the bullets were found, wrapped in a piece of newspaper, as stated. If, as had been suggested, Stagg had found his friend dead by his own hand, he would hardly have been so foolhardy as to have taken away the gun. As to the few words he was allowed to have with me, they were as follows, as near as I can remember: "I am quite content to die, but as an innocent man as to this crime. Do you believe, sir, I would have assisted him to escape, have ridden miles to have given him food, and money to pay his passage, and every way to help him, and after all to murder him? I am content to die. I have led a bad life, and confess to you I have previously committed crimes deserving death. I do not desire to live to continue a bad life. I hope you believe me. I would sooner have died in defending Joe, if it had been necessary. I have been a violent bad man, but I could not kill a friend." He requested to see me again before he was executed, but as he was in the hands of a minister of religion, I felt it better not to do so.

Private Lomas remained in the police force some time before he obtained his discharge, on the plea that he had by the death of a relative come into some property in England. He was a married man and left his wife behind him. He was not again heard of for some years, and after a time his wife consoled herself by marrying a second husband.

Many years after he left this colony the Governor received a despatch from the Secretary of State, giving the extraordinary information that a man of the name of Lomas had confessed that he murdered a man of the name of Gofton, in South Australia. At this time he was confined in a madhouse, but as he had given the information in a most clear and circumstantial manner, notice was taken of it, and our Governor was directed to make inquiries into the matter. This official communication naturally caused much excitement here. The confession was mixed up with many circumstances which had occurred, and described that on the Sunday evening, the day of the murder, he had been sent by Sergeant-Major Alford from the Little Para to the police camp at Port Gawler for rations; that on his way he met the man Gofton, and shot him. The Governor, as a matter of course, ordered a full inquiry to be made. Judge Crawford had some time before the arrival of this despatch been appointed second Judge, and he was called on by the Governor to conduct the inquiry. After taking the evidence of Inspector Tolmer and other witnesses, he started out, accompanied by Mr. Alford—at this time Inspector of Police—to the place where the tragedy was enacted. He was taken over the whole of the ground where Gofton had been in hiding, and from thence to the place where his body was discovered. Judge Crawford was informed by Inspector Alford that Lomas's statement as to being sent on the Sunday evening for rations was correct, and he showed Mr. Crawford where Lomas started from, and how far along the track he watched him; and was taken to the place indicated by Lomas, where he said he met Gofton and shot him. They then measured the distance from that spot direct to the place where the body was found, crossing several small salt-water creeks, and found the distance over three-quarters of a mile, thus proving that it was not possible for him to have conveyed the dead man to the place where the body was found. It was further manifest that the Inspector or one of the men must have heard the shot if it had been fired so near the encampment. Judge Crawford, from his careful examination of the ground, and of the evidence of the police who were on duty at the time, as well as of the other evidence given at the trial of Stagg, pronounced his opinion that there was not a doubt on his mind but that the confession of Lomas was a gross fabrication, and reported accordingly. A most inexplicable circumstance in the action of Lomas is that of his returning to South Australia after charging himself with such a crime.

Information some time after this reached the colony, that Lomas, although he did not succeed in getting out of the madhouse by obtaining a free passage to our colony as a prisoner on a charge of murder, did manage to escape from the asylum in which he was confined, and made straight off to the property he had unsuccessfully claimed, and set fire to the premises. He had been placed in the madhouse on the complaint of the persons whose property he claimed on his arrival in England, and who declined to accept him as heir-at-law. His conduct at that time had been sufficiently wild and eccentric to gain an order for his incarceration. He was tried for arson, and was sentenced to transportation to Western Australia, where, after serving his time, or obtaining a remission, he managed to make his appearance in South Australia, where he found his wife comfortably settled, and she, as may be supposed, declined his protection. He was brought before the Adelaide police-court for threatening her second husband, and was dismissed on his promising to leave the colony. He returned to Western Australia, where he said he had acquired possession of an island, and where it is to be hoped he will live and die a regular Robinson Crusoe.

CHAPTER II.

I NEXT give some account of a man who was not a convict before his arrival, but the son of convict parents. His name was Joseph Storey. He was born in Van Diemen's Land, now known as Tasmania. In all matters relating to those of the prison class or breed who joined us from that beautiful island I feel inclined to keep up its original name, as these persons were amongst early settlers known as Vandemonians. Storey arrived in the colony in 1837, or early in 1838, quite a young man ; he was by trade a shoemaker. He finished a criminal career here on the 24th August, 1841, when his sentence of death was commuted to transportation for life as a burglar and the head of a gang called the "Black-faced Robbers." Shortly after I arrived I was introduced to this criminal, and this, fortunately for me, was the only occasion on which he came in my way, and it certainly did not prove advantageous to him.

The colonial Treasurer (the late Mr. Osmond Gilles), whose house adjoined the hut I first occupied at the south-east end of the embryo city, had lost a pair of gray mares. He asked me as a favour to look out for them in my rides, and to order my people to do the same. He soon received information about them, brought by a man from the New Tiers, to the effect that he and his mate, Joseph Storey, had seen two light gray mares passing their hut on the dray track. This man offered for a reward of £10 to go after them and bring them in, urging that as the horses were travelling on as long as they had watched them, he supposed they would by the time he was speaking be a long way in the wild and unsettled bush. Mr. Gilles sent for me to speak to the man, who admitted he had come from Tasmania, on which an offer was made to him that if he or his mate, as a guide, would accompany two persons on horseback, who would bring a spare horse for the guide to ride to look for the mares, he should have five pounds on their being recovered. To this he agreed, saying his mate Storey would go, and it was arranged that the start should be as early as possible the following morning. I was pressed to go as one, as a favour to the owner, and consented, one of Mr. Gilles' clerks being chosen to accompany me. We started before sunrise, leading a spare horse for Storey, and followed the track of the spur then known as Chambers' Hill, and with the directions given found Storey's hut. After taking breakfast with these men, we started under Storey's guidance. The sun was obscured; the hills were wrapped in foggy clouds, and so remained during the day— very unfavourable for discovering lost horses in a thick forest, where we often had to pass through an undergrowth of dripping shrubs, but highly favourable for the game designed and carried out by our false guide. After beating about for several hours, Storey taking us across deep gullies and over steep-sided spurs,

I felt it was time to call a halt, to refresh men and horses. We had seen no tracks of horses. On a fresh start it appeared to us we were now taken on a wider course, and apparently across the same ridges and gullies, only more to the eastward. As the sun remained obscured, and we had no compass with us, I took great notice of the ground we passed over, and of the direction of the spurs and watercourses, for I began to suspect we were being "sold." After going over many miles I found my horse showing signs of distress, and pulled up and dismounted, my companion and Storey doing the same. Watching an opportunity when Storey was some distance from the horse he had been riding, I said to my companion, who was no bushman, and acting under me: "Now is our time; I will mount Storey's horse, you also mount and take my horse by the bridle, and I will treat with Storey." I drew out of my pocket a small pistol, and presenting it at him as he came up, said: "Now you may make the best of your way home on foot; you have been leading us about long enough." Then we left him and continued up the spur at the foot of which we had dismounted, believing that the many spurs we had crossed ran from the east side of the Mount Lofty range, and this conclusion we found to be correct, for in less than an hour we attained the top of the main ridge, very wet and somewhat tired, after being in the saddle full twelve hours. Not long after we gained the summit the sun dipped below the bank of clouds, and to our joy we saw beneath us the infant city of Adelaide. On our right and north of us we could see Chambers' Hill, and we had time to make observations, by which we were convinced that the designing Storey had been leading us backwards and forwards in circles over ground entirely to the south of his hut, and so it did not require a conjuror to decide that the direction to expect to find the mares in was to the north of the ground over which he had been misleading us, and that the mares had been planted, and might be only a short distance from the confederates' hut. Horses and men weary, we passed down a main spur and direct across the then open plain, and reached home an hour after sunset. On the following day two mounted men were sent out with directions to search only to the north of Storey's location, and to be on the ground so early as to give no time for the mares to be replanted. They were soon found in a snug gully, about a mile from the hut, and so the scoundrels who planted them did not get even five pounds.

The police had plenty of work cut out for them by burglars as well as by cattle-stealers. About this period a gang of four cattle-stealers had been playing their game some time before the police got reliable information as to the principal parties engaged, and the locality where the slaughtering of the stolen beasts took place, as so many of the timber workers were deriving profit from this sort of crime. The information came to the police in this way. A man known as Black Joe, not a coloured man, but a European of dark complexion and of doubtful character, who kept a coffee-shop and worked a team of bullocks in the Tiers, having lost one or more of his cattle, suspected they had been slaughtered by this gang, and gave the names of four men as the guilty parties, and said one of them was Joseph Storey. He said this gang was in the habit of bringing into certain gullies in the Mount Lofty range, where sawyers and splitters were located, small drafts of cattle, with which they supplied the tiersmen. Their custom was to furnish their confederates, any one of whom, on the mob being brought near his hut, could choose a beast. which was there shot and slaughtered. The skinning being partly accomplished, the part carrying the brand was cut off as quickly as possible, and thrust into a fire ready prepared. Afterwards the whole skin was cut up and burned. The carcass, on being separated into convenient pieces for removal, was carried into the hut of the man to whom the beast had been delivered, and there immediately placed in the salting cask. Acting on this information, Inspector Tolmer and Sergeant-Major Alford, with three troopers, took up a position on a spur or ridge at the back of the New Tiers shortly after sundown, as directed by Black Joe. It was not long before they discovered two fires at a distance in the gully below them. The darkness was increased by a drizzling rain. Two men were ordered to make their way down the spur to the mouth of the gorge and patrol there, and to arrest any men escaping. The officers gave their horses to a third man to hold, and as they thought they perceived a person about the fires, hastily started down the steep side of the spur, but owing to the darkness they soon found it to be more precipitous than they anticipated, and they quickly lost their footing, and after rolling over rocks found themselves at the bottom; but as they had their swords on a great rattle had been made, and they found no one at the fires. Here they waited till morning. On searching the partly-burned pieces of hide they could not discover any brand marks in letters, but they secured some pieces with figure brands on them, which were quite plain. They next commenced the search of huts in the gully they were in and in others, and found men at work salting meat, which had been killed over night. Portions of the skins secured were taken to town, and three of the men found salting the beef were taken into custody, and, after the usual delay, were put on their trial, but sufficient evidence could not be brought against them. The cattle were supposed, and with good reason, to have been stolen from the South Australian Company's cattle station at Inverbrackie. Tracks of a small mob were traced from that run to the neighbourhood of the gullies where cattle had been recently slaughtered. The Company's stockkeeper produced in Court their figure brands, which exactly fitted the brand marks on the hide, but as he could not positively swear that the beast or beasts from which the patches of skin had been removed belonged to the Company, the men were acquitted, and escaped punishment. These men were the receivers. Eleven of the jury stood out for conviction against one, but at length gave way. Although the man who had given the information to the police gave the names of four men, Storey being one, sufficient evidence was not obtained to justify the arrest of Storey and his mates, but evidence was got that twenty-two head of cattle had been killed in different places at the back of the New Tiers. The proceedings of the gang were, however, stopped, and a good look-out was kept up in that neighbourhood afterwards.

A few months after this, Joseph Storey was arrested and lodged in the old gaol, on charges of various burglaries. He had associated with him three others, of which gang he was the head, and they were called the "Black-faced Robbers." One of the four (Maitland, who arrived as an immigrant) was taken with him, but the evidence as to his identity was not clear enough, and he was discharged. Storey was committed to take his trial at the next Criminal Sittings, on a capital charge, but, getting impatient, managed to escape from the insecure make-shift prison, and the police had again to spend much time in search for him. Two of his mates managed to evade the police, and, as was afterwards discovered, cleared out of the province. These four depredators, during the time they were engaged in their nefarious pursuits, occupied huts in the New Tiers, where they assumed the characters of sawyers or splitters, but their real pursuit was (after the cattle-stealing was put an end to) to turn out after dark and visit the plains to plunder where they could. On their committing a robbery on a publican at Kensington, of the name of Ball, they were recognised, and it was on his evidence that Storey was committed for trial. At the time Storey's gang were at work as burglars, two youths were also occasionally associated with them. They, however, were caught on charges of stealing in dwelling-houses, in which the others were not implicated, and were committed for trial; but both managed to escape by jumping the gaol fence, as so many others had done. This was frequently accomplished, although guards were placed, armed with carbines, at the corners of the premises, after this manner: When an escape was to be made, some row was created by the numerous prisoners out in the yard, and then when the attention of the guard was taken up, who was placed to cover a certain part of the fence, that part was rushed by one, or by two, as in this case, and they were soon out of sight down the steep banks of the river, and their passage over the fence perhaps not observed.

Postscript.—Storey was subsequently recaptured by Sergeant-Major Alford. In one of the many parties of police who were from time to time ordered out to retake the prisoners who had escaped from the custody of Mr. Ashton, Inspector Gordon was out with Sergeant-Major Alford and three troopers, who, when passing along the top of a high ridge to the north of the New Tiers, discovered Joseph Storey, one of the men whom they were after, scrambling up the opposite ridge. They were near enough as the crow flies to identify him. Mr. Alford, seeing a kangaroo dog following him, took particular notice of the dog, that he might know him on any future day, when he might make use of him. Storey was away out of sight even before they could make their way into the intervening gully. As night was drawing near, the Inspector ordered the return to quarters. On their way back, before they left the ranges, one of the troopers informed Inspector Gordon that he caught sight of a man escaping into the scrub. On his pointing out the spot, the party were ordered to spread, so as to intercept the fugitive. This movement was quickly made, and shortly after the Inspector called out to the Sergeant-Major: "I see a man squatting in the centre of that patch of thick dwarf tea-tree." This was a swamp. The men were ordered to dismount and arrest the man, who proved to be one of the youths; so, although they did not succeed in catching Storey that day, they caught one of the escaped prisoners. His mate was also soon afterwards taken, and these two were tried, found guilty, and transported to Sydney. Although these were not, on their arrival, of the convict class, their miserable exit may be justly attributed to the extensive impregnation of evil our community suffered from the large number of convicts sent out to the adjoining colonies.

Great exertions continued to be made to secure Joseph Storey and his two mates. Inspector Tolmer, in one of the police excursions for this purpose, had with him Sergeant-Major Alford and more troopers than usual, so as to thoroughly scour the various gullies in the New and Old Tiers. On reaching the part where the timber-splitting was going on, Mr. Alford was called on one side by a man of the name of Josh. Lines, who was a connection of his. This man said to Mr. A.: "Harry, who are you after?" "Storey." "Well, you will never catch him, there are too many of you, and you make too much noise with your swords. I saw Joe this morning close by. You go away and return in an hour, and I will tell you in what hut you will find him, but do not let out I gave you information, or I shall be killed. He is armed with pistols." Mr. Alford: "Has he a kangaroo dog with him?" "Yes; and mind you look out, Harry, as he has threatened he will take your life." Having gained this clue, the Sergeant-Major followed the Inspector and overtook him at Crafer's pub. He then asked his superior officer to allow him to return with two men to follow up some trace of Storey he had gained, to which he consented, and Alford selected privates Dawson and McMahon, with whom he returned to the rendezvous, and met Lines, who said: "All is right, Storey is in Brown's hut; he has got his dog with him." Arrived at the hut they saw a little boy at the door, and Storey's kangaroo dog not far off. The boy was asked, "Have you seen anybody about to whom that dog belongs?" "Yes," he replied. "Do you know where he is now?" "No." "Has he pistols on him?" "Yes." "My boy, if you speak the truth I will give you sixpence. Tell me if you know where the man is." "I do not know." "Where are your father and mother?" "Up the rise, working." "Go and tell them I want them." Mr. A. with the men then searched the hut, but did not find any one within. He then supposed the escaped prisoner might be secreted outside. After examining the floors of the two rooms, to ascertain if under the bed or elsewhere there might be an opening to a cellar, but finding none, he left one man at the door. With the other one he searched the scrub and ground around the hut. The dog was still hanging about, and would not be driven away. From this the officer concluded that his master was secreted not far off. On the boy returning he said "his father and mother had gone away." Mr. Alford now re-entered the hut, and observing a wide slab shelf above the bed, which he had passed before as too narrow to cover a man, he ordered private Dawson to jump on the bed and see what use it had been put to. On Dawson doing this he cried out : " There is a man lying here." " Jump down and both of you cover him with your carbines." The Sergeant-Major also drew a double-barrelled pistol, and cocking and raising it, called out : " Storey, surrender yourself quietly, and first give up your firearms, handling the pistols by the muzzles, and present the butts to me, as you will be shot if you raise your weapons in any other manner." On this summons, and seeing four loaded barrels presented at him, he quietly succumbed, and after giving up his pistols as ordered came down, and was handcuffed. The loaded pistols which were found on him he had stolen after escaping from gaol from an armourer in King William-street. The prisoner was escorted to the horse police barracks, where they arrived a few hours after the Inspector, who was at the time taking a meal, and was called out to see the prisoner in the yard in charge of the two troopers, much to his surprise and pleasure, and exclaimed : " Alford, how did you manage to take him so soon after you left me?" "Well, Inspector, I had the assistance of his dog."

CHAPTER III.

AFTER the early experiences colonists had to endure from visitors from the convict colonies, I now give the closing scenes of two of the shipments of convicts, which will add materially to the dark side of the history of the opening days of this colony, which in so many other respects were so bright and pleasing.

On the 17th of April, 1850, the *Lady Dennison* was chartered by our Government to convey ten long-sentenced prisoners to Tasmania under the charge of three constables. Sixteen passengers were also in the ship. It was afterwards reported that amongst the passengers were some confederates of the convicts on board. Of this unfortunate ship no tidings have ever been heard. It is unknown whether she went down with all hands or was taken by the prisoners; and, if so, as a matter of course Captain Hammond—her commander—his crew, constables, and passengers, were all killed, excepting any who might have assisted or joined the prisoners. Written information was received by the Government shortly after the discovery of gold in Victoria that one or more of the escaped prisoners had been seen on the Victorian diggings, but no confirmation of such a statement has been made public.

To follow the brief and sad account of the missing *Lady Dennison*, I may with propriety quote the description of the narrow escape the captain of the brig *Punch* and his passengers and crew experienced, on a voyage shortly afterwards from Port Adelaide to Hobart Town. What took place on board I have learned from a gentleman, one of the cabin passengers, who, shortly after he made the trip, committed the occurrences to paper, and has obligingly allowed me to use the same.

"The brig had been chartered by our Government to convey twelve long-sentenced prisoners, to expiate their breaches of the law by penal servitude in Tasmania, or Van Diemen's Land, as it was then called; but this I did not know till I got on board. At this time, and for a short period afterwards, our prisoners were sent to one of the convict colonies, either to Sydney or Tasmania. In addition to twelve prisoners, the captain accommodated two cabin passengers. I should say three, for a female, the wife of one of the prisoners, was allowed to take a cabin passage, and she brought on board a considerable quantity of luggage; there were also four steerage passengers.

"The brig had amongst her prison passengers one at least who had been sentenced to a long term of imprisonment under a first conviction, and so had not joined ours from a convict colony. As I know the respectability of his connections, I do not publish his name, as no good purpose has to be served thereby; and as I suppose he may have obtained his liberty long before this account appears in print, I trust his bitter experience of the consequences of wrong-doing will have produced a favourable change in him.

"On the day the brig *Punch* was advertised to sail for Hobart Town I found myself under the necessity of visiting

Tasmania without delay. To take advantage of the *Punch*, I only had time to make hurried business arrangements and to pack up a carpet-bag. Thus prepared I started in one of the Port passenger-carts. On arriving at the bank of the Port Creek, I found the brig already in the stream ready for a start, and was put on board by a Port boatman. On stepping on deck the first thing which attracted my attention and surprised me was to perceive two armed sentries pacing the deck. On entering the captain's cabin, I inquired of him the cause of the sentries being on board, and he, as if it was a matter of no consequence, informed me he had a number of prisoners between decks, but that if I wished for a passage with him I could have half a cabin with a gentleman passenger already on board. I felt rather dashed by the position in which I found myself, but as my business was most pressing I took my passage with a sort of desperation, feeling prepared to defy any ordinary discomforts; but I certainly little expected what did occur.

"I had arrived on board in an excited state from the hurry I had been put to in the short notice I had, and did not feel in my usual spirits, perhaps in part occasioned by this being my first trip on shipboard since my voyage from England, and with a very lively recollection of a narrow escape from wreck on that occasion, causing me to feel an undefined dread of a coming calamity; but I certainly did not anticipate such fright as we experienced, before we arrived at our destination, which was nothing less than an attempt of the prisoners to take the brig, and for which well-laid plans had been made before we left the port of departure, which to the captain, crew, and passengers would have resulted in violent death in the contest, or in walking the plank if the ruffians' designs had succeeded; but in their attempt to recover freedom they were most providentially frustrated. Our captain was a man over six feet in stature and stout in proportion, with a fist and voice to create dread whenever called into play, so that when the first intimation of the prisoners' designs was revealed to us, and arms put in our hands, our courage and confidence in our leader were aroused. Before any alarm was given, I had observed in the captain's cabin a goodly supply of weapons in good order. Our captain had the look of a jolly Irishman, who rather had a taste for a scrimmage. We were soon making good way down the Gulf, having been towed to the Lightship. I was informed that amongst the prisoners were several 'lifers,' as they were called, and the remainder transports for seven or fourteen years, and some returned runaway prisoners from the convict colonies, and that many desperate characters were amongst them. On receiving this anything but cheering information, and seeing only three guards in charge of them, the nervous state of feeling which I have described as mine at starting, was not diminished, and I heartily wished myself on shore again; but this I knew to be an impossibility, as no boat would be allowed to leave a chartered convict ship.

"I may mention here, to account for so many criminals being sent away at one time, that runaways from the neighbouring colonies were retained in gaol until after a session, when a sufficient number of sentenced men could be added to make up a number to justify our Government in chartering a suitable vessel. To some readers it may be necessary to repeat that for some years after the founding of this colony, the Governments of New South Wales and Tasmania still received our own sentenced prisoners, and justly so, as we had been supplied with plenty of runaways and expirees from those colonies. Now we have to provide for our own criminals, and laws have been passed by our legislature to forbid the landing of persons of that class on our shores, either from the mother country or from the neighbouring colonies.

"I now describe our passage. After leaving Port Adelaide everything seemed to go on favourably. The wind was propitious, and after turning in, I passed a quiet and comfortable night. On passing Kangaroo Island we encountered a much rougher sea. Our brig was a smart craft, and our captain, as he afterwards explained, having the unknown fate of the *Lady Dennison* present in his mind (which was the convict ship previously despatched from South Australia), had under the conditions of his charter made every suitable arrangement to keep secure his prison passengers, and he was resolved, if possible, to avoid the supposed fate of the captain and crew of that lost ship. The 'tween decks were fitted up in a substantial manner, the chain cable so arranged that refractory prisoners could be made fast to it by shackles, and also his cabin was well furnished with loaded firearms, cutlasses, &c. The cook was an old servant of the captain's, and had made many trips with him. When we were well at sea he came to the master with an appearance of having something serious to say. On being asked: 'Well, cook, what do you want?' he replied: 'Captain, I don't like your lady passenger, Mrs. B——, the wife of one of the prisoners. She has a good deal of luggage in her cabin, and I think there is something suspicious about it. I noticed one of her trunks as being very heavy, and putting this and that together, I feel I must tell you what I have on my mind. I have an engagement with a young woman ashore in Adelaide to marry her, and she was quite upset when I parted with her. I told her we were only bound on a short trip, but she kept on crying, and at last said: "You will never come back, nor will the brig ever reach Hobart Town, as I have overheard a conversation between the passenger (Mrs. B——, whose service she had just left) and one of her friends to that effect."' On receiving this vague tale the captain became more than ever on his guard, and on hearing on a subsequent night an unusual noise among the prisoners, he went, accompanied with the guards and part of the crew, all armed, and shackled the worst of the men to the chain cable. The prisoners had the appearance of men under the influence of drink, which must have been smuggled to them. To explain how this might have been done, I must state that an arrangement had been carried out soon after starting of bringing three or four of the prisoners on deck for air and exercise, and on these occasions the prisoner B—— had been granted the privilege by the guards and the good-natured captain to hold a few minutes' conversation with his wife in her cabin. Before the captain went below after hearing the noise, Mrs. B—— begged of him, in an excited manner, not to do so, but he did not feel inclined to follow her advice, and, after securing some of the prisoners, turned in for the night, but like a miller, who is said to sleep with one eye open, he was alive to the slightest noise. When he was ruffled he was a sort of demon, but when things were going on smoothly, he was quite amiable and anxious to make all hands happy. We had not long retired again to rest, before midnight, when the sea had become very rough, and the brig laboured heavily; but above the noise of the elements a cry of one of the guards was heard. The crew and myself and the other cabin passenger had been supplied with arms, and told to keep ourselves in readiness, and we were all soon on deck. We found the guards doing their best to beat the prisoners back from escaping up the main hatch, which was half open. Our captain was at the opening roaring with such vehemence and language as I never heard before, 'that he would cleave in two any man who dared to come within his reach.' After a short struggle the revolting prisoners were driven back, and every man chained to the cable, with the threat from the captain that on any fresh attempt every blessed man should go over the side fast to the cable. On the following morning the captain, accompanied by the cook, visited Mrs. B—— in her cabin, and addressed her in these words. He was very polite in his rough way:—

"'Mrs B——, I am sorry to intrude on you so abruptly and early in the day. My only excuse is my anxiety for the safety of my ship and passengers.'

"'Captain, I do not understand you. What can I do to secure the safety of your ship? what can you mean?'

"'Well, madam, it is no use mincing matters. I will be plain, and not keep you in further suspense. I have sufficient grounds to know that there is a conspiracy between you and your husband and the other prisoners to take the ship.'

"On hearing this, Mrs. B—— became as white as death, and quickly exclaimed: 'It is false, it is a lie! I know nothing of such a conspiracy; it is cruel to bring such a charge against me—an unfortunate woman,' and, with a woman's last resource, she burst into tears.

"The answer she got was: "Madam, I must be firm; and so I have at once to demand of you the keys of your trunks.'

"At this she became abusive and refused to comply, and when she was told the cook would be ordered to break them open, she produced the keys. On the heavy suspected trunk being opened, pistols ready loaded, with cutlasses, &c., were found, also sundry charts and other requisites for a voyage. During this exposure the woman, dejected, with her head depressed with shame and fear, kept silence. The skipper ordered the confiscated arms, &c., to be placed in the store, and addressed the wretched woman thus :—

"'Madam, you see our information was correct as to what was intended to be carried out. I have hitherto granted you every indulgence in my power. Now it becomes my duty to order you to keep close to your cabin for the remainder of the passage, and you will not hold any communication with your husband in the ship. I shall take care of your personal comforts and see that your wants are all attended to; but you must not attempt to leave your cabin, or to hold any secret communication with any person on board.'

"On this the captain went on deck, and called the passengers and crew to hear him. He ordered us to keep our arms in readiness, and to be ready to attend promptly to any call, night or day, and he added one of the crew to the guards.

"There must be one universal opinion that the South Australian Government were highly to be blamed in sending so many prisoners with only three policemen as guards, especially as before we left the opinion had become general that something fatal had happened on board the *Lady Dennison*, which had been despatched such a short time before us with prisoners, and of her no tidings had been heard. The weather during the remainder of the passage still continued rough, dark, and foggy. The captain became quite anxious, as he supposed he was in the neighbourhood of the dangerous rocks called the Sow and Pigs, but we fortunately passed without sighting them, and made the mouth of the River Derwent, and with a fair wind sailed up that beautiful river, and soon obtained a pilot. On his coming on board his first question to our captain was if any tidings had been heard of the *Lady Dennison*. On our nearing the wharf the usual officials came on board. The prisoners were ordered on deck, and were ranged, and their names called over. Before they were ordered over the side, where a file of soldiers were ready with fixed bayonets to receive and guard them, the privileged prisoner had the face to request to speak to our captain, and said:—

"'Captain, I wish to ask you if you will accept a small token from me as a memento of this voyage? Amongst my wife's luggage there is a trunk which I wish you to accept with its contents. In it you will find charts and other articles which we intended to use if an opportunity had occurred. It is useless to deny that it was our intention to have seized the ship, and to have compelled part of the crew to steer for California; but we were foiled in our purpose, and we must now submit as patiently as we can to our destiny.'

"The captain thanked him for his candid confession, but informed him that the present he offered had been in his safe keeping some days, and would be handed over to the South Australian Government. And then the miserable fellow was marched off in a chained gang under a strong escort, the wretched wife from the side of the brig witnessing with floods of tears her husband's departure. It was reported that she afterwards entered into a small way of business, and in a certain time applied for her husband, and obtained him as an assigned servant under the convict regulations."

CHAPTER IV.

THE narrative of the original settlement of Port Lincoln has been withheld that the advantage of a consecutive account may be given of this western part of South Australia, which has been from the first so sparsely occupied and by widely separated squatting stations, so that stock-owners and their servants were exposed to the attacks of the wild natives, being without adequate police protection; this extensive portion of the colony being adapted only to grazing purposes, and cut off from the more settled portions of the province by two wide gulfs.

It is necessary to explain that I have received full information as to the "experiences" of the first settlers in this district of the colony, from two gentlemen who were of the party which arrived there in 1839 to form the settlement, and were amongst the most active in that work. From them and others I have been favoured with descriptions of the first trials endured, and of a sad accident which occurred at the opening scene, as well as all accounts of the first murder by the blacks of a youth a short distance from the township.

The visit to, and inspection by Colonel Light of the unsurpassed natural harbour of Boston Bay and the neighbouring anchorages, proved to him that the previous navigators were perfectly correct as to the beauty and capacity of the harbour; but of the adjacent country no information was extant. Arrived in Boston Bay, he found the harbour all that could be desired; and if they had been backed up by such a country as he had seen on the eastern side of Gulf St. Vincent, no doubt he would there have fixed Adelaide as the capital; but from every point of vantage as an elevation from which to view the interior, the picture was so unfavourable that he quickly made his decision against Port Lincoln.

Early in 1839 an association was formed in Adelaide, called "The Adelaide Association," by whom a party was organized and sent out to examine the shores of the Gulf of St. Vincent.

U

The party sailed from Adelaide in the schooner *Victoria*, Captain Hutchinson. Messrs. Hughes, Robert Cock (sometime Government auctioneer), George James, and W. B. Lucas, with six men, formed the party deputed by the Association to examine land, with the view of taking up special surveys, embracing suitable sites for ports, with good land adjoining. The object in giving a brief account of this first exploring party is to show in what a favourable manner these intruders were received by the natives.

The account of this is furnished by Mr. George James, who says :—" On one occasion, after we had landed to the south of Port Lincoln, on May the 18th, we had proceeded some miles inland when we observed a large body of natives ; at first we were alarmed, friendly signs were made to them, and thinking I would divert them from making an attack on us, I threw off my coat, and commenced to dance and sing "Jump Jim Crow," when they at once came to us in great glee, laughing and yelling. One of them came to me and began to pat me, and to open my shirt front, as if to assure himself and the others that my body was white as well as my face. Before they approached us they laid down their spears and waddies." This party of explorers selected Port Lincoln for a special survey, as well as one on each side of Yorke Peninsula. The first was taken up, but the others were abandoned.

I now give the narratives of Captain Hawson, Mr. T. N. Mitchell, and others, taken down from their lips. Mr. Mitchell was one of the passengers by the *Abeona*, Captain Hawson, and also on board were Messrs. C. Fenn, R. Todd, W. Williams, J. M. Phillipson, and others, whose names may appear in the course of this narrative. The landing was made in March, 1839, in Boston Harbour, at Happy Valley. By the captain and passengers it was arranged that those on shore should fire a volley and hoist the British flag, and that after a certain interval of time, the mate, named James Hunter, should answer by firing the one and only carronade on board. The volley on shore having been fired, the first discharge of the gun on board took place, and shortly after they were surprised by a second discharge of the gun on deck contrary to orders, and also by witnessing a splash in the water following the report. It was evident an accident had occurred, and Captain Hawson, with Mr. Mitchell, immediately pushed off in the boat. On arriving on board they were horrified at finding one of the seamen lying in a pool of blood on the steerage deck. He was begging to be thrown overboard : his eyes were literally blown out, one of his cheeks was lacerated, his hands shattered, and his body otherwise injured. Mr. Mitchell, having previously operated on animals, and having fortunately with his luggage a medicine chest and a case of surgical instruments, in the absence of any surgeon amputated part of one hand, and dressed his face and wounds in the best way he could. The captain at the same time set about the discharge of passengers' luggage and cargo, so as to lose no time in returning to Adelaide, and placing him, if then surviving, under professional treatment. It was ascertained that poor Hunter had most improperly, in ramming down the powder, used an iron bar, and thus the powder had exploded, the splash seen by the captain and others on shore being the iron bar striking the water. The running up of the British flag, part of the introductory ceremony, happening almost at the same moment as this accident, the unfortunate occurrence was looked upon as a sad opening of the settlement. The brig was soon under way, and made a quick and comfortable passage to Holdfast Bay, and the sufferer was conveyed to Adelaide. Mr. Mitchell accompanied Hunter to attend to him, and to alleviate his agonies as much as possible. The patient arrived in the Adelaide Hospital alive, much to the surprise of Dr. Wyatt and other medical gentlemen, who were soon in attendance. The building then used as the public hospital was situated near the Black Swan, on North Terrace, and was a small thatched hut. The maimed man recovered, and survived some years. This was the first unfortunate experience of the Port Lincoln settlers.

Captain Hawson returned with his ship and passenger, Mr. Mitchell, and anchored again in Boston Bay. No time was lost by the few arrivals in organising an exploring party to view the country and discover its capabilities, Captain Hawson being leader, with about nine men, all on foot, an overlander, called Yorky, carrying the bulk of the provisions. The direction first taken was about south-west. After passing over a barren and sandy country, and travelling three days, they made Coffin Bay, where a little fresh water was found, but not sufficient to satisfy the wants of the party. They then turned in a north-west direction to reach a range of hills in sight, on arriving at which it was decided that the bulk of the party should rest, and remain at a certain spot, while the leader,

Mr. Mitchell, one other member of the party, and Yorky, with his load, should surmount the range. This was carried out, and the active party struggled up the steep and rocky range, which was named by them the Marble Range, from finding large masses of quartz, and what was taken to be marble. The prospect not being promising in any direction from the summit, no open country being in view, it was decided to continue N.E.; and, unfortunately for the explorers, by some accident, Yorky, the bearer of the main portion of the provisions, separated from the descending party, and was no more seen until they returned to the encampment at Happy Valley. The party had now to depend entirely on their return journey on the small quantity of provisions which they had in their wallets, and on brackish water, until a black was caught, who was induced to point out some of their watering-places in the direction of the new settlement, and the party had to subsist for four or five days on a few small birds. On arriving at the settlement at Happy Valley, as they had called it (but where they had not yet experienced much of that feeling), they found their provision-carrier had arrived before them, and without much inconvenience to himself. The black, who may be said to have saved the lives of the explorers by pointing out good water, remained with them a short time, and for a time his friendship was secured.

The first water shown by this blackfellow was on a rise near a hill, which they named Mount Gawler; and here the first sheep-station was afterwards formed, by Mr. John Brown, from Shields, who soon afterwards was killed by the blacks, as was also a Mr. Biddle, who subsequently formed a station about five miles from Brown's place, with some others employed on these first stations.

It was not long before the inhabitants of the small settlement were cheered by the arrival of Captain Porter, with his brig *Porter*, named after himself. His cargo was chiefly provisions, of which the inhabitants had run short, and, much to their inconvenience, he refused to sell. His brig *Dorset*, which he had sold at Port Adelaide to Messrs. Smith and Shane, also soon after arrived, with a number of Van Diemen's Land labourers—old lags—under engagement to them.

The next unfortunate circumstance which occurred was the pecuniary difficulties in which Messrs. Smith and Shane shortly found themselves at the commencement of the general crisis, when they could not continue to employ the rough characters whom they had introduced into the infant settlement; nor could they complete their bargain for the brig *Dorset*, which then fell into the hands of Mr. Emanuel Solomon, of Adelaide, who employed her to the great benefit of the older settlement of Adelaide. The rough characters who were thus thrown out of work by the difficulties of their employers, commenced to supply their own wants by committing robberies on the small stocks of the already needy settlers, who, few in number, and not altogether in harmony, did not combine together to resist the depredators, who carried on their actions with impunity, helping themselves frequently in open daylight. At this time no police had been provided or sent by the Government.

The Government were appealed to for protection, and Mr. Matthew Smith (some years afterwards Commissioner of Insolvency) was sent as Resident Magistrate, with Mr. John Irving Barnard as clerk; also Sergeant McEllister (who subsequently rose to the dignity of M.L.C) and four policemen. After these disorders were quelled the settlement went on in a quiet jog-trot way until the inhabitants, were aroused and delighted by the arrival of a French whaler, the *Recovery*, Captain Latham, who remained to water and refresh, and, having given and received hospitalities, continued his cruise after the monsters of the deep, promising to return. He soon fulfilled his promise; and, to the joy of the settlers, shortly after he dropped anchor, two more whalers arrived, both foreigners, and took up their stations and anchored without the aid of pilots. Now Boston Bay presented an interesting and unusually lively appearance. The next arrival was a most remarkable one, namely, a large whale, come in as it were to offer sport and a voluntary sacrifice of a body burdened with a superfluity of fat or blubber. Boats from all the vessels were soon in chase. Although the bays are spacious enough to shelter and accommodate the largest fleet ever afloat, the space afforded for the sport of fastening on to a full-grown whale, and keeping hold till death of the game, was found to be limited by the monster, which was at length made fast to the side of the whaler, *Nile*, the boats of which ship were successful in the race. The whale was longer than the ship to which it was lashed, and the affair was a sight the inhabitants were gratified with, such as seldom has been afforded to landsmen on shore. It is somewhat remarkable that before the whalers left their anchorage, two more whales were sighted but escaped.

Before the settlement of South Australia was made, the southern sandy beaches and sheltered coves were favourite places of resort for the female mammals to visit once a year; but now, with the numerous ships, especially the steamers, which are so constantly passing to and fro, the whalers have to visit other seas, and such profitable visitors are not now caught in our province, and only occasionally a stray one may be seen off Encounter Bay, or to the south of the Great Australian Bight.

I give an extract from the *South Australian Magazine* of November, 1841 (long defunct), furnished by the late Mr. Bentham Neales, who was one of the first supporters of the settlement at Port Lincoln, as he was of the general business of the colony. The extract is as follows:—

"I have as yet taken my stand on solid land, and have said nothing of the open sea. Look at the map, and you will see from this port (meaning Port Lincoln), to the westernmost extremity of the province, barren sand-hills. Says the traveller, these in fact are universal. True, so are the bays, coves, and inlets universal, literally teeming with live oil, which the prevailing winds, with the requisite amount of human industry, would at once bring up to the head-quarters provided by nature—Boston Bay. Last year (1840), four French whalers and one American, fished between this place and Fowler's Bay, and this year at least six foreigners are on the fishing-ground, taking away the riches which we neglect. A small branch of the Adelaide Fishing Company, at Sleaford's Bay, is all that has been yet attempted; although it is well known that no less than thirty-two whales have been seen in Boston Bay this year. Should a larger company be formed, as several excellent spots can be pointed out, it appears quite evident that the whale fishery will be ere long one of the principal sources of the wealth of the Port Lincoln settlers."

The most interesting visitor with whom the inhabitants were afterwards favoured was Lady Franklin, who, with her daughter, arrived in the brigantine *Abeona*, from Hobart Town, commanded by Captain Blackburn. This amiable lady and devoted wife had undertaken the duty of paying this visit, encountering in her own person the hardships of this early period of the settlement, when no suitable accommodation could be afforded her, or means to aid her in her toilsome work. Her object was to prosecute the difficult search for the spot on Stamford Hill from the highest part of which Captain Flinders, under whom her gallant husband was an officer, had taken his observation when on his visit some years before he was engaged on a marine survey in the ship *Investigator*. On the spot, when found, Lady Franklin's determination was to cause to be erected a suitable work as a memorial to commemorate Captain Flinders' visit and its accomplished object. Captain Blackburn, with some of the inhabitants, accompanied Lady Franklin and her daughter on foot to fulfil this arduous duty. When reached, the steep and rocky range had to be climbed, and on the summit being attained, the exact spot had to be worked out and discovered by observations, until a correspondence with Captain Flinders' record was obtained. The range was found to have so large an amount of metallic ore in its body that it was necessary to work the instrument placed upon the bent back of one man, resting to give steadiness on another. The person on whose back was placed the instrument was Mr. T. N. Mitchell, his support one of the Hawsons. After many trials a correspondence was obtained, and then the spot was marked, where the contractor (Mr. Kellet, of Adelaide), afterwards erected a monument dedicated to Captain Flinders. Anything I can write to record this devoted action of the gallant wife of a gallant sailor, whose life was afterwards lost, as is so universally known, in command of the party sent to seek the North-West Passage, will very inadequately record Lady Franklin's many virtues in this instance, which is in keeping with her untiring and self-sacrificing actions in sending out naval expeditions to recover the remains of her lost husband. Never was there a nobler man than Sir John Franklin, or one blessed with a worthier wife.

In this history, written after a residence in the colony extending over a period of over forty-five years, which the compiler has spent in active colonial pursuits, have been recorded to the best of his ability the "experiences" of the working bees who have, in their various employments, contributed their quota to establish and build up a new kingdom or dominion, and no class of events has caused him so much pain in relation as the collisions between the white intruders and the aboriginal races.

I have now to narrate the painful details of the murders of

detached settlers engaged in peaceful pastoral callings in the Port Lincoln district. The first and quite unprovoked case of murder was committed on Master Frank Hawson, youngest son of a respectable and early inhabitant of the town of Port Lincoln, and brother of Captain Hawson. This courageous youth was under 13 years of age, and happened to be left alone in the hut on their station, seven miles from the township, in the early part of the month of March, 1840. The sad occurrence was entirely unexpected, as the most friendly dispositions had been to all appearance entertained by the white and coloured races towards each other. The fine and bold boy was surrounded in the hut by twenty-two men and boys. He was pierced through by a war spear. On receiving this, which ultimately proved his death wound, he seized a gun and shot one native; the remainder retired, carrying away the wounded man.

Master Hawson survived the wound only eight days. After great sufferings, he gave descriptions and names of some of his assailants, but for want of further evidence none of them were brought to justice by process of law. The object of the attack no doubt was plunder, and the hut had been watched until they knew the poor boy was alone, and they supposed he would from fear offer no resistance to their plundering intentions.

On March the 28th, 1842, intelligence was received in Adelaide, that, on the 2nd of the same month, Mr. John Brown and his hut-keeper, a boy of the name of Lovelock, had been barbarously murdered on Mr. Brown's station, not far from Port Lincoln. Mr. Brown was for a time a large sheep farmer. At the commencement of the attack, in resisting his assailants, he knocked one of them down with the butt end of his gun, but he was soon overpowered by numbers, and fell, after receiving several wounds; he afterwards struggled and got upon his knees, and whilst in the attitude of prayer he was despatched. Although great exertions were made to bring his murderers to justice, they were not caught and punished in the ordinary way.

In the early part of the following month an attack was made by forty or fifty natives on the station of Mr. Biddle, a few miles from the locality of the previous murders, and, as is pretty certain, by the same unpunished and bloody aggressors. Mr. Biddle was on the station, and had with him in his employ one man as a shepherd, named Jas. Fastings, and an aged married couple of the name of Stubbs. When the party saw the natives approaching the hut, Jas. Fastings was passing from a fowl shed; the blacks threw several spears at him, and he received a spear wound in one of his legs, when he returned to the hut as quickly as he was able. The time was midday. The blacks soon surrounded the hut. They next pulled up some of the paling fence which enclosed a small garden, and then retired, but returned in about an hour; on which the man Fastings left the hut to release the dog, and exposed himself with remarkable courage to another flight of their war spears, and received one which pierced one of his arms, when he again gained the cover of the hut. Now the determined assailants set fire to the tarpaulin which formed the roof of the dwelling (they had left to provide themselves with fire-sticks) and threw spears through the open window into the hut. Mr. Biddle fired two pistols at them, and immediately received a spear wound in the heart and dropped dead. The old man Stubbs, who was standing by the side of his master, then fired a double-barrelled gun, and killed one and wounded another native. Stubbs then went to endeavour to relieve Fastings of the spears which were in his limbs, when several spears entered the hut, and he was brought to the ground, where he lay for a time in a state of insensibility. In a few moments Fastings fell dead across Stubbs. Prior to this the poor old woman, his wife, had secreted herself under one of the beds; she was sixty-nine years old. The murderous blacks now entered and soon found the poor old woman, and after dragging her out from her cover, put an end to her life by stabbing her in various parts of her body with a pair of shears. They then went out and procured hatchets, with which they shattered the heads of those whom they had already killed in such a shocking manner that their countenances were completely destroyed. As the head of Stubbs was covered by the prostrate body of the shepherd he providentially escaped death, although on his becoming sensible he felt himself faint with loss of blood from his numerous wounds. He took care to simulate death until the wretches departed, after clearing the dwelling of all they could carry away. It is quite evident that the white men deferred action until the natives had approached the premises too near, and had become the actual assailants. It is safe for persons who never expose themselves to be attacked by wild natives to say they must not have shots fired at them until they actually cast their spears, but here is an example of the consequence of such forbearance. But to return to the survivor. As soon as he was able he arranged the bodies as well as he could, and managed to crawl to the nearest station, which belonged to Mr. White. He there found Mr. Driver, the Resident Magistrate, who soon formed a party, and started off after the depredators and overtook them about four miles from the place where they had so far accomplished their horrid work. On seeing a strong party approaching, they bolted, but did not get clear off without leaving one of their number, who was fetched down by a long shot, and "bit the dust." They abandoned all their plunder—flour, silver spoons, &c., &c. Immediately after the above distressing news reached Adelaide a deputation of gentlemen waited on Governor Grey, and in consequence of their urgency a party of soldiers of the 96th Regiment, two companies of which were quartered in Adelaide, were sent. Lieut. Hugonin had under him one sergeant and fifteen privates. After their arrival at Port Lincoln they were marched out on an expedition against the tribes which had committed the murders and depredations. The party were supplied with a bullock-dray and team, also horses to carry provisions, baggage, &c., by Captain Hawson, who also accompanied the party to guide and direct the commander in his actions in endeavouring to capture prisoners of the offending tribes or families. This party was out three months; as the soldiers were all on foot, the natives, even when found, escaped in the scrub, and with the greatest ease avoided capture. The only result was the shooting of three of the blacks. This was a most unsatisfactory result of the expedition. At the time the orders were given to despatch such a party, strong remarks were made in the papers of the day, and decided opinions were expressed by colonists in Adelaide on the bad policy of the orders given. It will be felt, on comparing the upshot of this expedition, sent out by Governor Grey, with the one under Major O'Halloran, despatched by Governor Gawler against the Milemnura tribes or families, how unreasonable was the outcry raised against the previous Government measures.

The detachment under Lieutenant Hugonin was left at Port Lincoln some time. I have the advantage of the use of the diary of Major O'Halloran during the time he was subsequently out in the Port Lincoln district to endeavour to *catch and hold* natives, naked and greasy. Before the military were recalled by their Colonel, they were out a second time, accompanied by

Mr. Driver, S.M., and three mounted troopers, on which occasion one native was shot. By these measures the natives were thoroughly frightened, and for some time no more murders occurred. Before removal of the soldiers Major O'Halloran and a party of mounted police were sent from Adelaide, and were out six weeks.

Extracts from the Major's diary are now given :—" Nov. 7th, 1842. Embarked at Port Adelaide with Inspector Tolmer, in the *Alpha*, cutter, for Port Lincoln, and reached our destination on the 10th. I found to my great regret that Mr. Driver, the Resident, had taken the police party into the country in search of the blacks who had been guilty of the late murders. I was making arrangements for immediately following, when the return of Mr. Driver prevented me from doing so. He had left the party on their return; they had been absent one week. They yesterday fell in by accident with twenty-one natives, all of whom escaped except two, who were in charge of the police on their way in as prisoners. Both of these blackfellows have been identified as being concerned in the late murders. I decide with the police to proceed in search of the other actual murderers, who belong to the Midland or Battara tribe, amongst whom the Missionary Protector says there are not more than thirty fighting men. Port Lincoln appears at present a deserted place, more than half the houses have been abandoned, and the remainder are barricaded to protect the occupants against the attacks of the natives. I believe they have no more reason to fear an attack than the inhabitants of Adelaide have. The timid conduct of the settlers in leaving their stations, with a few honourable exceptions, has emboldened the natives. We must teach them to respect us, and give them high notions of our power and speed. The party consists of Inspector Tolmer and five constables, Mr. Driver, the Resident, Mr. Schurman, the Missionary Protector, and Messrs. Hawson and McEllister, who accompany me as volunteers. I notified to the party the orders I had received from His Excellency as to our conduct towards the aborigines. Before I started I had a long conversation with the Protector, who exhibited great reluctance to accompany the party when he became acquainted with the strict orders under which the party were held to act. He at length consented to join the party; nevertheless, if he had declined I should have used my powers and compelled him to proceed as interpreter. His original residence was at Happy Valley, where he had cultivated a small patch of ground, and had a promising crop of wheat growing, but, in fear of the natives, had taken up his residence in the township. A Protector is of no use if he is afraid to live and mix amongst the natives to whom he has been sent. To place himself between the settlers and aboriginals, and to mediate and reconcile differences, and by his politic training to lead those among whom he should be able at all times to mix and to exercise pacific habits—such a man so placed would do more to keep up peaceful relations between the white and coloured races than sections of military or police forces."

The following is an extract from a memorandum made by Major O'Halloran after an interview with the Governor, April 18, 1842, and certified :—

"Having sought for instructions from His Excellency to guide me in case I might be called on, during his contemplated visit with Captain Frome to Lake Albert, to proceed against the blacks if they continued troublesome in the North, I asked the Governor what would be the extent of any powers and instructions if sent on such a service? He replied that I must treat the blacks, if armed and likely to resist, as I would any hostile party who were resisting the law; and that I should be fully justified in becoming the aggressor in such a case; or if I thought the life of a single individual of my own party was threatened or endangered, I must act with vigour until all resistance ceased. The Governor further added that the law might have to decide upon the legality of such proceedings. I might rest assured that the Government would give me every support and protection in their power.—T. O'HALLORAN, Commissioner of Police."

Major O'Halloran started from the township with the above-mentioned party on the 14th of November, twelve in number, to the country north-west of the township, with one of the prisoners named Moullier, who was caught and brought in by Mr. Driver's party. He promised to lead them to the waters where the tribe would be likely to be found. He was placed on the back of a pony, and made fast by a chain looped round the neck of the animal he rode. A friendly black named Utulla, who had been depended on to guide the party, was missing. The first day Pillaworta Water was made—30 miles. Here two police were left with stores in charge. The next day several men of the detachment were supplied with three days' provisions, and guided by the prisoner made a start. Towards evening they came upon a place where the natives had been recently encamped, and where a patch of grass had been fired a few hours before. The prisoner said they had gone north. The Major in his diary says:—

"Next day had much thunder and lightning. After riding sharp a few miles came in sight of and gave chase to a number of natives. On coming up with them, found our missing friend Utulla, who ought to have been with us. Intimated to these friendly blacks that we sought the murderers only, and desired to be at peace with all other blackfellows. These blacks took us to a waterhole, where we refreshed men and cattle. They told us the part of the tribe with whom were four of the murderers (whose names they gave, and which corresponded with some of the men who were on the list we had), were ahead of us, so ordered an advance at speed. We had already travelled miles enough to fatigue our horses, and made out we would have to travel twenty-five miles before we could reach the next water. Mr. Tolmer was suffering from the effects of a fall he had experienced on his late expedition to Mount Arden, in the far North, but I could not allow him to return back alone. We were now about sixty-five miles from the township. At 1 P.M. the party mounted and continued chiefly through scrub, and sometimes on the beach of the Gulf. To our great joy we came upon a rock waterhole filled with recent rain, and carefully covered up with fresh-cut green boughs, proving the natives were not far ahead. After refreshing at this water, kept on at a sharp pace, and at about four o'clock saw about a mile in advance of us a mob of retreating blacks, to whom we gave chase over a terribly rough and scrubby country, but only caught one man. In this last gallop through high scrub, three of the party lost their swords, dragged out of their scabbards in tearing through high and strong bushes. We found the man we had taken was not one of the offenders, and so he was allowed to follow his friends, with the assurance we gave before to the others. He informed us we had passed two of the men we wanted, who had secreted themselves in a thick part of the scrub. We returned to the chance water, after being in the saddle over ten hours.

"*Thursday, 17th November.*—Returned to the depôt, a distance of from forty to fifty-eight miles by the shortest course we could take. Our native guide or prisoner, poor wretch, must have been greatly astonished at his rapid ride, frequently tumbling out of the saddle. His nag was led by a trooper latterly; he held on, one hand grasping the pommel and the other the crupper. Memo.—I must not forget to represent to the Governor and Judge how faithfully he has acted as a guide, while Utulla had been unable to act, as he was under the process of being made a man and a warrior by his tribe.

"20*th*.—Left the depôt, party now eight in number, on a W.N.W. course. The black guide has now to tramp on foot, much apparently to his satisfaction, as the pony's back was seriously galled. After passing over several miles found no blacks, now travelling nearly due west. Moullier says this party must be in hiding, aware of our approach. He knows the whole of the natives now in this part of his country, and that his lubra and children are with them. He has no fear we shall hurt his family. He says four of the murderers are with this section of the tribe. After twenty miles, mostly through scrub, we arrived at several salt lakes, and now perceived ahead of us two smokes, and made a dash onwards. On coming up to the fires, found the birds flown. In the deserted wurlies, amongst other abandoned properties, was a fresh skin of a kangaroo. We were now thirty-five or forty miles from the depôt; the natives had abandoned spears in their hasty flight; the horsemen divided into parties, and rode round the nearest lakes; tracks of the runaways were, after some time, found, where they had waded through the shallow lakes; and if so we had come up in sight of them; horsemen could not have followed through the lakes with rotten boggy bottoms, and the only course to stop them was by the use of firearms, which I should not have resorted to."

After this second failure to secure any of the murderers, the Major adds :—" One source of consolation I have, that this party has come across, and greatly alarmed, the whole of the Battara tribe, and visited all their usual haunts, by which much good may have been done in alarming the tribe, and in giving confidence to the settlers.

" I do not consider myself justified in entering on the country of the Coffin Bay tribe, which is immediately to the south of us, which tribe has done the settlers no harm except in the case of the murder of young Hawson about two years ago. I am not sure that the tribe has not suffered at the hands of the white settlers. We are now about fifty-five miles from Port Lincoln, from whence we have been absent nine days.

"*Friday, 24th.*—Embarked in the cutter *Alpha* with two prisoners in charge. Owing to foul winds had to land horses and men at Yankalilla, and made head-quarters on the 29th." And so ends this expedition.

It had been well if the anticipations of the gallant Major had been realized as to the effect of his scouring the country of the Battara tribe and had extended to other tribes. A reference to a return from the Sheriff to Parliament opens a black record of the execution of twelve natives from the Port Lincoln side, at various times within ten years of the Major's return for murders of white people engaged in pastoral pursuits or in exploring, of which particulars will be given in another chapter.

CHAPTER V.

HAVING given the sad accounts of the murderous attacks by the natives on three of the Port Lincoln out-stations, which caused horror and alarm to the inhabitants of that settlement and anxiety to the inhabitants in Adelaide, I am now enabled to continue this discouraging part of our history by the use of the diary of Mr. James Hawker, who started overland from Adelaide in the hope of meeting Mr. C. C. Dutton (once sheriff of the province), who was known to have broken up his station in consequence of the hostile actions of the natives, and to have started with his people and stock to make his way round the head of Spencer's Gulf. The party consisted of the following gentlemen, and started on the 14th of September, 1842, viz.:—Messrs. James Hawker, William Peter, James Baker, Charles Hawker, with a Sydney native (Billy). The Governor ordered Inspector Tolmer with four troopers to accompany and aid the volunteers, who had one saddle-horse each and two pack-horses to carry about six weeks' rations of flour, tea, sugar, and a small quantity of bacon—trusting to fowling-pieces to procure some game in aid of the small supplies of meat. The troopers had three pack-horses to carry their necessaries.

The furthest out-station from the town of Port Lincoln was

Mr. Dutton's, which he had found quite untenable from the number of natives in that quarter, and in consequence started on his unfortunate overland journey. He left in July, 1842, escorted by part of the detachment of soldiers as far as one day's journey. When twelve weeks had elapsed after Mr. Dutton's departure, and no tidings had reached even the outermost settlements on the Adelaide side of the Gulf, it was decided to start a light party to meet him or to obtain information as to what had befallen him and his party. Amongst other things feared was that he had been unable to reach the head of the Gulf from deficiency of provisions. The relief party, after making their way north to head the Gulf, on the 18th September had the misfortune to lose a pack-horse, which left the other horses in the night. As every hour saved was an object, no time was spent in seeking the absentee, the anxiety being to push on, hoping to find Mr. Dutton alive. To do this there was no alternative but to abandon part of the small supply of provisions, and this in the face of such a journey as they had to encounter, with the prospect of meeting a destitute party. For the next five days in journeying along they found both feed for the horses and water growing scarcer and scarcer, and at the same time the weather proved exceedingly hot. They were one night without water for man and beast. The volunteers, after a consultation, decided to go on alone and allow the police to return, as it was evident that water and feed could not be depended on to be found in sufficient quantity for so many horses. On this account the police returned to head-quarters, and the volunteers pushed on alone. On the 24th they reached Eyre's old Depôt Creek, at Mount Arden, distance 236 miles from Adelaide. They found the feed during the last three days' travel most wretched. They remained at the depôt three days to rest and recruit the horses. Here was found Eyre's tarpaulin tent lying on the ground rotten, where it had been left two or three years before. Two pigeons were here shot, which were very acceptable, as the party had been reduced to about one ounce of bacon each man in twenty-four hours, and even with that small supply it was seen it would not last many days. The diary of Mr. J. C. Hawker states:—

"On the 28*th* we started, horses much refreshed. Had great difficulty now in crossing the channel above the head of the Gulf, owing to the numerous quicksands which were found in its bed. No feed for the horses, except stunted salt bushes.

After twenty-five miles advance found a dirty pool of water, which the horses would not drink.

"*29th.*—Pushed on to Baxter's Range, forty miles over a wretched country. Found a small supply of water; could only give three quarts to each horse, poured into a basin formed by the use of Peter's mackintosh cloak. Barked a tree here, and wrote, 'Volunteers in search of Mr. Dutton, 29th September.' We had found Mr. Eyre's tracks plain here, and conceived it possible Mr. Dutton by following the same might reach this place.

"*30th.*—As I and my brother could work the direct course we desired to take, it was decided to leave the guidance to us, and from this camp we struck out a course through a thick gum scrub, and could not make more than eighteen miles. No water found; horses nearly done up.

"*October* 1.—Still a thick scrub in heavy sand. Crossed the dry beds of several salt lakes; the salt, as fine as dust, most annoying to horses and men. A packhorse unable to travel, although all his load had been taken off his back; his tongue was hanging out. Large patches of skin peeling off our own faces; our mouths so dry we could hardly articulate a word, and were adopting signs. It now became to us a matter of life or death to the whole party, men and horses, and it was determined that I and Billy the Sydney black, our horses being in best trim, should push forward and endeavour to reach a cluster of rocks which, according to Eyre's chart which we had with us, should be ahead of us, and at which was shown a permanent spring. Providentially, before I and the black had proceeded more than a mile through scrub we came upon the rocks, around which were green tussocks of grass, at sight of which our poor exhausted beasts were quite frantic. But imagine our horror when, on our first searching around the rocks, we could find no spring or water. The efforts of the horses to climb the rocks, and their whinnying, assured us that there was water somewhere near; and shortly we found in a cleft of the rocks several gallons, about five feet down. We lowered our pannikins and got a small quantity up, and although it was full of insects, dead and alive, by us it was taken as nectar. We lost no time in returning to our comrades, and found them considering whether they should kill a packhorse, and drink his blood, to save human lives. The news we brought saved the life of the horse, and all hastened on to the rocks. Here we afterwards found other clefts, but all the water in such a polluted state that we had to strain it through saddlecloths, long used beneath the saddles (think of such a remedy to render water pure!), so we did not swallow insects. We remained here two days and turned off for the Gawler Ranges. After making our way through scrub, and travelling eighteen miles without finding any traces of Mr. Dutton, and discovering neither feed nor water, we returned to the rocks. The weather was fearfully hot. On our return we perceived the place had been visited by a considerable body of blacks. Their fires were still alight, so that they must have bolted in alarm on hearing the clatter of our approach. After dark we set a watch. At this time the ammunition which we had retained was nearly exhausted. During the night the men on guard heard a blackfellow among the horses, who had a narrow escape from a shot fired at him.

"5th.—Made an early start, the country all around us being alight with native signal fires. This day we were without water, but at night came upon a little grass for the horses, which were suffering much for the want of water.

"6th.—Started at 6 A.M., travelling still in scrubs, with occasional bare ridges. After riding twenty-three miles came on a green patch, like an oasis in a desert. Here was a puddle of water on a clay pan, to which the horses could get themselves, and was quickly used up by them. Before this Peter's mackintosh had been the only means by which we could give them water for the last nine days.

"7th.—A shower fell here, during which we caught water in our pannikins, from the dripping grass. We found dense scrub in travelling all day, and came upon no feed or water.

"Two days after this we came upon a good supply of both, scuh a treat as we have not met with for eleven days, and during that time, until this improvement in our prospects, we had not experienced the indulgence of a wash (think of this, ye daintily nurtured stay-at-homes!). The skin was still peeling from our faces in flakes, caused by the scorching rays of the sun and the hot sand drifting against our exposed countenances. The poor horses had suffered from the same causes, and their heads had been denuded of hair as if they had undergone a close shave. We this day rationed upon gruel composed of flour and the addition of the remains of mutton suet which we had brought with us to lubricate our firearms to prevent rust. With the exception of two pigeons our daily allowance of meat had been during the previous seven days one inch of bacon to each man. On the second day after this we shot an emu, and made a good meal out of the liver. In the afternoon we made the bare and deserted station of poor Dutton. Although we found no traces of him, it was afterwards ascertained through some of the natives that he and all his party were killed by a murderous tribe, and such of his cattle as were not used by them were dispersed and scattered through this wild and scrubby country. It is sad to relate that the bodies of the slaughtered men have never been found.

"We had now a difficult matter to arrange, viz., how we were to appear in decent costume and to present ourselves to the Port Lincoln inhabitants. Our garments were in the last stage of dilapidation. We had not made any change of clothing for sixteen days; we had been under the necessity of abandoning all our spare changes. The gum scrub had torn our nether garments to ribbons, and patches had to be made of pieces of blankets of any colour obtainable; it might be dingy scarlet, deep blue, striped, or dirty white, or in some cases with fancy-coloured, much-worn saddle cloths. These had in a great measure to take the place of the original materials left behind on the bushes. Our inventive faculties had to be taxed to the greatest possible extent, for the work was a crying necessity, and the fact was none of us were experienced or skilful in such work. I must not omit to mention that the legs of our boots had remained to us to our great benefit, but the soles had parted company. Well, in this motley array, the party started next morning for the Residency, a distance of thirty-two miles, and many a laugh we indulged in on the way. But I must change the subject to one of grief, for on our way we first came to the deserted and destroyed stations of the murdered Brown and Biddles, and here a more melancholy sight could not be imagined than that which met us. The flowers in one of the gardens were in full bloom, displaying the beauties of peaceful nature, growing up around the shattered furniture, recklessly destroyed and cast about here and there. There was one table standing on its legs, with its top stuck full of nails, which had been driven into it for amusement. On the legs and other parts were still to be seen dried blood and human hair clinging, as they had been dashed from the mangled heads of the already dead bodies. We shuddered on viewing such devastation on peaceful stations. The first inhabited station we reached was the Hawson's, three miles from the township, and here ourselves and horses were most hospitably received and treated.

"In the evening we reached Port Lincoln, and surely such a grotesque troop breaking the stillness of the quiet township never was seen; nor such a reception—with barking of dogs, rejoicing shouts mingled with peals of laughter—as greeted the arrival of our volunteer relief party, supposed to be lost and dead. We were here detained some days, as there was no vessel leaving the bay for Port Adelaide. One evening, to our astonishment and great surprise, a party came in overland from Adelaide, which proved to be under the command of Mr. Eyre, who, on the return of Mr. Tolmer and the troopers who had left our small body of men, had been speedily equipped and ordered by the Governor to follow the volunteers, to aid and lead them, and to seek for Mr. Dutton and his servants and stock. It had been rumoured that we had all been killed, as well as the unfortunate gentleman whom we went out to save; but our proposed rescuers, instead of finding our remains, discovered us with a jolly party discussing egg-flip.

"Mr. Eyre had suffered more severely than we had; for on finding the waters exhausted by us, he had to push for the beach of the Gulf, after losing one horse. His party consisted of three troopers and one black man."

The account of these treacherous murders will be fitly concluded by quoting a return which was made by Sheriff Boothby, to Parliament, of the conviction and execution of the native murderers of detached white settlers of the South-East Lake country, and in the out-districts of Port Lincoln.

COPY OF REPORT.

First, the murder of Geo. MacGrath, on the 3rd of June, 1844, at MacGrath's Flat, South-East, by Werd Maldera, *alias* Peter. Hung in front of Her Majesty's gaol, Adelaide, 29th March, 1845.
Murder of Captain John Beevor, in Port Lincoln district, May 3, 1849, by three natives, Neulatta, Pulluruninga, Keelgulta. Hung at Port Lincoln, November 9, 1849.
Murder of Peter Brown, near Franklin Harbour, June 1, 1855,

by three natives, Wadmiltie, Pamgulta, Ilyelta. Hung at Franklin Harbour, January 14, 1856.
Murder of John Jones, near Franklin Harbour. Murderer hung at Franklin Harbour, May 13, 1860.
Murder of Thomas G. Bergeest, at Fowler's Bay, by two natives, Nelgerrie, *alias* Peter, Telcherrie, *alias* Harry. Hung at Fowler's Bay, January 19, 1861.
Murder of Margaret A. Impey, in Port Lincoln district, by two natives, Karrabidne, Mangeltie. Hung at Port Lincoln, May 2, 1861.
Murder of William Walker, near Venus Bay, by Mangultie. Hung at Venus Bay, September 8, 1863.

The natives who had committed the crimes of murder in the previous melancholy list were first caught, after infinite trouble, then with witnesses brought to Adelaide, and after being tried and found guilty, after sentence were conveyed by the Sheriff and a sufficiently strong party to the respective districts in which the crime had been committed, and there hung at the several dates given.

This closes the history of the experiences of the difficulties encountered by the first settlers in the Lake and Port Lincoln districts from attacks of the natives. It is a subject painful to reflect upon; but all such experiences in every part of Australia have proved that in situations where a state of safety for the lives and properties of white intruders has been attained, without exception it has been where in the first instance of occupation large and concentrated bodies of whites have settled down; or in other cases where the blacks, having taken advantage of a few individuals venturing to occupy lonely places, have killed them, safety for succeeding parties has not been secured until a dread has been created in the minds of the offending tribe by speedy and severe punishment inflicted on the offenders and accomplices, and on those who sheltered them. It is a fact which cannot be denied that there has been no safety for the lives and properties of the whites until such a dread has been established.

The now lost or defunct Adelaide or Cowandilla tribe has been held up as a pattern tribe, because the members of it committed so few aggressions of a serious nature against the settlers on their arrival; but then it must be remembered, in proof of the preceding statement, that the first settlers landed in overwhelming numbers, and poured out of large ships, producing a great awe of the powers of the strange race arriving.

On reflecting on the long list of executions, it will not be unjust to say that through the weak measures adopted, and the mistaken instructions issued by Captain Grey at the beginning of the outbreak, he left a legacy of difficulties which culminated in additional massacres of the whites, and the necessary legal executions of the murderers. Many, without doubt, have, however, at different times been shot by the whites rather than risk the tardy and uncertain legal punishment.

It is also a fact, not for the whites to be proud of, that advantage was taken by the intending settlers of the normal weak organization of the natives, who, from the very nature of the climate and country, in the original scarcity of water and food, especially in the absence of natural and edible fruits and roots, could only exist in small scattered families or tribes, and maintain life, chiefly dependent on such food as snakes, reptiles, and insects. These tribes, although weak and degraded, were only held in check by the large numbers of whites arriving. With such a low class of aboriginals scattered about a vast extent of country, there was no necessity forced upon the Government here, or the governing powers at home, to treat with such a race in the same manner as would be required with a superior and less divided people.

There is one fact patent that the natives favourably placed as to superior food and abundance of water were found to be specimens of humanity finer in bodily development, and possessed of superior brain power, than other less favoured tribes, and were also more dangerous to cope with. Under the above circumstances it was incumbent on the rulers and founders of the colony to have acted as the real protectors of such people when embracing them among its subjects, and not to have rested satisfied with the appointment of a few nominal aboriginal protectors to dole out a scanty supply of necessaries, and to employ themselves in persuading the supplanted and helpless natives to refrain from attacks on those who were taking their land from them, and destroying or driving away their game without adequate compensation.

CHAPTER VI.

GOVERNOR YOUNG arrived 2nd August, 1848. The appointment of Sir H. Fox Young as fifth Governor of South Australia must be recorded as a red letter day for the colony. He was an enlightened man eminently qualified to govern and advance a young colony just emerging from an early and serious depression. One of his highest qualities was to know no party, and to be uninfluenced by any section of the community bent on pushing their private interests to the injury of the community at large.

The first Council under the new constitution was assembled on the 1st of August, 1851, and consisted of 24 members: 8 nominated, and 16 elected by the constituents. In his Excellency's address, he informed the house that "Her Majesty had, with a wise liberality, placed in their hands the power, subject to her approval, to modify the details of the constitution in such a manner as experience might show to be necessary."

One of his first legislative actions was to assent to the repeal of the obnoxious and impolitic royalty on minerals, 14th August, 1849. Amongst his earliest propositions was that of raising a loan of half a million, one-third to be applied to increase the immigration fund, and the balance to the construction of roads and railways. It is remarkable that the labouring classes at this time were in favour of this proposition, involving an increase in the number of their class; nevertheless, the elected members of the Council did not approve of fixing a burden, which might fall on property holders, and the measure did not pass. On the 5th February, 1851, the fearful atmospheric disturbance took place known as Black Thursday. To describe it, it must be explained that there was no violent action of wind, but the atmosphere for many hours remained charged with a black dust combined with smoke so dense that the writer, who was driving with his family, having started early from the hills, was soon immersed in all but utter darkness, and was reduced to drive at a foot's pace, and had to require one of his sons to walk beside the horse to avoid a collision, and to keep the centre of the road. This was in the day-time from about 9 o'clock until 12. His course was through the city of Adelaide, but it was necessary to keep along the terraces, to gain the Port Road. All public-houses were closed: nor would any publican open his doors to give us shelter. On the Port Road, Tanner the driver of the port and city coach, was met at a foot's pace with a man walking at his leader's heads. The same extraordinary state of the atmosphere extended, as reported, to the neighbouring colonies. All business for that day was impossible.

On the 31st October, 1851, an Act was passed for the construction of a railway from Port Adelaide to the city. The engineer employed was B. Babbage, Esq. Prior to this a company had been formed in London to construct this line, but the offer was declined. The cost of the construction under Mr. Babbage was most extravagant. Mr. Harcus in his work uses the words, "at a frightful and wasteful cost." Leaving the Port Road for a line direct, saving a short distance, was by some persons considered unnecessary, as land had to be purchased from the park lands of the city within a short distance of the port, whereas Colonel Light had laid out the Port Road with a width sufficient for both a macadamised road and a railway line. The line from the city to the port is 8½ miles.

In the following year the opening of the goldfields in New South Wales and Victoria produced an extraordinary migration from South Australia; the exodus tempted from their homes nearly the whole of the male population. In rural districts the wives, daughters, and younger boys had to take upon themselves what work they could do. Even in the town and suburbs, on seeing a man, children would call out to their mothers, "Look here, mother, there is a man." When the earliest absentees returned with their bags of gold, the Governor was advised to establish an overland escort, and this was quickly acceded to. In consequence of the stagnation of trade, the Governor, early in the year, ordered a further reduction of the police force, one having already been made, this time to the extent of thirty troopers and twenty men from the foot police.

Mr. Tolmer claims to have, in an official letter, suggested to the Governor the scheme of an overland gold escort. After a delay of a few days he was sent for, and met his Excellency the Colonial Secretary (B. T. Finnis), and the late Sir R. Hanson (Attorney-General).

After this interview Inspector Tolmer was instructed to draw off certain troopers from out-stations, and make a start with these men, and a strong spring cart, horses, and a driver.

There was no track between this colony and the Mount Alexander goldfield in the province of Victoria. The start was made on the 10th of February, 1852. It is not necessary to give the details of this difficult journey; it is sufficient to state that the party reached the diggings at Forest Creek in eight days, the distance estimated to be 338 miles. The escort party was met by the Adelaide diggers most warmly. The gold was received in a tent lent for the occasion, which was used by its owner as a druggist's shop. A great crowd was in waiting before the hour at which it was announced gold would be received. Dr. W. Gosse and Mr. Carleton assisted the Commissioner, as Mr. Tolmer now was, for South Australia. The work of receiving the small parcels of gold, weighing, sealing, and ticketing the same, with furnishing receipts, was continued until dusk, when the bulk was conveyed under police escort to the Commissioner's camp. It must be here stated that the commander of the party and his men were treated with hospitality by Mr. Wright, the Commissioner, although some soreness had been exhibited at the dividing the great stream of gold which had commenced to flow to Melbourne. The amount of gold brought to Adelaide by this first escort, in money and gold dust, was £21,000, deposited by 318 persons.

The return party reached Wellington on the Murray in twelve days from the Commissioner's camp on the diggings. At the return of Mr. Tolmer, a meeting was held at which resolutions were passed highly complimentary to the leader of the escort party. A resolution was passed, moved by John Hart, Esq., M.L.C., "That a suitable testimonial be presented to Mr. Tolmer, &c."

Before Mr. Tolmer started (*i.e.*, in the previous month a Bullion Act had been passed under which gold tokens were issued), Captain Hart remarked that "the previous resolution spoke of the success of the expedition, but it was to the skilful diplomacy of Mr. Tolmer with the diggers who had been made acquainted with the principles of the Bullion Act, otherwise a very small portion of the gold brought by the escort would have found its way into this colony." To the action of Mr. Tinlin must be attributed the passing of the Bullion Act, which, in a short time, produced such an amazing revolution in the pecuniary condition of the Government and the colonists in general. The gratitude felt by the people resulted in the raising and presenting a munificent offering to Mr. Tinlin, then manager of the South Australian Banking Company, of a purse of 2,000 sovereigns and a silver salver with a gold centre.

It may not be out of place here to mention that the author was on the gold-fields in Victoria when the first escort arrived and relieved him as well as so many fathers of families of the anxious state in which they all were; it is impossible to describe the state of excitement and thankfulness felt. He cannot help expressing here the wonder he felt at the order and good conduct which prevailed amongst such a motley gathering from all parts of the world which was there to be seen. One or two anecdotes he will give. Near the Red Hill, where he was encamped and working with his two boys, he daily saw a man pass with one leg and a crutch, who always with jolly good humour bid good-day to us; he was working underground alone, and was seen to pass daily down a small hole under a large gum tree. In passing by his hole one day he came out and paused to speak; it could be seen that he was undermining the heavy-topped tree, and he was asked if he was not afraid in his disabled state to expose himself to such danger, to which he replied, "I can go down and come out again as quick as if I had two legs" (his leg had been removed at the hip joint.) He then said, "Go down and see how I work," he quickly followed. He showed the nuggets of gold he had that day fossicked out in a small opening, and said, "See if you can reach to the end," that was not to be done; then he said, "Clear out of my way," and placed himself so close that he could easily reach, and with his small pick work out with clay a small vein of gold nuggets; he then said, "Now, mate; what do you think of it? You see the advantage I have in having lost that leg; you see a man with two legs must have grubbed the tree and then mayhap have lost the gold." Not many days afterwards in passing along one of the dray tracks leading from the camp, I met a bullock dray guarded by six old pensioners each with an old brown bess and fixed bayonet; prisoners were sitting in the bottom of the dray. Suddenly, a voice was heard, "Sergeant, please halt, here is a friend I want to speak to," a halt was allowed, and then I saw it was the man with one leg, who held out his hand to me and said, "I am going to have a spell in Melbourne." On being asked what he was going down for, he replied, "It's only a grog business; I and my mates had been doing a little business in grog; we were bowled out, and as we had no money," with a wink, "one of us had to take it out in a couple of months; my mates said a rest would do me good, and as you know I cannot march, they have to give me a ride. I say, old chap, I don't want to be pitied; I am all right, good-bye, mate."

"March," was the word, the jovial fellow used, laughing.

The next tale is of a pair of men who were working in the same neighbourhood who I knew were Adelaide men, and who were reported to have a very rich claim. One of them was suddenly laid up by sickness; a doctor was soon in attendance; as it was soon known to be a case of virulent fever no nurse could be procured, and neighbouring tents were soon struck, ours was some distance from the sick man, and we had taken up claims lower down in Triangle Gully. We soon heard that the men's rich claim was jumped as the mate would not leave his partner, who soon was relieved by death. It was talked of far and near that the deceased's faithful friend was the only mourner to follow the remains to the grave, and that then he sold the infected property at a low price, and left for Adelaide. On my return home some months later, I met the survivor in King William Street, Adelaide, driving a horse and cart loaded with vegetables; he pulled up to speak to me, and on my asking him questions, he told me his mate had left a widow and six children, and that as their gold was principally lodged in Melbourne, he had hastened down to draw out their funds, that he had paid doctor's bill, and funeral expenses, and had hastened to Adelaide to his mate's widow with whom he had divided the balance of gold and money, and with his own share had purchased a place and a horse and cart, and hawked vegetables which he grew, and was doing well.

On my expressing a word or two of commendation, he said, "Oh, that's nothing, my mate would have done the same by me." I have related these two cases of rough working men, and of their actions in a scene and in a moral atmosphere generally supposed to be corrupted almost to an approach to outlawry and not to be restrained or purified by a high tone of religious and moral surroundings, yet such or similar traits of character in the lower walks of life are not scarce; my experience of the world under very varying circumstances has taught that more real charity is to be met with in the lower than in the higher walks of life.

Those readers who have not visited an extensive goldfield with thousands of migratory gold-diggers vigorously at work cannot realise the scene. There are to be seen broken down gentlemen, graduates, young men from the upper classes, all such who previously had never handled pick or shovel, working on the same level as to their present station not only with honest but rough men, ordinary labourers and seamen of all nations, but also with men whose previous careers had been stained by long-continued criminal actions. Let my gentle readers fancy such a mixture of men almost without the presence of women, and of the few of those softeners of men's lives (say one in a hundred of men) could be found a small proportion only whose influence would be beneficial,—the conclusion would naturally be that such a community would represent a "hell upon earth." But such a conclusion would be erroneous.

Take a picture perfectly true. Here are four gentlemen working a claim; next claim on one side, four Californians; on another side, four Tasmanians (coarse fellows), and not far off a party of Melbourne men. All these men are on an equality as to their pursuit. Did the well-bred men descend to the general manners of their surroundings? As a rule, no. Civil and sociable remarks pass, perhaps all are doing well, and some of the parties may have led a very pinched life who are now gaining capital, and have their acquired gold sent to Melbourne or Adelaide by escort, and hold the representative of it in a Commissioner's receipt. The roughest of the men see and adopt, as far as they can, the manners of the gentlemen, and begin to feel themselves to be respectable.

Then Sunday comes, and what then did we witness?

Take the post-office square, near the Red Hill, at first the centre of the richest part of the Forest Creek digging. Here was a small square of tents, on a gentle rise. The post-office on one side, with a small store or two on other fronts. About eleven o'clock a cluster of quiet-looking men, with prayer and hymn books in their hands, have assembled, when a way is respectfully opened, and a clergyman of the Church of England, the Rev. Mr. Gregory, takes his place in the centre, prays silently, and then gives out a hymn; a pause occurs, a leader, without arrangement, strikes up and fixes the tune; all join, then morning service is devoutly said, the congregation doing their part heartily in the responses. An outer circle gradually increases the number of worshippers. A short and eloquent sermon, a hymn and silent prayer, and the service ends. Then out of sight, at a short distance to the west, a stump of a tree is occupied by an independent preacher, and a larger congregation are engaged in earnest worship. On the lower ground, east, a third congregation, addressed sometimes by a Methodist, a Primitive Methodist, or a Baptist preacher, or one of any other denomination, and at a sufficient distance north, a fourth. These four Protestant services were, without fail, carried on during the time the author was in that neighbourhood. Then he was aware, by seeing Roman Catholic priests moving about, that their services were doubtless well attended elsewhere.

Now, who shall presume to say that these services had not a benign influence on the manners and conduct of such masses of men so associated as described?

I must not omit to mention that Bishop Perry, that eminently good man, on one Sunday preached from a stump, at the place previously described, the author present, to an immense congregation, whose united voices echoed far through that old forest, where, but a few years earlier, might only have been heard the yells of the natives, the songs of the magpies, or the howls of the wild dogs. I remark that the levelling of ranks and behaviour was not at all downwards, but both ways, which in any re-arrangement of society is the only principle to be safely carried out.

My readers must not suppose that I wish to hold up communities of gold-diggers as patterns of a high state of morality, but in giving truthful accounts of what occurred early on the part he was engaged on, as evincing the beneficial influence he witnessed, where a considerable proportion of the diggers were, I may say, gentlemen who had at that time adopted that pursuit, and who mostly returned to their distant homes.

Not the least important work during the government of Sir H. F. Young, was the navigation of the river Murray, projected by him in a despatch to the home authorities, on the 6th April, 1860, and approved by the Secretary of State. The Governor's scheme, which was recommended by Captain Lipson, R.N., then Harbour Master, Port Adelaide, and supported by Mr. R. T. Hill, surveyor, unfortunately included the connection of Port Elliott with Goolwa by a tramway. The error was in attempting to make Port Elliott a port for ocean vessels, which was too shallow, and liable to be silted up. The project was strongly opposed by the Legislative Council, the vested interests of Port Adelaide being arrayed against any project likely to interfere with the trade of the central port. Nevertheless, the Governor having the uncontrolled power of the disbursement of the Crown moiety of the Land Fund, carried out his scheme, the mistake being that he adopted Port Elliott instead of the more westerly portion of Encounter Bay, Victor Harbour, as now so successfully carried out. Governor Young's determination to take this first step towards utilising the grand waterway provided for this part of Australia by nature, created against him an ill-feeling amongst the holders of vested interests in the city and central port.

Now such opponents, if surviving, must feel what a mistake they made. They were quite right in opposing the scheme, as embracing the making use of Port Elliott, as well as to the cost of protecting it by a breakwater, but they had selfish reasons in addition, as has been subsequently proved. At the time of this first move, Captain Cadell came forward, to carry out the main work, viz., the navigation of the river Murray by steamers. A reward having been offered for the first steamer which passed in by the mouth of the river Murray, Captain Cadell encountered the task, and succeeded in entering with the *Lady Augusta* on the 16th August, 1853. Governor Young was not only the projector, but accompanied, with a party, the captain in his river boat on its first trip up the Murray. The party proceeded safely to Swan Hill, a distance of about 1,300 miles from Adelaide, and a cargo of wool was brought back.

This successful opening of the river trade was soon supplemented by other steamers being placed on the river.

It is fair to record, that before Captain Cadell started with the *Lady Augusta* (named after Lady Young), Mr. W. Randall, of Gumeracha, launched a small steamer at Mannum, on the river, and steamed up in advance of Captain Cadell, but as this boat was too small, Mr. Randall was not entitled to the reward of £2,000 which the Government had offered for the steamer which should first reach the junction of the Darling after entering by the river mouth.

Mr. Randall afterwards had a larger boat constructed, but his success was not much greater, in a pecuniary sense, than that of Captain Cadell. He was more unfortunate in one respect, for his boat was destroyed by fire, with a large and valuable cargo on board.

On the 29th September, 1853, a Constitution Bill was passed by the Legislative Council, but was not confirmed by Her

Majesty, as before the Royal Assent could be given, a petition, signed by upwards of 6,000 persons, was sent home, praying Her Majesty that it might be disallowed. It was then referred back to the colony for further consideration. The term of office of Sir H. F. Young expired on 20th December, 1854. Although his official actions had so greatly advanced the colony, and his private character and that of Lady Young merited the highest commendations, yet a section of the port people did not in any way demonstrate any regret at his departure. I may here give a little anecdote, petty enough, to exhibit the narrow and selfish feeling before alluded to. I, with my friend, the late Osmond Gilles, drove down, forming part of a small cavalcade to do honour to the departing Governor and his lady. In passing the first hotel in the port, was to be seen the landlord of the same, in front of his house, in a chair tilted back against the wall, with a newspaper held open before his face; further on, no crowd, no demonstration. On returning to put up the horses, I was met by the landlord, when I said, "Well, Carleton, what did you mean by the ridiculous posture you adopted as the Governor passed?" His reply was, "I wished to show what I thought of him for his opposition to our interests."

Postscript.—To show that Governor Young's ideas respecting the importance of the navigation of the River Murray to South Australia have been subsequently borne out by facts, I append the following extracts from an article on "The Murray and Darling Trade," by a special reporter of the "S. A. Register," of June 13th, 1883:—"The large cattle runs for which the Darling was noted a few years ago have nearly all been stocked with sheep, and, as has already been indicated, this means increased production and consumption. In considering the ultimate destination of this large and growing trade, an important element is provided by the fact that South Australia is well represented on the river, and it is only natural to suppose that the influence of these gentlemen will be cast in favour of the colony to which they are greatly indebted for the wealth they now enjoy. Some of the Darling stations have already assumed proportions that would never have entered into the dreams of the most sanguine in former days. Albemarle, between Menindie and Wilcannia, belonging to Messrs. J. & T. Phelps, and managed by Mr. Vandaleur, last year shore 212,500 sheep. The wool from this station—about 2000 bales—formerly went to Melbourne, but last year over 1000 bales found their way to Port Victor, and the manager was so satisfied with his experience of South Australia that in all probability in future the greater part of the wool from this station will be sent to Port Victor. Occasionally stores have been carted to Albemarle from Terowie, a distance of 400 miles. The largest single station on the Lower Darling is said to be Tolarno, belonging to the Messrs. W. L. & R. Reid, but the properties owned by Messrs. Cudmore, Pile, H. B. Hughes, and other South Australians are also very extensive.

* * * * * * *

"At the present time the sentiment of the business people for the most part is with South Australia, which is regarded as being much more energetic and anxious to extend her commercial relations with that part of the colony than New South Wales.

* * * * *

"The cost of carriage from Morgan or Goolwa to Wilcannia varies somewhat between £3 and £4. If the river were continuously navigable, goods could be landed for about £1 10s. a ton. It is needless to point out that no railway could compete with such rates; but that is an aspect of the question that can be discussed more appropriately further on. Last year wool was taken from Wilcannia and up the river to Adelaide and Port Victor, and to Melbourne viâ Echuca, f.o.b. in both cases, at the following rates :—To Adelaide and Port Victor, scored, £4 2s. 6d.; greasy £3 10s. To Melbourne, scoured, £5 10s.; greasy, £4 10s. These rates included receiving and shipping agency charges, while by both routes the insurance was the same. It must be remembered, however, that the wool goes down-stream all the way to the South Australian ports, and up-stream from Wentworth to Echuca, which represents an advantage of three or four days in favour of the former."

Port Victor Breakwater.—The length of the breakwater at present completed is 333 yards, composed of large blocks of granite blasted from Granite Island, many weighing 20 tons each; the island forms part of the breakwater. The present extent is only about half the distance to which it is ultimately to be carried at low water on Sir John Coode's recommendation.

This portion of the breakwater was finished on the

VIEW OF ADELAIDE IN 1836, SHOWING THE VICE-REGAL RESIDENCE.

Life in South Australia. 321

31st August, 1882, and will accommodate several ocean steamers at anchor, where they receive river-borne wool, brought from Goolwa, the terminal river port, by a railway eight miles long, thus connecting the navigable river with a safe port, possessing a capacious and direct entrance from the Southern Ocean. The greatest depth at low water is 35 feet. The cost of the present portion of the structure has been £85,500.

CHAPTER VII.

The Honourable B. T. Finniss occupied the post of Acting Governor from 20th December, 1854, until the 8th June, 1855, when Sir Richard Graves MacDonnell assumed the reins of Government.

The new Constitution Bill was received back from Lord John Russell at this time. The Governor, desirous of ascertaining the opinions of the colonists, dissolved the Council. The new Council (mixed nominees and elected members) met on the 1st November in the same year, and threw out the Bill which had been returned, and one of an altogether different character was presented and passed, and in due time received the Royal Assent, and has been in force ever since. The Act provided for two Houses of Legislature, *both elected*—an Upper House, the Legislative Council ; and a Lower, the House of Assembly. A civil list of £13,500 was reserved to Her Majesty.

The first elections for the two Houses took place in March, 1857. James Hurtle Fisher was elected President of the Legislative Council, and George Strickland Kingston was elected first Speaker of the House of Assembly, both of whom were subsequently knighted.

The first Parliament was opened on the 22nd April, 1857. The members of both Houses having been sworn in, and the necessary preliminaries settled, Sir Richard MacDonnell met the new Parliament in the Legislative Council and delivered the inaugural speech. His Excellency was enabled to congratulate honourable members upon the prosperous condition of the colony, and to inform them that with the enlarged powers of self-government bestowed upon the colonists, had also been yielded to them the entire control of the waste lands

Y

of the Crown, the proceeds of which were to be appropriated to such objects, and in such proportions, as the Legislature might deem most suitable to the varying wants of the community. Referring to the new system which had been inaugurated, Sir Richard said :—"The personal satisfaction which I experience at thus meeting you on an occasion so auspicious as the opening of the first Parliament of South Australia, wholly elected by the people, is much increased by the confidence with which I anticipate a no less prudent than energetic exercise of their extensive powers by the representatives of the people. Yet whilst relieved by the existing constitution of much responsibility which till lately had attached to my office, I feel that a new and equally grave responsibility will arise whenever, with none between the representative of the sovereign and the people, it may become the duty of the former to give the fullest constitutional development to the wishes of the country. That responsibility I do not shrink from, satisfied that a fearless and honest desire to act up to the liberal spirit of the constitution will always ensure the support of a South Australian Parliament."

Thus, then, was launched in a colony with a population of little over 100,000 souls, and placed 16,000 miles away from any controlling authority, a system of responsible government, involving the principles of universal suffrage, vote by ballot, equal electoral districts, and triennial parliaments. And to a community thus governed was granted the whole territory of the Crown, embracing nearly 300,000,000 acres of land.

The history of the advance the colony made during Sir Richard MacDonnell's term of government shows that great public works were accomplished. Roads were made and improved, and bridges built, so that journeys for hundreds of miles from the city could be made without inconvenience. Surveys for railways were also pushed on. The first railway opened was the eight and a-half miles from Adelaide to the Port. This was constructed at an enormous cost, over a level plain without one impediment. The rails were placed on longitudinal timbers, and the lower part of the line was ballasted with sand, which was in a very short time pumped out from below the sleepers, and carried away with every wind that blew. The next extension was from Adelaide to Gawler, being the first link in the Great Northern line. Subsequently this line was extended to Kapunda, fifty-two miles from Adelaide ;

Life in South Australia. 323

and afterwards a branch (now the main line) was carried further north to the Burra, making the distance from Adelaide about 100 miles. These lines were well built, and have been successfully worked up to the present time—1883.

The telegraph line between Adelaide, Sydney, and Melbourne was commenced on the 9th August, 1857, and the same year saw the commencement of the Glenelg Jetty, and the discovery of the Wallaroo Mine.

On the 6th August, 1859, the steamer *Admella* was wrecked on the rocks off Cape Northumberland, with a sad loss of life.

During this Governor's administration Government House was enlarged, and Government Offices, Mounted Police Barracks, and the South Australian Institute were built.

The *Real Property Act* was passed in the year 1857, and received the Governor's assent 27th January, 1858. The amendment in laws relating to real property, transfer of ownership, or mortgaging, it appears, was first broached in a series of leading articles in the *South Australian Register*, with a view to put an end to the enormous charges made in the transactions of sales or mortgages. Some old colonists will remember that this desirable change was in the mind of Mr. Jas. Hurtle Fisher, when he held the office of Commissioner of Crown Lands. It appeared at the time (*i.e.*, about the year 1838) to those to whom Mr. Fisher spoke of this desirable reform that he designed to inaugurate it, but soon after Mr. Fisher lost his Government appointment on the arrival of Colonel Gawler, when he had to turn to his profession, and became the leader at the bar, and no more was heard from him of the project of transfer of land by registration. But the articles in the *Register* brought to the fore Mr. R. R. Torrens (now Sir R. R. Torrens), who was at that time Registrar-General for the colony. Mr. Torrens having been convinced of the superiority of the system of transfer by registration, soon associated with himself a gentleman as strongly impressed as himself of the benefits which would be conferred on the colony by such a radical change. The gentleman with whom he went into harness had received a legal education, and was well acquainted with the principle of transfer by registration in practice in one or more of the German states. This was Dr. Hubbe. Mr. Torrens published a pamphlet in the year 1859, in which he informed his readers that his attention had been "painfully drawn to the grievous injury and injustice inflicted under the English law of real property by the misery and ruin which fell on a relation and dear friend," and so he was resolved to strike a blow at the expensive and tedious old-established system. In commencing this crusade, nothing but his unwavering determination to accomplish his object could have borne him to the success he gained in carrying the Real Property Act, in the face of an almost unanimous phalanx of the lawyers in the colony. In the House of Assembly the Bill was carried by a majority of nineteen to seven. In the Legislative Council it met with strong opposition, but in the end was carried there also; and on the 27th January, 1858, the Real Property Act was assented to by the Governor. Mr. Torrens and those who worked with him to effect this great reform had been greatly aided by the arrival in the colony of the Report of the Royal Commissioners on the Registration of Titles, which had been presented to the House of Commons in May, 1837. To show what an uphill fight Mr. Torrens had, it may be mentioned that he met with grave discouragement from Sir Charles Cooper, then Chief Justice, as well as from Wm. Belt, Esq., a highly-respectable legal practitioner. Mr. Torrens had formerly held the position of Collector of Customs in South Australia, and was well acquainted with the laws relating to registration under the shipping laws.

The first extension of the colony was on its western side, in October, 1861, when the slice of country called No Man's Land, between the province and Western Australia, was annexed. This additional piece of country up to this time has been of no value to South Australia, as it is a level waterless desert.

Mr. J. McDouall Stuart started in October, 1861, on his last and successful trip across the continent, but as his return was not during this Governor's term of office, it will be recorded with the rest of his explorations in the next chapter. On the 16th August, 1861, Mr. McKinlay started with a strong party to search for Burke and Wills, the Melbourne explorers. About this time the following gentlemen were out on exploring trips : Messrs. Goyder, Surveyor-General, Freeling, Babbage, and Warburton, but as no great or important discoveries were made, no great interest attaches to their reports.

Sir Richard MacDonnell was not only possessed of great energy, but also exhibited much tact, judgment, and taste in inaugurating the work of the new constitution, so that the introduction of the popular element did not disturb the smooth

Life in South Australia.

and efficient work even of the first session. His early popularity was maintained until the end of his term of office.

The Governor, on the expiration of his term of office, retired on 4th March, 1862.

Sir Dominic Daly assumed the office of Governor on the 4th March, 1862. He had had great experience in the several Governments he had administered, and soon became very popular by his mild manners, and for the easy approach he accorded to all classes, rich or poor. He was a Roman Catholic, but most judicious in his liberality as to differences of creed, never obtruding his religious belief into the region of politics. He took the greatest interest in all the pursuits of the colonists. On the 4th May, 1863, the foundation-stone of the Town Hall was laid. During Sir D. Daly's term of office the annexation of the Northern Territory was made, a short account of which will be given subsequently. On the 26th September, 1866, McKinlay returned. He discovered the grave and the bones of Gray, one of poor Burke's party. The body had been dug up by the natives, by whom, it was supposed, the flesh had been cut off.

In the year 1867 the colony had the honour of receiving His Royal Highness the Duke of Edinburgh. Great preparations were made, and his Royal Highness expressed himself highly gratified with his visit. He arrived on the 30th October, when the winter rains had given the hills and plains a pleasant green aspect. The Duke laid the foundation stone of our noble and commodious Post Office. The weather was most enjoyable. Suitable equipages were placed at his command, and he was also escorted across the River Murray to witness and join in a great kangaroo hunt. Races were also held on the Adelaide race-course, on the spacious City Park Lands. He left on the 21st November. It is a pleasant retrospect that there occurred nothing to mar the great holiday which was kept up in his honour.

On April 13, 1865, an accident occurred on the Port Railway. The Governor, Lady Daly, and Lady Charlotte Bacon, and a Ministerial party were in the State carriages when the train was run off the line, at a part where repairs were being made on which the rails were not properly fastened. The manager (Mr. C. S. Hare) himself was on the engine driving, and did not slacken the speed. Fortunately the passengers received no worse injury than a violent shaking. The manager made an extraordinary excuse, knowing the state of the rails; he thought that, under such circumstances, the greater the speed the greater the safety; nevertheless he lost his office.

In July, 1867, Judge Boothby was removed from the Bench, and died in June of the following year at the age of 64.

On the 5th October, 1867, the first Torrens Dam was swept away. This structure was of timber, and on a pattern of which it might be said "warranted not to stand."

On the 19th February, 1868, Governor Daly departed this life, universally respected. It may truthfully be said that no jar or friction occurred between him and the people over whom he was appointed Governor. His remains were followed to the grave by an immense number of mourners of all classes and creeds, and no greater grief was ever exhibited at the death of any public servant. He was interred in the Roman Catholic Cemetery.

Lieut.-Colonel Francis Gilbert Hamley, on the death of Sir D. Daly, assumed the reins of Government, and continued to hold the office of Acting Governor until the 15th February, 1869. Lieut.-Colonel Hamley was senior officer in command of her Majesty's forces in the colony.

Amongst the mementoes left by the Duke of Edinburgh not the least is the laying the foundation stone of the Prince Alfred College on the 7th November, 1867. The total cost of the land and buildings, as now completed, has been over £25,000; the greater part of that amount has been paid by voluntary contributions, and but a comparatively small balance remains to be liquidated.

The central part of the building was opened for the reception of pupils in June, 1869; the Governor, Sir James Fergusson, being present. The Waterhouse wing (named after the largest donor) was added in 1877. The second, the Colton wing, was erected in 1882, named after the Hon. John Colton, M.P., a large contributor. The present number of scholars is 375; of these 74 are boarders. The school will accommodate 400. To the other necessary buildings has been added a capacious and well-appointed gymnasium. The school fees are moderate as compared to those of high schools in England.

In connection with this College four scholarships are awarded annually, viz.: The Old Collegians' Scholarship, value £15; and the Colton, Longbottom, Robb, and Foundation Scholarships, each of the value of £12 12s.

The course of instruction and methods of management are much the same as those followed in English public schools—embracing classics, mathematics, and scientific training to prepare for entrance to the Universities.

Some of the past pupils have graduated at the Adelaide University and at London, Cambridge, and Edinburgh, and entered the professions. Amongst these must be mentioned Mr. Thomas Hudson Beare, who, after taking three scholarships during his course at the Prince Alfred College, subsequently gained his bachelor's degree at the Adelaide University, and carried off the first South Australian Scholarship of £200 per annum, tenable for four years, which is annually offered by the Education Department, and has since taken the degree of Bachelor of Science at the London University. It may be added that Mr. Beare is the youngest son of the late J. H. Beare, one of the first arrivals at Kangaroo Island, and his maternal grandfather was the late Rev. John Bull, M.A., Oxon. Another pupil, Mr. Percy Ansell Robin, who passed his B.A. examination at the same time as Mr. Beare carried off the South Australian Scholarship the second year it was offered, and is now pursuing his studies at Cambridge.

Mr. Frederic Chapple, B.A., B. Sc., is the present Head Master, and there are sixteen under masters, besides visiting lecturers and professors.

The College is incorporated by Act of Parliament. The South Australian Wesleyan Conference appoint the governing body. The course of religious instruction is undenominational. In the year 1882 the College was visited by the Royal Princes Edward and George, accompanied by his Excellency the Governor, Sir W. F. D. Jervois, and the youthful Princes were greatly interested in viewing an institution the foundation stone of which was laid by their royal uncle.

Postscript.—By the obliging action of Sir Thomas Elder, the author is enabled to give the following full and satisfactory account of his far-seeing and *extensive* expenditure in the introduction of those invaluable beasts of burden—camels. By the employment of these patient and efficient workers in a hot climate, such an important work has been already carried out in this colony, as the Transcontinental Telegraph line. In the year 1860, Mr. Samuel Joseph Stuckey was despatched to India, with ample means at his command, to purchase a breeding herd of camels. His instructions were to travel through the districts in India where the camels were chiefly bred. He was to procure all necessary information as to the breeding and general management of the animals, and to engage a sufficient staff of natives of the country, experienced in work. Mr. Stuckey purchased the required number, but on his return to the port of shipment he was unable to charter a suitable vessel, and on account of this difficulty, he returned to Adelaide to report himself to Sir Thomas Elder. He returned to India, and succeeded in shipping 117 camels, and 40 Afghans, with the loss of only one camel at sea, the men and the remainder of his charge were safely landed by Mr. Stuckey at Port Augusta, in 1862. The skin disease, to which these beasts are subject, had greatly increased during their close confinement on board ship. The remedy for this disease (the scab or mange) used in India is extracted from a shrub growing in the camel districts. Mr. Stuckey had been surprised and pleased on this plant being pointed out to him, as he had observed the same growing in the far north in South Australia, in which part he had resided some years in management of a station. The South Australian plant, on being prepared and chemically examined, was found not to contain the virtue required. Although all care was taken of the diseased camels, a serious loss occurred six weeks after landing by the death of fifty-two of them.

Thus the stock was reduced to sixty-three; amongst them ten males. The survivors were removed as soon as recovered from the effects of the voyage, to Beltana, where they quickly improved in condition, and commenced to increase until the number amounted to six hundred. In consequence of the loss after landing the staff of Afghans had to be reduced to twenty-two. The value as given by the liberal owner of the camels at this time was £70 per head.

The following expedition of McKinlay is mentioned here as an early instance of using camels in explorations, and to them may fairly be attributed the salvation of Mr. McKinlay and his party. Almost the last meal on animal food the party partook of was the flesh of the last camel which remained; sheep, bullocks, and many of the horses having been first eaten. This sole-surviving camel, after bringing what burden they had not abandoned and buried to within one day's journey of one of the outmost stations in the colony of Queensland, was also slaughtered, and partaken of without bread, vegetables, or condiments. A graphic picture of this loathsome breakfast is given in the words of one of the party, Mr. Davis, as published in his diary. "30th July.—Camped at a running stream of beautiful water. Here we shall kill our faithful ally, 'Swee'; he has been such a noble animal. I shall be sorry to see him drop, spelled here in a comfortable cool camp. 31st.—Boiling down camel all day, preparing for a start. Poole sick with a touch of fever and ague, and cannot eat anything. There is not much choice, that's quite certain. Preparing for a start to-morrow. Four days' meat left—so that if we don't hit a station in that time look out for those that have not got good boots, as we must kill another horse, then we shall have all to walk in our turn; my boots, happily, are good. The old camel is worn out, with sores all over him. He will be a nice morsel without a bit of fat to be seen. He is dead, and we are to have his liver and kidney for our evening's meal. I was once offered a bit of tiger, but never a bit of old camel. Rhinoceros I have helped to eat in pies, but this ulcerated old quadruped goes against the 'grain.' Remarks piquant and racy are made, and we all sit down round the pot, and get our portions on our tin plates. All helped, but no one seemed inclined to begin. At last, the Governor said, 'What's the matter, boys,' and he put a bit of liver in his mouth. We all looked at him, and at it we went. A few still held back, when I spoke the word of command used to make the camel lie down, 'Ushe Nan'! That was a settler for one or two. I tried to finish mine, but the liver was so tough that none of us could eat it." The following day, the 2nd of August, the worn-out party made the cattle station of Messrs. Harvey and Somers, and were most hospitably entertained.

To return to the history of the Beltana Camel station, as appeared in an article in the *Australasian*, the first use of the camels was to perform the station work in journeys from Beltana and other stations, belonging to the firm of Messrs. Elder and Smith, for some considerable time. Mr. Samuel J. Stuckey managed the camel station. After a time these useful animals were employed by the owners of other stations in conveying up supplies and in carrying produce down to Port Augusta.

After a time their number increased sufficiently to be otherwise employed than in merely bearing pack-saddles. A commencement was made to break them into harness. At first, Mr. Phillipson found some difficulty in this matter; it had first to be proved whether to yoke them as bullocks are worked with yokes and bows and chains, or with collars and traces. The style at length adopted was with suitable collars and what is called spider harness—collar, backstrap, and traces. This form of gear has ever since proved most successful. The advantages of such use of the camels in the hot central and northern portions of this large colony soon attracted the attention of distant settlers and of the Government.

At first they were taken up on hire. Soon afterwards the Government purchased the animals for the Telegraph Line, the Police, and the Crown Lands' Departments for the work of the outer districts. Settlers in the north also became buyers. The use they have been in the explorations since they were available, Mr. Giles, the explorer, shows, who reports he travelled for sixteen days from water to water, through almost impenetrable scrub, on his way from Beltana to Perth, Western Australia. Instances of their wonderful powers of endurance could be multiplied, of what they have undergone here; but such are not required, as their characters are so well known. The confidence with which explorers may now feel on starting in a direction where waters are not known to exist, is a great gain to this colony, which possesses such an enormous extent of country yet unknown as to its value for out-stations.

Several station-holders some time ago purchased camels, and in proof of the benefits they have derived from their use, are still buyers. Distances between some of the waters during the late years of drought in some cases have been from eighty to a hundred miles. It was by means of camels, both by pack and waggons, that the famine at Mount Brown Goldfields was relieved. Cobb and Co. also relied on them to convey the mail from Wilcannia to Milparinka till rain set in. Another advantage possessed by camels is the fact that when the ground is as bare as the road, there are generally plenty of bushes which they can do very well on, but that sheep and cattle cannot reach. Some time ago a Camel Carrying Company was formed in Port Augusta, and camels and waggons, &c., were purchased from Beltana. This has turned out a successful speculation, and is a strong factor in the carrying business of the far north.

It cannot but be acknowledged that the last three years have been of the most trying description for all kinds of stock; and yet there are plenty of camels which have had no spell whatever for that time, working away—carrying and drawing heavy loads through difficult country—frequently encountering long stages without water, and this at a time when it was quite out of the question for bullocks or horses to travel. In fact, it was more than many of the latter animals could do to keep alive, much less work. It is calculated that fully 75 per cent. of the working stock of horses and bullocks have died during the last two years, and yet the camels have worked through it all, in the most admirable way.

Thus it has been shown that camels in this country are an unquestionable success. The great secret in getting the most benefit from camels is keeping them constantly at work; it is not good for them to be turned out for a spell like horses or cattle. "Keep on doing it," is the best motto. I have often heard the question asked, "How long will a camel do without water?" I can only say, after eight years' experience, that I do not know. As long as the bushes are green, when they are not working, they will not drink if you take them to water; but in the summer time, when everything is dry, it is customary to take the herd to water twice a week, though sometimes then only the female camels with calves will drink. I heard it said by those who know camels in India and here, that they get far fatter in Australia than in India; and that in this very thing lies their liability to contract the terrible disease I have spoken of already—the scab.

The pack camels are mostly worked by Afghans, but the waggons are all driven by Europeans, and any man who is a decent horse or bullock driver, soon learns to drive camels and work them to the best advantage.

The Camel Carrying Company, and most of the station-owners who possess camels, have European drivers, both for pack and camel waggons, and they seem quite *au fait* at the work. One hears some very amusing camp-fire stories told of camels by those who worked amongst them in the early days of their experience, and the wonderful stages done by riding camels in such marvellously short periods, completely put in the shade any record of "tall" doings by horses.

CHAPTER VIII.

BEFORE giving Mr. Stuart's final exploring trip, when he succeeded in crossing the continent and planting the British flag on the shores of the Indian Ocean, it is my intention to give an account, condensed as much as possible, of the five expeditions he commanded, subsequent to the expedition with Captain Sturt, in which he was engaged as draughtsman, and which unfortunately was attended with very few beneficial results.

It will be seen even in the necessarily brief account of these toilsome but eventually successful explorations, that Mr. Stuart has placed himself high in the ranks of the brave and self-denying men who have devoted themselves to such hard contests with life destroying climates, desolate regions, and hostile natives.

Mr. Stuart's first trip as leader was in 1858, when his expedition occupied six months, and he discovered pastoral country to the west of Lake Torrens to the extent of 16,000 square miles. Mr. Stuart reported this discovery to the Government, claiming as a reward for himself and for those who contributed to his outfit and expenses, a lease of 1,000 square miles, to be free from rent for four years, and at the end of that term to be subject to the usual grazing rental.

After some hesitation on the part of the Government, this was granted on the conditions he offered, viz., to hand over the maps and diary of the expedition.

The land was to be rent free for four years from the 1st January, 1859, for stocking, and the fourteen years' lease was to date from the expiration of that term, when the runs were to be subject to the regulations which might then be in force. This concession was not availed of by Mr. Stuart.

On this expedition he had been despatched by Mr. John Chambers, after he had surveyed the runs which Messrs. James and John Chambers had taken up on leases from the Government in the Flinders Ranges; his instructions were to endeavour to discover a large fresh-water lake which the natives had described to Mr. J. Chambers to be to the west of Mount Deception, which they called Wingilpin. Though Mr. Stuart discovered good country for grazing purposes in that direction, he did not find Wingilpin, nor has it since been met with.

Life in South Australia.   333

An account of Mr. Stuart's second expedition in the neighbourhood of Lake Torrens, is condensed from his diary :—

"*2nd April*, 1859.—Started from Mr. Glen's station. On the 6th camped south of Mount Delusion (Deception) ; on the 8th camped two days at Gum Creek ; 10th prevented from starting being too unwell, but sent Hergott and Miller to find water in advance. Hergott did not return till noon on the 13th, and reported he had found a batch of springs, twelve in number (now called Hergott Springs) from whence a survey for a railway is at this time being made to the boundary of Queensland, the Great Northern Railway having been extended as far as Farina, Government Gums.

"*18th April.*—Resting the horses. Went to the top of Mount Attraction ; found copper with iron-stone on the top of the mount, and some native copper adhering to the sides of large pieces of iron-stone.

" On the 26th arrived at Chambers' Creek ; remained to fix the positions, latitude 29° 39′ 9″.

" *8th May.*—Started from Chambers' Creek and made Hamilton Springs ; 10th, made Beresford Springs.

" *11th.*—Arrived at Elizabeth Springs, water brackish ; named Elizabeth after Miss Chambers. There is water enough to drive a flour mill, they are most remarkable as being at such a height above the level of the plain. On the previous day passed Paisley's Ponds. The white deposit seen round the springs is soda.

" *16th May.*—Miller found a spring ; not hot, but a little warm.

" *3rd June.*—Miller found two large springs covered with long reeds—Hawker's Springs.

" *4th June.*—Hawker's Springs. Started towards the highest point of the next range ; struck a gum creek at 12¼ miles ; came upon a small batch of springs in a broad grassy valley. At seven miles came on a broad gum creek named Blyth, after the Hon. A. Blyth ; a range to the east, named Hanson Range, after the Hon. R. D. Hanson. On the highest point of the range built a cone of stones, and named it Mount Younghusband. On rounding the mount found eight springs. To the north-west is another isolated range—say 700 feet high —named Mount Kingston. 6th, started at 10. Passed Mount Kingston on the south-west side. At three-quarters of a mile came upon springs flowing in a stream strong enough to supply any number of cattle the country would bear, named the Barrow Springs. At four and a half miles struck a large broad valley, in which are the largest springs yet seen, named Freeling Springs, after the Hon. Major Freeling, M.L.C. Hergott and Miller, old gold diggers, say the country resembles the Victorian gold fields. At 11 miles struck a salt-water creek; at three-quarters of a mile a gum creek, with very long water holes slightly brackish, but might do for cattle, named Neale's Creek.

"*7th June.*—At four miles ascended one of some detached hills, named it Mount Harvey, and the next Mount Dutton. Approaching Hanson's Range on the north side found a few springs.

"*8th June.*—At three-quarters of a mile passed a batch of springs, some fresh, other brackish.

"*9th June.*—Miller discovered two large water-holes in a large creek running for about four miles north-west, one a hundred yards wide and a quarter of a mile long. Can it be Cooper's Creek?

"*10th June.*—Very unwell.

"*12th June.*—Still very unwell. Camped on the large water-holes found by Miller on the 9th.

"*15th June.*—Started at 9.15. On approaching the Hanson Range found two large water-holes, with ducks upon them, in the gap a quarter of a mile long and very deep, deemed to be permanent.

"*17th June.*—Made the Neale. Found another large quantity of water supplied by springs; this is a wonderful country for water.

"*1st July.*—Chambers' Creek. At 24 miles camped on a water-hole in Gregory Creek. Remarkable peaks north of the water, one having a white face to the east.

"*3rd July.*—Arrived at Mr. Glen's station, thus ending the search for water in the country where runs had been recently taken up."

This short expedition is recorded in this history as showing how successful Mr. Stuart was in this, his second exploring trip, in discovering permanent waters, thus enabling him to form a new base from which to resume his onward course north.

Mr. Stuart's third expedition was in the vicinity of Lake Torrens, to fix corners of runs and lay down base lines, and to make searches for permanent waters.

"*4th Nov.*, 1855.—Started from Chambers' Creek for the Emerald Springs.

"*5th.*—Reached the top of a high hill, from which we could see Lake Eyre, north, about three miles distant. No land visible in the distance.

"*6th.*—Rode to the lake; had to dismount, the ground being too soft. Walked some distance, found a number of small fish dried and encased in salt left by the receding waters, and driven on land by a heavy wind. They were scattered over a surface 12 yards in breadth, all along the shore, one found measuring eight inches by three inches, another six inches by two and a half, and another five inches by two. They resembled bream. Such products are a proof of the depth of the water.

"*7th.*—Sent Keckwick and Miller to examine lagoons seen yesterday.

"*8th.*—The men did not return till 12 noon from Paisley Ponds; found to be brackish.

"*10th.*—Found large salt lagoon two miles broad and five miles long. On south-west point a spring surrounded with soft ground, covered with reeds dark green. Going round the lagoon came to a hill upward of 100 feet high, upon the top of which appeared to be green reeds; on ascending it, found black sand and clay, over which water trickled from a spring, filtering through sand into the lagoon. This discovery brings us one day's journey nearer the Spring of Hope. We can now make that in one day if we get an early start. On this trip the road can now be travelled, to the furthest water I saw on my last trip, and not one night need be passed without water. These I named William Springs. Remained here. The men found to-day a similar spring about three miles east.

"*14th.*—Started for the Hope Springs. At twenty-one miles crossed the Douglas. As we approached the Hope the country improved. Distance thirty miles.

"*15th.*—Spring of Hope. Reached with two men the top of a hill. Named it Mount Anna.

"*17th and 18th.*—Arrived at Mount Margaret. Cone of stones built at top. Commenced survey. Obtained bearings from the hill at Hawker's Springs, of Mount Margaret, Mount Younghusband, hill at Parry Springs, Mount Charles, and Mount Stephenson.

"*19th.*—Sent the men to form camp at Fanny Springs. Went

to the top of Mount Margaret. After descending, rode about three-quarters of a mile, and found a spring. Numerous native camps in the creek. Arrived at the camp after dark.

"*20th Nov.*—Fanny Springs. Got up at daybreak and went to the top of Mount Charles, where men had built a cone of stones as ordered. Began with Keckwick, the base line from the top of Mount Charles. Chaining continued.

"*24th.*—Found hot springs. A staff was thrust through soft sand, and, on withdrawing it, was quite hot. Survey continued over the country in which the springs and fresh water had been discovered in the previous exploring trip. A few additional springs found.

"*14th December.*—Saw Lake Torrens. Rode to the shore, and found it composed of sand mixed and gravel too soft to bear the horse.

"*8th January*, 1856.—Confined with a severe attack of lumbago. Eyes still very much inflamed.

"*10th.*—Milne Springs. Latitude 28° 15' 45". Keckwick and the other man returned, and reported they had found to the west two springs, one about nine miles, and the other about thirty distant.

"*11th.*—Started with Keckwick to examine the country to the west, which he had reported on. Provisions are now running short. At 28 miles reached the spring country. Found them in what appears to be the basin of a large salt lagoon three miles broad and upwards of eight miles long, at the south end. A brackish creek with fresh water springs on the bank, with very good water flowing from them.

"*12th.*—West springs. A number of blacks. Their smoke is seen, and plenty of tracks, new and old. Many places where water is to be obtained a few inches below the surface.

"*15th.*—On return to camp found that two men left at camp had opened the plans, and so damaged the principal one that I did not know what to do with it.

"*16th.*—At about 22 miles found four other springs. Named them the Keckwick Springs.

"*21st.*—Chambers' Creek. Arrived and found provisions awaiting, but the two labourers exhibited non-compliance with orders, and refused to proceed again north, bent on returning to Adelaide to obtain their discharge and pay. As they had broken their engagement, sent Keckwick on to Mr. Chambers' station with despatches, and to procure other assistance if possible."

Mr. Stuart and party, failing to obtain hands, returned to Mr. Baker's station, and found Mr. Baker had left for Adelaide some weeks before. Under these circumstances the party was broken up, and Mr. Stuart had to organise a fresh and stronger party.

The fourth expedition was for the purpose of fixing the centre of the continent, and occupied from March to September, 1860.

"*2nd March.*—Chambers Creek. Left this week with thirteen horses and three men. Next day camped at Beresford Springs. Here it was evident there had been a native fight. There were the remains of a body of a very tall native, lying on his back; his skull was broken in four places; animals and birds had left the bones nearly bare. Scattered about on the rising ground were waddies, spears, boomerangs, and a number of broken dishes. The owners of the wurlies which were on the rise appear to have been driven away by a hostile tribe.

"*14th.*—Freeling Springs. Found the creek to be impassable from recent floods.

"*15th.*—The Peak (River).—Started to cross the creek, but had a tearful job, the banks being boggy and the current so strong the horses could hardly keep their feet. Water up to saddle-flaps, and some under water. Obliged to leave one old horse to his fate, after trying several hours to save him. It took five hours in getting across.

"*16th.*—Camped at Keckwick Springs, found on last trip. There are six springs; the reeds on them are very thick, and twelve feet high. At sundown it rained heavily, and continued the greater part of the night.

"*17th.*—Keckwick Springs. Found the banks of the Neale River very boggy.

"*18th.*—Neale River. Observed in the bed of the river a bulb springing like the Egyptian arum.

"*22nd.*—Side Creek of the Neale. Found great difficulty in crossing, where four creeks join.

"*23rd.*—Myal Creek. At three miles struck another myal and gum creek. Good grass. At ten miles struck another creek, spreading over a large plain, very boggy. After passing a thick scrubby country of mulga and other shrub, the soil changed to a dark red, covered splendidly with grass. At twenty miles struck a large creek, running at the rate of five miles an hour; breadth of water, 100 feet. Gum trees on the bank; apparently other channels.

"*March* 24*th*.—Large gum creek. Unable to cross. To the south-west are seen two high peaks, the highest named Mount Ben. After leaving the creek, at eighteen miles, found no water. In the Neale we saw fish eight inches long. This creek must have permanent holes in it. Had to camp out with water.

"25*th*.—Mulga scrub, of which there appeared no termination. On this course had previously followed to the thick mulga scrub, therefore changed course more westerly and cut the Neale. Found sand ridges with spinifers, an indication of desert to the westward.

"26*th*.—Neale River west. Remained to repair damage from water.

"27*th*.—Same camp. Rained very heavily during the night. About noon the sky cleared. Keckwick was sent out to get a notion of the country west of a low range. Feed excellent south-west from the camp. Too cloudy to take an observation.

"28*th*.—Started on a north-west course to get through the mulga scrub. At ten miles changed from scrub to sand hills. Altered course to north-east range. Cut water at five miles where three branches join. This is supposed to be the River Frew, one branch from south-west, the others from N.N.W.; water running; on the banks good grass.

"29*th*. —The Frew. The natives had only just left their fires, which were still alight. Came on a large native grave of a circular form, about four feet six inches high and from 20 to 24 yards in circumference. Struck the creek where a branch comes in, with splendid reaches of water. Found winter as well as summer native habitations. From these and the native grave, the water here may be taken to be permanent. Changed course to the north, which appears to be open. Struck another large gum creek running to the south-east. The country passed over to-day was covered with grass and salt bush.

"30*th*.—Small branch of the Frew. At sixteen miles struck a large sandy creek; named the same the Ross; not apparently promising to hold water. Struck another creek. These large creeks spread over a grassy plain one mile wide. The wild oats on the bank were four feet high; some of the grass on the plain resembled drake; some, wheat.

"2*nd April*.—At six miles struck a gum creek with water in it. Three miles good country : gypsum, chalk, iron-stone, and quartz prevail. No water.

"3*rd*.—Gum Creek. At three miles ascended a hill, Mount

Beddome. The country appears open on a bearing of 330°. A large isolated table hill to the north; a large number of broken hills, the highest point named Daniel, after Mr. D. Keckwick. Still no water; distance, 20 miles.

"*4th April.*—Mount Humphrys. From the top broken ranges all round; beyond, an open and grassy country; also seen, about two miles distant, a gum creek with water in it. On Keckwick examining same, found to have plenty of water, and the finest gum trees yet seen. Feed most abundant. Named this creek the Finke.

"*5th April.*—Good country.—*6th*, started on same course 330°. In the distance a most remarkable hill like a locomotive engine with a funnel. At six miles met with a large gum creek: the largest seen with running water, much trouble in crossing it. A black fellow was seen amongst the bushes. On being called he was off like a shot. The creek appears to come from the south-west; numerous tracks of blacks; the pillar is of sand-stone. From its base to its top is about 150 feet, quite perpendicular. It is 20 feet wide by 10 feet deep. Named this Chambers's Pillar, after Mr. James Chambers. By observation, the situation was found to be 116° 26' 15".

"*7th April.*—Rain water in sand-stone hills. From the top of a sand-hill can see a range which our course will cut. Expect to find water. Arrived at the foot of the range. Found water and camped. Creek broad. Named it Hugh Gum Creek, and the range James Range.

"*9th April.*—Hugh Gum Creek. Passed through a thick mulga scrub. On the north a high broken range with two remarkable bluffs about the centre; had great difficulty in crossing the range; stopped by a second range nearly perpendicular; huge masses of red sand-stone on its side. Scurvy beginning to show itself on some of the party.

"*12th April.*—The Hugh. Could not ascend the creek for precipices. Camped at a good spring. Found a remarkable palm tree with light green fronds ten feet long, having small leaves; they spread out like the top of a grass tree. The fruit has a large kernel about the size of an egg, and the taste of a cocoa-nut; when roasted, tastes like a potato. The East Bluff named after Captain Brinkley, the other named Hanson. This is the only real range met with since leaving the Flinders Range. Named it, after his Excellency the Governor-in-Chief of South Australia, McDonnell Range.

"*13th April.*—Brinkley Bluff, McDonnell Range. On ascending the bluff with much difficulty, was able to decide on a course. To the north-west the view is intercepted by another point of the range, which was named Mount Hay, after the Hon. A. Hay, Commissioner of Crown Lands. On passing down with much trouble, found we had taken the wrong creek to get through the range. Camped on the creek. An abundance of water, believed to be permanent, the feed splendid.

"*14th April.*—Got through the range further down (north); it took the whole day to make five miles. Camped north of the bluff.

"*15th April.*—North gorge of McDonnell range. The country in the ranges is as fine a pastoral country as can be wished, with abundance of waters. The nut found a few days ago not fit to eat; made the men vomit violently.

"*16th April.*—Started to cross the scrub for high peak seen. Made 30 miles. No creek, leaving the range found.

"*17th April.*—In the scrub. Started through scrub and spinifers. Three Reap Hook Hills seen to the west. Followed the range till after dark; passed nothing but sandy or rocky watercourses. Grass dried up.

"*18th April.*—Keckwick sent out to look for water. Ascended the range and saw on the other side of it a gum creek very promising; Keckwick found water in a creek about two miles off; horses very badly in want of it. A small cone of stones built on the peak; named it Mount Freeling.

"*19th April.*—Moved to the east side of the mount to the place where water had been seen at this camp. Marked a tree J.M.D.S. At two miles a creek with more water, and a little higher up is a splendid reservoir of water about 100 yards in circumference in a ledge of rocks. Where it was tried it was 12 feet deep; also two other similar lodges of water. Native tracks all about.

"*20th April.*—East side of Mount Hugh. The range is well grassed, with gum creeks leaving it. Here was discovered a new tree whose dark green leaf has two wide prongs; the seed or bean is of a red colour.

"*21st April.*—At seven miles across the scrub made another high hill; the scrub had been open with splendid grass, afterwards it became much thicker, and a quantity of burnt timber was lying about; clothes and saddle-bags torn to pieces. At about 22 miles on the plain, met with large granite rocks lying even with the surface. Found rain water in holes in them. Camped on a small gum creek.

"*22nd April.*—Under Mount Stuart. In the morning an observation was taken, when it was found that the camp was in the centre of Australia, 111° 0' 30". Thus was gained by Mr. Stuart the honour of having reached the centre of Australia after so much toil and suffering. A tree was marked, and the British flag hoisted. There is a high mount about two miles and a half to the N.N.E. Wish that it was in the centre. , Camped here.

"*23rd April.*—Centre. Ascended with Keckwick to the top of this mount, which was found to be as high or higher than Mount Serle. A cone was formed; in the centre of it a pole was erected with the British flag nailed to it. Near the top of the cone a small bottle was placed with a slip of paper in it, with the signatures, stating by whom it was placed, when three hearty cheers were given for the British flag, the emblem of civil and religious liberty; and may it be a sign to the natives, that the dawn of liberty, civilization, and Christianity, is about to break upon them. Named the range John, after Mr. John Chambers."

Mr. Stuart, although he had thus by his indomitable pluck, marvellous endurance, and natural talents, established his fame as one of the most successful explorers of the day, was still not satisfied, and without delay started, with his willing party, to endeavour to finish, in this expedition, the work of reaching the shore of the Indian Ocean. With this intent he continued on northwards without rest, from Central Mount Stuart on the 25th April, and kept up his system of beating about east and west on his northerly course, to discover feed and water, and to establish a practicable line on which to progress or to return.

" On the *26th June.*—Arrived at a large gum creek with long sheets of water in it, the banks in some places steep, the lower part formed of concrete. Here saw some blacks, but they did not come near, but walked off as fast as they could. From the top of a rise was seen their camp on the banks of a large sheet of water. After leaving this spot at 15 miles, cut the creek with a sandy bottom and no water, was then compelled to return and camp about nine miles above the previous camp. At half-past one, when about three miles from the creek, we came upon our tracks, and found numerous foot-marks of the blacks, as if they had been examining the horse tracks. Found the natives had left their camp, and concluded they had done so on seeing the party pass their camp in the morning. On approaching the creek to cross, suddenly behind some scrub which they had entered, three tall black fellows sprang up; they were fully armed with war spears, boomerangs, and waddies. The distance was about 200 yards; it was so nearly dark that we were placed at a disadvantage. I wished to pass without taking any notice of them, but such was not their intention, for they continued to approach us, calling out and making all sorts of gestures, apparently of defiance. I then faced them, making every sign of friendship. They seemed to be in a great fury and performing some sort of a war dance; now they were joined by more of their tribe; in a few minutes they numbered upwards of thirty; every bush seemed to produce a man. The horses were placed near the creek, and seeing they were bent on mischief, as they disregarded my friendly signs, I ordered my men to load their fire-arms. They were still gradually approaching, and their leader, an old man, who was in advance, made signs which were taken as a signal for us to be off, but they were signs of defiance. I had no sooner turned my horse to comply as I thought with their wishes, than we received a shower of boomerangs accompanied by a fearful yell; they then set fire to the grass, jumping, yelling, throwing up their arms, like so many fiends. In addition to the number already fronting us, I could now see others getting up from behind the bushes; still I felt unwilling to fire upon them, and tried again to make them understand we wished to do them no harm. Having approached within forty yards of us, they made another charge, and threw their boomerangs, which came whizzing about our ears, and one struck my horse. I then gave orders to fire, which stayed their mad career for a little. Our pack-horses, which were on before us, took fright at the firing, and rushed for the creek. Seeing some of the blacks running from bush to bush to cut the pack-horses off—meanwhile those in front were yelling and throwing their boomerangs, and approaching nearer to us—I ordered another volley to be fired, and sent Ben to drive the horses to a more favourable place, while Keckwick and I covered our rear. The natives still followed yelling, but they kept out of reach of our guns. It was now quite dark; the country scrubby, and the natives bold and daring. We could easily have been surrounded and destroyed by such determined antagonists as they had proved themselves, more than ten to one against us. I decided to push on to our last night's camp; after we had done so, after some consideration I decided that it was not safe to remain there for the night, and thought it better to return to the grassy plain or gum creek; wishing I had only four more men, as my party is so small, that I can only fall back and act on the defensive; as now if I were to stand and fight them, our pack-horses would be left without protection. Their aim evidently was to capture our supplies; but so far they have found out their mistake, as we have not turned out of our way for them."

It was Mr. Stuart's intention, after stopping a day at Keckwick's Ponds to give the horses a rest, to have continued his northern course, but after a night's due consideration he reluctantly decided to abandon the attempt to reach the Gulf of Carpentaria. He says: "Situated as I am, it would be most imprudent. In the first place my party is far too small to cope with such determined and wily natives as those I have just encountered. If they had been Europeans they could not have better carried out their plan of attack; they had observed us pass in the morning, and having examined our tracks, knew on the course we had taken that we should not find water, and must return to obtain it above them; therefore they lay in wait for our return. Their charge was in double column, open order, and we had to take steady aim to make an impression. With such as these in our rear, and most probably with worse in advance, it would be destruction to all my party to go on. All the information of the interior I have already obtained, would be lost. Moreover I had only half rations for six months, four of which are passed. My men complain of weakness, and are hardly able to perform what they have to do. The poor horses are greatly reduced in condition, and unable to stand more than one night without water. Finally, my health is so bad that I am hardly able to sit in the saddle. After taking all these things into consideration it would be madness and folly to attempt more." Seeing signal fires around him, he decided to give his "black friends" a wide berth, and turned south to Bishop's Creek.

Mr. Stuart made out a course for a larger party to take his tracks to feed and water, and returned, arriving safe at William Springs, 25th August, 1860, and next day he found Mr. Brodie camped three miles south-east of Mount Hamilton.

Mr. Stuart reached Adelaide in October, 1860, and reported that he had penetrated to the northward, almost as far as the 18th degree of south latitude, and had been driven back by the hostility of the natives. The Parliament of South Australia voted the sum of £2,500 for a larger and better armed and organised party, of which Mr. Stuart was to be the leader. The ill-fated Victorian expedition, under Burke and Wills, had already started.

On the 20th November, Mr. Stuart was ready to start once more from Adelaide, having lost no time in getting together his party, consisting of 12 men and 49 horses.

On the 29th November, 1860, Mr. Stuart left Moolooloo with 7 men and 30 horses.

"1st December.—Mr. Glen's Station. Here he was delayed by some of the horses being unmanageable, and unsuited for the work.

"12th December.—Chambers Creek. Delayed here, on account of knocking up of some of the horses, one was lost, one died, and several went blind. On this being known in Adelaide, Mr. Finke sent up four fresh horses. The party was increased both by men and horses.

"1st January, 1861. Left Chambers Creek with 12 men and 49 horses. As in the previous trips, Mr. Stuart laid a good foundation in the discovery of many waters, chiefly at convenient distances, having obtained as well the knowledge where feed could be depended on.

Although Mr. Stuart had on this occasion a much stronger party and larger outfit than on any previous occasion, he had to return. After proceeding only a few miles north beyond the Attack Creek of the last expedition, he was driven back by impenetrable scrub forests and by want of water. He penetrated nearly five degrees north beyond Central Mount Stuart, which brought him within four degrees of the north coast of Australia. He returned to Adelaide on the 23rd September, disappointed but not daunted.

The final entry in Mr. Stuart's journal, of this expedition, is as follows:—"*Sunday, the* 15*th September.*—I shall leave to-morrow for Port Augusta, and proceed by steamer for Adelaide. I cannot close my journal without expressing my warmest thanks to my second in command, Mr. Keekwick, and my other companions. They have been brave, and have vied with each other in performing their duties to my entire satisfaction. I also tender my best thanks to Messrs. Chambers and Finke, and the Government, for the handsome manner in which I was fitted out."

CHAPTER IX.

IMMEDIATELY on Mr. Stuart's return, he made his report to the Government, on the 23rd September, 1861.

Almost at the same time, the Victorian Government obtained the first news of the survivors of the unfortunate expedition which had been despatched, under Messrs. Burke and Wills, to endeavour to reach the northern shores of the continent.

Although Mr. Stuart's report had explained his disappointment at the results of his last trip, the Government still felt such confidence in his skill as an explorer, that they accepted his services to make another effort to cross the continent.

On the 26th October, 1861, the new expedition started from Adelaide. Mr. Stuart accompanied it to see them well off. When they had proceeded a few miles, one of the led horses turned restive. On Mr. Stuart observing that the rope on his neck was choking him, he attempted to cut it, when the brute reared and struck him on the head. He fell senseless, and the horse sprang forward and stamped on Mr. Stuart's right hand, and discolated two joints of his first finger, tearing the flesh and nail from it. By careful treatment he was able to overtake his party in five weeks. He joined the rear portion of the party at Moolooloo, 20th December, and the advanced portion on the 29th, at Finnis Springs.

The names of the party were as follows :—

John McDougal Stuart, leader of the expedition ; William Keckwick, second officer ; F. W. Thring, third officer ; W. P. Auld, assistant ; Stephen King ; John Billiat ; James Frew ; Heath Nash ; John McGorery, shoeing smith ; J. W. Waterhouse, naturalist (subsequently Curator of the Adelaide Museum).

"*15th February.*—Marchant's Springs. The blacks became troublesome. On the 17th, when Auld was approaching the water, some natives set the grass on fire, with the supposed intent of making an attack on the camp. Thring, who was out looking up the horses, was met by some blacks, one of whom threw his boomerang at him, which did not strike him, but feeling the necessity of quickly repelling them, Thring drew his revolver and shot one man in self-defence. After leaving the Hugh on the 25th, they again showed their hostility. The party had passed

about half through the gorge, when the natives set fire to the
long grass, which blew in their faces, and through the smoke
three fully armed natives appeared, about twenty-five yards off,
with spears and shields, defying them; they placed their spears
in their womeras (propellers), yelling out at the top of their
voices. Auld was ordered to dismount and to fire a shot to one
side of them; the ball struck a rock and stopped their yelling,
but seemed not to affect them otherwise. He was then ordered
to fire at the rock on which the middle one was standing; the
ball struck the desired spot, which sent them flying at their
best speed.

"5th March.—Again, in crossing the plain under Mount
Hay, when watering the horses at some rain-water, seven fully
armed natives appeared. A shot was fired at a long distance
to frighten them, but this had no effect. With the aid of a
telescope a number of others were discovered concealed in a
belt of scrub. After crossing a creek they again showed
themselves. One, a fine tall fellow, with an unusually long spear,
seemed very anxious to commence an attack. They came running, but were received with a discharge of rifles, which caused
them to retire. About sundown the party arrived without
further annoyance. A week later, March the 12th, passed
Centre Mount Stuart.

"28th March.—The party camped at Attack Creek.

"31st March.—At Tomkinson's Creek.

"5th April. — Newcastle Water. Here, fifteen natives
appeared, but were given to understand they must not approach
near the camp. Some looking-glasses and handkerchiefs were
given them.

"16th April.—Frew's Water Hole. Started on a course
302°; general course north-west for ten miles; changed to
275'. Came on some fine ponds one and a half miles long,
20 feet wide, and three and a half feet deep, and camped.
Named these ponds after Mr. Jno. Howell, of Adelaide.—17th
April.—Started on a bearing of 10° N. of W.; returned to the
ponds, seeing no chance of finding water on the course.

"19th April.—Returned to Newcastle Waters. Remained to
correct our latitude.

"21st April.—Proceeded six miles to the water discovered
on the 14th; thence changed course to 301° 30', for nine
miles, then to 275'. At two miles camped at the ponds discovered on the 16th; the day very hot.—23rd April.—Howell's

Ponds. Left Keckwick in charge of the party, and took Thring and Frew to explore for water ahead. Course at first 284°; at seven miles changed to 320°; at four and a half miles changed to 40° to find water. At one mile changed W., at one mile changed to N.W., and so on during the day to find an opening in the scrub. After searching in all directions to find water, gave up all hopes of making the Victoria River, the horses having suffered greatly; and as they would not stand two days more without water we returned to the camp.

"*25th April.*—Started with Thring and Frew on a northerly course, 360°; penetrated 22 miles. Grassy plains, after that a thick forest and scrub. At 28 miles, seeing no chance of penetrating, returned two miles to a small plain to tether the horses, but found no water.

"*26th.*—Returned to the camp. Howell's Ponds.

"*27th, 28th,* and *29th.*—Sturt's Plains. Started on an easterly course, following the flight of some birds; again encountered a thick forest. Returned.

"*30th April* and *1st May.*—Howell's Ponds. Started with King and Thring to the water discovered on the 15th named Frew's Water Hole. This is about 20 feet below the level of the plain, surrounded by a conglomerate of iron-stone rock.

"*2nd May.*—Frew's Water Hole. Started course 335°. At ten miles a dense forest scrub; changed 10° east of north at half a mile. Struck a water-shed; followed it north for two miles; at three miles changed to 30° east of north; at three miles and half changed to 330°, and struck some fine ponds of water; at two miles further found shallow ponds, which seem to be the last. Returned to the deeper holes and camped; later in the day was delighted at the sight of a chain of fine water-holes; named these King's Ponds. Following the watercourse found more water.

"*3rd May.*—King's chain of ponds. A start was made, course 350°; at 24 miles changed to 45°; at three miles and a half to north; at two and a half miles camped. At two miles from last night's camp found an easy passage through the forest, but no water. Dense forest.

"*6th May.*—Frew's Water Hole. Some friendly natives seen. They called water nimloo. They were armed with spears about ten feet long, with sharp flint points, and at the other end a piece of bamboo. They pointed to the west as the place where they get bamboo and water. On returning to the camp were nearly surrounded by the bush on fire. It came rolling along in one immense sheet of flame and smoke, destroying everything before it.

"*7th May.*—Howell's Ponds. Another disappointing expedition. Started with two men followed by two others with led horses carrying water-bags on a west course, about a mile beyond where the former trial on this course ended. A mile beyond the forest, in the middle of a small plain, found a small water-hole or opening full of water, which seems to have been dug by the natives; this appears to be the water that the natives pointed to. Named it Nash's Spring.

"*8th May.*—Howell's Ponds. The water-bags in coming the distance of 21 miles have lost about half of the water.

"*9th May.*—Nash's Springs. The men sent back with the horses which brought the water-bags. With two men proceeded on a bearing of 29°. Found gum-trees blaze on one side, with a slice of bark cut off. The marks are very old. At 18 miles another belt of gum-trees blazed. This was never seen before as done by the natives. Changed the course frequently. At four o'clock camped at a place with good feed, but no water.

"*10th* and *11th May.*—Forest. Pack-horse found dead. Attempt to reach the Victoria abandoned.

"*12th May.*—Nash's Springs. Proceeded slowly with the knocked-up horses to depot. Found all right; the natives had again visited them.

"*15th May.*—Started the whole party to Frew's Water Hole.

"*16th May.*—Frew's Water Hole. Started, course 345°, latitude 16° 54′ 7″, for King's Chain of Ponds. Arrived to-day; exceedingly hot.

"*17th May.*—King's Chain of Ponds. King and Thring report, these ponds are lost on a flat surrounded with a thick forest of scrub.

"*19th.*—King's Chain of Ponds. Party remain, as the leader has so constantly to change his course, and the sun remaining obscured, an observation cannot be taken. A lunar one must if possible.

"*20th May.*—King's Chain of Ponds. Started with Thring and King on a southerly course; at little more than a mile struck a small water-course; at two and a half miles came upon some ponds of water, smaller than those at the depot, about three and a half feet deep. The plain is covered with gums; a few white gums around the ponds; plenty of grass. The ponds named Auld's Ponds. Latitude, 16° 28′ 16″.

"21st May.—Auld's Chain of Ponds. Took course north. At three miles found another chain of ponds; named them McGorery's Ponds. At 17 miles found deep ponds without water; country dipping north, changed to that course. Travelled over splendid grass country; more deep holes dry. Latitude, 16° 8′ 39″.

"22nd May.—Fine grass country. Horses suffering for want of water. Returned to McGorery's Ponds; horses drank an enormous quantity of water.

"23rd May.—McGorery's Ponds. Started on course 20° east of north. Followed a small creek, which appeared to be getting larger; occasionally, a little water in it. On both sides of course, ponds which, when full, must hold a large supply; further on, fine holes of water, which will last at least three months. At five miles the creek broader and deeper; taken to be permanent. Course changed to 20° east of north. Ponds named Daly Waters. The creek has many bends; on coming upon it, it is found to have fine reaches of water. Return to depot to bring forward the whole party.

"24th May.—Chain of Ponds, large creek.—25th.—Auld's Ponds depot.

"27th.—Proceeded with party to Daly Waters.

"28th May.—Daly Waters. Thring and King sent round the swamp into which this creek flows; on their return reported a small water-course running 10° east of north; in one mile, another large swamp covered with water.

"29th May.—Started with Thring, Auld, and Frew; ascertained the creek found yesterday to be running about 30° east of north; changed course 20° east of north to examine a flat on which Thring saw from the camps smoke of blacks yesterday. At 18 miles from depot crossed the gum plain; no water; passed on to rising ground, and changed course to 90° east of north. At three miles changed to former bearing of 20 east of north. No water-courses; latitude, 15° 56′ 11″.

"30th May.—N.E. of Blue Grass Swamp. Returned to depot.

"31st May, 1st June, 2nd June.—Daly Waters depot. Started with Thring, Auld and Frew. Course north. All day passed through splendid grassed country. Latitude 15° 50' 20"; day very hot.

"*3rd June.*—Returned to depot.

"*4th June.*—Daly Waters. —*5th June.*— Same. Started with Thring and Auld, taking King and Billiatt with all the water-bags. At sundown camped; no water.

"*6th June.*—King and Billiatt sent back with pack-horses. Started on a course 70° east of north. At a mile and a half came upon a scrubby iron-stone rise, from top of which a good view was obtained of surrounding country, and a more dismal and black prospect never was beheld. At seven miles met with what appeared to be a water-shed, trending to west of north; on following it, found a shallow pool of water; watered horses. At three miles came upon a fine large pond, which terminated in a swamp. This last pond will do for the party.

"*7th June.*—Returned to depot.

"*10th June.*—Camp was struck and start made.

"*11th June.* - Blue Grass Swamp. Start made on course 70° north to cut the chain of ponds named Purdie's Ponds after Doctor Purdie, of Edinburgh. Camped at the largest pond.

"*13th June.*—Started with Thring and Auld, King and Billiatt with pack-horses and water-bags. Course north, following what seemed to be a water-shed. Changed to north-west to follow the water-shed, which gradually became a small creek. At seven miles found water; allowed the horses to drink up what there was in the hole. The cabbage-tree palm was growing here; plenty of grass, but all dried up. The cabbage-trees appear to be all along the banks of the creek. The first time the tree has been met with growing to a height of 15 feet. Latitude 15° 30' 27".

"*14th June.*—River Strangways. Named after the Hon. H. B. Templer Strangways, Commissioner of Crown Lands, South Australia a patron of explorations. King and Billiatt were sent back with the horses to depot. Channel of creek now running north; the bed is very rough and stony. On climbing to the top of a precipice at three miles and a half was delighted to see a large hole of water; in the creek large masses of sandstone; found the water deep and beautifully clear. Further down another large water-hole; decide to return, and send the party to this large water-pond.

"*18th June.*—Gorge, River Strangways. Horses shod; sent Thring and King down the creek. Some of the party succeeded in catching a few fine large fish, some weighing over two pounds ; they were of the perch family. Latitude, 15° 30' 3".

"20th June.—First Camp, River Strangways. A great deal of good timber in the valley. Latitude, 15° 10' 30".

"22nd June.—Rock Camp, River Strangways. The party are now in the country discovered by Mr. Gregory.

"23rd June.—Same. Started following the river. At 12 miles struck a creek from S.W. junction with the Strangways. In the creek found enough water for the night. Latitude, 14° 58' 55".

"24th June.—Mussel Camp, River Strangways. Followed down the bed of the creek ; after breaking into branches, it was found to spread into a large area. Mr. Keckwick found cane in the bed of the river. Found a beautiful new lily. The whole party joined and camped on clear ground, the country splendidly grassed, and seems to be thickly inhabited ; fires to the east and north-east.

"25th June.—River Strangways. Started on course about 70° east of north, following the channel ; at three miles struck a large sheet of water, deep and clear, on which were a number of natives with their lubras and children ; they set up a fearful yelling and ran off. At a mile three men were seen to be following the explorers, who tried to make them understand that a ford across the river was wanted. They pointed further down ; on following the course, decided we had arrived at the junction of the River Roper, tried to cross, but could not do so. It is divided into a number of channels, very deep and full of running waters. The country is still of the same fine description. The journeys have been very short during the last week, on account of weakness from an attack of scurvy. Latitude, 14° 51' 51".

"27th June.—West Roper River. A horse fell into the river, and was impounded by fallen trees across the channel ; had great difficulty in getting him out. Another horse fell into the river in a deep and rapid channel, and was drowned. Latitude, 14° 47' 26".

"28th June.—Roper River. Being short of meat, the drowned horse was skinned and some of the flesh was dried. The water of this river is excellent, the soil of the finest description, the grass dry but abundant. This is certainly the finest country I have seen in Australia.

"29th June.—Roper River. The party are now enjoying fresh meat ; the horse was found to eat remarkably well.

"*30th June.*—Roper River. Although the party had made 20 miles, yet on their various courses they had progressed only ten miles direct. Country level, with a single peak just visible. On arriving at a different branch named it Chambers River. Some natives joined, and Mr. Keckwick gave one of them a fish-hook, which he had stuck in his hat; they wanted more. Latitude, 14° 27′ 24″.

"*1st July.*—Reedy Swamp, River Chambers. This swamp shows a mass of springs. Started, following the course of the river 30° east, passed fine ponds, camped early, as the nature of the ground had tired the horses. Latitude, 14° 41′ 39″.

"*2nd July.*—River Chambers. Started, keeping nearly a north-west course; at one o'clock, the river suddenly turned east. Frew picked up a small live turtle. Latitude, 14° 32′ 30″.

"*3rd July.*—Chambers Creek. Started on a north-west course, reached the top of one of the tributaries of the Chambers. This is apparently the last water-hole in the Chambers, which is in a grassy plain to the east.

"*4th July.*—Last water-hole in the Chambers. Started, course north-west. Crossed a lime- and iron-stone ridge, and on following it about five miles came upon a nice running stream. After crossing several stony ridges entered a broad valley with a creek running through it. At a mile it received a large tributary, with melaleuca and bean trees in it. This creek was first taken to be a tributary of the Alligator or Adelaide River, but after following it for five miles, it seemed to run south. A great disappointment. Camp at the gorge of this creek. Changed course to 325°, and at four miles struck another large branch from the north-east, with plenty of water in it. Named it the Waterhouse, after the naturalist to the expedition. The country of the very best description.

"*7th July.*—Waterhouse River. Struck the river. Plenty of water. The cabbage palm still growing in the creeks. Named a hill after Lieutenant Helpman. Latitude, 14° 9′ 31″.

"*8th July.*—Waterhouse Creek. Stony Rises. Found the creek running too much to the west of the course. Six miles came upon a large and broad creek, with permanent water; this was named the Fanny. In a small tree on this creek the skull of a very young alligator was found by Mr. Auld. Now passing through a basaltic country. Met another large creek having a running stream to the south of west; this was named the Katherine. Latitude, 13° 58′ 30″.

"*9th July.*—The Katherine. Started on a north-west course.

A high hill named Stow. At six miles and a half crossed a creek with water in it. The basaltic country suddenly changed to slate, limestone, and sandstone. Found water at 13 miles; feeling very unwell camped here. About a mile to the west are springs called Keckwick. Latitude, 13° 54′ 12″.

" 10th July.—Keckwick Springs. A large group of springs. Proceeded on a north-west course. Came upon more springs with running water, the ground too boggy to cross it. For the first time the fan palm is seen, growing upwards of 15 feet high; the leaf much resembles a lady's fan set on a long handle. Now the Adelaide River is arrived at. Latitude, 13° 28′ 24″. This branch was named the Mary.

" 12th July.—The Mary-Adelaide River. Started, and at one mile and a half struck a running stream coming from the north. Camped to get the horses shod on the front feet. This day were seen large clumps of bamboo, from 50 to 60 feet high, and six inches in diameter at the butt.

" 14th July.—One of the horses missing, very weak, supposed to have gone away to die. All the horses shod on front feet. Started on a north-west course. Crossed six creeks, the third a large one, called William; all these creeks running at right angles to the course. Latitude, 13° 29′ 25″. Springs named Billiatt.

" 15th July.—Billiatt Springs, named after Billiatt, as a token of approbation of his thoughtful, generous, and unselfish conduct throughout the expedition. Continued the course through a granite and quartz country, splendidly grassed, and timbered; the river was found running to the west, between ranges. In the plain are four or five lines of trees, indicating that the river is divided. At one mile and a half struck the river running north. At two miles and a half camped. The country had been recently burnt; obliged to stop where feed can be found; one channel comes close to the bank, about six yards wide and two feet deep, the main channel in middle of the plain. Latitude, 13° 17′ 22″.

" 16th July.—The Mary-Adelaide River. Started, course north; crossed several creeks. To the north-west and north are a number of stony hills. From twenty to twenty-five miles distant another range, at foot of which is seen a blue strip like water. The banks of the river, when first struck to-day, were high and rocky; crossed some stony hills and broad valleys with splendid alluvial soil. On a course 3° north of west struck a branch of the river. A large number of kangaroos seen, not so large as those found south. A number of new birds seen. Latitude, 13° 7′ 21″.

"17*th July*.—Tide Creek, Adelaide River. Started on a course north-west; at three miles again struck the branch of the river, with bamboos. At five miles changed course to 15° west of north, passed over a rich alluvial plain. Thring reported he had seen high hills to the north-west. Did not desire to follow the course of the river, as Lieutenant Helpman had already described it when he entered it in a boat. The branch creek was named the Priscilla. Latitude, 12° 56′ 54″.

"18*th July*.—Priscilla Creek. Started, course north-west. At three miles changed course to 310°, passed over a grassy plain with grass which must have been high when green, but now is so dry and tender that it breaks off and is carried by the horses before their legs, and the men have to dismount to remove the accumulation. At six miles and a half crossed a deep bamboo creek called Ellen Creek. At fifteen miles came upon the Adelaide River, about eighty yards wide, and so still that it could hardly be seen which way the current flowed. High tide supposed to be at the time. The banks thickly lined with bamboo, very tall and stout, banks very steep and 12 feet down to the water's edge. The range on the opposite side of the river being the highest seen in this new country, it was named the Daly Range, after his Excellency the Governor-in-chief. The marsh is covered with fine grass, in which is growing a new kind of lily, with a large broad heart-shaped leaf, a foot or more across. The blossoms are six inches high, resembling a tulip in shape, and are of a deep brilliant rose colour; the seeds are contained in a vessel resembling the rose of a watering-pot. The marsh had to be rounded, which took a little more than an hour; then got upon some undulating rises, not far from Mount Goyder. Camped on the side of the marsh for the benefit of the horses, that they may get some of the green grass.

"19*th July*.—Lily Marsh, Adelaide River. Started, course 20° east of north. At 14 miles struck a creek with water and camped; about a mile to the eastward came upon a large body of springs which feed the creek; this was named the Anna. Latitude, 12° 39′ 7″.

"20*th* and 21*st July*.—Anna Springs and Creek. Passed a miserable night, unable to sleep on account of mosquitos. Started, course north-west and north. At three miles came upon an extensive fresh-water marsh, too boggy to cross. At seventeen miles came upon a thick clump of trees with beautiful palms growing amongst them. At a mile was again stopped by a continuation of the large marsh; it was to be seen to the south-west, north-east, and south-east. Camped on a point of rising ground running into it. Latitude, 12° 28′ 19″.

"22nd July.—Fresh Water Marsh. Thring found sound ground and succeeded in reaching the banks of the river; the breadth of it here is one hundred yards, very deep, and running with some velocity; the water quite fresh. Thring, King, and Frew, mounted on the strongest horses, found the banks not available to travel on. This will give two days' longer journey before the sea-shore can be reached. No natives seen since leaving the Roper. On this camp the party found numerous fish bones and mussel and turtle shells. A curious frame was here standing, eight feet high, supposed to be designed and used to smoke-dry the dead bodies of the tribe.

"23rd July.—Fresh Water Marsh. Course 22° east of south, one mile round the marsh, thence one mile south-east, thence east for six miles, then struck a large creek, deep and long reaches in it, named Thring's Creek; thence east one mile and a half, thence north for nine miles; struck the marsh; have travelled twelve miles to endeavour to round the marsh, but have not succeeded. Camped where the Thring spreads out over a portion of the marsh.

"24th July.—Thring's Creek; course north to strike the sea-shore; at eight miles and a half came to a broad valley, rather more than a quarter of a mile wide, crossed the valley and entered the scrub from the valley; could hear the wash of the sea; did not tell any of the party, except Thring and Auld, how near they were to the salt water. On crossing the valley, entered the scrub, which was found matted with vines, and a passage had to be cut through, when the horses were stopped. Advanced a few yards on the beach, and was gratified and delighted to behold the water of the Indian Ocean in Van Diemen's Gulf. Thring, who had ridden in advance, called out, 'The sea,' much to the astonishment of the party. They gave three loud hearty cheers. They found the beach covered with a soft blue mud, being ebb tide. The horses were kept where they were halted. Half the party came on the beach at a time." Mr. Stuart adds: "I dipped my feet and washed my face in the sea, as I had promised the late Governor, Sir Richard

McDonnell, I would do if I reached it. The sand has nearly covered all the shells. A few were collected." The party returned to the valley, when the initials of Mr. Stuart were cut on a large tree, J. M'D. S. He did not intend to put up his flag until he arrived at the mouth of the Adelaide. So proceeded west, to endeavour to work his way among impenetrable swamps, and to cross the oozy channels of creeks, until he came to a small flat covered with beautiful green grass, kept moist by a running creek of fresh water; here a halt was made, to give the horses the benefit of it. Mr. Stuart took counsel with himself, and after considering his heavy responsibilities, with the lives of his faithful and long-enduring men depending on his care and judgment, and on Thring's return with a most discouraging account of the line necessary to take to reach the mouth of the River Adelaide, he decided not to attempt to do so. Mr. Stuart gives his decision as to what is left for him to do, as follows : " The great object of the expedition is now attained, and the mouth of the river is well known. I do not think it advisable to waste the remaining strength of my horses in forcing them through (to the river's mouth). They have still a very long and fatiguing journey in crossing the continent to Adelaide, and my health is so bad that I am hardly able to bear a long day's ride. I shall, therefore, cross this creek, and see if I can get along by the sea-beach or close to it." (He might also have added the deficiency in stock of stores, no vessel having been sent to meet him with a fresh supply of medical comforts, &c.)

" To cross the creek, logs and a quantity of grass were thrown in, but even with this improvement of the crossing, one horse was nearly lost, and got out after much loss of time ; several others were bogged. The party then proceeded on a west-north-west course, over a firm soil of alluvial black earth. At two miles came upon another part of the beach. Again tried beach and found it to be of the same nature as first seen." Mr. Stuart then ordered one of the tallest trees near the verge to have all the lower branches cut off, and a space cleared around the tree, and the Union Jack was then nailed to an upper limb, with his name sewn in the middle, and the party gave three cheers. Mr. Keckwick addressed Mr. Stuart in a few words on the successful work done, and congratulated him on his achievement. Mr. Waterhouse also spoke, and concluded with calling for three cheers for the Queen and three for the

Prince of Wales. At one foot south from the foot of the tree an air-tight tin case was buried, about eight inches below the surface, in which was a paper with the following words: "South Australian Great Northern Exploring Expedition. The exploring party, under the command of John McDouall Stuart, arrived at this spot on the 25th day of July, 1862, having crossed the entire continent of Australia from the Southern to the Indian Ocean, passing through the centre. They left the city of Adelaide on the 26th day of October, 1861, and the most northern station of the colony on the 21st day of January, 1862. To commemorate this happy event they have raised this flag bearing his name. All well. God save the Queen." Here followed the signatures of myself and party.

Mr. Stuart adds: "As this bay has not been named, I have taken this opportunity of naming it Chambers Bay, in honour of Miss Chambers, who kindly presented me with the flag which I have planted this day, and I hope this may be the first sign of the dawn of approaching civilization. Exactly this day nine months the party left North Adelaide. Before leaving, between the hours of eleven and twelve o'clock, they had lunch at Mr. Chambers' house. John Bentham Neales, Esq., being present, proposed success to me, and wished I might plant the flag on the north-west coast. At the same hour of the day, nine months after, the flag was raised on the shores of Chambers Bay, Van Diemen's Gulf. On the bark of the tree on which the flag is placed, is cut, 'Dig one foot.—S.'

"We then bade farewell to the Indian Ocean, and returned to Charles' Creek, where we had again great difficulty in getting the horses across, but it was at last accomplished without accident. We have passed numerous and recent tracks of natives to-day; they are still burning the country at some distance from the coast. Wind, south-east. Latitude, 12° 14′ 50″."

Mr. Stuart continues his diary with the following suitable remarks:—"Thus have I, through the instrumentality of Divine Providence, been led to accomplish the great object of the expedition, and to take the whole party back safely as witnesses to the fact, through one of the finest countries man could wish to behold, good to the coast, and with a stream of running water within half-a-mile of the sea. From Newcastle Water the horses have been only one night without water, and then got it within the next day." He continued with the following remarks:—"If this country is settled, it will become one of the finest colonies under the Crown. What a splendid country for the growth of cotton, and suitable for any and every tropical production!"

Mr. Stuart's diary of the return journey continues as follows:—

"*Saturday, 26th July*, 1862.—Charles' Creek, Chambers Bay, Van Diemen's Gulf. This day I commence my return, and feel perfectly satisfied in my own mind that I have done everything in my power to obtain as extensive a knowledge of the country as the strength of my party will allow me. I could have made the mouth of the river, but, perhaps, at the expense of losing many of the horses, thus increasing the difficulties of the return journey. Many of them are so poor and weak that they have not been able for some time to carry anything like a load, and I have been compelled to make the $\bar{C}$ horses (Chambers' brand) stand the brunt of the work of the expedition. As yet not one of them has failed; they have all done their work in excellent style. The sea has been reached, which was the great object of the expedition, and a practicable route found through a splendid country from Newcastle Waters to it, abounding, for a great part of the way, in running streams well stocked with fish; and this has been accomplished at a season of the year during which we have not had one drop of rain. Started, following my tracks back. Passed my former camp on the Thring, went on and crossed it. Proceeded on my east course to the west, about one mile and a-half, to some small, green, marshy plains of black alluvial soil, with a spring in the centre, covered with fine grass. Camped. Wind, south; latitude, 12° 30′ 21″."

The return journey over the same ground is not of sufficient interest to relate *in extenso*.

The next entry of any interest is :—

"*5th December*, 1862.—Chambers Creek. I shall require to rest my horses here to-day. I was in great hopes that when I reached this place, I should have been again able to have ridden on horseback; but the waters of the spring country through which I have just passed have reduced me nearly to my former state of weakness, and I shall be compelled to continue in the ambulance a little longer. I feel a little better this morning—I suppose, in consequence of drinking fresh water. Hot wind from the north. Towards evening a heavy thunderstorm coming from the westward.

"*6th December*, 1862.—Chambers Creek. Started at eight o'clock with the ambulance, towards Termination Hill. After crossing numerous sand-hills, we frequently found rain-water. Towards sundown, arrived at the south side of Porter Hill.

"*7th December.*—Porter's Hill. Mounted, and started at 6 A.M. I find that I can endure the motion of the horse better than I expected; but about mid-day began to feel it very much. Camped at Termination Hill.

"*8th December.*—Termination Hill. During the night experienced a heavy thunderstorm and shower from the south-east. Started at 6 A.M., and arrived at Mr. Glen's station at sundown, quite done up. Received a hearty welcome. Encountered a heavy storm of thunder and lightning, a few miles from the station.

"*9th December.*—Mr. Glen's station. Proceeded to Mount Stuart station, where I had the pleasure of meeting Mr. John Chambers, who received me with great kindness.

"*10th December.*—Mount Stuart Station. Accompanied by Mr. Chambers, proceeded to Moolooloo, and arrived there in the afternoon completely tired and exhausted from riding in the saddle. Day, hot; wind, east. In conclusion, I beg to say, that I believe this country (*i.e.*, from the Roper to the Adelaide, and thence to the shore of the Gulf), to be well adapted for the settlement of a European population, the climate being in every respect suitable, and the surrounding country of excellent quality and of great extent. Timber, stringy-bark, iron-bark, gum, &c., with bamboo fifty to sixty feet high on the banks of the river, is abundant, and at convenient distances. The country is intersected by numerous springs and watercourses in every direction. In my journey across, I was not fortunate in meeting with thunder showers or heavy rains; but, with the exception of two nights, I was never without a sufficient supply of water. This will show the permanency of the different waters. . . . .
My party have conducted themselves throughout this long and trying journey to my entire satisfaction; and I may particularly mention Messrs. Keckwick and Thring, who had been with me on my former expedition. During my severe illness, every attention and sympathy were shown to me by every one in the party; and I herewith beg to record to them my sincere thanks. I may here mention that the accident which occurred to me at

the starting of the expedition from Adelaide has rendered my right hand almost useless for life."

The journal concludes with the following letter:—

"*To the* HON. H. B. T. STRANGWAYS, *Commissioner of Crown Lands and Immigration.*

"ADELAIDE, *December* 18*th*, 1862.

"SIR,—For the information of His Excellency the Governor-in-chief, I have the honour to report to you my return to Adelaide, after an absence of twelve months and thirteen days; and I herewith beg to hand you my chart and journals of the expedition from which I have just returned.

"To you, sir, and the Government, my special thanks are due for the liberal manner in which the supplies were voted, and for the kind and ready assistance I at all times experienced. Also to George Hamilton, Esq., Chief Inspector of Police, for the efficient manner in which my party were fitted out. The original promoters of my various expeditions, Messrs. James and John Chambers, have always shown the most lively interest in my success, to which they have cheerfully contributed."

In the next chapter will be introduced, though not in chronological order—but as explaining the peculiar difficulties Mr. Stuart met with at the finish of his work—an account of Mr. McKinlay's extraordinary escape with his exploring party from the East Alligator River on a float or raft formed of poles lashed together with strips of horse-hide, and covered with horse-hides and canvas. The author is favoured with this account by Mr. R. H. Edmunds, who was surveyor and second in command.

CHAPTER X.

NORTHERN TERRITORY.

THE acquisition of the northern territory by cession from the Crown to South Australia in 1862 was by some of the colonists deemed an impolitic act. The addition of so large a tract of country to a colony already very extensive, and at the time only partially occupied, was certainly a great increase of liability to such a comparatively small population. The successful termination of Mr. Stuart's explorations had, however, induced the Government, with the sanction of a considerable portion of the colonists, to apply to the Home Government for the cession, and as no opposing interests intervened the grant was made.

The quantity of land annexed amounted to over 300,000,000 acres, the northern boundary of which was the Indian Ocean, the southern the original boundary of the acquiring province, the eastern the western line of Queensland, and the western the ocean and the West Australian boundary line.

One of the first steps by the Government of South Australia was to offer a considerable quantity of land for sale in the north-western portion of the territory. The sale took place in Adelaide in March, 1864 (*i.e.*, before any survey was made), in order to raise funds to cover the cost of survey and for other requirements.

A number of land grants were purchased, including some for English speculators. Priority of choice was arranged to be by lot, and each purchaser of a country section was to receive a town allotment. The first town was to be named Palmerston, and to be at a port. The survey was to be completed before the end of five years from the date of sale.

The next grave matter was to arrange the appointment of a Government Resident and staff of officers. Lieutenant-Colonel Boyle Travers Finniss received the appointment of Resident, he having had great experience in occupying high public offices in South Australia. The other officers appointed were J. F. Manton, surveyor, and second in command; F. E. Goldsmith, surgeon, and Protector of Aborigines; E. Ward, clerk and accountant; S. King, storekeeper; J. Davis, assistant storekeeper and postmaster; Pearson, Wadham, and Hamilton, surveyors; Watson and Bennett, draughtsmen; also a strong party of labourers and seamen. The ship *Henry Ellis* was chartered to convey the expedition to the Northern Territory, and started from Port Adelaide in April, 1864.

The first camp was fixed on the 1st of July, 1864, when the party were landed at Adam Bay. It was a most unfortunate circumstance that on the voyage round, differences occurred between the chief and his officers, which continued after landing. Mr. Finniss had lost all control over the party. He had decided to fix on Escape Cliffs as the first settlement, against the opinions and remonstrances of his officers.

The blacks in the neighbourhood of Escape Cliffs were numerous and hostile, and after robbing the stores, made an attack on the party, which resulted in Mr. Pearson being severely wounded, and one of the natives being killed. After this affray, Mr. Finniss sent a despatch by the *Henry Ellis*, to the Government in Adelaide, containing a disheartening account of the affray with the natives, and urging on the Government the necessity of sending a relief party at once. The survey hung fire through the disorganizations of the party, some of whom purchased a boat, which they named the *Forlorn Hope*, and made sail for Adelaide, and arrived safely at Champion Bay, Western Australia, a distance of 1,600 miles, and thence sailed for Adelaide. These parties (one of them Mr. J. P. Stow, who had gone as agent for purchasers), laid their complaints against Mr. Finniss, the Government Resident, before the Government, and a Board of Enquiry was appointed to examine into the matter. It must not be omitted in the short account of this miserable beginning of such an important work that the report of the Board of Enquiry says, "although the actions of the Resident did not show he had acted with proper tact or temper, that amongst the party he had to work with were many individuals unsuitable for the work they had gone to perform, and that some of the witnesses in their evidence and by their demeanour had shown a bias which rendered their evidence against Mr. Finniss unreliable."

The steamer *South Australian* was despatched on the 29th October, 1864, from Port Adelaide with a relief party, consisting of three officers and forty men, under the charge of Mr. R. H. Edmunds. Upon the arrival of this contingent, the survey of a township at Escape Cliffs, and another at the Narrows, was commenced. These places had been condemned by Mr. Jefferson P. Stow and others, and the Government was finally prevailed upon to suspend operations until the country had been further explored. The late Mr. John McKinlay with a properly equipped party was despatched from Adelaide for this purpose, and arrived by the *Ellen Lewis* early in November, 1865. At the same time, Mr. Finniss was recalled, and the settlement was placed under the charge of Mr. Manton. Mr. McKinlay had arrived too late in the season, and even then more valuable time was wasted before a start was made.

On January 14th, 1866, the exploring party, consisting of John McKinlay in command, R. H. Edmunds, second as navigator and surveyor, 12 men, 45 horses, and a few sheep, finally left Escape Cliffs and camped that night at the Narrows, where they were detained three days by heavy thunderstorms, when with the assistance of the officers and crew of *H.M.S. Beatrice* the river was crossed. McKinlay proceeded up the river in a large boat with the stores, the remainder of the party with the horses and sheep following by land, on the west side of the river. On the 19th a man (Thomas Crisp) was sent back after two dogs which had returned to the last camp, and he lost his way. The country was searched, and Crisp's horse, blankets, and gun were found, but no trace of the man himself, until the 31st January, when the search party decided to return, as their provisions were exhausted; it was also considered that the man had either died of starvation or had been killed by the blacks.

Just before sunset, and when everything had been prepared for a start by daylight next morning, Crisp appeared over some cliffs above the camp. He was in a most deplorable state, having been eight days without food, and his mind was so unhinged that he could not recognise his companions, and would have escaped from them if he could.

On the 2nd February the land party reached the fork of the Adelaide River, where the boat with the stores was awaiting them (latitude, 12° 54′ 52″ S.; longitude, 131° 17′ E.). On the 4th the boat left on its return journey, about 120 miles distant. On the 5th a fair start was made about 3 P.M. Owing to a heavy thunderstorm, and the soft nature of the ground, only about six miles were made. After camping on the 7th, McKinlay went on ahead to test the country, and by some means missed the camp; he did not return until early next morning wet through.

On the 12th the first horse died; a large stream was met with, which was taken to be the Adelaide of Stuart, who never saw the Adelaide proper. After following this river up for some distance, a large tributary also was met; owing to the slippery and rotten state of its banks, only a few of the party were able to cross; the remainder had to follow it up for some miles before another crossing could be found. At dark camp was pitched on an extensive wooded flat, between the tributary and the river; here heavy tropical rains prevented further progress. On the 14th a fresh start was made, the ground was so soft and treacherous, that only three miles were made up to 10 P.M., the horses getting continually bogged. Just before dark a gravelly hill was seen on the opposite side of a fork of this branch, but the loaded horses could not approach within a hundred yards, and the packs had to be unloaded and carried over.

Gaining this hill was a providential escape, as the rain continued, and the flat became a sea of water, and further progress was here stopped for six weeks. Two trees were marked, one thus " JK FEB. 14 TO MAR. 29—DIG ", and the other " R.H.E. 1866 ." The word "dig" indicated that a bottle had been buried containing information as to the position, stay, and contemplated route of the party, and the hand pointed to the spot. This creek was named Escape Creek. The provisions were much damaged, and the store of flour was reduced to 53 lbs. Here also another horse died, he had been badly bogged; as the stores were getting short he was eaten. The continued wet weather and soft country had so reduced the horses, that they were frequently knocking up, although there was plenty of feed. About the middle of April the last sheep was killed. At this time the flour and other stores ran out, and before this each man had only a piece of cake for the day, about as large as a coffee biscuit. Nothing was left now for food but the horses, and of these the weak and knocking up ones were selected for killing, and while the meat was being jerked (dried in long strips in the sun), the party managed to live on the head, blood, and liver, which generally brought on diarrhœa. The jerked meat was served out very sparingly to the cook twice a day, and after being divided as fairly as possible lots were cast for each plate. Occasionally additions were made to the larder in the shape of a few kites, lizards, or a snake or two, all of which went into the pot. On May 2nd the camp narrowly escaped being burnt down. Day by day the difficulties increased, and by the 31st May, 19 horses had been lost by poison, besides those which, being unable to travel, had been killed for food. Every one had an intense longing for salt and fat, and had become very weak. Three of the men through weakness were unable to walk any distance, and most were without shoes, and with clothes sadly torn. At this camp (31st May) the country appeared to get more difficult than ever, being part of that peculiar line of precipitous sandstone hills, or rather walls, which Leichardt and Stuart, although widely apart, had such difficulty in descending. McKinlay and two men endeavoured to scramble up one of these perpendicular cliffs to obtain a view of the country ahead, and returned so disheartened, that he suggested to give up his charge, and let each man do the best he could for himself, but he was after strong remonstrance dissuaded from doing so. That night several schemes were discussed by the officers, one of which was to abandon everything, kill the remaining horses and jerk the meat, and try to reach Cape Hawkesbury, where the *Beatrice* was supposed to be waiting with a supply of provisions; but this was decided to be impracticable, as some of the men were unable to walk through weakness. McKinlay eventually took some of the strongest men and horses, and pushed on ahead to find a way out of the difficulties of a broken and precipitous country on the one side, and the boggy flats on the other. After an absence of two days he returned with the news that he had found a large river with steep muddy banks which no horse could cross, and that he intended to get to this river and make a raft and attempt to reach the coast. Three days afterwards the whole party moved on and reached the river, which McKinlay named the Alexandria, but it proved to be the East Alligator. Upon the arrival of the party the raft scheme was given up, being opposed by Mr. Edmunds, and after much discussion it was decided to make a kind of punt or boat, with saplings which were growing on the banks, to be covered with horsehides sewn together, and outside these the canvas of the tents. The framework before being covered had the appearance of a large crate 20 feet long and 8 feet broad. The hides and canvas were lashed with strips of horse-hide to the top rails and strained tight. The floor was made of saplings, the oars of small saplings with short boards (sides of pack saddles) pegged on the ends for blades, and another small sapling was stepped as a mast, a sail being constructed out of a calico tent. The only tools available were two chisels, which had been brought for the purpose of marking trees on the route, a small saw, an axe, and some horse-shoe nails.

Shortly after arrival at this camp (June 7th) large parties of natives made their appearance and preserved friendly relations until the 26th, when they showed signs of active hostility, setting fire to the country and making an attack on the explorers through the smoke. A few shots fired over their heads made them alter their tactics, and they retired to the dense scrub behind the camp, and although at only a short distance could not be seen, but their horrible yells were plain enough. Had they then made a rush they would have exterminated the whole of the worn-out explorers, but a well-directed volley in the neighbourhood of their yells effectually settled the affair. Early on the morning of the 29th the punt was successfully launched, and the voyage commenced. Before leaving, two trees were marked, on the edge of the bank, so as to be plainly visible from the water. One bore this inscription :—

JVK

41

MADE PUNT OF
HORSE HIDES &
TENT & START?
DOWN RIVER
7 TO 29 JUNE
DIG IN TRACK
FOR BOTTLE
8 FEET S.W.
R.H.E.

and the other

A NATIVES TREACHEROUS

The bottle contained a short account of the journey, addressed to the Government, by Mr. McKinlay, and a farewell letter to his wife. The few horses that were left had been killed, and the meat jerked, and this formed the sole provision for the voyage. No means were available for cooking on board.

Two water-bags were made out of the canvas of the pack-saddles, and had to be filled at low-water, the water being very brackish at high-water, even at the head of the river; the tide at the camp rose about seven feet, and at the mouth the rise and fall was found to be about eighteen. All the luggage that was not actually necessary in the punt was abandoned, the last act being the shooting of the two dogs, survivors of the seven that had left Escape Cliffs. The morning of the start was very fine, with a light breeze down stream. The men were divided into two watches of an hour each, the oars were manned, and a final adieu bidden to the head of the East Alligator. Mr. Edmunds, at the steer oar, made a survey of the river, as the voyage proceeded.

A sharp look-out had to be kept for crocodiles; two or three of them generally followed in the wake of the punt, and when they approached too close a shot or two soon increased their distance. As the flood tide made, the boat had to be brought up, as both flood and ebb stream ran from two to three knots an hour. During these stoppages attempts were made to find fresh water, the bags leaked very much, and all the men suffered considerably from thirst, pulling as they were under a tropical sun. It was also found that there were other dangers besides crocodiles, in the shape of rocks, sand-banks, and strong eddies, and there were several narrow escapes of knocking a hole in the bottom of the punt. In one place, with the sun glistening on the water right ahead, some large white birds were seen standing on a large shoal, not showing above water, in the middle of the river—there about a mile wide. As the punt had to be pulled something over the tide to give her steerage way it was approaching the danger at a rate of about five miles an hour, and it was impossible to tell which way to steer. The lead (a piece of iron tied to a fishing-line) was cast and the water found to be shoaling rapidly; some of the men had therefore to jump overboard to arrest the punt's progress. The ground, however, was full of holes and quicksands, and in the strong tide all efforts were useless. Another danger was now seen—rocks in the direction in which the punt was drifting, so the oars were taken in and a dash made for the difficulty, and fortunately the punt at once slid into deep water.

Just before dark good banks were seen, and as the timber indicated good water the punt was brought up for the night; a fresh-water swamp was fortunately close at hand, so the quart pots were soon filled, and with a little dried horseflesh a supper was made. An anchor watch was set with instructions to make as much noise as possible, in order to keep off the crocodiles, while the remainder tried to sleep with one exception, Mr. Edmunds, who remained awake to get some observations of the stars so as to fix the position. Before daylight next morning every one was astir, and an air-bed which had been brought to assist in crossing unfordable rivers, but which had not been required, was filled with fresh water and placed on board. More water and dried horse for breakfast, and the party set sail with a fair breeze, down a beautiful broad reach, which widened as it went for miles ahead, evidently approaching the sea. Just below the last camp the river was nearly a mile in width, about 3 P.M. The point at the mouth of the river, here about five miles broad, was rounded, and named Point

Farewell. And when fairly out at sea a course was shaped between Field Island and the mouth of the South Alligator, which was reached at 1 A.M. the following morning close in with the land; here the punt came within the influence of a strong ebb-tide, and had to be brought up until daylight; a canvas pack-bag filled with the horseshoes and the ironwork of the pack saddles, with a tether rope, making an excellent anchor. At the first peep of day the anchor was hoisted; during the morning a stiff breeze and a heavy sea, the rip of the South Alligator (the mouth of which is about three miles wide), were encountered, so sail was set and the oars double banked until the wind steadied in the afternoon, and the punt ran into smoother water. It was thought impossible on board that such a frail craft could live in such heavy seas as had been met with, and various exclamations were made as each successive wave struck the punt, such as, "My God! another sea like that will put an end to us." The men, however, worked well; it was a struggle for dear life, and they knew it and stuck manfully to the oars, although well-nigh exhausted. There was now no more rest, each watch took its turn of an hour, day and night, Mr. Edmunds generally at the steer-oar. On the 3rd July a narrow escape from foundering was experienced; a heavy breeze sprang up, and the punt was blown far out of its course to sea. Sail was taken in and the oars double-banked, and for four hours the unfortunates were buffeting with wind and sea, without being able to make any progress. On the afternoon of the 4th, in spite of all efforts to avoid it, the punt was carried over a sunken reef by a strong current, but providentially slipped into deep water, all expecting shipwreck momentarily. To add to the miseries of their position, one of the best men was seized with violent pains, and rendered unable to assist in the work. The water in the air-bed had become so impregnated with the taste of the vulcanized india-rubber that it was all but impossible to take more than enough to wet the tongue and lips, though suffering from intolerable thirst. At the same time the hides slowly rotting sent up such a horrible stench that it was impossible to keep the head below the gunwale. Sharks and sawfish became very numerous, especially during the night, and on several occasions knocked some of the men off their thwarts by running foul of their oars —had they run foul of the frail craft they would have sunk it. By sundown of the 4th, a point within two or three miles of

Cape Hotham was reached, and here the tide ran so strong that the punt was obliged to be brought up again. Bearings having been taken of the gaps in the reef stretching out from the Cape for about two or three miles, a start was made in the dark, and by the aid of frequent soundings the Cape was doubled about midnight, and at nine in the morning Mr. Edmunds was able to point out the blue outline of Escape Cliffs to his suffering companions.

When within three miles of the cliffs, and approaching land, some natives were seen fishing, three of whom put off to the punt in a canoe. For some time they were too suspicious to come alongside, but were eventually persuaded to do so, and it was found that they were camping at the settlement. Mr. McKinlay tore a leaf from his note-book, and prevailed upon them to carry it to the people at the cliffs. The natives, however, did not deliver it as requested, but joined a mob of their tribe already there; they had taken the voyagers for enemies. The hubbub they created brought out some of the officers of the party at the cliffs, who seeing the letter in their possession, soon found out its contents, which ran thus— "Pioneer. Will arrive in an hour—please have dinner ready." There being no signature attached, this missive greatly puzzled the readers, who never dreamed of the exploring party returning in that way, and thought it came from the crew of some shipwrecked vessel. The position of the punt was completely hidden from those at the cliffs by a dense fringe of mangroves, until within a few yards of the cliffs. Rounding this fringe, the cliffs and the beach were seen to be lined with whites and blacks, the latter with their spears poised ready for a fray, if necessary. The voyagers were soon recognised, and their friends waded out to greet them, seizing hold of them and carrying them ashore; some of the men were so overcome with joy at finding themselves once more amongst their friends that they could not speak. The punt could not have lived many hours longer; directly it touched the beach the covering literally fell to pieces, and the water flowed in and out. Every attention was paid to the unfortunates by Dr. Goldsmith, who first administered a glass of porter to each man. With the exception of the time they lay at Cape Hotham, Mr. Edmunds had not rested for three days and nights. A meal was soon prepared—a kid killed, and some chops fried—but, strange to say, very little satisfied the

B B

starved explorers, probably owing to the excitement. For a week great pain was experienced by all after eating, and their bodies and limbs swelled very much.

On the 11th July, the barque *Ellen Lewis* arrived from Port Adelaide with stores, mails, &c., the only communication with head-quarters for eight months.

After the officers and men had somewhat recovered from the wretched state in which they landed at Escape Cliffs, Mr. McKinlay decided to form a boat party to explore the coasts as far as Anson Bay. He was again accompanied by Mr. R. H. Edmunds, and left the Cliffs on the 27th July at sundown, and steered direct to Anson Bay, arrived and anchored on the 30th, about a mile off the Daly River at 7 P.M. The mouth of the river is divided by an island about two miles long. The next day after clearing the island the boats entered a fine reach fully two miles wide—met a strong ebb running at about four knots. The voyage was continued up the river until the 3rd August about 36 miles—the banks generally low. Some fine deep reaches were passed through; high land was seen in the distance, on the right hand a large dome-shaped hill was prominent. On the banks 30 feet high were growing trees showing flood marks 20 feet high. On the 4th the small boat was taken on until stopped by fallen timber at the foot of a high range of hills. The boat party then returned to the anchorage, and here a slight difficulty occurred with the natives. On the 5th the boats headed down stream. Mr. Edmunds made a survey of the river, marking dangers discovered.

This was the first party of Europeans which had entered the Daly River. On the 7th the mouth was cleared, and a course for the Cliff Head was made. These cliffs run from 60 to 70 feet high, with a fine sandy beach beneath. On the 8th a a course was shaped for Channel Point, from which the course was Foggey Bay where anchors were dropped one and a-half miles from Blaze Point, in five fathoms. On the 9th the boats passed between a reef and Quail Island over a peculiar tide race, the least sounding being three-and-a-half fathoms. On the 10th, a landing was effected at Port Darwin under Point Emery. On the 11th August a course was taken through the inner channel, and at 8 P.M. the Beatrice was discovered at anchor, and at once boarded. The boat party were most kindly received by the officers. The Beatrice had waited seventy days at the Liverpool River for Mr. McKinlay's land party, until all provisions had been used, and all rockets, ammunition, etc., expended in the hope of attracting their attention, had they been successful in reaching the appointed neighbourhood. The Beatrice had then steered for Adam Bay for further supplies, and on returning to Mount Morris Bay, obtained some scanty information to the effect that a tribe had attacked the exploring party, when several of the blacks had been killed, that the whites then went to an island to build a ship, and then had gone somewhere. The Beatrice then returned to the settlement, and heard the good news that McKinlay and his party had returned, and of the voyage they had made, which could scarcely be credited as having been accomplished in the punt, the frame of which they saw on the beach, and of which Lieutenant Gay took a photograph. On the 14th August, the Beatrice sailed for Port Adelaide *viâ* Kolpang. On board were Mr. Jno. McKinlay, R. H. Edmunds, Glen, and Mayo, and arrived on the 26th September, 1866. The remainder of the party were recalled by the Government.

The reduced condition of these explorers when they arrived after their punt voyage can be fully endorsed by the author from the appearance on landing in Adelaide of Mr. Edmunds, even after the nursing and rest he had enjoyed between landing at Escape Cliffs on the 5th July, and his arrival in Adelaide on the 26th September, say three months, and Mr. Edmunds had apparently suffered less than any man of the party.

An account of the first abortive attempt at settlement having been introduced here, the history of the Northern Territory may be further continued. As the term of five years, contained in the conditions of sale of Northern Territory lands, had nearly expired, Mr. G. W. Goyder, Surveyor-General, was sent by the Government in his official capacity to the Northern Territory with a competent and thoroughly equipped party, to complete the survey, to enable them to carry out the contract made with the purchasers. Captain Cadell was, about the same time, sent to the Gulf of Carpentaria to report on the advantages offered there, and on his return made a most flattering report of his investigations.

Bearing in mind the serious objections which had been raised against Escape Cliffs as a site for the principal city of the territory, the Government instructed Mr. Goyder to fix, if possible, on a better position, and, after mature consideration, his choice fell on Port Darwin, which has a splendid harbour with deep water close in; and here the city of Palmerston, which at some time in the future will be the terminus of a Grand Trans-Continental Railway, was soon laid out. Through the unwearied personal exertions of Mr. Goyder, assisted by the cordial co-operation of his efficient staff, the work of surveying the country lands was quickly accomplished, and the Government put in a position to fulfil their agreements with the original purchasers of land orders. The English purchasers, who had become impatient at the delays in the survey, had demanded a return of their money, with interest, with which demand the South Australian Government did not comply, but gave each purchaser an additional quantity of land as compensation. Many colonists considered, before the despatch of Mr. Goyder, that the best policy would be for the Government to have submitted to the first loss, and complied with the demands of the land speculators, but at this time very different opinions prevail, as will be seen in the relation of the present condition of that portion of our great colony, it will not long be as it was at first called, a "white elephant," but a most valuable addition. The present Minister of Education, the Hon. J. L. Parsons, M.P., in whose department the Northern Territory is included, has kindly favoured me with returns containing the latest information respecting the condition and prospects of the Northern Territory, in which he exhibits much interest. From these returns it appears that the whole of the land set apart in the Northern Territory for pastoral purposes has been applied for. Extensive blocks have also been chosen for sugar, coffee, and other tropical productions, some of which have been partly occupied and planted.

From 14th August, 1880, to 31st December, 1882, the amount of gold exported reached 61,990 ounces, of the value of £219,200, and a considerable quantity, in all probability, has evaded the export duty. It is here necessary to add one more of the calamities which so often occur in opening up new colonies to relieve the mother country, and carry on the spread of civilisation. It must first be explained that for some years all the prisoners committed for trial in the territory had to be conveyed to the courts in Adelaide, where civil cases had also to be tried, and prisoners and witnesses to be sent. To avoid this expensive administration of law and justice, the

Government determined to hold a circuit court at Palmerston, to be presided over by one of the judges of the Supreme Court, and Mr. Justice Wearing, third judge, with the necessary officers, was sent for that purpose. The voyage up, in the steamer *Gothenberg*, was made in safety, the court business despatched, and the party embarked once more on board the same steamer for the return voyage. Sad to relate the vessel ran on a reef near the coast of Queensland, and became a a total wreck. The greater part of her passengers and crew perished, over a hundred persons, men, women, and children, being swept off the wreck. Amongst these were Judge Wearing, his associate, Mr. Pelham, Mr. Whitby, Acting Crown Prosecutor, the Honourable Thos. Reynolds, long a leading politician in Adelaide, and Mrs. Reynolds, with the captain and his chief officers. No previous calamity in the history of South Australia had produced such an overwhelming panic of grief as this. On the public arousing from their intense sorrow, the question quickly presented itself, what could be done to relieve those unfortunates who had been left widows and fatherless, and a sum of between nine and ten thousand pounds was at once raised and distribubted amongst them. The Parliament took care of the families of those who died in its service, and made liberal provision for them.

The law has now been altered, so that all offences not punishable with death are tried by a local court at Palmerston. Port Darwin is in latitude 12° 23′ 30″ south; longitude, 130° 52′ east. The harbour contains many miles of water, from four to fifteen fathoms in depth. The chart shows numerous branches, the principal one running to Southport, 24 miles from Palmerston, the chief inland depôt for the gold fields.

In 1869 Captain Douglas was appointed Government Resident; he retired in May, 1874. W. Price, Esq., has for many years held the post of Government Resident, and has performed his arduous duties in a most commendable manner.

Mr. J. G. Little, of the Telegraph Department, describes the climate as follows:—" The year has two climatic divisions, consisting of the wet season from October to April, and dry from May to September; these changes can be relied on almost to a day. With regard to the suitability of the country for European labour, after four years' experience there is nothing to prevent a moderate day's work being done; there is an almost entire absence of those enervating influences which prostrate the European labourer in other tropical countries; the eight hour system being usually adopted. The country is free from cholera and other scourges of hot countries. Intermittent fever is prevalent at times, especially in low-lying localities, or immediately after the wet season; but this complaint is not dangerous in itself, and can often be prevented by a moderate and judicious use of medicine, and a little bodily exercise."

The following account of the Roper River has been communicated by Captain Sweet:—" The River Roper debouches on the west side of the Gulf of Carpentaria, in latitude 14° 45' south, longitude 135° 28' 15" east, with a somewhat difficult entrance, as it has many sand-banks for a distance of about seven miles; though there is a very good channel if buoyed, carrying fifteen feet of water right into the river, when it deepens to thirty-four feet, and gradually decreases as you proceed up, varying from forty-five to eleven feet according to the width or narrowness of the reaches. The writer took the *Omeo* and *Tararua*, steamers, and *Bengal*, barque, ninety miles up (the *Omeo* drawing fourteen feet), and when moored at the jetty, lashed close to gum trees, there was thirty feet of water. Seven miles above all navigation was stopped by a rocky bar; the river then continues in a series of long reaches, and water holes for many miles further. Rains, &c.—The rainy season is during the westerly monsoons, and lasts from November till March, when the river is subject to very heavy floods. During my stay there I saw one in which the river rose thirty feet in as many hours, being ten feet over the jetty, the level of which was twenty feet above the normal condition of the river; at that time I found that the sea was perfectly fresh fifteen miles from the entrance of the river. In passing down from the landing-place I found the flood gradually decreased, and on arrival at the mouth found it was not over two feet above the average height.

" The country, almost right up to the landing, showed large plains of rich loam many feet deep and almost ready for the plough; we dug down several feet and still found it the same quality. A bag was taken and brought to Adelaide, and was reported by our respected Curator of the Botanic Gardens to be fit to grow anything. At another place we dug up a small space and sowed several kinds of vegetable seeds, and, on the next visit in about three weeks, we could scarcely find the place, as the native grasses, &c., had completely smothered everything else in their rapid growth. Trees are mostly to be found near the parts of the country where there are many hills cropping up, which stand out very prominently. The banks of the river are generally lined with dense mangroves and creepers here and there, growing over half-withered stunted gum-trees in beautiful profusion; large trees are scarce. The plains appeared to me to be grand for the cultivation of sugar, rice, coffee, and maize. On some of the hills grew the cyprus pine, which run about from six to twelve inches in the butt, and straight for fifteen to twenty feet, and of very smooth grain, and I believe a very lasting wood.

"Birds of various kinds were plentiful, wild ducks in thousands; also emus, a small kind of kangaroo, wild geese, swans, native companions, and white and black cockatoos. The place seemed alive with living creatures, amongst them a large kind of bat in large flocks, which, when they pitched in the trees, hang down just like a leg of mutton. The fish I did not find in large quantities, I suppose owing to the swarms of alligators which I have seen come half out of the water on the edge of a sandbank to devour them. Sharks are also numerous at the mouth of the river.

"I remember sailing up from the Cara, after a day's surveying, when a splendid fish weighing six pounds jumped into the boat and into the lap of one of the crew, which startled him to such a degree that he rushed forward, and I thought he certainly was going right over the bow, when I sang out, ' Hold on, hold on, it's not the blacks.' Alligators are dangerous customers, still, while you are moving about, there is not so much danger. When the horses went down to the riverside for water they managed to take three away while the poor brutes were drinking. I will relate a sad occurrence which happened to my second officer; I sent him up the river to bring fresh water down to last the vessel to Sweer's island, where I was bound, and as the boat was lying at anchor in the stream for the night, the second officer lying on his bed placed on the stern-sheets of the boat aft, and only about six inches from the top of the gunwale, was in a very exposed position. In the dead of the night the boat gave a sudden lurch, which woke up all the crew, when to their horror they found the second officer was missing; one of the crew exclaimed, ' My God, the second mate's gone.' They immediately lifted the anchor, and, looking astern, they saw an alligator come to the surface with the man in his mouth, apparently to let him go to get a better grip of him. They were so near the boat, poor fellow, that the men put out an oar and could reach him, and begged of him to get a hold, but he was dragged down under water, and was never seen again; though they pulled about the spot and searched until daylight, when all they could see were several alligators following the boat, which they did for two days and nights, until the distressed men got back to the ship. They were in a terrible state of excitement and melancholy; in fact, with all my thirty years' of a sea-life I never saw men so completely unnerved as at that time."

CHAPTER XI.

THE following extracts from the voyage and the visit of the Parliamentary Party to Palmerston are taken from the reports of the Special Reporter of the *Register*, the additional interesting matter was obligingly forwarded to the Author by the Hon. the Minister of Education, and of the Northern Territory, J. L. Parsons, M.P.

"Port Essington is situated on an inlet on the most northern headland of the Northern Territory and was 'settled' in 1831 by Sir Gordon Bremer for the Imperial Government, as a military post and harbour of refuge for shipwrecked sailors. It was abandoned nineteen years afterwards, and the only remains of the settlement now are ruined buildings and an enormous tamarind tree, the wonder of the place. There are numbers of buffaloes, the descendants of herds turned loose by the settlement party, many years ago. A speculator owning land in the neighbourhood tried some time since the experiment of hunting these cattle, and jerking their flesh for sale, but he was not successful, owing mainly to circumstances which could be controlled in future. A number of Adelaide capitalists are about to take the industry in hand. Then you get a glimpse of the Cobourg Peninsula, where a cattle station is, but where little has been done. But chiefest of all sights, is that of Melville Island, about thirty-four miles, as the crow flies, from Port Darwin, and separated by Clarence Straits from the mainland by about fourteen miles.

"The island is seventy-five miles long, and thirty-eight broad. It is said to be fertile, and to possess several good harbours. I was fortunate enough to interview one of the very few Europeans who have visited it, and he assured me that the reports as to the character and the number of the blacks there are fully sustained. The island is overrun with them, and they are as fierce as the bulky mosquitoes that congregate in the thick mangrove-lined coasts. For these reasons scarcely any whites have visited the island since 1840, when the military post of Fort Dundas on King Cove was abandoned, after having been kept up sixteen years, during which time there were several affrays with the natives. The country for the greater part is low, thickly wooded, and in a great many places fronted by rocks. The highest elevation is 320 feet. The trees and undergrowth stretch down to the coast, and there are two or three rivers on the island—one navigable for a short distance. Separated by Apsley Straits (nearly a mile broad) from Melville Island is another named Bathhurst, which is about thirty miles in extent, and which has a grand natural harbour in which a fleet might float. The soil almost exactly resembles that of the adjacent mainland. In the more open parts the sago, fan-palm, bandana, gum, and other trees grow, and everywhere almost there is evidence of fertility. I have described these islands at such length because they are absolutely unproductive bits of South Australian territory, supporting no one but the swarming tribes of blacks. The hostile Melville natives had better make the most of their opportunities; ere long we shall have begun to civilize them. If, by the way, there is a missionary to spare in South Australia or elsewhere, here is a good opening for him. But he must be hardy and plucky; as bold in demeanour as in opinion." . . . . .

"At one o'clock on Monday, February 21st, we passed the entrance to Adelaide River opposite Vernon Islands, where the passage is intricate and difficult of navigation, and where the efflux from the river discolours the sea water. We arrived at our destination shortly before six o'clock in the evening, when the sun shone brightly and the weather looked as unlike the wet season as it could possibly be. A perfect cloud of vari-coloured flags went up over the Government residence in sign of welcome, and the leading townsfolk, headed by Mr. Price, S.M., the Government Resident, as soon as possible came off to the vessel, and expressed the welcome gracefully.

Mr. Price imparted the cheering information that the District Council and a host of supporters had been marshalled for some time on the beach, to the end that they might fire off an address of welcome to the distinguished travellers; but the Minister decided not to go off that night, and consequently the eager crowd had to nurse their complimentary sentiments till next morning.

"At ten o'clock on the morning of the 22nd February, the Government Resident came off to the ship in the official cutter, and conducted the Parliamentary Party to the shore, where they were received by the leading residents.

"After an inspection of the Government residence, they proceeded to the Court-house, where the principal officials, and about a dozen other folk (Northern Territory musters are not over-large) had gathered in the hall, to witness the presentation of an address to the Minister, by the District Council of Palmerston, represented by Messrs. P. R. Allen, Joseph Skelton, V. L. Solomon, James Pickford, and J. G. Kelsey. The address was graceful enough, and sufficiently in conformity with tradition not to need republication; and what more need be said? The ceremonial trouble was soon over, the Minister, by a thoroughly hearty little speech, winning at once the regard of the Palmerstonians. That regard, to their honour be it said, they freely extend to all eligible strangers in the most practical manner. The next three days the party spent in preparations for the exploration of the interior, and in a deserved *dolce far niente*, if the dolce qualification may be allowed by the critical reader, when consideration is given to the fact, that eager deputations of sand-flies and mosquitoes, made with embarrassing importunity the most perplexing demands. There were demands, too, by human deputationists, the most tempting being that the party should attend a 'welcome' banquet ere they entered upon their adventures; but the Minister bravely resisted all their blandishments, deciding to do the work first and the feasting afterwards.

"The start was made on the 23rd. The Parliamentary Party, accompanied by Mr. J. G. Knight (Special Magistrate, Goldfields Warden, Clerk of the Court), and Mr. David Lindsay (Government Surveyor), left Palmerston and boarded the steam launch which was to convey them to Southport, amidst the cheers of the Government Resident and his friends from the shore. To reach Southport the steamer had to go straight

down the middle of the harbour, and through the Middle or
South Arm, which is the most extensive of the inlets from Port
Darwin. Its entrance is about three miles wide, but an islet,
two and a half miles south, makes it bifurcate. The branch
we followed trends south-east eight miles from the inlet, and
seven miles nearly due south, when the channel narrows down
to a mere creek at its end, dignified by the name of the Black-
more River, on which the township of Southport is situated,
about twenty-six miles from Palmerston. We did the distance
in less than three hours, but then we had a swift current with
us. There is nothing particularly inspiring about the trip.
Save for a little patch of open land and one hill 250 feet high
or thereabout, you see little change from swampy flats densely
covered with mangroves; though when, after an hour's broiling
below, backs to the engine boiler, to escape the rain, we came
on deck, a few verdure-clad hills were overlooking us in the distance. The water, which varies in depth from six to thirteen
fathoms, was muddy but salt, and the best sight you are struck
with is the thought of what a grand provision Nature has made
for future wharfowners. The river, for a very long distance
thence, varies from two to three chains in width, and the depth
of water in many places is as great as that in the new dock at
Port Adelaide, at ordinary low tide. All that would be needed,
besides population, to make this a great shipping place, would
be to drive down piles and reclaim a little land. Vessels of
three hundred tons could come down and take away without
lightering the produce of all the plantations, and the output of
every factory the circumjacent land is likely to contain for half
a century.

"Southport is pleasantly situated, considering the character
of the surrounding country. It will not be on the route of any
intercolonial or other railway, probably, but it will ever be the
port of shipment for the south-western hundreds—Glyde and
Milne and Hughes at least. In public institutions it boasts a
telegraph office, a police station, and a cemetery. The telegraph station is one of those in connection with the overland
line. There are a few flourishing Chinese vegetable gardens,
and plenty of fish—rock cod and a sort of bream, mostly—are
got in the river, which has a tidal rise and fall similar to that
at Palmerston. Public religious services are unknown in the
township, and there is no school in which the children can be
educated. But in the dry season Southport—though in the

wet a dull, shambling, dingy, fifth-class, disordered, commonplace little village—is an actively important centre. Thence all the diggers' supplies go down to the goldfields, and thither comes all the gold. The horse and bullock teams, that do no work from December to April, make it their terminus, and the mail contractor has his head-quarters there, getting the postbags from Palmerston by steamer, which runs down one day and returns the next. The farthest post office south is Pine Creek, but the Catherine, further still, will soon probably be the final point at which the mailman will call. By the coach in the dry season, and by it and pack-horses in the wet, a weekly mail is carried between the terminal point and Southport.

"The previous day the pack-horses provided for the convenience of the party arrived at Southport, and next morning the first grand muster came off by the telegraph station. Altogether, there were twenty-two horses in the cavalcade; and the order was, they must only be walked: a miserable lot, but there was no choice. Behold the party mounted! The Minister, the Honourable J. L. Parsons in a slashed slouch hat with veil—à la bushranger—light tweed trousers, with singlet, black umbrella, and long white oil leggings, on (as was fit) the best horse of the lot—a horse that, judging by an occasional caper, evidently indulged sometimes in youthful reminiscences; Mr. Bright (with his seventeen stone distributed over a disheartened-looking nuggety roadster), with a wideawake brown hat, a tight light singlet, trousers and brown leggings, and a light umbrella; Mr. J. H. Bagster, M.P., like the Minister, save a dustcoat; Mr. L. L. Turner, M.P., ditto, with slight deviations; Professor Tate with leggings, which left a white blank above his shoe-tops, and buccaneer-like in look but for a good humoured, semi-cynical smile; and Mr. Knight somewhat like H. E. Bright, M.P., and each laughing heartily at the grotesque appearance of the other; and all immensely amused at the sight and sound of the cavalcade, with its halting pack-horses, their vociferous drivers, and the loud crack and wild flourish of the stockwhips, which oft and again interviewed the steeds' raw backs and sides. Thus the auspicious start.

"I should have recorded before an interesting event—the distribution by the visitors of largesse to the blacks, in public half-circle assembled in front of the hotel. The gift was in the shape of flour—next to tobacco the best esteemed native luxury—doled out in a grocer's scoop in anything but grocer fashion by Mr. Knight. The sight was certainly the most interesting seen on this trip. Oh, such degraded specimens of humanity!—less manlike some than a grinning and chattering monkey. And then, their quarrelling over the food as pigs quarrel over a bone, and quite as thankless to the donor, with a profuse spitting (not to have seen a tobacco-chewing native salivate is something to be thankful for), and a screeching and jabbering and a discordant whirr like the alarm-note of a quail, but more discordant—the dusky crowd moved off to their camp to put their different lots of flour together and to have, for once at least, 'one big, big fellow feed,' the while their benefactors went upon their journey. That journey began at about ten o'clock on the morning of the 24th, when the sun shone down with great fervency. The horses bore the infliction with great fortitude for the first hour, which was engaged in going through rather poor-looking flat country, little different from an ordinary bush landscape in South Australia proper in point of vegetation, save that the grass was higher and more rank, and the road bore deep water-channels—mementos of recent wet-season rains. At the end of that time, Mr. Bagster's horse determined to stand the conveyance of that honourable gentleman no longer, and without any notice took the bit between its teeth and galloped off the road, in amongst the thickly planted trees, winding in and out in such an erratic fashion, and so nearly colliding with them, that it was by nought else but a miracle that the Parliamentarty party were not under the necessity of leaving one of their number behind them."

Having given the account of the start, space can only be found for reports on the capability of the country. As extracts will follow from Professor Tate's report of the mineral productions of the province, only one account of a goldfield will be given from the special correspondent's report, from whom he now borrows a natural-history paragraph.

"I have left till the last mention of one of the most peculiar features of the scenery passed through so far, and continuing throughout. I mean the ant-hills. For hundreds of miles the landscape is relieved by these erections. The busy little ants are fond of fantastic designs. The Gothic they follow most. The forms are of six or seven turreted columns, triple pinnacles, gables twenty feet high, sugar-loaves of two feet, and apparently shapeless masses, yet perfect in their mathematical proportions.

One was almost exactly like a bust of Shakespeare, only the immortal Will's face, thus portrayed, looked as though the cast had been taken after he had been battered somehow. Others of the hills run in nearly regular succession due north and south, and the builders of these are called the magnetical ants. Their houses are an unerring guide—a compass to the traveller. These ant-hills are so hard, that they are used, when the position is convenient and the inside is scooped out, as chimneys, and it takes a great deal of heavy battering to break them in, though the shell be not thicker than your palm. The ants mortar together the different lumps of clay of which the hill is composed, with a glutinous substance, which hardens more rapidly and effectively than the most valuable coagulation which ever quack puffed. Outside the hill you find only a few hundreds of blackish ants, doing very little; on 'Change, when shares are at a discount, I should say, judging by their leisurely look; but break a piece off it, and you see myriads of the oft-cursed white ants, in a section of what looks like nothing else so much as a huge rough sponge. The white ant is a puffy, fat, contented little creature, with a round head like the pink top of a lucifer match; and collectively you will see him in this broken section, after he has cooled down his disgust at your intrusion; you will see him sitting in council in the cosiest, cleanest little cells, or rushing to others—the granaries—to protect his wet-weather stock of grass-seeds and stalks, and other food. Then, if you wait an hour, you will be a witness to the readiness with which he sets about repairing the damage you have done to his tenement. Some of the ants, instead of building independent houses for themselves, cut their way into the heart of trees; raise a tiny mound outside, and sometimes a little way along the trunk, and then actually eat nearly the whole of the firm wood of the tree, leaving, as they advance higher and higher, earth deposits in lieu of the timber. By-and-by the tree falls, and then it makes, and is used as, a capital water-duct. This is one of the effects of the ant nuisance."

The following account of one of the Union Reefs, the Extended Union is given:—"Messrs. Noltenius and party were, at the time of our visit, the holders of the Extended, which has since been sold. Started about eight years ago, and at sundry intervals allowed to remain idle since, it has given as much as 75 ounces to the ton, from 9 tons of a shoot sunk down upon from the surface. The country is permeated by most peculiar quartz leaders, some no thicker than a knife-blade, but all rich. The last returns from the top ground averaged 30 dwts. to the ton, the stuff being taken the whole width of 23 feet. In sinking, the course of the shoot has been followed, and as it was erratic, the workings also are eccentric, beginning in a huge excavation, and forking off into a downright and an underlay shaft, continuing in a tortuous direction, and winding up with a downright 170 feet from the surface. The workings are almost full of water now, but they will be drained by an engine, to be erected near the main shaft. A ten-head battery will also be furnished to help the five-head one, a little erection which has put through £21,000 worth of gold. That exact information respecting the broad totals might be in possession of my readers, I got a statement copied from the battery books, which show that 4,000 ounces came from the Extended claim, 1,177 from Lorrance's, in the neighbourhood (average 6 ounces), 882 ounces from Fiveash's (average about 4 ounces), 150 ounces from Walker's, and 122 ounces from Stuart's ;—in these cases the averages not given. Besides these, other little claims adjacent are being worked. Towards dusk we crossed the banks of the McKinlay, and reaching the Twelve-mile on Saturday night, rested on Sunday.

"About twelve miles from Southport the party were met by the mail-coach, sent to convey them to the port, should they wish to be relieved from the inconveniences of further horseback travel. All save the Minister accepted the pleasant alternative; but he thought it would be cavalier treatment of his steed—the long-since historical Gaylad—if he deserted it, and so he stuck to his saddle the whole journey through, and came in at the head of the little troop. The arrival at Southport marked the close of 300 miles travel on horses—and such horses! It is only justice to the party to say, that from the time when Mr. Bright returned, they all went through the inconveniences, the slight dangers, and the many discomforts of the trip with more energy than one would expect, opposing to obstacles a cheerful good-nature which won the ready assistance of the residents wherever they went. Especially is this the case with regard to the Minister, who was ever to the fore, and, in season and out of season, interviewed sundry bores and far more numerous intelligent imparters of information."

CHAPTER XII.

[COMMUNICATED BY THE HON. THE MINISTER OF EDUCATION, J. L. PARSONS, M.P.]

THE NORTHERN TERRITORY AS A COUNTRY FOR THE GROWTH OF SUGAR AND OTHER TROPICAL PRODUCTS; AND THE ADVANTAGES OF COOLIE LABOUR FOR THE NORTHERN TERRITORY.

It is not necessary, after the success which has attended the operations of Mr. Holtze, the Government gardener at the nursery, Fannie Bay, to demonstrate by description or statistics the suitability of the Northern Territory for tropical agriculture under proper management. Mr. Holtze has shown that sugar-cane, indigo, cotton, tapioca, rice, and other tropical products grow and thrive. The report of Mr. W. H. Thompson to the directors of the De Lissa Company is highly satisfactory, so far as soil and climate are concerned; and as Mr. Thompson has had many years' experience in sugar growing in the West Indies, he is entitled to speak as an expert. Very fine cane has been grown on the land of the Palmerston Plantation Company, on the Daly River; and the latest accounts give good ground for believing that a large extent of suitable land exists on the banks of the Adelaide. In addition, there is the great unexplored region which stretches up to Cape Arnheim, where those who are most competent to form an opinion anticipate that large areas of agricultural land will be discovered. A party is now organized to thoroughly explore this country.

CULTIVATION IN THE NORTHERN TERRITORY.

Mr. Maurice Holtze, of the Government garden, at Port Darwin, contributes the following interesting information:—
"I may state at the outset that the Fannie Bay experimental nursery, covering thirty-two acres, was started under my management in November, 1879, and is, therefore, only about two and a half years old, so that it may be rather premature to pronounce a decided opinion upon the various plants which have been tried in the garden. I think, however, that those which have thriven during the three growing seasons without being affected by climatic influences or disease, may fairly be said to be suited to the country; especially when we know that the first two seasons have been unfavourable on account of the

weather being unusually dry, and that some of the soil in the nursery is rather poor.

"To simplify these notes it will be best to class the plants under three heads, viz. :—

"I. Those proved fully suitable to the country during each of the three past seasons.

"II. Those which from any cause have failed during one or other of the above seasons, but seem otherwise suitable for cultivation if the cause of failure be removable ; and

"III. Those which have failed to thrive in the nursery.

"1st. Amongst the plants fully suitable I am glad to say that the most valuable portion of those which succeed well includes sugarcane, indigo, tapioca, arrowroot, rice, maize, ramie, ground nut, castor oil, sesame, and ginger.

"All of these have grown in such luxuriance, and have been so completely free from disease or vermin, that I have not the slightest hesitation in recommending their culture.

"2nd. Plants having failed in one of the seasons, through any cause, but otherwise apparently adapted to the climate of the territory. These include cotton, jute, and tobacco, though it is scarcely fair to put cotton in any other than the first division, as the cause of its failure last year was due to the seed being taken from deteriorated plants. I have since imported fresh American seed of Upland and Sea Island varieties, and the state of their growth this year leaves nothing better to be desired.

"Jute for the first two seasons was strong and healthy, but this year, probably from the unusual dryness of the weather, the plants have been attacked by borers and have been completely destroyed.

"Of tobacco I had a good crop in the season of '78-80, but '81 was rather too dry to bring it to perfection, though the produce was by no means a failure. Of the present plantation I cannot yet give an opinion as it is yet too young. Tobacco should be grown during the first part of the dry season, it being a sub-tropical production, and would best thrive in the moist gullies which are so numerous in the territory, where I believe it would flourish in great luxuriance.

"3rd. Of plants which have not thriven well in the nursery may be mentioned coffee, cocoa, nutmeg, cinnamon, cloves, pepper, tea, vanilla, poppy; but I have not the slightest doubt that in many parts of the country, in sheltered moist gullies nearly all the above might be successfully cultivated, though I would not advise any large outlay to be incurred before a special trial.

"Liberian coffee, which I received only a few months ago, stands very well, but it would be too early to give a decided opinion as to its fitness.

"It must not be forgotten that our nursery is close to the sea, and exposed to its breezes, and that while many plants are not injuriously affected thereby, the air and saline moisture are too strong for other kinds.

"I may here refer to another plant tried this season for the first time, and therefore still unproved ; but when I mention that the seed was only put in the ground last September, and has already made a stem over 12 feet high and 3 inches through, there are grounds for hoping that it will turn out a success. This is the indiarubber plant (*Ceara* or *Manihet glazious*), seeds of which, with other valuable products, I received from my greatly esteemed friend Baron F. von Müller, the celebrated Victorian Government Botanist.

"In the foregoing I have only referred to those plants which have a commercial value, and are the common staple produce of tropical countries ; but I might add that many tropical and sub-tropical fruit trees are being tried and propagated in the nursery, most of which are doing well—such as the mango, jackfruit, breadfruit, custard apple, sweetsop, soursop, orange, citron, lemon, lime, shaddock, fig, peach, pomegranate, luchre, longan, bambootan, jujube, almond, quince, granadillar, banana, plantain, pineapple, &c., as well as a collection of fodder plants and grapes, together with ornamental trees and shrubs in considerable variety.

"Intending colonists may feel interested in vegetables as well as in the above-enumerated productions, so I may in conclusion state that a fair variety of tropical as well as European vegetables are successfully grown and sold at reasonable prices by the Chinese market gardeners."

The Government Resident (E. W. Price, Esq.), in his report under date June, 1882, referring to agriculture, says : "The growth of the cane this year, which was rather backward, has been materially assisted by the May rainfall, and the canes on the De Lissa Company are growing vigorously, and even should the crop not realise expectation this year, owing to the lateness of the rainy season, still there must be a splendid crop from the ratoons next year. The crop at Bean's plantation at the Palms is very healthy, and there is a very thick crop. These canes were only planted in March, and of course could not mature this year, but there will be a fine crop for nursery purposes, and the present growth proves what the land on Cox's Peninsula will grow. Messrs. Erickson, Cloppenburg, Harris, and Head, who have taken up land on the Peninsula, in small blocks, are all doing well with sugarcane, tobacco, maize, and other produce. Their cane is splendid in size and quality, and there is some hope of their being able to obtain a small mill, as they are rather far away from the De Lissa Company's mill. The above men have been the real pioneers of tropical agriculture in the territory. The only capital they started on was a stout heart and a strong hand. Some samples of the cane growing on the Daly have been brought by Mr. Owston to Palmerston; they are quite as fine as any in the Government garden, and there are twenty acres similar on the plantation, ready for nursery purposes this year. The maize from the Daly is also first-class, and the cobs much larger than any hitherto grown here. It now remains to test the land on the Adelaide for sugar growing; and there, although the top soil is very rich, the subsoil of clay seems to frighten intending planters. In my last report I quoted from Dalton's British Guinea, to show that such subsoil is good for sugar, and I now supplement by quoting from 'The Coolie,' by Mr. Jenkins, the author of 'Ginx's Baby,' and who was sent out at the same time as the Commission ordered by Earl Granville, then Secretary of State for the Colonies. Mr. Jenkins made a most minute inspection of the sugar lands in British Guinea; and there, where the finest sugar is grown, he reports the subsoil 'as like the London blue clay.' Another fault found with our alluvial soil on the river banks is the excessive quantity of water, and therefore people say ' it is only fit for rice." Now the Chinese at Mindale, one mile from Palmerston, have been trying patches of sugarcane on some low swampy land, and the result is fine cane, long and thick, the density of which has not yet been tried."

EXTRACTS FROM PROFESSOR TATE'S REPORT TO THE GOVERN-
MENT ON MINERALOGICAL AND OTHER FEATURES OF THE
NORTHERN TERRITORY. BY FAVOUR OF THE HON. J. L.
PARSONS, M.P.

"*Gold Reefs.*—The gold-fields extend from the river Stapleton, *via* Bridge Creek, the Howley, Port Darwin Camp, Twelve-mile, McKinlay River, and the Union to Pine Creek, a distance of sixty-five miles, and thence to the Driffield, thirty-five miles farther. The width of the auriferous country, as at present known, is only a few miles. The chief centres of gold-reefing are the Howley, Twelve-mile, McKinlay, the Union, and Pine Creek. The quartz veins are included in the felspathose sandstone. In some cases the crest of the range coincides with the outcrop of a quartz vein of two feet or so in thickness; this phenomenon is well exemplified at the Union, where one reef is traceable along the summit of the range for over two miles; in other cases, a close series of strings of quartz determines the outline and direction of the ridge. Many of the hills carry one or many reefs, the majority of which are auriferous; most particularly are the smaller veins and strings rich in gold. From prospects taken at random, I have no reason to doubt the statements made, that their yield is from four to six, and even twelve ounces per ton. Were these reefs located in a country better circumstanced, they would have been made to yield handsome profits. An unfortunate feature of most of the auriferous lodes is that the gold is compressed into a small compass; whereas, if it were disseminated throughout a wider and more solid body of stone, there is no doubt it would be easier and more profitably extracted, and offer less uncertainty as to its permanence. Quartz-reefing is chiefly carried on by small parties, whose capital is their bone and sinew. The returns for a time are large, but, on encountering water or other impediments, which bring down the earnings, the reef is abandoned, in order that the same process may be repeated elsewhere. In this way the multiplicity of auriferous reefs has been a comparative disadvantage, as very few of them have been followed to any depth. The mining operations are of the simplest kind: the quartz is raised to the surface in buckets by hand windlass. There are only two pumping-engines on the whole field. The period at which the bulk of the quartz veins can be advantageously worked will not entirely depend on their yield, but will be more or less influenced by the general price of labour and the materials in the district. The supply and consequent price of labour is materially influenced by the distance at which the goldfields are situated from the great centres of trade. The history of gold-mining in Victoria offers a striking illustration of these axioms. Year by year the amount of gold derived from the working of gold quartz has gone on gradually and rapidly increasing; as, by the introduction of efficient and powerful machinery, ores of a very low produce are treated with advantage; but in this connection it must be observed that to obtain a satisfactory profit, it is necessary not only that large quantities of ore should be treated, but also that the greatest economy should be observed in every department of the manipulation. To develop the gold resources of the Northern Territory, it is necessary that more capital be introduced, to be chiefly applied to improved machinery for the extraction of the gold, and to cope with water; more experienced and honest management be secured, and a reduction of working expenses be effected. The batteries which I examined are discreditable; they are all of the same pattern, and no attempt has been made to adapt them to particular requirements. There is a total absence of labour-saving appliances. All the batteries which I saw at work are in the highest degree wasteful; the slimes in every case are highly charged with amalgam, and no attempt is made to save the auriferous pyrites, as indeed no appliances are in use for their treatment. I do not hesitate to estimate the loss of gold at from 50 to 75 per cent. involving among other disadvantages a loss of considerable revenue to the State. If to the above fact we add that the price of carting and crushing has been hitherto at the rate of £3 10s. to £4 per ton, and that the wages of the skilled miner are £5 per week, and that the gold realises only about £3 6s. per ounce, there can be no reason for wonder that quartz reefs carrying an average of 3 oz. of gold per ton are barely remunerative. It must be obvious that unless the quartz is really good, our gold mines could never have kept so many men employed with these expensive appliances for so long a time. Mines employing native labour, with a minimum number of European overseers, compatible with successful and economic exploitation, have yielded steady profits to the proprietors. The St. John del Rey Mine, in the Brazils, makes a noble profit, with a quarter of an ounce of gold per ton. To reduce the working expenses of our gold mines it is imperative that we employ cheaper labour—that of Chinese or Negroes.

"*Alluvial Goldfields.*—These are located in the immediate vicinity of the auriferous reefs, and occupy the lower slopes and bottoms of the short gullies which feather in and out among the ranges. There the 'pay-dirt' lies on the surface, or rarely at a greater depth than two feet. It is obviously of local origin. Here and there the gold has been retained in pocket-like depressions fronting rocky barriers across the gullies, from which considerable stores of the precious metal have been obtained. The main lines of drainage into which these gullies lead have not been systematically prospected, and it is a moot question whether or no the broad valleys have 'pay-dirt' beneath them. The ground may easily be tested, as there seems to be a very limited depth of drift-deposit filling the depressed surfaces; indeed, the slight rises on the plains are all composed of bed-rock. As long as rich gold shall continue to be found in shallow ground, so long shall we despair of the deep ground being tried, or the auriferous reefs being energetically prospected. Considering the primitive methods employed for gold-washing (I saw in use only the tin dish and small cradles), I have no doubt that the employment of more efficient appliances, will result in much larger returns of gold than have hitherto been obtained: even the residuum of the deserted goldfields may be again gone over with profitable results.

"*Tin.*—Stream-tin was seen *in situ* at two places, ten miles apart in a straight line. Samples of tin-stone were inspected which were reported to have been obtained at other localities than those visited. The first site is the gravelly bed and east bank of one of the tributaries of the McKinlay River. Good prospects were obtained here. The tin-stone is well rounded, but the pebbles do not exceed half-an-inch in diameter. As prospecting was limited to two holes near to each other, it is impossible to arrive at any approximate estimate of the quantity of stream-tin that is here present. One excavation is twenty feet by thirty feet, and six feet in depth, from which it is said 11 cwt. of tin-stone was taken. The tin-stone at this locality is small and angular, and shows the fine ruby colour characteristic of the purer state of the mineral. From the physical features of the country, and the condition of the mineral, it is evident that the tin-stone has been derived from the adjoining slopes, which are composed of a sub-metamorphic micaceous sandstone. These stream deposits are of comparatively small importance in comparison to the supply to be derived from stanniferous lodes, but they will doubtlessly afford employment to a number of the poorer miners for some time to come. The formation most abundant in tin veins is the granite, but in neither of the two deposits of tin-stone did I find evidence of such an association, nor is it definitely known if stream-tin has been found in the *débris* from the known granitic masses.

"*Copper.*—The existence of ores of this metal in the Northern Territory is beyond dispute. The sites of the discoveries are a little south from Pine Creek, in Cruikshank's Gully, and at another point near the Howley Battery. The prospects are, in each case, in the highest degree encouraging; but, apart from the question as to the quality of the copper in these ores, their utilisation under existing surroundings must not be attempted. Other minerals are galena (not seen *in situ*) and hæmatite, in massive beds.

"*General Conclusions and Recommendations touching the Mineral Resources.*—The development of the mineral resources is but in its infancy, and I believe that rich stanniferous lodes will yet be found, whilst the prospects already unearthed indicate the presence of good percentage copper ores. Rich auriferous lodes abound over a large tract of country. Hitherto adventurers have made a show of developing the mineral resources, but their action has been protractive rather than otherwise, whilst the honest efforts of the nomadic miner cannot count for much. It is my honest conviction that, with the introduction of more capital, the gold reefs can be worked profitably, and to considerable depth. To hasten the advent of this, however, there must be a railway to cheapen carriage, and make the country accessible to mining and other speculations, and that the railway may also be the means of opening up the copper deposits known to exist along the route to Pine Creek. Alluvial digging is only pioneer work, and should be strenuously encouraged, as leading to permanent settlement—by it the poor miner may acquire sufficient capital to open out additional sources of revenue to the State of a more enduring nature.

"*Agricultural Resources.*—So very little has been done to test the agricultural capabilities of the country that the question,

"Are the climate and soil of the Northern Territory suitable for the growth of tropical plants of economic value?" is still open for discussion. The soils of the valleys and of the hill slopes are, in my opinion, ill-suited for agriculture, and, with a few exceptions, the land seen under cultivation was only that reclaimed from the jungle scrub. The chief of the exceptions to which I allude is the soil formed by the decomposition of the diorite rock massed between Port Darwin Camp and Yam Creek Telegraph Station; it shows great capabilities, if I may judge from the healthy growth of the great variety of culinary and fodder plants under cultivation by the Chinese. Corroborative evidence of its richness is afforded by the reappearance of the graceful palm, *Kenta acuminata*, and, if it really be that species, in a more luxuriant state than it assumes in its northern stations. It abounds about Fannie Bay, near Palmerston, and occurs at intervals as far south as the Stapleton; then its place is taken by the fan-palm, *Livistonia humilis*, which is less choice in its habitat. I believe that in several parts of the colony various species of *Gossypium* (cotton-plant), rice, and indigo could be cultivated, and a fair and even prolific crop obtained. Indeed, good cotton has been produced within the Murray Basin (see F. von Müller, 'Select Plants for Cultivation,' p. 99, 1876). The rice-plant is indigenous to the Northern Territory, having been found by Baron F. von Müller in the marshes about Hooker's Creek, by Mr. Wilson in the marshes of the valley of the Norton-Shaw River, and by Mr. J. A. Giles in the valley of the Birdum Creek. The Tamarind is also a native, having been noticed first by Leichardt at Port Essington, and subsequently by Müller on the cliffs at the entrance to the Victoria River. Another useful plant indigenous to the country has been overlooked. It is *Tacca pinnatifida*, from the tubers of which the main supply of Fiji arrowroot is prepared. I noticed it growing in rather humid gravelly soil here and there from Palmerston to Pine Creek.

"*Pastoral Resources.*—The humidity and high temperature of the air during a portion of the year cannot be conducive to the rearing of sheep within the region of the northern rivers. Jukes says: 'Sheep, if they lived at all, would soon have their woolly coats changed into hair.'—*Op. cit.* p. 361. Landsborough writes that: 'The Kangaroo grass, though of itself possessing excellent properties, is so certain an index of humid soil, which is, on the whole, unfavourable to sheep, that I cannot agree with many squatters in their estimate of the country on which it is found.'—'Narrative Explor. Gulf of Carpentaria," p. 36. What is true with respect to the unsuitability of the climate for sheep will be true in a less degree for horses, both of which, however, may find more congenial conditions on the table-land country, especially along the course of the southern creeks, which are well known for luxuriance of vegetation and richness of soil. These creeks take their rise in basaltic formation, and it is to its presence that is due the oases in an otherwise desert country. Landsborough, in describing the Barkly table-land, which is drained by the Herbert, says: "In the course of the day we had travelled thirty miles, chiefly over fine country, doubtless destined to rank as a first-class sheep-run.'—*Op. cit.* 53. Tropical South Australia has truly been said to be a land of grasses; the number of known species is about 130, and of these I collected over fifty between the Adelaide River and Pine Creek, but only some four or five are constituents of the grass plains and adjacent hill slopes. Some flats are almost exclusively occupied with *Anthistra*, or with *Andropon triticus*, or with another congeneric species, whilst not infrequently the three are found in company. The two latter grasses acquire on the flats a height of from six feet to eight feet, and exceptionally attain to fourteen feet, but on dry hill slopes the same species dwindle down to two feet or less. The exuberant growth of grasses in the plains of the basin of the northern rivers should be capable of keeping alive large herds of cattle, but I very much doubt if there are all the requisites for the production of marketable beef. I have observed that there is an absence of the rich fodder grasses, and the much valued kangaroo grasses (*Anthistira ciliata* and *A. frondosa*) are only locally abundant in the country traversed, whilst *Antropogon triticus*, or tall spear-grass, and its congener, *A. Australis*, seem to me ill-adapted for fattening stock. The tall spear-grass is everywhere abundant in the open country, its hard and cane-like flowering stalks growing to fourteen or sixteen feet in height; the other common grass, *A. Australis*, is not so strong a plant, but is equally deficient in succulency and leaf. The density of the growth of the grasses on the flats defies all opposition to the establishment of other herbaceous species; but when external agents exercise their sway, then a herbage of panick grasses and some sedges take possession of the soil—the former on the drier ground chiefly, the latter on the more humid surfaces. Whether or not this improvement can be maintained without the intervention of man and domestic animals, or can be extensively brought about, is a question which I doubt if any one can yet answer; but, nevertheless, it is true that such a change has supervened over very limited areas, where the balance of nature has been disturbed and maintained by the agencies referred to."

CHAPTER XIII.

THE Right Honourable Sir James Fergusson, Bart., arrived on the 16th February, 1869, to occupy the post of Governor, Lieutenant-Colonel Hamley having occupied the post of Acting Governor after the death of Sir D. Daly. Sir James Fergusson had previously held office under a Conservative Government at home as Under Secretary of State for India, and came with high credentials. He possessed high talents and attainments, was liberal in his expenditure, and in that respect pleased the Adelaide people. He was an able orator and a clear thinker. Though his higher qualities were not duly appreciated, he was yet esteemed a high-minded gentleman, and felt to be an able representative of our gracious Queen Victoria.

Whilst resident here Sir James suffered a great family affliction in the death of his wife, Lady Edith Ramsay, daughter of the late Marquis Dalhousie. Lady Edith exhibited a bright example in her almost constant attendance on the daily morning services of the Anglican Church, and in her support of charitable institutions. The province has never been favoured by the residence of a lady excelling her in all the high qualities of a high-born lady. The official career of his Excellency Sir James Fergusson was so commendable that he was promoted to the government of New Zealand. He left South Australia 7th December, 1872.

In August, 1872, telegraphic communication between the Australian Colonies and Europe was opened through the means of the South Australian through telegraph line. The Governor's active support in carrying out this great work was duly acknowledged by Mr. Gladstone.

No work of greater magnitude or of such vast importance as this knitting of our distant colonies with the rest of our great empire has ever been recorded as having been carried out by one colony without any outside aid whatever.

This work naturally followed the successful operations of Mr. John McDougall Stuart; and not long after that indefatigable explorer succeeded in finding a practicable track across this southern continent, Mr. Todd, then Superintendent of Telegraphs, estimated that a line from Port Augusta to the north coast could be constructed at a moderate cost. He brought this scheme before Sir R. G. McDonnell in the year 1859, but the subject was allowed to remain in abeyance until 1869, when several schemes were made public; the first of which was to join the North-West Cape with Ceylon, the next, the same cape with Java, and a third was to join Normanton, on the north-east, with Java. Not long after this the British Australian Telegraph Company was established, and proposed to reach our north coast, if aided either by subsidy or guarantee. At that time Mr. R. D. Ross, who had been connected with the imperial commissariat in this colony was in London, and a letter from him appeared in the *Times*, in which he forcibly pointed out the importance of opening up a trade between India and the Australian Colonies. He also drew attention to the probability of telegraphic cable communication being opened between Australia, India, and Europe, within a few years. There is no doubt that Mr. Ross's letter was the means of advancing the proposed work. It was not then thought probable that a line would be laid to Port Darwin at any time. To obtain correct information Commander Noel Osborn was sent by the company to Australia, and Mr. Todd was successful in persuading him that a line from Adelaide to Port Darwin possessed superior advantages over any other project put forward, in that it would be the shortest, and that Queensland could easily tap it by a line from Normanton. Mr. H. B. T. Strangways, then in office as Chief Secretary, brought his whole influence to bear in support of Mr. Todd's proposal, and offered on behalf of the Government to construct a line from Port Augusta to Port Darwin to meet the cable of the company at that port, and so relieve the Cable Company of all cost and trouble of the land line. This offer was accepted by Commander Osborn.

A bill was brought in to construct the overland line, and

although there had been a change of Ministry, it was passed with enthusiasm. Our Government bound themselves to have the line completed in eighteen months, *i.e.*, to be open for traffic on January 1st, 1872. It was only a few months before this that the office of Postmaster-General had been conferred on Mr. Todd, in addition to the office he had previously held, and to his increased duties was added the construction of the telegraph line over a distance of 2000 miles, through a country the greatest portion of which was unknown to white men. The country for 350 miles had no white inhabitant, and for hundreds of miles no suitable timber could be found. All the wire had to be ordered from England and landed in the colony. It was also found that iron posts would in some sections have to be used, from the numerous white ants.

The cattle and conveyances had to be hastily procured, tents and provisions provided and despatched, and the line selected and marked out. This last portion of the work fell on a Mr. Ross, a skilful bushman; and well he did his duty, with a lightly equipped flying party. Various sections of the line had to be let on contract; but the central portion, the most difficult, was retained by Mr. Todd, as it was impossible to estimate the difficulties to be overcome with anything like the accuracy necessary either by the manager or the contractor. The most northerly section had to start from Port Darwin as a base, the next from the Roper River, and the parties were to work from both ends, so as to meet in the centre. These two sections and the southern one, from Port Augusta, were let on contract. The central section, which Mr. Todd had retained, was entrusted to a party of five young men, who went to work with a hearty good will. The Government parties started from Adelaide in August, 1870. The first pole was erected at Port Darwin in the middle of September, and the first at Port Augusta on the 1st of October, 1870. All preliminary arrangements having been carried out, Mr. Todd started to the Peake, to make that the central base of operations. There Mr. Ross received his final instructions as to the disposition of his forces. The general start being made, Mr. Todd returned to Adelaide. For a time satisfactory progress was made, and sanguine hopes were entertained that the work would be done within the promised time. Of the Port Darwin section it was expected that no hitch would occur, as fewer difficulties were thought to exist there; but here the first breakdown occurred.

Life in South Australia. 397

Early in July, Mr. W. McMinn, the Government overseer, returned to Adelaide with the annoying news that the contractor had failed in his work, and he had been compelled to terminate his contract. The other parts of the line were progressing satisfactorily, but only six months of the term remained.

In this dilemma Mr. R. C. Patterson was sent with a large party and ample materials to complete the work. Mr. Todd and Mr. Patterson desired to start the work from the Roper River, but their opinions were overruled, and the expedition was sent to Port Darwin. The season was unfavourable, and the difficulties of transport were almost insurmountable. Mr. Patterson sent back a most melancholy report. He then despatched materials to the River Roper. Before this was done, a number of horses, and one-third of the bullocks died. Before the work could be resumed the monsoon set in with unusual severity, and all further progress was suspended for months. The men were shut up in their tents fretting away their strength.

At this time of adversity the cable fleet arrived at Port Darwin, and the shore end of the line was fixed. Mr. Patterson wrote asking for an immediate despatch of large reinforcements. Mr. Todd, with his accustomed energy, decided to go to the scene of the difficulties. He quickly got together an ample supply of all necessaries, and started all in well-appointed steamers to the Roper River, himself accompanying the reinforcement. The day before he started he heard that communication had been opened with the McDonnell Ranges, that the central part had been completed, and that the section beyond was progressing well. When the *Omeo* steamer reached the mouth of the Roper, Mr. Todd gave the captain an indemnity against damage, on behalf of the Government, if he would force the passage of the bar. The vessel safely reached the jetty which had been erected to facilitate the unloading of materials. All through February and March heavy rains fell. When the fine weather set in, drays were loaded and a start was made, Mr. Patterson taking the command. Mr. Todd left for Port Darwin, to arrange matters there, and made a thorough examination of the line from Palmerston to the Catherine. He found many poles destroyed with white ants, which had to be replaced with iron posts. After this he returned to the Roper, where he arrived on May 31st. As the work was now going on well, he started to return overland along the telegraph line, that he might inspect the work already done. He arrived at Daly Waters station June 22nd, between which place and Tenant's Creek was an unfinished gap. Mr. Todd soon established a pony estafette to ride express to cover the gap, and communication by this means was established between Australia and the Old World. He sent a message to our Agent General in London, informing him of the progress of the work and its approaching completion. Several messages came through from London the next day, and then there was silence, as a break occurred in the cable. This was a favourable accident for South Australia, as the Cable Company had threatened to apply to the Government for compensation for breach of contract on the non-completion of the land line in the promised time. During this period the gap in the land line was being shortened, and on the 22nd of August, 1872, the junction was made, and the successful work accomplished of a telegraph line from south to north, a distance of 2000 miles. This work was performed by South Australia unaided, having a population of less than 200,000 souls.

The contractors of the north section, who, when they failed to carry on their contract, had experienced a loss of most of their draught stock by death, had erected about 220 miles. The contractor for the south section had completed nearly the whole distance for which he had contracted, when he was assisted by the Government party.

At the time when the difficulties which Mr. Todd met with became known in the neighbouring colonies little sympathy was expressed in the papers: the people of the colony of South Australia were upbraided with being rash and presumptuous in attempting to accomplish such a stupendous work, which was beyond their power to complete single-handed; but the current soon took the opposite course when the first recipients of a message from London were the firm of Messrs. McEwan and Co., of Melbourne, and when within six months of the opening, the colony netted nearly a quarter of a million sterling extra on the wheat harvest, through sales being effected in foreign markets direct.

At the time the line was finished, Mr. Todd was at Central Mount Stuart in the centre of his work, and must have felt that he occupied a position never before enjoyed by any other scientific man. He was master of the position, and could talk

Life in South Australia. 399

with exalted personages in Europe and America, and exclude for the time all other communications to or from the new fifth quarter of the world. Mr. Todd did not let the grass grow under his feet in returning to the city, and on arrival he was received with becoming enthusiasm. A banquet was prepared, at which Sir James Fergusson presided, during which he announced that the services of Mr. Todd had been recognised and acknowledged by Her Most Gracious Majesty, in conferring on the Chief Secretary, the Honourable Mr. Ayres, the honour of K.C.M.G., and on Mr. Todd and the Agent General, Mr. F. S. Dutton, the honour of C.M.G.

Out of the published remarks of Mr. Todd on this his great work may be selected the following as coming home to all :— "Telegraph might check unhealthy speculation, but it made commerce safer, tended to equalise prices, put the farmer, merchant, and consumers on a footing of equality, and by the more speedy liberation of capital it cheapened all the commodities and the necessaries of daily life." To this may be added, that the occupation of the country has been advanced to an extent which was not previously deemed possible.

CHAPTER XIV.

FROM the departure of Sir James Fergusson, on the 7th December, 1872, the Chief Justice, Sir R. D. Hanson, held the post of Acting Governor until the 8th June, 1873. Sir Richard D. Hanson died on the 4th March, 1876. On the 9th June Sir A. Musgrave, K.C.M.G., arrived and entered on his duties as Governor. His actions and bearing were those of a highly-educated gentleman, and he fulfilled his high duties in an efficient manner. The opinions of those who were brought into contact with him officially were expressed greatly in his favour. One important incident occurring during Sir Anthony's administration was the proposition of Bishop Bugnion to introduce a considerable number of Memmonites (a Protestant sect in Russia who were at that time suffering persecution) into the Northern Territory, on terms which, however, were not accepted by the Government. Sir A. Musgrave resigned his office early in 1877, on receiving the appointment of Governor of Jamaica.

During the time of the three Governors who last filled the office, the salary attached to it had been £5000 a year; the private secretary receiving £506; aide-de-camp, £150. The next representative of royalty was Sir William Wellington Cairns, K.C.M.G., who, after filling several offices in the Civil Service of Ceylon, including that of Postmaster-General, was, in the year 1867, made Lieutenant-Governor of Malacca, Straits Settlement, and in 1868 of several of the West Indian Islands, until 1870, when he was transferred to British Honduras. In 1874 he was appointed Governor of Trinidad, with the rank of Companion of the Order of St. Michael and St. George, but from ill-health was compelled early in 1878 to resign this Government. He was next appointed Governor of Queensland, and received the honour of Knighthood in 1877, and retired from that Government on March the 24th in the same year, being transferred to South Australia, but only held this Government until May 17th, as through continued ill-health he was compelled to resign his appointment and return to England. The various offices he filled in unhealthy climates had so impaired his health that he reluctantly found it necessary to relinquish official life. During the short time he remained in South Australia he won golden opinions by his urbane and dignified manners, his departure being much regretted by all classes who had approached him.

On the 2nd October, 1877, Sir William Francis Drummond Jervois, G.C.M.G., C.B., R.E., was appointed to the vacant office. Sir William commenced his military career in the Royal Engineers in the year 1839. In 1841 he was ordered to the Cape of Good Hope, where he continued in active service until 1848. In 1842 he acted as Brigade Major in an expedition against the Boers. In 1845 he was appointed acting Adjutant, and in 1846 Major of Brigade, and subsequently accompanied Sir J. Berkeley, Commander-in-Chief against the Kaffirs. From 1848 to 1852 he commanded a company of Sappers at Woolwich and Chatham, and in 1852 he was ordered to the Island of Alderney to design and carry out plans of fortifications. In 1854 he received the rank of Major. In 1855 he was in command of the Royal Engineers in the London district. In 1856 he was appointed Assistant Inspector-General of Fortifications. In 1861 he attained the rank of Lieut.-Colonel, and in 1862 was appointed Deputy Director of Fortifications. During 1863 he was engaged in Canada, Nova

Scotia, and New Brunswick, inspecting their defences. On his return, in 1864, from a special visit to Canada, his report on the defences of Quebec was laid before the Imperial Government, and his plans were approved. The Indian Government commissioned him to inspect and report on the defences of Aden, Bombay, &c. His great services to the Empire were acknowledged and rewarded by Her Majesty by appointment as Knight Commander of St. Michael and St. George, and Governor of the Straits Settlements. He was next appointed by the Home Government to examine and report on the best means of defending the Australian Colonies, and before he had quite accomplished this extensive and important duty, he entered on his office as Governor of South Australia. The necessity of completing the work of inspection and laying down the necessary fortifications, required him to leave his government several times, and on each occasion the office was filled by His Honour the Chief Justice, S. J. Way. In 1878 Sir William proceeded on a visit to England, when he was created a Grand Cross of the Order of St. Michael and St. George.

This history of the progress of a young colony cannot have a happier conclusion than the following interesting extracts from the speech of Sir W. F. D. Jervois, delivered at the farewell banquet given in his honour on the 5th of January, 1883, in the City Banqueting Hall.

After a graceful opening Sir William continued,—" Gentlemen, I should be guilty, I think, of over-weening vanity did I not remember that the honour you have done me must be in large measure due to the fact that I am the representative of Her Majesty the Queen, who rules over an empire such as the world has never seen before, and who lives in the affections of her subjects, not only in Great Britain, but in all her possessions throughout the habitable globe. . . . . Gentlemen, as the mayor has hinted, I feel myself, as I am just about to leave you, so placed that I may rather throw off for the moment the position—if I may so call it, the constitutional position—of Governor, and speak on some matters in my individual capacity. . . . Let me turn for a moment to matters relating to the progress of the colony during the five years that I have had the pleasure to dwell among you. . . . First, then, as regards the progress of the colony. The population has gone on steadily increasing. It has increased during the last five years upwards of 62,000 souls. . . . .

Driving about the suburbs, as I have been in the habit of doing, I have been astounded to see the number of houses and townships that have been created whilst I have been here. . . Then, again, if you turn to the country, you see the number of additional towns that have been established. See how Port Augusta has been almost created and extended. See, again, what great improvements have taken place in your means of communication, both local and imperial. . . . Well do I remember in the year 1877, laying the first rail of a tramway in Adelaide. . . . I must also refer to the extension of railways. Whilst there were 321 miles of line open when I came here, there are now 946 miles open, and that irrespective of 276 miles which have been authorised, but which have not yet been constructed. When you come to consider the progress of the country in matters relating to trade you find, comparing the banking statistics of five years ago with those of the present day, that whilst the liabilites of the banks in 1877 were £4,000,000 and their assets £6,300,000, the liabilities now are £5,500,000 and the assets nearly £8,500,000. This is a considerable increase, and now the banks have a balance of £3,000,000 assets over liabilities. I observed it stated the other day in one of the papers that the assets amounted to £5,000,000 over the liabilities, but that must refer to a later period than that with which I am dealing, as I am taking the returns of 1881. . . . Then, again, if you look at the imports and the exports of the colony, you will find a considerable increase. But, on the other hand, you will observe that the imports for the year 1881—and, I suppose, for the present year as well—considerably exceeds the exports. . . . I must next direct your attention to the fact that the revenue has gone on increasing. It has increased £749,680 during the five years I have been amongst you, whilst the expenditure has been added to the extent of £600,597. On the other hand, the public debt of the colony has also increased from £5,217,100 to £11,369,600, amounting to an increase of £6,152,200. . . . I pass on, to say a few words with reference to what has been done in connection with educational matters. Since I first came to the colony, the number of private schools has increased to a large, and I have no doubt a salutary extent. In 1877, there were 382 public schools, and this year there are 422, *i.e.*, forty have been established during the five years I speak of. The number of pupils on the roll has gone up from 27,305 to over 37,500, and the average attendance has increased from over 14,400 to over 22,000, the increase in the percentage being 63·6. I may add that the whole of the model schools except the model schools of Adelaide have been built during the period of my government among you. I can remember—and I look back upon the time with great satisfaction—that the very first public act I performed after I was sworn in here as your Governor was the opening of a primary school at Willunga, when I first had the honour of addressing a South Australian audience. Then, if we pass from school to other institutions, we find that the institutes, and especially the Adelaide Institute, have taken a tremendous stride. . . . The present institution is . . . one of national importance. There is as you know a fine new building erected at a cost of something like £40,000. There is also an art gallery on which £3,000 have been spent, and donations worth £1,000 have been received besides. . . . I feel bound to refer to the action of Sir Thomas Elder in voluntarily giving £3,000 towards establishing a South Australian scholarship in connection with the Royal College of Music, under the auspices of the Prince of Wales, and it must be a matter of great satisfaction to Sir Thomas Elder that not long ago he received a telegram signed by His Royal Highness the Prince of Wales, and His Royal Highness the Duke of Edinburgh, thanking him heartily for his splendid munificence in this respect. The University is, I believe, at present in a satisfactory condition. There is a gradual increase in the number of students, and the law school which is to be established will, I believe, still further add to this. There are various classes for those who do not intend to graduate; and by the various examinations, junior and matriculation, which are provided for, the University affords many advantages to students, especially those who work up to the examinations in the public schools. . . . Considering, gentlemen, the position in which I came here, or at any rate to Australia, it is almost a matter of necessity that on the present occasion I should offer a few observations as regards the question of defence. I must say that I think—and this is an opinion which I have previously expressed—that the Volunteer Military Force, and generally the volunteers of South Australia, are certainly second to none, if indeed they are not superior to any of the forces of the other colonies on this continent. . . .

Whilst speaking of the Military Forces, I cannot but refer to the splendid offer that was made by 300 volunteers of South Australia to go to the Transvaal, when going there, meant hard work, great danger, and many difficulties ; and it is a great satisfaction to know that that voluntary act was recognised personally by Her Majesty the Queen, who sent a telegram to me through Lord Kimberley, begging me to express her gratification at this loyal movement. I am glad to see that the Parliament has passed a resolution authorising the purchase of a war vessel, because, as I have often stated, naval defence is after all and must be from the condition of the coast, a very considerable and indeed the main element in the defence of South Australia. . . . I observe that there is a very pretty fight going on about which route the intercolonial railway is to take. Well, of course, I cannot on the present occasion go into the merits of the question, I will only say that it appears to me that on the whole, taking the fact of the existence of the Murray Bridge, that it would be much better to leave the matter alone and let the railway go over the Murray Bridge. The Bill has been passed sanctioning that route, and although no doubt you may inquire as much as you like, I think you will ultimately come to the conclusion that the route *via* the Murray Bridge is the proper route. As regards railways yet to be carried out, I am sure you cannot overrate the importance of making a railway to the north-eastward, to the south-west of Queensland, and to the north-west of New South Wales. I know that not only will such a railway be a good thing for the people of South Australia, but it will be a good thing for the people in the south-west of Queensland and the north-west of New South Wales; and I have reason to believe that the people in the south-west of Queensland are exceedingly anxious that you should carry out such a work. Then there is the much-talked-of railway to Port Darwin. I hold a rather different opinion from that which is expressed in public with regard to the construction of that line—that is to say, the mode of its construction. I believe that if you allow a company to do it it will be done. I believe, on the other hand, that whatever may be the arguments adduced on the other side, if it is left to be done by the country itself it will be postponed indefinitely. . . . .

"I must before leaving the question of works refer to the Victor Harbour Breakwater. I believe in it thoroughly. I has gone up from 27,305 to over 37,500, and the average attendance has increased from over 14,400 to over 22,000, the increase in the percentage being 63·6. I may add that the whole of the model schools except the model schools of Adelaide have been built during the period of my government among you. I can remember—and I look back upon the time with great satisfaction—that the very first public act I performed after I was sworn in here as your Governor was the opening of a primary school at Willunga, when I first had the honour of addressing a South Australian audience. Then, if we pass from school to other institutions, we find that the institutes, and especially the Adelaide Institute, have taken a tremendous stride. . . . The present institution is . . . one of national importance. There is as you know a fine new building erected at a cost of something like £40,000. There is also an art gallery on which £3,000 have been spent, and donations worth £1,000 have been received besides. . . . I feel bound to refer to the action of Sir Thomas Elder in voluntarily giving £3,000 towards establishing a South Australian scholarship in connection with the Royal College of Music, under the auspices of the Prince of Wales, and it must be a matter of great satisfaction to Sir Thomas Elder that not long ago he received a telegram signed by His Royal Highness the Prince of Wales, and His Royal Highness the Duke of Edinburgh, thanking him heartily for his splendid munificence in this respect. The University is, I believe, at present in a satisfactory condition. There is a gradual increase in the number of students, and the law school which is to be established will, I believe, still further add to this. There are various classes for those who do not intend to graduate; and by the various examinations, junior and matriculation, which are provided for, the University affords many advantages to students, especially those who work up to the examinations in the public schools. . . . Considering, gentlemen, the position in which I came here, or at any rate to Australia, it is almost a matter of necessity that on the present occasion I should offer a few observations as regards the question of defence. I must say that I think—and this is an opinion which I have previously expressed—that the Volunteer Military Force, and generally the volunteers of South Australia, are certainly second to none, if indeed they are not superior to any of the forces of the other colonies on this continent. . . .

Whilst speaking of the Military Forces, I cannot but refer to the splendid offer that was made by 300 volunteers of South Australia to go to the Transvaal, when going there, meant hard work, great danger, and many difficulties; and it is a great satisfaction to know that that voluntary act was recognised personally by Her Majesty the Queen, who sent a telegram to me through Lord Kimberley, begging me to express her gratification at this loyal movement. I am glad to see that the Parliament has passed a resolution authorising the purchase of a war vessel, because, as I have often stated, naval defence is after all and must be from the condition of the coast, a very considerable and indeed the main element in the defence of South Australia. . . . I observe that there is a very pretty fight going on about which route the intercolonial railway is to take. Well, of course, I cannot on the present occasion go into the merits of the question, I will only say that it appears to me that on the whole, taking the fact of the existence of the Murray Bridge, that it would be much better to leave the matter alone and let the railway go over the Murray Bridge. The Bill has been passed sanctioning that route, and although no doubt you may inquire as much as you like, I think you will ultimately come to the conclusion that the route *viâ* the Murray Bridge is the proper route. As regards railways yet to be carried out, I am sure you cannot overrate the importance of making a railway to the north-eastward, to the south-west of Queensland, and to the north-west of New South Wales. I know that not only will such a railway be a good thing for the people of South Australia, but it will be a good thing for the people in the south-west of Queensland and the north-west of New South Wales; and I have reason to believe that the people in the south-west of Queensland are exceedingly anxious that you should carry out such a work. Then there is the much-talked-of railway to Port Darwin. I hold a rather different opinion from that which is expressed in public with regard to the construction of that line—that is to say, the mode of its construction. I believe that if you allow a company to do it it will be done. I believe, on the other hand, that whatever may be the arguments adduced on the other side, if it is left to be done by the country itself it will be postponed indefinitely. . . . .

"I must before leaving the question of works refer to the Victor Harbour Breakwater. I believe in it thoroughly. I have heard people say, 'Oh, Victor Harbour!—you can't lie alongside the jetty.' No ; and who supposed they could ! because the breakwater had only been made for 1000 feet, whereas the project was to make it for a length of 2000 or 3000 feet ; and, in order to afford protection to vessels, it will have to be carried out to that extent. Then you will have what Sir John Coode said you would have, and what I believe you will have—an excellent harbour. But in connection with this work it is necessary to cut a canal from Goolwa to Port Victor, a work which the best engineers of the old country would regard as a mere flea-bite. With these facilities you would have ocean steamers at Port Victor, and you would, moreover, have the trade of the Murray in your hands. . . . I shall be glad also to see an outer harbour carried out here, because I confess that there is a great want in regard to the embarkation and disembarkation of stores and passengers, when the P. & O. steamers come in. . . . In the past the money used for this purpose (public works) has been—and I suppose it will continue so—borrowed money. Well, now, what is the present position of affairs as regards our indebtedness ? The loans authorised up to June, 1882, were £12,481,800. Last session of Parliament additional loans were authorised to the extent of £1,433,535, and this brings up the total to £13,920,335. The interest on this sum at four per cent. is £556,812 per annum. Now, this must be paid. . . . You have the ability to pay if you only take the proper measures. But to meet or greatly reduce the pressure of such a possible crisis as that to which I have referred, the pastoral, agricultural, and mineral resources of the colony should be developed to the utmost. Exports thus would be greatly increased, and the revenue would be greatly increased as well. Immigration should also be carried on to the utmost extent, consistently with the interests of all classes of the community. . . . Then, so far as gold is concerned, I believe that very much more gold might be found in large quantities in our hills, if proper steps for its discovery were only taken. I am told by some people who have had considerable experience of gold mining in Victoria, that they are confident that such is the case, and that it only requires a proper expenditure of capital to tap these reefs and find a large supply of gold. . . . The operations of Mr. Malcolm on his ostrich farm near Gawler, are such as to indicate that something of importance will yet be done in that direction. I merely mention these facts with a view of hinting what may be done in the agricultural interest towards developing the resources of the country, and so help the payment of the interest on your loans, and of the expenses of the government of the colony. . . . I may state that Mr. Malcolm, who commenced operations with nine birds, has now seventy-five, and an ostrich may, under favourable circumstances, produce £30 worth of feathers a-year. But, gentlemen, you must after all recollect that a very small portion of South Australia is fit for agriculture. South Australia is, and must be, mainly a pastoral country. . . . You should remember that in this country it is important that the growth of wool should be encouraged. Whilst wheat can be grown in almost any part of the globe, merino wool can only be produced in a very narrow part of latitude, and you are in that part. The people of the world must come to you for merino wool, and there will be an increasing demand for it, and I shall count the development of the pastoral interest as almost at the root of the progress of the country. . . . And now it only remains for me to thank you again for your hearty reception, and for the great kindness and consideration I have experienced at your hands during the five years I have been amongst you—those five years, I say it with all sincerity, being as happy a time as I ever spent in my life. I now wish you a hearty, a sincere, a cordial, and an affectionate farewell."

CONCLUDING REMARKS.

THE Author on concluding this volume cannot omit to express his grateful thanks to the following gentlemen for their kind help in enabling him to complete and publish this his last work, viz., to Sir Thomas Elder, the Hon. A. B. Murray, M.L.C., John Chambers, and H. T. Morris, J.P., Esqrs., for substantial aid; to Mr. G. S. Wright, J.P., Secretary to the Commissioner of Crown Land, and Mr. T. Gill, Treasury Clerk, for important information; to Captain Sweet, for photographic views and for other assistance; and generally to the gentlemen who have so readily subscribed for the work.

APPENDIX.

AUSTRALIAN STATISTICS.

IN a return recently compiled by the Treasury of New South Wales, showing the relative positions and aggregate importance of the various Australian Colonies at the close of the year 1881, and also information of a like nature with regard to New South Wales up to the end of the year 1882, we find the following figures relative to New South Wales, Victoria, South Australia, Queensland, Tasmania, Western Australia, and New Zealand :—Area in square miles, 3,086,128 ; estimated mean population, 2,774,353 ; revenue, £20,613,673 ; proportion raised by taxation, £7,329,862 ; rate of taxation per head, £2 13s. : value of imports, £52,708,556 ; value per head, £18 19s. 11½d. ; exports, £48,368,941 ; exports per head, £17 8s. 8d. ; total value of trade imports and exports, £101,077,497 ; value of trade per head, £36 8s. 7¾d. : miles of railway open, 5,470½ ; in course of construction, 1,310 : telegraph lines open, 29,428 miles ; telegraph wire open, 49,112 ; lines and wires in course of construction, 1,899 : acres under crop, 6,405,001 ; number of horses, 1,197,638 ; number of cattle, 8,292,766 ; number of sheep, 74,627,354 ; pigs, 905,281 : estimated population (December 31, 1881), 2,826,635 : public debt, £95,965,582 ; indebtedness per head, £33 19s.

NOTES OF A TRIP AMONG THE MACKAY SUGAR PLANTATIONS.

THE following notes of a trip amongst the Mackay Sugar Plantations in Queensland have been kindly supplied by the Hon. J. Langdon Parsons, M.P., Minister of Education. His zeal in the performance of the duties of his office as Minister of the Northern Territory is shown by his exertions in travelling to obtain information on the cultivation of the sugar cane, and of the processes of extracting and refining of sugar from the same, in the adjoining colony, where the climate and soil are similar to those in the Northern Territory. The information thus gained will doubtless lead to the introduction of capital, to be applied in establishing that important and profitable branch of husbandry in our province, which has peculiar advantages of its own in numerous navigable rivers, and an unsurpassed harbour, occupying a most advantageous position on the Indian Ocean.

Mackay is situate 625 miles to the north of Brisbane. On reaching Mackay, I was most cordially met by M. Hume Black, Esq., M.L.A., who represents the Mackay district in the Legislative Assembly, who is one of the pioneer sugar planters, who has for many years closely studied the whole question of sugar cultivation and manufacture, and from whom I derived much information. Mr. Black's plantation is called "The Cedars," and is situate on the summit of a moderately high hill.

From a local paper the following description of "The Cedars" is given : "'The Cedars,' is situated on the north side of the river, and affords a good example of the hill system of cultivation, which has proved eminently successful in this district. The extent of the estate is 2,156 acres, of which 298 are under cultivation. Of the area cultivated, upwards of two-thirds are grown on scrub lands. The hills, which were originally covered with heavy scrub timber, have been cleared, and, though the surface then presented was found to be stony and precipitous to a great degree, the soil proved to be so rich, and naturally well drained, that very heavy crops have been and continue to be taken off. The mill is by the well-known maker Fletcher, and like all that manufacturer's work, is remarkable for the proportionate strength of all its parts. The boilers, of which there are two, have a joint capability of being worked up to about 40 h.p. The works themselves do not differ much from those on the majority of estates, with the exception of the battery, which is locally famous for being one of the quickest in the colony. It is of the description known as a flat battery, but the bottom is more curved than is usual in such batteries, and its extra efficiency is probably in a great measure due to the excellent draught of the flues and stack. The centrifugals here are Weston's patent, and being driven by a powerful small engine, can be worked up to a great speed, thus securing the best results in drying the sugars. There are four evaporating pans, built in the mill-house, on a principle closely allied to that known as the 'Gadsden.' In an ordinary season the works can produce 350 tons of sugar."

There is something very novel in the spectacle of so many dark faces and forms, and woolly heads, in the houses and on the roads, and in the fields. Judging from personal observation on a large number of plantations, many of which were visited without any notice, I have no hesitation in stating that they present a healthy and happy appearance. They are allowed practically as much bread and beef as they can eat with safety to their own health, and also a sufficient quantity of sweet potatoes and rice. They receive two suits of clothes every year, and are in every sense well cared for by the planters. On no occasion did I see any attempt at ill-usage. I did not even hear a harsh or angry word. In fact, the planters all feel that their interests are bound up with the welfare of their labourers—in a word, that it pays to keep them in comfort and contentment. They receive at the end of their three years' engagement £18, *i.e.*, at the rate of £6 per annum, which they usually spend in the purchase of a miscellaneous kit, beginning with a gun, with which they return to their islands, and mainly with a view to astonish their home-staying friends. Often, however, after the first novelty of their splendour is over, they become tired of the monotony of the Pacific isles, and the shortness and uncertainty of their meals, and they gladly re-engage for another three years' term on a sugar plantation in Queensland.

After a good look round at "The Cedars," Mr. Black and I started out on a tour through some of the plantations on the northern side of the river. Taking the main road to Bowen, we passed through the Miclere estate, formerly the property of Messrs. Carroll and Avery, but now owned by

Sir John Bennet-Lawes. This is a fine estate, and embraces both forest and scrub, or jungle land. The total area is 1,100 acres, of which a large portion is under cultivation. The mill is one of Walker's, of Maryborough, and can manufacture 400 tons per year. Crushing was commenced on this estate in 1872.

Passing on, the road goes through some dense scrub or jungle. This description of land costs from about £3 10s. per acre to clear, the work being done by Europeans.

On the north side we passed the Narbrook plantation, which comprises about 640 acres, in which but few permanent improvements have been made. Notwithstanding this, however, the estate was recently purchased by Sir J. B. Lawes for the sum of £10,400, or over £15 per acre. The Farleigh plantation, also owned by Sir J. B. Lawes, we reached about one o'clock, and received a planter's welcome from the general manager of Sir J. B. Lawes' estates, Mr. Robert Walker, who is also the chairman of the divisional board. Before lunch, we examined the numerous and complete plans of the mill, which have been supplied by Mirlees, Watson and Co., of Glasgow. This mill, which contains all the latest improvements in sugar manufacturing, will cost, when erected, from £25,000 to £30,000. Fully 2,000 tons will be manufactured in the season. The weight of the rollers is 6½ and 7 tons, the weight of the three being over 20 tons.

After lunch we had a thorough inspection of the premises, visiting the quarters for Kanakas, Europeans, and overseers, which are very extensive, and all brand new. There are 250 Kanakas employed on the estate, and over forty Europeans are on the monthly pay-sheet. The stables are 250 feet long. The stall accommodation is for eighty horses, being forty on each side, with a tramway between for the running up of fodder from the stores.

The cost of getting this plantation, which contains 2,500 acres, into working order, including machinery, clearing, and cultivating, up to the time of crushing (but entirely exclusive of the purchase of the land), will be £60,000—*i.e.*, that amount of money, in addition to the purchase of the land, will be spent before there will be a single penny of return upon the outlay. It is a fact like this which indicates the confidence which capitalists must have in the prospects of the sugar industry. It also clearly indicates that, if the cultivation of sugar is to be successfully carried on in the Northern Territory, it will be absolutely necessary to win the confidence of capitalists, as well as to make provision for the introduction of Coolie labour.

Leaving Farleigh, we soon entered on the Pioneer estate, and for three miles drove through the fine undulating country on which the sugar-cane is planted and is richly thriving. This estate was at one time known as the Ashburton estate, and was the property of Mr. J. Spiller. It consists of 4,242 acres. The mill, which is one of Mirlees, Tait, and Watson's, of Glasgow, is very complete, and is equal to a production of 1,500 tons annually. There are eight centrifugal and seven steam pumps. The water for the mill is conveyed from the creek, a distance of 1,300 feet, in a six-inch main. There are two batteries in the works, one round and one flat, and a five and a half ton vacuum pan. There is also a railway, two and a half miles long, for bringing cane and fuel to the works. This estate employs about 200 Kanakas and 60 Europeans, and, in addition to several large bullock teams, works over 130 horses. This estate was purchased by Mr. McKinnon, of Melbourne, for £95,000, and the first year he took off it a crop of sugar worth over £20,000.

The Foulden plantation was next reached. Sir J. Bennet-Lawes is now the proprietor of this plantation. It is a very compact estate, and the mill is furnished with excellent machinery. The charcoal process is in use, and as a consequence the sugars produced are among the finest in the district. Golden syrup is also manufactured in this mill. The premises are very complete, and the manager's residence is very prettily situate.

Our next halt was at the River plantation. This is the property of Mr. J. Spiller. It comprises about 2,355 acres, and the area under crop this year is about 1,400 acres. This mill is one of the finest in the district, and is by Mirlees, Tait, and Watson. There is one multitubular and two Cornish boilers, five engines (with a total of 48 h.p.), four Weston's and two Manlove and Alliott's centrifugals, two round batteries, six clarifiers, 23 coolers, cane and megass (the dried crushed cane) carriers, and vacuum pan. There is a railway more than three miles in extent, on which a small locomotive with trucks conveys the cane or firewood to the works, where a 10-ton weighbridge keeps check upon the deliveries of both. The manager of this mill, Mr. Percy Creece, most obligingly conducted us over the mill and outbuildings, which are undoubtedly in a very complete state. The yield of the crushing last year was 1,400 tons, which realised an average price of £23 per ton. We were shown white sugar which is realising £33 per ton in Mackay. The prospective yield for the coming year is estimated at 2,000 tons. The plantation is one of the oldest in the district, and has been under cultivation about twelve years. One hundred and twenty working horses are in constant employment, and the horse-feed account has amounted during the past three months to over £100 per month. The butcher's bill for the supply of meat to the plantation hands averages nearly £90 per month. Here, as elsewhere, the Kanakas, in various degrees of light garments, with here and there a gay colour somewhere shown on the attire, looked plump and happy.

Early on Friday morning, February 9th, we started, and after crossing the river, followed the main Homebush-road, which passes through heavily-timbered forest land, in which gums, blackwood, and acacia are the prevalent varieties where the soil is good, and the poplar gum where the soil is poor. The distance from the Cedars to the Homebush mill is about 18 miles.

The Homebush estate, with adjacent lands, which is now the property of the Colonial Sugar Company, comprises an area of about 13,000 acres. This year on the Homebush plantation there are about 300 acres planted. There are 700 acres in course of planting, which will be ready for crushing this season, and in addition the company have made arrangements to purchase about 400 acres of canes from small growers. About 14 miles of permanent tramway on the 2 ft. gauge of Fowler and Co., is being laid down, and about 15 miles of portable tramways will be in operation to bring in the cane from the company's, and the local growers' fields. The labour at present located at Homebush is 87 Kanakas, 80 Chinese (who are under engagement at 13s. per week with rations), and 120 Cingalese, out of 198 who were recently imported. With these 120 Cingalese the company have entered into new arrangements under which, instead of receiving £20 per annum and finding themselves, they now are to receive tenpence per day and rations. The mill is one of the largest and completest in Australia. No expense has been spared to put down the latest improvements in manufacture. It is expected, when in full working order, to produce 5,000 tons per year.

From Homebush we made for the plantation of the Oakenden Sugar Company. This estate is about 5,000 acres in extent, and recently belonged to Mr. A. Kemmiss, an old settler in the district. It has now been disposed of to a Melbourne company, Mr. Kemmiss retaining a fifth share, and holding the appointment of general manager. There are between 300 and 400 acres in cane this year, and arrangements have been made on certain conditions for the purchase of the cane grown on the plantation during the next two years by the Colonial Sugar Company, for crushing at Homebush, at 10s. per ton in the field, *i.e.*, the company cut and carry the cane from the fields to the mills.

Mr. Davidson drove me for some miles through luxuriant cane fields, and on the return we called at the Pleystow estate. This property belonged, up to a short time since, to Messrs. A. Hewitt and Co., but was then sold to a Melbourne company for £58,000. The area is about 5,000 acres, with about 1,000 under crop. The mill is estimated to be equal to the production of 1,200 tons of sugar. Here also there is a still, where the famous "Anchor" brand of rum is made, which secured a first prize both at the Brisbane Show in 1877, and at the Sydney International Exhibition in 1879-80. We looked through the mill, and also the Kanakas' quarters and hospital. The manager, who accompanied us, informed me that when any of the "boys" appear to be shamming, they are ordered into the hospital and kept on the prescribed hospital diet and physic. If they are playing the old soldier they soon get well and offer themselves for work. In case of real sickness they receive every care and attention. The plantations in the district, it should be mentioned, are regularly visited by a medical man.

Close by is the Branscombe estate, which formerly belonged to G. H. M. King, Esq., but is now the property of the Melbourne-Mackay Sugar Company, of which Mr. King is a large shareholder. The extent of land is about 1,400 acres, of which over 600 are cultivated. The mill can produce 600 tons of sugar, and the Branscombe sugars have secured medals in Brisbane and Sydney. After leaving Pleystow we reached the Palms estate, also the property of the Melbourne-Mackay Sugar Company. This is one of the most valuable plantations in the district, and the mill is the largest and most complete in working order in Queensland. The mill will, however, be eclipsed by those now being erected at Homebush and Farleigh. The Melbourne-Mackay Sugar Company now own about 10,000 acres, and have, I was informed, a larger quantity of rich land than any other proprietors in the district.

After spending a most splendid day at Alexandra we left, and on our return passed the Te Kowai estate, another of the Melbourne-Mackay Company's properties. This plantation lies to the north, and on the south side of the road the land is chiefly occupied by small selectors, who grow cane and sell it to the neighbouring mills. The mill at Te Kowai can produce 1,500 tons in the season.

QUEENSLAND GOVERNMENT RETURN SHOWING THE QUANTITY OF SUGAR, RUM, AND MOLASSES EXPORTED AND CONSUMED, LAND UNDER CROP (SUGAR-CANE), POPULATION, &c., DURING EACH OF THE FIVE YEARS ENDING 1881.

		1877.	1878.	1879.	1880.	1881.
Number of sugar mills		61	61	70	83	103
Number of distilleries		11	12	—	9	7
Number of sugar refineries		1	—	1	1	1
Area under sugar-cane	Acres	15,220	16,584	17,652	20,224	28,026
Area of sugar-cane crushed	Acres	8,043	10,702	11,409	12,306	15,550
Quantity of sugar made	Tons	12,243	13,525	18,714	15,564	19,051
Quantity of sugar exported (raw)	Tons	4,605$\tfrac{15}{20}$	3,380$\tfrac{10}{20}$	8,215$\tfrac{10}{20}$	7,559$\tfrac{18}{20}$	6,631$\tfrac{10}{20}$
Quantity of sugar exported (refined)	Tons	1,336	754	2,097$\tfrac{5}{20}$	2,717	965$\tfrac{10}{20}$
Total value of sugar exports	£	180,668	119,018	275,769	292,041	207,210
Total quantity of sugar for consumption	Tons	6,809$\tfrac{11}{20}$	9,680$\tfrac{12}{20}$	8,799$\tfrac{10}{20}$	5,569$\tfrac{9}{20}$	11,709$\tfrac{5}{20}$
Population		203,084	210,510	217,851	215,054	226,968
Quantity of molasses manufactured	Galls.	510,260	570,301	641,486	602,960	753,658
Quantity of molasses exported	Tons	182$\tfrac{2}{20}$	279$\tfrac{2}{20}$	268$\tfrac{13}{20}$	742$\tfrac{17}{20}$	1,222$\tfrac{2}{20}$
Value of molasses exported	£	1,190	1,335	2,438	5,238	10,661
Quantity of rum manufactured	Galls.	196,001	216,395	238,710	201,111	157,325
Quantity of rum exported (Jan. 1 to Dec. 31)	Galls.	93,776	43,809	80,723	58,659	95,702
Value of rum exported	£	10,915	6,199	9,814	7,762	13,312

413

STATEMENT SHOWING PROGRESSIVE DEVELOPMENT OF THE COLONY FROM ITS FOUNDATION IN DECEMBER, 1836, DIVIDED INTO QUINQUENNIAL PERIODS FROM 1st JANUARY, 1838, TO 31st DECEMBER, 1882, WITH AVERAGE RESULTS.

Period.	Popula-tion.	Revenue.	Expendi-ture.	Acres under Cultivation.	Acres under Wheat Crop.	Number of Sheep in Colony.	Value of Imports.	Value of Exports.	STAPLE PRODUCE EXPORTED.			Shipping Inwards and Outwards.
									Bread-stuffs.	Wool.	Minerals.	
		£	£				£	£	£	£	£	Tons.
Year 1836	546	†	†	Nil.	Nil.	*	*	*	Nil.	Nil.	Nil.	2,592
Year 1837	3,000	†	†	8	Nil.	28,000	*	*	Nil.	Nil.	Nil.	*
1838 to 1842	†12,000	20,125	5,283	5,945	3,850	†200,000	248,857	46,891	Nil.	13,475	68,566	†48,725
1843 to 1847	23,034	39,583	88,526	30,311	22,574	526,708	230,759	197,555	†	64,612	318,311	34,546
1848 to 1852	58,094	179,185	46,420	60,000	40,000	†960,000	663,807	773,513	108,079	120,553	258,302	155,768
1853 to 1857	96,619	504,788	145,080	†166,000	126,000	†1,965,000	1,768,777	1,635,432	424,394	323,720	416,125	258,026
1858 to 1862	125,489	505,538	494,066	407,268	262,277	†2,984,900	1,742,622	1,825,977	584,960	547,491	686,408	206,681
1863 to 1867	156,135	832,547	540,994	670,952	429,057	4,033,247	2,542,068	2,061,513	1,024,535	844,556	650,040	323,572
1868 to 1872	183,818	725,293	823,998	965,461	624,450	4,627,475	2,396,533	3,110,568	808,658	1,207,000	680,368	324,070
1873 to 1877	215,163	1,176,310	770,287	1,068,566	954,124	6,029,735	4,249,335	4,647,693	1,559,242	1,812,327	398,721	617,232
1878 to 1882	271,132	1,908,432	1,166,835	2,418,793	1,602,560	6,434,130	5,649,422	5,091,980	1,737,789	2,155,988		1,129,355

No returns. † Returns incomplete.

On 30th June, 1883, there were 966¼ miles state railways working, and 255½ miles in course of construction ; 174 telegraph offices ; and 519 post offices open ; and 8,170 miles of telegraphs in operation. Telephones have recently been extended, of which 628 miles of telephone wire are now worked.

Total area of the Province (exclusive of the Northern Territory), 243,244,800 acres. Area sold to 30th June, 1883, was 10,029,134 acres, leaving unsold (June, 1883) 233,215,666 acres.

T. GILL, *Treasury.*

FIRST STEAMER FROM LONDON TO ADELAIDE, SOUTH AUSTRALIA.

THE *Courier* steamer from London, in 1840, was the first steam boat arriving at Adelaide. She came to Mr. W. S. Whitington, from his London firm, and was put into sailing order by him under the management of Mr. Rd. Bless, the Engineer (lately deceased), but the traffic at that early time between the Colonies was found not sufficient to pay for trading her.

RUM JUNGLE CREEK NURSERIES, NORTHERN TERRITORY (NEAR SOUTHPORT).

NOTE.—The following extracts are taken from a report, which the Author did not see till the body of the work had been despatched to London for publication. Mr. Henry Poett, manager of the plantation, states as follows:—

"In 1881, I selected in the Northern Territory, three sections containing 3,793 acres. The first seed received was planted during the second and third weeks of December, 1882. In 50 beds I have about 200,000 plants, enough (allowing for loss), to plant 100 acres with this coffee. The second batch of seed I received should produce plants enough to stock 100 acres. The plants look so well and healthy that they may escape the disease so common in Ceylon and Figi. There are at present engaged on Poett's Nurseries, 25 Coolies and white labourers and mechanics; but with 250 men, say, 550 acres can be planted and brought into bearing at a cost of £45,000, which, in five years, will be returned by a yield of coffee and cinchona bark worth £48,000.

"After this period the property could be worked with Malabar and Cingalese labour at an average expenditure of £8,000, and the return would be:—

  Yearly return of coffee 1,800 cwt. £7,200
  Cinchona, every alternate year, 400,000 lbs.
   (1,600 per acre), or annually   ...   ... £20,000."

It must be remembered that the above favourable anticipations are entertained in a country where tropical rains can be depended on, and bearing in mind the actual returns in the young sugar plantations of Queensland, with the same climate, soil, and rainfall, the above is not an over estimate. Indiarubber, Cotton, and Maize, are also being very successfully grown on this, at present, miniature plantation.

Appendix. 415

USEFUL INFORMATION FOR PARTIES WHO INTEND TO VISIT OR TO INVEST FUNDS IN SOUTH AUSTRALIA.

Agent-General for South Australia—SIR ARTHUR BLYTH, K.C.M.G. *Office*—8, Victoria Chambers, Westminster, London.

FULL information can be obtained of recent liberal amendments in Land Laws, Emigration Regulations, &c., on application at the office.

Under present regulations blocks of land can be obtained up to 1,000 acres at the upset price of £1 an acre. Payments in redemption as follows : 10 per cent. on day of purchase, 10 per cent. at the end of three years, and the balance by annual payments of 5 per cent. during remainder of term of twenty years, when a registered title will be granted.

LAND ORDER WARRANTS of the value of £20 for Adults, and £10 for Children, are issued by the Agent-General to suitable persons proceeding *direct* to South Australia. On arrival in the Colony the Warrants are exchanged for Land Orders, which are received by the Government as cash for purchase of land.

ASSISTED PASSAGES are granted to the industrial classes on payment of £4 for Adults under 40, and £8 for those between 40 and 50. Children under 12 are allowed to accompany their parents free of charge. (Free passages are also given to good female domestic servants.)

By paying the difference between the deposit and £15 within 12 months after arrival in the Colony (provided such intention is stated within one month after arrival), a Land Order is granted to each adult under 45.

CORPORATION OF THE CITY OF ADELAIDE.

THE Council consists of the Mayor (H. R. Fuller, Esq., J.P.), six Aldermen, and twelve Councillors. The Mayor and Aldermen (two of whom retire every year), are elected by the whole body of the citizens ; the Councillors by the ratepayers in the wards ; there are six wards.

The assessment of all the city properties, exclusive of all public buildings, the property of Her Majesty's Government, all schools, churches, and charitable institutions, is, for the year 1883, £485,068. Upon this the rates are levied as follows :—

General of 1s.; *Lighting*, 3d. ; *Health*, 2d. ; *Park Lands*, 1d. ; *equal to* 1s. 6d. *in the £* ... ... *Total* £36,380 2s.

Estimated income of the Corporation amounts to... ... £95,000

The value of the freehold property belonging to the Corporation £250,000

The bonded debts of the Corporation £84,000

Population of the City on December 31st, 1882 ... 41,241

THOMAS WORSNOP,
Town Clerk.

BANK OF SOUTH AUSTRALIA.

INCORPORATED BY ROYAL CHARTER, 1847.
Capital, £800,000.   Reserved Fund, £250,000.
Head Office—54, Old Broad Street, London.
General Manager—WILLIAM GILMOUR CUTHBERTSON, ESQ.

ADELAIDE ESTABLISHMENT.

Inspector and Colonial Manager—JOHN CURRIE, ESQ.
Assistant Manager—THOS. D. SMEATON, ESQ.
(With Branches and Agencies throughout the Colonies.)

NOTE.—There are eight additional Banks, each with many Local Branches in South Australia, whose aggregate Capital amounts to over Seven Million Pounds Sterling.

The Savings Bank of the Colony holds Deposits to the amount of £46,388, being the average of £32 6s. 9d. of each Depositor.

ELDER, SMITH & CO.

ADELAIDE.

Merchants and Commission Agents.
Lloyd's Agents for South Australia.
Agents—Comité des Assureurs, Maritimes de Paris.
  ,, Peninsular and Oriental Steam Navigation Company.
London Offices—122, Leadenhall Street, E.C., and 25, Cockspur Street.
Agents—Elder Line of Clipper Ships.

ORIENT LINE OF STEAMERS.

Agents—JOSEPH STILLING & CO.,
Adelaide and Port Adelaide, South Australia.
Managers in London—F. GREEN & CO., and ANDERSON, ANDERSON & CO., Fenchurch Avenue, London, E.C.
JOSEPH STILLING & CO., Agents for the Stilling Line of Sailing Ships.

www.ingramcontent.com/pod-product-compliance
Lightning Source LLC
Chambersburg PA
CBHW020534300426
44111CB00008B/655